THE JERUSALEM ANTHOLOGY

ꙮ A Literary Guide

A Special Edition
Presented by
United Jewish Appeal
Prime Minister's Council
Spring - 1996

Library of Congress Cataloging-in-Publication Data

The Jerusalem anthology : a literary guide / [compiled by]
Reuven Hammer. — 1st ed.
        p.   cm.
      "JPS Jerusalem collection deluxe ed."
      Includes bibliographical references and index.
      ISBN 0–8276–0554–4 (travel edition)
      1. Jerusalem—Literary collections.   2. Jerusalem in the
Bible.   3. Jerusalem in rabbinical literature.   4. Jerusalem in
Judaism.   5. Jewish literature.   6. Jerusalem—History—
Sources.   I. Hammer, Reuven.
   PN6071.J38J45   1995
   808'.032569442—dc20   95–17222
                                                  CIP

Designed by Elizabeth Anne O'Donnell
Typeset by University Graphics

Cover Illustration: *Solomon's Temple*, serigraph by David Sharir,
Old City of Jaffa, Israel. Copyright © and courtesy of Pucker
Gallery, Boston.

THE JERUSALEM ANTHOLOGY

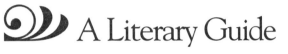 A Literary Guide

JPS Jerusalem Collection

Travel Edition

REUVEN HAMMER

 THE JEWISH PUBLICATION SOCIETY

Philadelphia • Jerusalem

5756   1995

For Raḥel, My Life's Companion

You are beautiful, my darling, as Tirzah,   יָפָ֨ה אַ֤תְּ רַעְיָתִי֙ כְּתִרְצָ֔ה

Comely as Jerusalem   נָאוָ֖ה כִּירוּשָׁלָ֑͏ִם

SONG OF SONGS 6:4

Publication of this volume was made possible
by a generous grant from

Geraldine and Harold Cramer

in honor of their parents

Esther and Charles Hassuk
and
Blanche and A. Harry Cramer ז"ל

✑ Contents

Illustrations   xv
Chronological Table   xxi
Foreword, *Teddy Kollek*   xxiii
Author's Preface   xxv
Sources and Acknowledgments   xxix

INTRODUCTION
Jerusalem in Jewish Consciousness,
Reuven Hammer   3

PROLOGUE   11

Jerusalem: A Tapestry in Time, *Samuel Heilman*   13

THE FIRST GATE
Jerusalem in Biblical Literature   19

The Torah and Historical Books   21
The Prophets   42
The Writings   59

THE SECOND GATE
Jerusalem in Second Temple Literature   71

The Letter of Aristeas   73
The First Book of Maccabees   77

The Psalms of Solomon   83
Noncanonical Psalms from Qumran   85
Second Baruch   88
Fourth Baruch   90
The Writings of Philo   92
      The Embassy to Gaius   92
      On Dreams   96
The Writings of Josephus Flavius   97
Antiqities of the Jews   97
Wars of the Jews   102

The Third Gate
Jerusalem in Rabbinic Literature   111

Jerusalem—the Chosen   113
Jerusalem—the Unique   117
The Destruction of Jerusalem   123
The Western Wall   129
Heavenly Jerusalem   130
Jerusalem—in the Future   132
Laws concerning Jerusalem   137

The Fourth Gate
Jerusalem in the Literature of the Geonic Period   141

Redemption, *Saadia Gaon*   143
Heavenly Jerusalem: Midreshei Geulah   145

The Jews Return to Jerusalem   147
No Jerusalem   149
Burial Kaddish Prayer for Jerusalem   150

THE FIFTH GATE
Jerusalem in Writings of the Middle Ages   151

Travelers' Accounts of Jerusalem   153
    Jacob HaCohen   153
    Rabbi Benjamin of Tudela   154
    Rabbi Moshe ben Nahman   157
    Isaac Chelo   159
    Obadiah Da Bertinoro   163
    Moses ben Israel Naphtali Porges Praeger   168
Jerusalem in Mystical Literature   174
    Zion and Jerusalem   174
    The Foundation Stone   175
    The Temple Above   176
    For Her Sake   177
Customs Relating to Jerusalem   178
    Rabbi Joseph Karo   178
    Maimonides   178
Jerusalem in Medieval Poetry   180
    Joy of the Whole World, *Yose ben Yose*   180
    I Remember, *Amittai ben Shephatiah*   180
    My Heart Seethes, *Shmuel Hanagid*   181
    Earth's Beauty, *Judah Halevi*   182
    My Heart's in the East, *Judah Halevi*   183
    Ode to Sion, *Judah Halevi*   184
    Lament for Zion, *Author Unknown*   188

Shalom to the City Shalem, *Judah Alharizi*   189
Cry, O Zion, *Author Unknown*   190

THE SIXTH GATE
Jerusalem in the Literature of the Turkish and Mandatory Periods   193

Life in Jerusalem (1834–1863), *Avraham Yaari*   195
A Narrative of a Forty Days' Sojourn in the Holy Land,
Sir Moses Montefiore   197
Coming to Jerusalem, *Eliezer Ben Yehudah*   202
Truth from the Land of Israel, *Ahad HaAm*   204
My Memoirs, *Yosef Yoel Rivlin*   206
Raise a Banner to Zion, *Saul Tschernichovsky*   209
In Palestine, *Theodore Herzl*   211
Land of Delight, *A. S. Hirschberg*   222
A Visit to Jerusalem in 1907, *Chaim Weizmann*   224
How the Glorious Day of Deliverance Came to Jerusalem,
Hemda Ben Yehuda   226
The Renaissance of the Jewish Soul, *Chaim Weizmann*   233
Pogrom in Jerusalem, *Chaim Weizmann*   235
A Jerusalem Diary, *Simon Greenberg*   239
Sound the Shofar!, *Moshe Segal*   240
To S. Z. Schocken after the 1929 Riots, *S. Y. Agnon*   242

THE SEVENTH GATE
Jerusalem in Modern Nonfiction   257

Jerusalem Is Called Liberty, *Walter Lever*   259
The Faithful City, *Dov Joseph*   265

The Siege of Jerusalem, *Pauline Rose*   271
Going into Captivity, *Aharon Liron*   278
A Generation's Dream Is Realized, *Uzi Narkiss*   286
Redeeming the Vow, *Rabbi Shlomo Goren*   294
The Seventh Day   296
    Like a Psalm of Praise   297
    Tonight We're Making History: A Discussion   299
The Lions' Gate   301
    Fear and Trembling, *Moshe Amirav*   301
At the Western Wall, *Elie Wiesel*   303
Strange City, *Amos Oz*   307
Jerusalem of My Childhood, *Muki Tzur*   313
Jerusalem—A Charismatic City,
Abraham Joshua Heschel   314
Next Year in Jerusalem!, *Anatoly Shcharansky*   316

THE EIGHTH GATE
Jerusalem in Modern Fiction   319

City of Many Days, *Shulamith Hareven*   321
Tehila: The Praise of Jerusalem, *S. Y. Agnon*   333
The Debt of Blood, *Elisha Porat*   338
A Journey through the Land of Israel,
Pinchas Sadeh   343

THE NINTH GATE
Jerusalem in Modern Poetry   351

From Jerusalem: A First Poem, *Gabriel Preil*   353
The First Day, *Marcia Falk*   353

In the Jerusalem Hills, *Leah Goldberg*   354

Jerusalem, *David Rokeah*   355

On Nevi'im Street (The Street of the Prophets),
Yehoash Biber   356

Longing (i), *Ruth Finer Mintz*   357

Religious Quarter, *A. C. Jacobs*   359

Building Partner, *Elisha Porat*   360

To My City Jerusalem, 1967, *Amir Gilboa*   361

Homage to Jerusalem; Jerusalem 1967,
Yehuda Amichai   362

Lesson in Geology, *Elisha Porat*   368

Jerusalem, 1968, *David Rokeah*   369

Jerusalem, *Else Lasker-Schüler*   371

Autumn in Jerusalem, *Oded Peled*   372

A View of Jerusalem, *T. Carmi*   373

City of Wound, *Haim Guri*   377

House Dog, *Uri Zvi Greenberg*   378

Jerusalem, *Moshe HaNa-ami*   378

The Warm Stone on the Hill of Jerusalem,
Ayin Tur-Malka   379

Jerusalem's Walls, *Israel Efrat*   380

Abu-Tor, *David Rokeah*   381

Evening in Jerusalem, *Yehuda Karni*   381

Jerusalem Moon, *Gabriel Preil*   382

I Don't Know If Mount Zion, *Abba Kovner*   383

Moriah, *Levi Ben Amitai*   385

City of David, *Zerubavel Gilad*   386

Jerusalem, *Yaakov Fichman*   386

Penalty Kick, *Ronny Someck*   387

·Leaving Jerusalem, *Marcia Falk*   388

Jerusalem: Ladders of Love, *Gabriel Preil*   388

From the Streets of Jerusalem, *Abba Kovner*   389
Tourists, *Yehuda Amichai*   390

THE TENTH GATE
Jerusalem in Jewish Folklore   393

King David's Tomb in Jerusalem, *Folktale*   395
Legends of Jerusalem, *Zev Vilnay*   396
> How Did David Conquer?   396
> The Synagogue of Elijah the Prophet   397
> The Miracle in Elijah's Synagogue   397
> Mount of Abraham   399
> Where are the Stones From?   400
Did King David Erect the Tower of David?
Abraham E. Millgram   400
700 Years of Sanctity, *Meir Ben Dov*   402

THE ELEVENTH GATE
Archaeology of the Old City   409

Walking the Old City: A Jerusalem Tour,
Herbert Alexander   411
Twenty-five Years of Excavations in Jerusalem,
1967–1992, *Hillel Geva*   419

THE TWELFTH GATE
Jerusalem: Toward the Future   441

Jerusalem, *Avraham B. Yehoshua*   443
Jerusalem—Today and Tomorrow, *Teddy Kollek*   453

EPILOGUE   461

Jerusalem, Holy City, *R. J. Zvi Werblowsky*   463
Jerusalem the Irreplaceable, *André Neher*   469
Pray for the Well-Being of Jerusalem, *S. Y. Agnon*   470

Afterword, Ehud Olmert   474
A Selected Jerusalem Bibliography   476
Index   481

ꙮ Illustrations

Jerusalem. The Tomb of David on Mount Zion, 1880.   2

Aerial view of the Temple Mount and the remains uncovered in the Ophel area south of it; looking west.   11

Entrance to the Old City, Jaffa Gate, 1925.   19

City of David.   25

Jerusalem with Temple of Solomon, *Liber Chronicorum*, Nurenberg, 1493.   28

The Silwan tunnel cut by Hezekiah. September 1967.   32

The Broad Wall, built at the end of the First Temple period, uncovered in the Jewish Quarter; looking northeast.   37

Map of Jerusalem at the end of the First Temple period. The dots represent excavated Israelite sites.   62

The Citadel of David, late 1960s.   71

Herodian construction of large ashlars at the southern wall of the Temple Mount.   75

Menorah and other objects incised on plastered wall in the Jewish Quarter during the Herodian period.   81

The Temple Mount and the monumental stairway at the Ophel along its southern wall; looking north.   105

Paved Herodian street at the foot of the Western Wall of the Temple Mount, north of Robinson's Arch; heaps of fallen stones from the wall cover the street.   108

The Damascus Gate at night. July 1968.   111

Hebrew inscription from the southwestern corner of the Temple Mount: "to the house of the trumpeting to pr[oclaim]."   127

Model of the Second Temple, Jerusalem, at Holyland Hotel, 1967.   128

Arrival of the Messiah in Jerusalem and Return of the Jews; woodcut from an Italian Passover Haggada; Venice, early 1600s.   131

Jaffa Gate to the Old City; late 19th century.   141

Temple of Solomon, *Liber Chronicorum*, Nurenberg, 1493.   151

Ayyubid tower (or gate) beneath the inner side of the southern wall of the Old City, uncovered in the Jewish Quarter.   154

Pool of Silwan storing the waters of the Gihon Spring. December 1978.   162

The Foundation Stone within the Dome of the Rock, 1898.   177

Zion Gate to the Old City, ca. 1898.   193

Bucharian Jew in Jerusalem.   199

Doorway to the School for Sewing at the Schneller Woods; date unknown; labeled as "the second house outside the city walls."   201

A "Moshav Zekenim" (Home for the Elderly) in Jerusalem.   204

"The Help of the Needy"—a settlement built at the foot of Mount Zion "with sixty houses to house sixty needy families who will be chosen by a lottery to be held every three years."   205

The Misgav Ladach Hospital in the Old City.   208

A 1950 picture of the house in which Herzl stayed in Jerusalem during his visit in 1898.   212

The Tomb of the Kings.   216

The Kaiser's procession near Jaffa Road in 1898.   218

A house in Motza, 1903.   220

Herzl's remains lying in state in the courtyard of the Jewish Agency building in Jerusalem prior to his burial on Mount Herzl; August 16, 1949.   221

The Wall in 1917 with Austrian soldiers and Jews in attendance.   225

General Allenby entering Jerusalem on foot near the Jaffa Gate.   232

The cornerstone ceremony of the Hebrew University, July 24, 1918, with Chaim Weizmann in front of the canopy.   234

Dedication ceremony of the Hebrew University Campus on Mount Scopus being addressed by the Earl of Balfour.   239

The smashed door of a home in Talpiot damaged during the riots of 1929.   248

Interior of a home in Talpiot damaged during the riots of 1929.   251

Torn and desecrated books in a home in Talpiot following the riots of 1929.   255

The Lions' Gate, ca. 1898.   257

The British compound—"Bevingrad"—on Princess Mary Street prior to the proclamation of the State in 1948.   261

The Stambuli Synagogue in the Old City after the liberation in 1967.   273

Rockets firing over Mount Zion in June 1948.   277

The Mandelbaum Gate passage between new and old Jerusalem, 1968.   288

Rabbi Shlomo Goren, then Chief Chaplain of the Army, blowing the shofar at the Wall; June 1967.   295

Paratroopers at the Wall immediately after its liberation in June 1967.   302

Crowds coming from the Wall soon after the end of the Six Day War in 1967.   304

View of the Jewish Quarter of the Old City, probably ca. 1937.   319

The dormitory of the Alliance School in Jerusalem in 1908.   324

The Hebrew University Campus on Mount Scopus, ca. 1928.   332

A monument to the soldiers of the Israel Defence Forces who fell in the 1967 War.   342

Haganah soldiers on King David Street, 1948.   345

The synagogue of Judah Chassid in the Old City, August 1937.   351

The Judean hills near Jerusalem, ca. 1935.   354

Street of the Prophets; date unknown.   357

Inhabitants of Meah Shearim; date unknown.   360

Jewish Quarter and New Synagogue, 1860.   370

Crowds looking at a building on Ben Yehuda Street demolished by a car bomb; February 22, 1948.   377

Mount Zion, the Dormition Abbey, and the walls of the Old City, ca. 1912.   384

Montefiore Quarter; date unknown.   389

Zion Gate, May 1968.   393

The synagogue of Elijah the Prophet restored following the Six Day War.   398

The Tomb of David on Mount Zion in 1900.   401

Jerusalem from the air photographed by a German pilot in 1917 or 1918.   409

Walking tour map.   414

Corner of an Israelite tower (right) and a Hasmonean tower abbutting it (left) as uncovered in the Jewish Quarter.   424

Remains of Hasmonean construction uncovered in the Jewish Quarter.   428

Remains of a columned room of the Crusader period uncovered in the southern part of the Jewish Quarter.   438

An aerial view looking toward the Rockefeller Museum with the Italian Hospital, now the Ministry of Education, in the front; 1937. 441

Ben Yehuda Street, May 12, 1937, decorated in honor of the coronation of King George VI and Queen Elizabeth.   450

The protective walls near the Jordanian section in divided Jerusalem prior to the 1967 War.   452

David's Tomb on Mount Zion, date unknown.   461

The animal market at the Sultan's Pool in 1900.   468

View of the Temple Mount and the horizon of new Jerusalem from Mount Zion, July 1981.   471

☙ Chronological Table

B.C.E. c. 3000 Earliest settlement of Jerusalem.

c. 2000–1800 Abraham visits Salem. Binding of Isaac on Mount Moriah.

c. 1200 Joshua's conquest of the Land.

c. 1004 David captures Jerusalem.

c. 960 Solomon builds First Temple.

701 Hezekiah's tunnel built.
Sennacherib's invasion. Siege fails.

586 Babylonians capture Jerusalem, destroy First Temple.
Exile to Babylonia.

520 Returnees from Babylonia build Second Temple and restore the city wall; Persians rule.

333 Alexander the Great conquers the Land.

164 Maccabean revolt.

c.20 Herod rebuilds the Second Temple.

C.E. 70 Jewish War (66–73); Jerusalem, Second Temple destroyed.

131 Aelia Capitolina founded by Hadrian.

135 Bar Kokhba Revolt.

326 Constantine legalizes Christianity (313) and

builds Church of Holy Sepulchre. Byzantine period (326–614).

640 Muslim Conquest.

691 Dome of the Rock built.

1099 Crusaders capture Jerusalem; Latin Kingdom of Jerusalem.

1187 Saladin captures Jerusalem; second Muslim period.

1212 City walls rebuilt but torn down seven years later.

1247–1517 Mamelukes rule.

1514 Ottoman Turk conquest.

1537 Suliman rebuilds walls.

1860 First settlement outside walls; New City begins.

1917 British conquest.

1948 Establishment of State of Israel. Arab Legion occupies Old City, destroys part of Jewish Quarter. Jerusalem divided between Jordan and Israel.

1967 Six Day War; Jerusalem reunited under Israeli rule.

1968 Jewish Quarter rebuilding begins.

☙ Foreword

For any city to celebrate its three-thousandth anniversary is an unusual and significant event, but for a city to celebrate three thousand years as the capital of the same people who first founded it is surely unique. In 1996 Jerusalem, the political capital of Israel and the unquestioned heart of the people of Israel, will commemorate three thousand years since King David made what was then a village into his capital. In order to unify all the tribes of Israel, he selected a site that did not belong to one particular tribe but to the entire people. He brought the Ark of the Covenant, the religious symbol of the Jewish nation, to an obscure threshing floor at the top of the slope on which the village was built and thus defined the site as both the royal and the religious center of power for Israel.

Since then, Jerusalem, in spite of many changes in control and changes in name over the centuries, has remained the City of David. There have been periods when Jews were not permitted to live in Jerusalem, though modern research indicates that such times were fewer than was previously thought, but there was never a moment when Jerusalem did not live within the Jews—as individuals and as a people.

Jewish independent rule over Jerusalem ceased in the year 70 C.E. and was not restored until 1948, and fully in 1967. We are the privileged generation of Jews who have seen with our own eyes the return to Zion. We are those spoken of by the psalmist: "When the Lord restored our exiles to Zion, it was like a dream" (Pss. 126:1). Unfortunately, life in a modern and complex city like Jerusalem is not always so dreamlike. The dream becomes a daily reality with which we must cope; that reality is frequently fraught with difficulty and even tragedy. As Mayor of Jerusalem for twenty-eight years, my work involved not only building Jerusalem physically, so that it would realize its potential of being a "crown of beauty" as well as a practical and livable place, but also finding paths of coexistence between Jews and Arabs and between Jews and Jews. This was particularly challenging, as Jerusalem is made up of so many diverse groups.

Yet Jerusalem must be the center for all Jews; tolerance must reign amongst us, and Jews and Arabs must live together in peace. For a united Jerusalem to exist and flourish, we have to forge mutual respect and a willingness to understand and accommodate each other.

It has been a privilege to serve Jerusalem and its people for many decades and to be the first Jewish Mayor of modern united Jerusalem. I prefer to think of myself and my work here not in terms of Herod, who for all his building cared more for himself than for the city, but as the heir of Nehemiah. It was Nehemiah who, at the end of the first exile, came back to Jerusalem in order to seek its "good" and energetically put the people to work. "Half my servants did work and half held lances and shields, bows and armor" (Neh. 4:10). His task, like ours, was not easy, but he succeeded in laying the foundations for the new Jerusalem which existed until the end of the Second Temple period.

We too have returned to Zion from exile. We too face enemies and problems, but we have dedicated ourselves to building and to creating a renewed Jerusalem that will be worthy of its past and able to endure into the future. May Jerusalem's next millennium be remembered as Jerusalem's true age of gold, a time of harmony and peace.

—Teddy Kollek

✌ Author's Preface

Compiling an anthology about a subject that has been under discussion for thousands of years in a variety of world cultures—as Jerusalem has—is a challenge of the first order. Before even beginning the work, it was necessary to determine the parameters that would be dealt with. One volume, no matter how large, could never encompass all the possibilities. Since this work is being compiled in honor of a specific celebration, the trimillennium of David's entry into Jerusalem, it was decided that only Jewish writings on the subject would be included. Wonderful and fascinating things have been written about Jerusalem through the ages by non-Jews, for many of whom Jerusalem has a sacred status, but this book will be confined to writings by Jews as an expression of their experiences or their feelings about Jerusalem. Thus the book really deals with Jerusalem in Jewish consciousness.

Another basic decision was to use original material rather than things written "about. . . ." There are extremely fine essays and books that tell about the history of Jerusalem and that describe Jerusalem during various periods of its history. There are also excellent essays in various languages that describe Jerusalem in the literature of certain eras. Some of these essays, which I read in order to discover the whereabouts of original sources, are listed in the bibliography. However, with the exception of some introductory material to set the scene and some concluding material to summarize it, the pieces here are material written at the time by people who were present at the events they describe. Thus, accounts of the Six Day War are by people who fought in it or witnessed it as civilians, and not by those who later wrote books about it. These latter will also be found in the bibliography. These pieces are reproduced as originally written, with their peculiarities of spelling and transliteration; thus, there are inconsistencies from piece to piece. Another decision was to avoid political polemics as much as possible In the section that discusses the future of Jerusalem, some political ideas are presented, but this is certainly not the main focus of this work.

These decisions having been made, the problems of what to include remained daunting. Building upon what I knew and spending untold hours in the libraries of Jerusalem, I uncovered layer after layer, book after book, and article after article. If it is true, as the sages said, that "one good deed leads to another," it is equally true that one good book leads to another. And so I went from clue to clue, from article to article, from generation to generation. As an organizing principle, I decided to build on historical-cultural eras and to include the outstanding literature of each era in connection with Jerusalem. In addition, other material—including a tour, music, Jerusalem Day services, and children's stories—has been added to make the book useful. Since the book is in English, it was necessary either to find material already translated into English (or, in more modern times, written in English) or to have it translated. It was simply not possible to translate into English everything I wished to include, but there are many selections of prose and poetry that appear here in English for the first time. In this connection, I am indebted to those who either made their superb translations available to me, such as David Simcha Segal and Gabriel Levine, or who undertook it especially for me, such as Aura Hammer. Some selections, including all of the rabbinic sayings, were translated by myself. Another problem was the availability of rights. There is nothing in this volume that I did not wish to include, but some things that I wanted to publish were simply not available. At all times the problem of space was acute. Even in the biblical selections, there was more material than could be included. Therefore, there are undoubtedly things missing that were worthy of inclusion, but in the end difficult and subjective decisions had to be made. There is enough worthy material left over for several other Jerusalem anthologies to be compiled from different perspectives. In condensing the work for this smaller edition, which is intended to be used by the traveller to Jerusalem when visiting the various areas of the city, I eliminated those selections which would be least helpful while viewing Jerusalem and those selections which were not pertinent to the actual sites. In order to gain greater background and depth, I urge the reader to consult the full version when at leisure.

It will be immediately obvious that a disproportionate amount of space has been devoted to works of the last hundred years. The reasons are equally obvious. The amount of such material available is enormous, varied, and of great interest. More people write and publish now than ever before. Furthermore, the variety of approaches is in itself of interest. This is our time and the events concerning Jerusalem that have occurred in it are unequaled for the last nineteen hundred years. They deserve our attention.

I am deeply indebted to the libraries of Jerusalem and the librarians of Jerusalem, without whom this book would never have been put together. Yad Ben Zvi is an absolute treasure-house of Jerusalem-related literature, and its librarians made everything easily accessible to me. The National Library at the Hebrew University was equally indispensable. I am extremely grateful to the library of Hebrew Union College in Jerusalem for the use of its fine facilities, and to the Schocken Institute for access to some rare volumes. I am also very grateful to those in charge of the collections of photographs and graphics at the Central Zionist Archives, the National and University Library, Jerusalem, the Israel Museum, the department of photography of the Israeli Government Press Office and the Museum of Photography at Tel-Hai Industrial Park for the extensive help given me and for making their vast collections readily available. I am especially indebted to the Central Zionist Archives, the Government Press Office, Mr. William P. Wolfe, and the Museum of Photography for their generosity in granting the use of their photographs.

In an enterprise such as this, it is necessary to turn to innumerable publishers, writers, and translators for permission to use their works. I am especially thankful to those who, either for personal reasons or because of their love of Jerusalem, went out of their way to be helpful and graciously to permit the use of their works. My appreciation is also extended to Dr. Ellen Frankel, Editor-in-Chief of the Jewish Publication Society, who originally broached this idea and helped in its realization and to my wife, Raḥel, without whom this book or any of my books would not have been possible. In the case of this work, that is so in a special way because her desire to live in Jerusalem preceded mine and inspired our decision to make Jerusalem our home. Living in Jerusalem since 1973, after having visited it many times starting in 1955, has been our privilege. We came to Jerusalem on the 9th of Av 5733, exactly twenty-one years ago today, remembering the tradition that on Tisha B'Av the destruction took place and on Tisha B'Av the messiah would be born. We felt that our aliya was a beginning of redemption. It is a decision we have never regretted. In a small way, this volume is the repayment of our debt to Jerusalem and voices our prayer that there may always be peace in Jerusalem and tranquillity in all her palaces.

—Reuven Hammer
　　Jerusalem, 9th of Av 5754

☙ Sources and Acknowledgments

Chronological Table, adapted with certain changes from "Walking the Old City," Herbert Alexander, from *Condé Nast Traveler* magazine, March 1993. Reprinted courtesy Condé Nast Traveler. Copyright © 1993 by The Condé Nast Publications Inc.

PROLOGUE

"Jerusalem: A Tapestry in Time," Samuel Heilman, from *A Walker in Jerusalem* by Samuel Heilman. Copyright © 1986 by Samuel Heilman. Reprinted by permission of George Borchardt, Inc., for the author.

THE FIRST GATE
Jerusalem in Biblical Literature

Biblical excerpts are from *Tanakh: The Holy Scriptures*, reprinted by permission of the Jewish Publication Society. Copyright © 1985 by the Jewish Publication Society.

THE SECOND GATE
Jerusalem in Second Temple Literature

"The Letter of Aristeas," from *Aristeas to Philocrates*, ed. and trans. by Moses Hadas, Dropsie College Edition published by Harper and Bros., New York, 1951.

The Psalms of Solomon, Second Baruch, Fourth Baruch, from *The Old Testament Pseudepigrapha* by James H. Charlesworth. Copyright © 1983, 1985 by James H. Charlesworth. Used by permission of Doubleday, a division of Bantam Doubleday Dell Publishing Group, Inc.

The First Book of Maccabees, ed. and trans. by Sidney Tedesche, Dropsie College Edition published by Harper and Bros., New York, 1950.

"Noncanonical Psalms from Qumran," Eileen M. Schuller, *Harvard Semitic Studies 28*, Atlanta 1986, by permission of Harvard Semitic Studies.

"Apostrophe to Zion," from *The Psalm Scrolls of Qumran Cave 11* by J A Sanders (1965), © Oxford University Press 1965, by permission of Oxford University Press.

"The Writings of Philo," from Loeb Classical Library, *Philo* Volumes V, VII, and X, translated by F. H. Colson, Cambridge Mass.: Harvard University Press, 1962, reprinted by permission of Harvard University Press and the Loeb Classical Library.

"The Writings of Josephus Flavius," from *The Life and Works of Flavius Josephus*, translated by Willian Whiston, The John C. Winston Co.

THE THIRD GATE
Jerusalem in Rabbinic Literature

Translations by Reuven Hammer.

THE FOURTH GATE
Jerusalem in the Literature of the Geonic Period

"Redemption," Saadia Gaon, from *Saadia Gaon, The Book of Beliefs and Opinions*, translated by Samuel Rosenblatt, New Haven, Conn.: Yale University Press, 1948. Reprinted by permission of Yale University Press.

"Heavenly Jerusalem" from *Midrashei Geula* (Hebrew), ed. Judah Even-Shemuel. Translated by Reuven Hammer.

"The Jews Return to Jerusalem," from *Texts and Studies in Jewish History* (Hebrew), Simha Assaf, Mosad HaRav Kuk, 1946. Translated by Reuven Hammer.

"No Jerusalem," from *Mahzor for Yom Kippur* (Hebrew), ed. Daniel Goldsmidt, Keren Yerushalyim, Jerusalem 1970. Translated by Reuven Hammer.

"Prayer for Jerusalem: Burial Kaddish" translated by Reuven Hammer.

THE FIFTH GATE
Jerusalem in Writings of the Middle Ages

"Jacob HaCohen," "Isaac Chelo," "Meshullam ben R. Menahem," "Obadia Da Bertinora," from *Jewish Travelers*, Elkan Nathan Adler, George Routledge and Sons LTD, London, 1930.

"Rabbi Benjamin of Tudela," from *The Itinerary of Benjamin of Tudela*, Marcus Nathan Adler, London 1907.

"Rabbi Moses ben Nahman, Letter to His Son," from *Sefer Yerushalayim*, (Hebrew), Talmi, translated by Reuven Hammer;

"Biblical Commentary" from *Studies in Judaism, First Series*, Solomon Schechter, Jewish Publication Society, Philadelphia, 1896.

"Rabbi Moses ben Israel Naphtali Porges Praeger," from *Roads to Zion*, Kurt Wilhelm; Trans. I. M. Lask, Schocken Books, New York, 1948.

Jerusalem in Mystical Literature

"Zion and Jerusalem," "The Foundation Stone," from *The Wisdom of the Zohar*, Fischel Lachover and Isaiah Tishby, translated by David Goldstein, Oxford University Press, Littman Library, Oxford 1989. Reprinted by permission of Oxford University Press and the Litman Library. University Press, Oxford 1989.

"The Temple Above," "For Her Sake," from *The Zohar*, translated by Harry Sperling and Maurice Simon, Soncino Press, London, 1933. London.

"Customs Relating to Jerusalem," translated by Reuven Hammer

"Joy of the Whole World," Yose ben Yose, translated by Zalman Dimitrovsky, from *Zion in Jewish Literature*, ed. Abraham Halkin, the Theodor Herzl Foundation Inc., New York 1961. Reprinted by permission of Theodor Herzl Foundation.

"I Remember," Ammitai ben Shephatiah. Hebrew text in *Sefer Yerushalayim* (Hebrew) Ephraim and Menachem Talmi, Tel Aviv, no year. Translated by Reuven Hammer.

"My Heart Seethes," Shmuel Hanagid. Translated by David Simha Segal. Printed by permission of David Simha Segal.

"Cry, O Zion." Translated by Reuven Hammer.

"Earth's Beauty," Judah Halevi, translated by David Simha Segal. Printed by permission of David Simha Segal.

"My Heart's in the East," "Ode to Sion," Judah Halevi. Translated by Gabriel Levin. Printed by permission of Gabriel Levin.

"Lament for Zion," Hebrew text in *The Penguin Book of Hebrew Verse*, ed. T. Carmi, Penguin Press. Translated by Reuven Hammer.

"Shalom to the City Shalem," Judah Alharizi, Hebrew text in *Anthologia Hebraica* (Hebrew), ed. H. Brody, Leipzig, 1922. Translated by Reuven Hammer.

THE SIXTH GATE
Jerusalem in the Literature of the Turkish and Mandatory Periods

"Life in Jerusalem," Avraham Yaari, from *The Goodly Heritage*, Avraham Yaari, Youth and Hechalutz Department of the Zionist Organization, Jerusalem, 1958. Reprinted by permission of Youth and Hechalutz.

"A Narrative of a Forty Day's Sojourn in the Holy Land," Sir Moses Montefiore, from *A Narrative of a 40 Days' Sojourn in the Holy Land*, Sir Moses Montefiore, Wertheimer, Lea and Co., London, 1875.

"Land of Delight," A. S. Hirschberg, "Sound the Shofar!," Moshe Segal, from *The Western Wall*, ed. Meir Ben Dov, Ministry of Defence, Tel Aviv, 1983.

"Coming to Jerusalem," Eliezer Ben Yehudah, from *Sefer Yerushalayim* (Hebrew), Ephraim and Menachem Talmi, Tel Aviv, no year. Translated by Reuven Hammer.

"Truth from the Land of Israel," from *Kol Kitvei Ahad Haam* (Hebrew), Ahad Haam, Dvir, Tel Aviv, 1956. Translated by Reuven Hammer.

"My Memoirs," Yosef Yoel Rivlin, from *Liyushalayim* (Hebrew), ed. Gedalya Alkoshi, et al, Agudat HaSofrim B'Yisrael, Yachdav, 5728. Translated by Reuven Hammer.

"Raise a Banner to Zion," Saul Tschernichovsky, from *Shirim*, Schocken Tel Aviv, 1951. Translated by Reuven Hammer.

"In Palestine," Theodore Herzl, from *The Diaries of Theodore Herzl*, ed. Marvin Lowenthal, Dial Press, New York, 1956. Reprinted by permission of Doubleday, a division of Doubleday, Dell Publishing Group, Inc.

"How the Glorious Day of Deliverance Came to Jerusalem," Hemda Ben Yehuda, from *Jerusalem: Its Redemption and Future*, Christian Herald, New York, 1918.

"The Renaissance of the Jewish Soul," Chaim Weizmann, from *The Jewish Anthology*, ed. Edmond Fleg, Harcourt, Brace and Co., New York 1925. Translated by Maurice Samuels. Reprinted by permission of Behrman House, Inc.

"Pogrom in Jerusalem," "A Visit to Jerusalem," Chaim Weizmann, from *Trial and Error*, Chaim Weizmann, Jewish Publication Society, Philadelphia 1949. Reprinted by permission of the Jewish Publication Society.

"A Jerusalem Diary," Simon Greenberg. Unpublished writing of Simon Greenberg. Used by permission of his estate.

"To S. Z. Schocken after the 1929 Riots," S. Y. Agnon, from *Me-Atzmi el Atzmi* (Hebrew), Schocken, Jerusalem, 1976, which appeared in *The Jerusalem Quarterly* 9, Fall 1978. Reprinted by permission of Schocken Publishers, Tel Aviv.

THE SEVENTH GATE
Jerusalem in Modern Nonfiction

"Jerusalem Is Called Liberty," Walter Lever, from *Jerusalem Is Called Liberty*, Walter Lever, Massada Press, Inc., Jerusalem, 1951. Reprinted by permission of Massada Press Ltd.

"The Faithful City," Dov Joseph, from *The Faithful City*, Dov Joseph, Simon and Schuster, New York, 1960. Copyright © 1960 by Dov Joseph. Copyright renewed © 1988 by Dov Joseph. Reprinted by permission of Simon and Schuster, Inc.

"The Siege of Jerusalem," Pauline Rose, from *The Seige of Jerusalem*, Pauline Rose, Patmos Publishers, London, no year.

"Going into Captivity," Aharon Liron, from *The Old City of Jerusalem in Siege and Battle* (Hebrew), Aharon Liron, Ministry of Defence Publications Department, Tel Aviv 1957. Translated by Reuven Hammer.

"A Generation's Dream Is Realized," Uzi Narkiss, from *The Liberation of Jerusalem*, Uzi Narkiss, Vallentine Mitchell and Co. Ltd, London, 1983. Reprinted by permission of Vallentine Mitchell and Co. Ltd, London.

"Redeeming the Vow," Rabbi Shlomo Goren, from *Jerusalem Eternal*, ed. Azriel Eisenberg, Board of Jewish Education, New York, 1971.

"Like a Psalm of Praise" "Tonight We're Making History, A Discussion" "Strange City," Amos Oz, translated by Dvora A. Susman and Edna Berlyn, "Jerusalem of My Childhood," Muki Tzur, from *The Seventh Day*, Andre Deutsch Ltd, London, 1970. English version © Henry Near, 1970. Reprinted by permission of Henry Near.

"Fear and Trembling," Moshe Amirav, from *The Lions' Gate* (Hebrew) as printed in *The Western Wall*, ed. Meir Ben Dov, Ministry of Defence, Tel Aviv, 1983.

"At the Western Wall," Elie Wiesel, from *Hadassah Magazine*, July, 1967. Reprinted by permission of *Hadassah Magazine* and Elie Wiesel.

"Jerusalem—A Charismatic City," Abraham Joshua Heschel, from *Israel: An Echo of Eternity*, Abraham Joshua Heschel, Farrar, Straus and Giroux, New York, 1967. Reprinted by permission of Mrs. A. J. Heschel.

"Next Year in Jerusalem!" Anatoly Shcharansky, from *Passover Haggadah: The Feast of Freedom*, Rabbinical Assembly, 1982.

THE EIGHTH GATE
Jerusalem in Modern Fiction

"City of Many Days," Shulamith Hareven, from *City of Many Days*, © 1993 by Shulamith Hareven, translated by Hillel Halkin and the author. Published by Mercury House, San Francisco, CA, and reprinted by permission.

"Tehila: The Praise of Jerusalem," S. Y. Agnon, from "Tehila," translated by Walter Lever. Reprinted by permission of Youth and Hehalutz Department of the Zionist Organization, Jerusalem.

"The Debt of Blood," Elisha Porat, from *Kametz Alef* by Elisha Porat, translated by Dalia Bilu, 1982. Printed by permission of Elisha Porat.

"A Journey through the Land of Israel," Pinchas Sadeh, translated by Hillel Halkin, from *The Tri-Quarterly Review 39*, Spring 1977. Reprinted by permission of Hillel Halkin.

THE NINTH GATE
Jerusalem in Modern Poetry

"From Jerusalem: A First Poem," "Jerusalem Moon," Gabriel Preil, from *Sunset Possibilities and Other Poems*, Gabriel Preil, translated by

Robert Friend, Jewish Publication Society, Philadelphia 1985. Reprinted by permission of the Jewish Publication Society.

"The First Day," "Leaving Jerusalem," Marcia Falk, from *This Year in Jerusalem*, Marcia Falk, State Street Press, 1986, copyright © 1986 by Marcia Falk. Reprinted by permission of Marcia Falk.

"In the Jerusalem Hills," Leah Goldberg, from *Mukdam U'meuhar* (Hebrew), Sifriat HaPoalim, 5719. Translated by Aura Hammer. Printed by permission of Sifriat HaPoalim. © All rights for the original Hebrew version are reserved by Sifriat HaPoalim.

"Jerusalem," David Rokeah, from *Modern Hebrew Poetry*, ed. and translated by Ruth Finer Mintz, University of California Press, Berkeley and Los Angeles, 1966. Reprinted by permission of Ruth Finer Mintz and the University of California Press.

"On Nevi'im Street" (The Street of the Prophets). Yehoash Biber. Translated by Aura Hammer.

"Longing (i)," Ruth Finer Mintz, from *Jerusalem Poems, Love Songs*, Ruth Finer Mintz, Massada Press 1976. Reprinted by permission of Ruth Finer Mintz.

"Religious Quarter," A. C. Jacobs. Reprinted from *Retrievements*, ed. Dennis Silk, Keter Press, Jerusalem, 1968. Efforts to trace the copyright owner, Mr. Jacobs, have not succeeded.

"Building Partner," "Lesson in Geology," Elisha Porat, translated by Riva Rubin. Printed by permission of Elisha Porat.

"To My City Jerusalem, 1967," Amir Gilboa, translated by Shirley Kaufman with Shlomit Rimmon, from *Tri Quarterly Review*, 39, Northwestern University, Evanston, Ill. Reprinted by permission of ACUM. © All rights for the original Hebrew are reserved by the author.

"Homage to Jerusalem; Jerusalem 1967," Yehuda Amichai, translated by Harold Schimmel, reprinted by permission of Harold Schimmel, Yehuda Amichai and ACUM. © All rights for the original Hebrew are reserved by the author.

"Jerusalem, 1968," David Rokeah, translated by Alan Brownjohn, from *Jerusalem: Most Fair of Cities*, Armon Press, 1977. Reprinted by permission of ACUM. © All rights for the original Hebrew are reserved by the author.

"Jerusalem," Else Lasker-Schüler, translated by Audru Durchslag and Jeanette Litman-Demeestere, from *Hebrew Ballads and Other Poems*, Jewish Publication Society, Philadelphia, 1980. Reprinted by permission of the Jewish Publication Society.

"Autumn in Jerusalem," Oded Peled, translated by Aura Hammer, from a series of Jerusalem poems (unpublished). Printed by permission of Oded Peled and Aura Hammer.

"A View of Jerusalem," T. Carmi, from *Selected Poems*, T. Carmi and Dan Pagis, Abelard-Schuman. Reprinted by permission of ACUM. © All rights for the original Hebrew are reserved by the author.

"City of Wound," Haim Guri, from *Flowers of Fire* (Hebrew), Tarshish Publishers, 1964. Translated by Aura Hammer. Printed by permission of ACUM and Aura Hammer. © All rights for the original Hebrew are reserved by the author.

"House Dog," Uri Zvi Greenberg, from *In the Midst of the World and Time* (Hebrew), Hakibbutz Hameuchad, 1929. Translated by Aura Hammer. Published by permission of ACUM and Aura Hammer. © All rights for the original Hebrew version are reserved by the estate of the author.

"Jerusalem," Moshe HaNa-ami, from *Lamerchav*, January 4, 1963. Translated by Aura Hammer. Printed by permission of Aura

Hammer and ACUM. © All rights for the original Hebrew are reserved by the author.

"The Warm Stone on the Hill of Jerusalem," Ayin Tur-Malka, from *Ken Shel Zardim* (Hebrew) Kerem Press. Translated by Aura Hammer. Printed by permission of Aura Hammer, Ayin Tur-Malka and ACUM. © All rights for the original Hebrew are reserved by the author.

"Jerusalem's Walls," Israel Efrat, from *How Deep It Is Planted* (Hebrew), Devir, 1966, translated by Aura Hammer. Printed by permission of Aura Hammer.

"Abu-Tor," David Rokeah, from *Keno shel Yam* (Hebrew), Arbeh Publishers, 5723. Translated by Aura Hammer. Printed by permission of ACUM and Aura Hammer. © All rights to the original Hebrew are reserved by the author.

"Evening in Jerusalem," Yehuda Karni, from *An Anthology of Modern Hebrew Poetry*, ed. and translated by Abraham Birman, Abelard-Schuman, London, 1968. Efforts to trace the copyright holder have been unsuccessful.

"I Don't Know if Mount Zion," Abba Kovner, translated by Warren Bargad and Stanley F. Chyet, from *Israeli Poetry*, ed. Warren Bargad and Stanley F. Chyet, Indiana University Press, Bloomington, Ind., 1986. Reprinted by permission of Indiana University Press and ACUM. © All rights to the original Hebrew are reserved by the author.

"Moriah," Levi Ben Amitai, from *Vilirushalayim* (Hebrew), ed. by G. Alkoshi, Yahdav Press, Jerusalem. Translated by Reuven Hammer. Printed by permission of ACUM. All rights for the original Hebrew are reserved by the author.

"City of David," Zerubavel Gilad, from *Hakichali* (Hebrew), HaKibbutz HaMeuchad, 5738. Translated by Aura Hammer. Printed by permission of Aura Hammer.

"Jerusalem," Yaakov Fichman, from *An Anthology of Modern Hebrew Poetry*, selected by S. Y. Penueli and A. Ukhmani, vol. 1, Institute for the Translation of Hebrew Literature and Israel University Press. Translated by Robert Friend. English © The Institute for the Translation of Hebrew Literature. Reprinted by permission of the Institute for the Translation of Hebrew Literature and ACUM. © All rights to the original Hebrew are reserved by the author.

"Penalty Kick," Ronny Someck, from *Panther* (Hebrew), Zemorah Bitan. Translated by Aura Hammer. Reprinted by permission of ACUM and Aura Hammer. © All rights for the original Hebrew version are reserved by the author.

"Jerusalem: Ladders of Love," Gabriel Preil, from *The Literary Review*, Winter 1983, vol. 26 number 2, Fairleigh Dickinson University, Madison, N.J. Efforts to locate the copyright holder have been unsuccessful.

"From the Streets of Jerusalem," Abba Kovner, from *Tatzpiot* (Hebrew), Sifriat HaPoalim, 1977. Translated by Aura Hammer. Reprinted by permission of ACUM and Aura Hammer. © All rights for the original Hebrew are reserved by the author.

"Tourists," Yehuda Amichai, from *Great Tranquility*, Yehuda Amichai. Translated by Glenda Abramson and Tidor Parfitt. Copyright © 1983 by Yehuda Amichai. Reprinted by permission of HarperCollins Publishers, Inc.

THE TENTH GATE
Jerusalem in Jewish Folklore

"King David's Tomb in Jerusalem," from *Folktales of Israel*, edited by Dov Noy with the assistance of Dan Ben Amos, University of

Chicago Press, 1963. Reprinted by permission of the University of Chicago Press.

Legends of Jerusalem, Zev Vilnay, from *Legends of Jerusalem*, Zev Vilnay, Jewish Publication Society, Philadelphia, 1973. Reprinted by permission of the Jewish Publication Society.

"Did King David Erect the Tower of David?" Abraham E. Millgram, from *Jerusalem Curiosities*, Jewish Publication Society, Philadelphia, 1990. Reprinted by permission of the Jewish Publication Society.

"700 Years of Sanctity." Meir Ben Dov, from *HaArtetz*, July 22, 1988. Translated by Reuven Hammer. Printed by permission of Meir Ben Dov.

THE ELEVENTH GATE
Archaeology of the Old City

"Walking the Old City: A Jerusalem Tour," Herbert Alexander, from *Condé Nast Traveler* magazine, March 1993. Reprinted courtesy *Condé Nast Traveler*. Copyright © 1993 by The Condé Nast Publications, Inc.

"Twenty-five Years of Excavations in Jerusalem, 1967–1992," Hillel Geva, from *Ancient Jerusalem Revealed*, ed. Hillel Geva, Israel Exploration Society, Jerusalem, 1994. Reprinted by permission of the Israel Exploration Society.

THE TWELFTH GATE
Jerusalem: Toward the Future

"Jerusalem," Avraham B. Yehoshua, from *The Jerusalem Quarterly*, Spring 1981. Reprinted by permission of A. B. Yehoshua.

"Jerusalem—Today and Tomorrow," Teddy Kollek, from *Jerusalem: Problems and Prospects*, ed. Joel Kramer, Praeger Publishers, New York, 1980. Reprinted by permission of Teddy Kollek.

EPILOGUE

"Jerusalem, Holy City," R. J. Zvi Werblowsky, from *Jerusalem 5000 Years of History*, Les Dossiers d'Archeologie, March 1992, Paris. Reprinted by permission of Les Dossiers d'Archeologie and R. J. Zvi Werblowsky.

"Jerusalem the Irreplaceable," André Neher, from *Jerusalem: Most Fair of Cities*, Armon, 1977, taken from "Dans tes portes Jerusalem," Albin Michel, Paris. Translated by Lida Schechtman. Reprinted by permission of Dr. Rina Neher.

"Pray for the Well-Being of Jerusalem," S. Y. Agnon, from *Meatzmi L'Atzmi* (Hebrew), Schocken Press, Tel Aviv. Translated by Reuven Hammer. Printed by permission of Schocken Press.

THE JERUSALEM ANTHOLOGY

෨ A Literary Guide

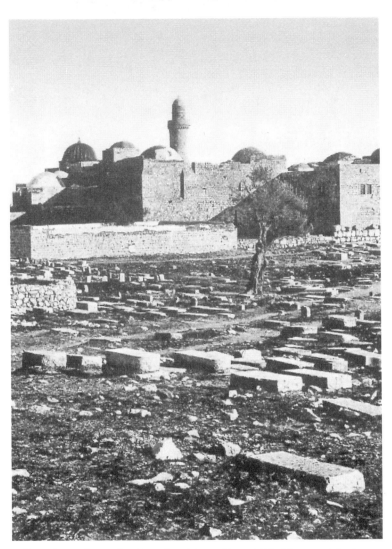

Jerusalem. The Tomb of David on Mount Zion, 1880. Photograph by La Maison Bonfils (The Museum of Photography at Tel-Hai Industrial Park; with permission)

☺ Introduction

Jerusalem in Jewish Consciousness

Reuven Hammer

For three thousand years Jerusalem has held a unique place in the mind and heart of the people Israel. Other cities played a role in the history of Israel centuries before Jerusalem did. Abraham lived in Beersheba. The first purchase of land in Canaan by a Hebrew was in Hebron. Jacob's sacred site was Beth El (which some later traditions identified with Jerusalem!). The Ark of the Covenant dwelt in Shilo before Jerusalem was conquered. The first capital of David's kingdom was the ancient city of Hebron. Yet, ultimately, none of these cities assumed the importance, the centrality, the sacredness, which was bestowed upon Jerusalem.

It would not be an exaggeration to say that no city in the history of the nations has been as important a part of the consciousness of a people for as long and continuous a period of time as has Jerusalem. For three thousand years it has been the capital of the kingdom of the people of Israel, whatever name and form that people assumed. Even when there was no kingdom, during the seventy years of the first exile and the nearly nineteen hundred years of the second exile, Jerusalem was the capital of the stateless people called the Jews. The eternal pledge made by the exiled levitical singers—"If I forget you, O Jerusalem, let my right hand wither . . ." (Pss. 137:5)—became the watchword of Jews from that moment to this. The symbolism of having it recited at the conclusion of each wedding ceremony—fulfilling the verse, "Let my tongue stick to my palate if I cease to think of you, if I do not keep Jerusalem in memory *even at my happiest hour*" (Pss. 137:6)—is a powerful expression of the desire to pass this

3

pledge from generation to generation. Even when they could not live in Jerusalem, could not set foot in it, Jews faced Jerusalem in devotion three times daily and prayed for its restoration not only during those three prayers but after every meal. Twice a year, at the conclusion of the two most impressive moments of the Jewish year, Yom Kippur and the Passover Seder, all participants pledge, "Next year in Jerusalem!" If modern leaders of the Zionist movement contemplated the possibility of a Jewish state devoid of Jerusalem or of an Israel with its capital elsewhere, they soon discovered that this was an impossibility and that the defense of Jerusalem and the proclamation of Jerusalem as Israel's capital were essential to Israel's existence.

There were ancient cities such as Babylon that were centers of civilization when Jerusalem was little more than a small village. They have long ceased to exist. Athens, which comes closer to playing a central role in the life of a people than any other of the world's cities, was nevertheless only one of the important cities of the various Greek states. Rome was the capital of a mighty empire and was indeed the metropolis of its time, but it also became a parasite, "the inveterate sponger" (Lewis Mumford, *The City in History* [New York: Harcourt, Brace and World, 1961], p. 228.) a condition that led to its eventual destruction. Furthermore, Rome assumed its role long after Jerusalem had become the "city of the great King" (Pss. 48:3) and later changed completely to become the spiritual center of a mighty faith rather than the capital of an empire. Jerusalem's three thousand continuous years of centrality to Judaism and the Jewish people remains unique.

There is no doubt that, although the original reasons for David's choice of Jerusalem were political and geographic, the driving force that created this eternal Jerusalem in the Jewish consciousness was religious. As Lewis Mumford wrote, "The first germ of the city, then, is in the ceremonial meeting place that serves as the goal for pilgrimage: a site to which family or clan groups are drawn back, at seasonal intervals, because it concentrates ... certain 'spiritual' or supernatural powers, powers of higher potency and greater duration, of wider cosmic significance, than the ordinary processes of life." (ibid, p. 10). It was the identification of Jerusalem with the earthly dwelling place of the Presence of God (the *Shekhina*) that ultimately rendered it unique. Jerusalem was chosen as "the place" where God would dwell and thus became the pilgrim site for Jews throughout the ages. The trip to Jerusalem at the Festivals during the period of the Second Temple attracted Jews from the entire Mediterranean basin and assumed gigantic, even legendary, proportions.

The designation of Mount Zion (the Temple Mount, not the hill called Mount Zion today) in Jerusalem as "the mountain of the Lord ... His holy place" (Pss. 24:3) was the culmination of a long process by which the tradition of the appearance of God upon Mount Sinai—"the mountain of God" (Exod. 3:1)—was transferred to Mount Zion. It is the presence of God that creates sanctity. There is no place that has sanctity built into it. Holiness is the quality of God, as we see from the words that Isaiah ascribes to the angels when he sees the Lord: "Holy, holy, holy! The Lord of Hosts! His presence fills all the earth!" (Isa. 6.3). Mount Sinai was holy because of God's appearance upon it, but when the Israelites left the wilderness, they took the mountain with them by erecting the Sanctuary containing the Ark of the Covenant, which served as a portable Sinai. There, too, the presence of God would appear to them: "When Moses had finished the work, the cloud covered the Tent of Meeting, and the Presence of the Lord filled the Tabernacle" (Exod.

40:33–34). By placing the Ark, the central feature of the Tabernacle, upon the mountain in Jerusalem (see 2 Sam. 6:12–19), David laid the foundation for the sanctity of that mountain and the holiness of Jerusalem. The erection of a permanent building by Solomon—"I have now built for You a stately House, a place where You may dwell forever" (1 Kings 8:13)—a revolutionary step in the faith of Israel, signaled the permanence of the Presence of God on the holy mountain. In this way, the Mountain of God, Sinai, merged with Mount Zion and became the holy mountain. Centuries later, this process was capped when the almost mythical Mount Moriah of the binding of Isaac—named by Abraham "Adonai-yireh, whence the present saying, 'On the mount of the Lord there is vision' " (Gen. 22:14)—was identified with Mount Zion as well: "Then Solomon began to build the House of the Lord in Jerusalem on Mount Moriah . . ." (2 Chron. 3:1). As the midrash put it so succinctly, "The foundations of Jerusalem exist because of the merit of two holy mountains: Mount Sinai and Mount Moriah" (Yalkut Shimoni Pss. 836).

Thus the sanctity of the Temple created an aura and eventually a legal status of sanctity for the entire city (J. A. Seelingman, "Jerusalem in Jewish-Hellenistic Thought" [12th Archaeological Convention, 1957] p. 194). But sanctity in Judaism is not divorced from worldly matters. Jerusalem was never to be turned into a "spiritual center" with no political reality. It had to play this dual role at all times.

If the presence of the Temple rendered Jerusalem holy, the presence of the king, also chosen by God, rendered it politically central. Again, Mumford: "In the urban implosion, the king stands at the center: he is the polar magnet that draws to the heart of the city and brings under the control of the palace and the temple all the new forces of civilization. Sometimes the king founded new cities; sometimes he transformed old country towns that had long been a-building, placing them under the authority of his governors; in either case his rule made a decisive change in their form and contents" (ibid, p. 35).

As early as the times of the prophets, a third, universal and eschatological, meaning was attached to Jerusalem. The same prophets who saw Jerusalem as all too real a city, an urban gathering of sinners, comparable to Sodom and Gomorrah, doomed to destruction unless redeemed by repentance, also saw it as the eventual site of the redemption. They had the unique vision of Jerusalem as the center of the hope of humankind:

Without for a moment losing its reality as an actual city central to a real nation living a this-worldly existence, the writings of the prophets turned Jerusalem into a symbol of messianic perfection. Lurking behind the Jerusalem of tailors and shoemakers, of sages, priests, and kings, is that mystic vision of a Jerusalem to which all nations will come to acknowledge the One God and from which instruction will issue to transform the world into a place of justice and peace.

A shadow of this vision was the eternal hope of Jews that the condition of destruction would eventually be reversed and that a rebuilt Jerusalem would welcome back her children as a mother embraces a long-lost child. "As a mother comforts her son, so will I comfort you and you shall find comfort in Jerusalem" (Isa. 66:13).

Jerusalem's centrality to Judaism and the Jewish people, then, ultimately stands on three pillars: its identification as the sacred place chosen by God; its political centrality as the capital and dwelling of the chosen king; its place in the prophetic and later rabbinic and mystic visions of the messianic era.

Even though the religious, mystical significance grew with the centuries, and certainly distance and exile tended to emphasize the other-worldly Jerusalem, the real Jerusalem never ceased to exist in Jewish consciousness:

> Said the Holy One, "I will not enter heavenly Jerusalem until I enter earthly Jerusalem" (Taanit 5a).

In the Middle Ages, the sacred poetry would mourn for Jerusalem and praise it in mystic terms, but the travelers would write of the real city—its problems of housing, food, and simply making a living.

In modern times, the attitudes became more varied. There was a time when, for the Zionist pioneers bent upon establishing a new political entity and in revolt against the traditions of the European-Jewish past, Jerusalem was in danger of becoming a symbol of the old ways they wanted to leave behind, whereas Tel Aviv, Rehovot, or Degania would be seen as the new image of the new Jew. In the long run, however, Jerusalem was irreplaceable, and the echoes of its sanctity created a special aura that could be reinterpreted but not replaced. Thus Boris Schatz, Usishkin, and Ahad HaAm all have visions of the future Jerusalem, which becomes a universal center for the greatest hopes and aspirations of Israel and all humankind. Chaim Weizmann cannot envision the great center of learning, the Hebrew University, anywhere else but on Mount Scopus. The efforts made during the War for Independence to keep control of the Old City and, above all, the events of the Six Day War testify to the unique place held by Jerusalem in the minds of the vast majority of Israelis and Jews, religious or secular.

In the minds of secular thinkers today Jerusalem is no less central. For some this may be a result of its long history. It is so interwoven with every event in Judaism, with thought and writings, with hopes and dreams, that it cannot be forgotten or dispensed with. And even the secular will suddenly find that there is a spiritual, almost a mystical meaning, which cannot so easily be dismissed. A. B. Yehoshua cannot write about Jerusalem without recalling the prophets who walked there, the deep connection of the Jewish people to it, and the "wonderful spiritual power poured out over this city," all the while struggling with the difficulties which Jerusalem presents in real terms today.

Although there is no lack of superstition in the attitudes of some toward Jerusalem and its most sacred site, the Wall, there is no doubt that in that one blinding moment of miraculous revelation in 1967 when the city of Jerusalem was "built up, a city knit together" (Pss. 122:3), the secular and the religious alike experienced some higher meaning than mere stones can convey. And if that moment cannot be sustained—as even the Israelites at the Sea were unable to sustain *that* supreme moment—it nevertheless became a transforming event for those who experienced it.

❧

Jerusalem is a city in which ancient writings have new meanings, in which one can walk the streets and read the words of the prophets, the psalmists, the rabbis, the philosophers, the mystics, the medievals, the poets, the travelers, and the moderns, the warriors, the theologians, and the statesmen on the sites where they were written or to which they refer, and find meaning in them. Somehow this city that was "knit together" also binds together the entire past of Jewry with its future and with the entire people of Israel wherever they may be.

It is the aim of this book to bind together somehow the three thousand years of Jewish Jerusalem and to create a feeling of unity—or at least of continuity—in the Jewish consciousness of Jerusalem. For, in fact, Jerusalem, both vertically through its history and horizontally in its present reality, can hardly be termed a unity. Each period of history has its own flavor and uniqueness. The Jerusalem of David, the Jerusalem of Ezra, the Jerusalem of Herod, the Jerusalem of the Romans, of the Byzantines, of the Mamelukes, of the Crusaders, of the Turks, the Jerusalem of the last century, and the Jerusalem of today are very different cities. And while the Jerusalem of today may share one civil administration, the life of Meah Shearim and that of secular neighborhoods, the Jerusalem of the *shuk* and that of Talbiah, of the Katamonim and Rehavia, of the Bucharian sector, French Hill and Talpiot Mizrah, to say nothing of Jewish versus Arab Jerusalem, seem anything but united. Yet they are at least intertwined. And in the Jewish consciousness—which is the basic concern of this volume—there is a binding together that connects the earliest writings of the Bible with the works of our own day. It is not the history of Jerusalem as such that concerns us, not its politics or geography, but the way in which the Jewish consciousness has perceived Jerusalem, has been created by it, and has in turn created a Jerusalem that includes streets and alleys but goes beyond that into feelings, values, beliefs, and prophetic hopes.

PROLOGUE

Aerial view of the Temple Mount and the remains uncovered in the Ophel area south of it; looking west (Ancient Jerusalem Revealed. Israel Exploration Society; with permission)

☙ Jerusalem: A Tapestry in Time

Samuel Heilman

Samuel Heilman is a professor of sociology at Queens College of the City University of New York.

Jerusalem: it is not one, but many. It is a place in which people actually live; it is a place which lives in them. It is a figment of the imagination, an idea. It is visible, open to discovery; it is unseen, hidden to all but insiders. It is constructed of mortar and stone and inhabited by flesh and bone; it is formed of spirit and faith and filled by belief and memory. It is the Omphalos Mundi—Navel of the World; it is a centuries-old but recently rebuilt city of Judean Hills, situated on the western edge of an arid wilderness.

Jerusalem is also called the city of peace; but throughout all memory, it has been a focal point of conflict. And so what is significant to some may be irrelevant to others. One people's shrine becomes another's ruin. The center for one group is the periphery for another. What one inhabitant wishes to save, another would destroy. What one would uncover, another would bury. One's dream and hope is another's nightmare and curse.

There are those who look upon the city as layers of history, a site to be archeologically uncovered, a place where one epoch is built upon another: the ancient Jebusite city lies beneath the City of David, which in turn merges into houses from the Second Temple and Hasmonean periods, built hundreds of years later. Then, with the Roman conquest of the city and the final exile of the Judeans, Jerusalem—or Aelia Capitolina, as the conquerors now called the place—went through two millennia of incarnations: Byzantine, Persian, Moslem, Umayyad or Syrian, Abbasid or Baghdadi, Fatimid,

Crusader, Mameluke or Egyptian, Ottoman, and British. After 1948, the city—a vulnerable border town—was divided for nineteen years by an armistice between the Israelis and the Jordanians. And in 1967, after the armistice was broken, it became at last the united capital of the modern state of Israel.

To those who dig, tracing the lines of history in the dirt and reconstructing it from the shards thus uncovered is what gives this city its ultimate meaning. Only in the journey toward the deepest layers, through other people's memories, down to the bedrock, does Jerusalem reveal itself and its attachments.

But everyone digs to the level of his interest and concern. For the Jews, only relics from the ancient period—a short spell in the days of the Patriarchs and then from David in 1200 B.C.E. to the destruction of the Second Temple in the year 70 C.E.—and the period of the Return to Zion, beginning under the Ottomans, growing under the British and blooming after the Israeli War of Independence, are important. All else remains a rime of exile.

Yet despite that long exile, to many Jews the memories and attachments of Jerusalem are visible, comprehensible, and undeniable. This is our land, say many of them, the land of our forebears. Here is our history and here is our future. We have never forgotten thee, O Jerusalem, and now that we are returned, we shall never leave.

And why? Because over the course of nearly two and a half millennia, Jerusalem remained the spiritual center of the universe, the crown of Jewish glory and apex of all hope. Distance from it was measured not in space but by intensity of yearning to be there. Six hundred and fifty-six times the city is mentioned in Scripture, and scores more in liturgy. On the summit of Mount Moriah, atop the *Even Sh'tiyyah*, or Foundation Stone, the Patriarch Abraham bound his son Isaac to be offered up to God, and upon that same stone, many believe, Jacob—the father of the children of Israel—rested his head during his prophetic dream. In Jerusalem, Kind David set up his capital, Zion, and on Moriah his son Solomon built the Holy Temple—God's resting place and, for the children of Israel, the holiest spot on earth. From Jerusalem and Zion, many have come to believe, began the Jewish exile, and here, the faithful say, upon arrival of the Messiah, bringing with him the resurrected dead, the final redemption will come. "The Lord loves the gates of Zion more than all the dwellings of Jacob," sang the Psalmist. "And the people blessed all those who were willing to dwell in Jerusalem," proclaimed the prophet Nehemiah.

Even in the face of that prophecy, some Jews ironically prefer a Jerusalem whose image in formed by the patterns of life that emerged in Eastern Europe, in the ghettoes of Sanz or Mattersdorf, Ger or Belz. If God happened to have placed His Holy Temple atop Moriah, they have only to close their eyes when they pray at its remaining stones, and thus be transported back to the Jerusalem of their Eastern European dreams, awaiting the days of the Messiah when those dreams will come true.

But Jerusalem is not important only to the faithful Jews. Others, for whom religion is but a relic or at best a part of national consciousness and folk life, hear more clearly the distant voice of Nehemiah and look upon the city as the soul of their homeland, the starting point of national history, the ground in which are planted the seeds of a growing national consciousness.

Many Jews who live the Zionist dream—call them Israelis—see Jerusalem in this way. For these people, beneath what *their* prophet Theodor Herzl called in his diaries "the musty deposits of two thousand years of inhumanity, intolerance and uncleanliness," lie the nuggets of collective memory in which are embedded all the hopes of an exiled people for national revival in the land of its origins, the

Promised Land. To retrieve and re-collect them and thereby over-come the estrangement of exile, Jerusalem must—these Jews believe—be penetrated, explored, plumbed and protected. As the Bible would have a man know a woman, so must the people of Israel know this Jerusalem: in body and spirit.

Since the days of its conquest by King David, no other nation has made Jerusalem its capital, the heart of its nation. To Jerusalem Nehemiah and Ezra returned to renew the days of old. Here Solomon's Temple which the Babylonians had destroyed was rebuilt. In Jerusalem began the short-lived revolt of Bar Kochba against the occupying Roman legions. From here, some believe, began the Diaspora, that most unnatural condition of the Jews; and here, some trust, the Return to Zion, the naturalization of the Jews, will at last be completed.

Although overlooked during the Zionist settlement process, in the days when Tel Aviv grew miraculously out of sand dunes and the swamps of the Hula Valley were drained while the fields of Degania were plowed, the return to Jerusalem remained the ends of hope. The last word of "Ha-Tik'vah," the song that would become the national anthem of the new Jewish State of Israel, was and remains "Jerusalem."

♏

And so in the end, Jerusalem must be understood as a tapestry in time. Woven into its present is an unforgettable past, and inter-twined with both is an idealized future. Normally, the sequence of time imposed by everyday life cannot be reversed or reordered; but in Jerusalem normal time can be rearranged. It is therefore not surpris-ing that people who wander within its borders often find the present least accessible or engaging, while they make their ways easily into the past or gain sudden access to some messianic timescape yet to come. Sometimes they can even grab hold of the ephemeral moment outside the flow of time as we know it—an interval which, although hardly more than a promise or hope, is clung to with the greatest fervor by those who are touched by it. So those who spend time in the city sooner or later find themselves somehow leaping back and forth from the ancient days to distant prophecies, occasionally getting caught up in the spaces in between.

THE FIRST GATE

Jerusalem in Biblical Literature

Entrance to the Old City, Jaffa Gate, 1925 (Central Zionist Archives; with permission)

THE TORAH AND HISTORICAL BOOKS

Considering its great importance in later historical and prophetic books, the entrance of Jerusalem upon the Jewish literary scene in the Torah, the most sacred part of Scripture, is modest indeed. It does not even appear by the name by which we know it, but is assumed to be referred to by the name Salem in the story of Abraham's victory in a war to liberate his nephew Lot. At that time:

> And Melchizedek, king of Salem, brought out bread and wine; he was a priest of God Most High. He blessed him, saying,
>
> "Blessed be Abram of God Most High,
>
> Creator of heaven and earth.
>
> And blessed be God Most High,
>
> Who has delivered your foes into your hand."
>
> (GEN. 14:18–20)

It has been suggested that the first part of the name of the city may have been like that of Ur-Kasdim, possibly from the Sumarian *uru* meaning "city." This was Ur-Shalem, i.e. Yerushalem, eventually Yerushalayim. Another suggestion in that it derives from the words *yarah*—"is found"—and *Shulmanu*—the name of a West Semitic deity. The popular etymology of "ir-shalom"—the city of peace—would then be no more than a midrashic invention of noble intention and poetic meaning. Although Jewish tradition has long identified Mount Moriah upon which Abraham is prepared to offer his son Isaac (Gen. 22:2,14) as the site of the Temple—that is, the acropolis of Jerusalem—this specific identification is found only in 2 Chronicles 3:1:

> Then Solomon began to build the House of the Lord in Jerusalem on Mount Moriah, where [the Lord] had ap-

peared to his father David, at the place which David had designated, at the threshing floor of Ornan the Jebusite.

Since Chronicles is a late book, dating from the Second Temple period, and since both the parallel story in the earlier book of Kings (1 Kings 6:1) and the story of David's purchase of the threshing floor (2 Sam. 24:18–25) do not mention this identification, scholars tend to regard it as a late invention. In any case, Jewish tradition made this identification between the two so that the verse explaining the meaning of Moriah:

> And Abraham named that site Adonai-yireh [that is, the Lord will see], whence the present saying, "On the mount of the Lord there is vision." (GEN. 22:14)

was understood as explaining the sacredness of the particular mountain upon which the Temple was built.

In view of the fact that Deuteronomy 16:16, in commanding males to appear before the Lord three times a year in the place the Lord shall choose, uses language which seems to echo deliberately the explanation of Mount Moriah in Genesis 22:14, it may well be that by the time Deuteronomy was promulgated in the seventh century B.C.E. the identification between Moriah and the Temple mount was already assumed.

Nevertheless, it is only when we come to the historical narratives referring to the conquest of the Land found in the Early Prophets that Jerusalem is called by name and explicitly enters the stage of Israelite history. The first specific mention of Jerusalem by name is found in Joshua 10:1–5:

> When King Adoni-zedek of Jerusalem learned that Joshua had captured Ai and proscribed it, treating Ai and its king as he had treated Jericho and its king, and that,

> moreover, the people of Gibeon had come to terms with Israel and remained among them, he was very frightened. . . . So King Adoni-zedek of Jerusalem sent this message to King Hoham of Hebron, King Piram of Jarmuth, King Japhia of Lachish, and King Debir of Eglon: "Come up and help me defeat Gibeon; for it has come to terms with Joshua and the Israelites."

Jerusalem appears next in the description of the borders of the tribe of Judah, which also mentions some of the major features of the city:

> Then the boundary ascended into the Valley of Ben-hinnom, along the southern flank of the Jebusites—that is, Jerusalem. The boundary then ran up to the top of the hill which flanks the Valley of Hinnom on the west, at the northern end of the Valley of Rephaim. (JOSH. 15:8)

Yet another name for Jerusalem is given when it is numbered among the towns of the tribe of Benjamin:

> Zela, Eleph, and Jebus—that is Jerusalem . . . (JOSH. 18:28)

The first Israelite conquest of the city came when the tribe of Judah captured it after the death of Joshua:

> The Judites attacked Jerusalem and captured it; they put it to the sword and set the city on fire. (JUDG. 1:8)

For whatever reason, the tribe of Judah does not seem to have retained it, for in the same chapter, it is described as being within the borders of Benjamin, who also does not dislodge its Cannanite inhabitants:

> The Benjaminites did not dispossess the Jebusite inhabitants of Jerusalem; so the Jebusites have dwelt with the Benjaminites in Jerusalem to this day. (JUDG. 1:21)

It remained for David to capture this city which had been so inconsequential and peripheral to Israel and make it the capital of the kingdom:

> The king and his men set out for Jerusalem against the Jebusites who inhabited the region. David was told, "You will never get in here! Even the blind and the lame will turn you back." . . . But David captured the stronghold of Zion; it is now the City of David. . . . David occupied the stronghold and renamed it the City of David; David also fortified the surrounding area, from the Millo inward. (2 Sam. 5:6–7, 9)

David had reigned in Hebron seven years and six months. His reasons for moving from Hebron to Jerusalem are not explained. It is generally assumed that a city which had not previously been occupied by one of the tribes, one which was on the border between two tribes, could more easily be accepted by all the tribes as their capital. Eventually, it was the amalgam of David, the chosen king, with Jerusalem, "the place I shall choose," which created the overwhelming importance and indeed centrality of Jerusalem in Jewish consciousness and history. Because it is the city of David, if for no other reason, it came to occupy the position it has today and has had for the last three thousand years.

David's building program to transform the city began at once:

> King Hiram of Tyre sent envoys to David with cedar logs, carpenters, and stonemasons; and they built a palace for David. (2 Sam. 5:11)

From that time on, the history of Israel and the history of Jerusalem become synonymous. All the major events of the rest of the book of

---

City of David (Ancient Jerusalem Revealed. Israel Exploration Society; with ⎯⎯⎯ permission)

Samuel—as well as of the two books of Kings, Ezra, and Nehemiah—
take place in Jerusalem.

Evidently, David's plan was to create in Jerusalem not only the
political capital of the kingdom, but the religious capital, as well.
After a disastrous first attempt (see: 2 Sam. 6:3–10), the ark was
brought to Jerusalem:

> Thereupon David went and brought up the Ark of God
> from the house of Obed-edom to the City of David,
> amid rejoicing. . . . Thus David and all the House of Israel
> brought up the Ark of the Lord with shouts and with
> blasts of the horn. . . . They brought in the Ark of the
> Lord and set it up in its place inside the tent which
> David had pitched for it, and David sacrificed burnt of-
> ferings and offerings of well-being before the Lord.
> (2 SAM. 6:12–18)

Nevertheless, David was not permitted to construct a building, as
opposed to a tent, to house the Ark. The desert tradition of a tent
was still understood to be authoritative (2 Sam. 7:4–7). The building
of the Temple was left for Solomon. See 1 Kings 5:19. Solomon was
an ambitious builder. He was not content with what David had built
but built his own palace and the walls around Jerusalem:

> He married Pharoah's daughter and brought her to the
> City of David [to live there] until he had finished build-
> ing his palace, and the House of the Lord, and the walls
> around Jerusalem. (1 KINGS 3:1)

With wood supplied by Hiram of Lebanon, with "huge blocks of
choice stone," with the forced labor of 30,000 men as well as "70,000
porters and 80,000 quarriers" (1 Kings 5:29–31) the house was built:

> In the fourth year, in the month of Ziv, the foundations
> of the House were laid; and in the eleventh year, in the

> month of Bul—that is, the eighth month—the House was
> completed according to all its details and all its specifica-
> tions. It took him seven years to build it. . . .
>
> Then Solomon convoked the elders of Israel—all the
> heads of the tribes and the ancestral chieftains of the
> Israelites—before King Solomon in Jerusalem, to bring up
> the Ark of the Covenant of the Lord from the City of
> David, that is, Zion. (1 KINGS 6:37–38; 8:1)

The great ceremony of the dedication and Solomon's monumental
prayer made it clear that although the house could never contain
God, nevertheless this was no mere sanctuary, but the special place
in which prayers would be heard and toward which God's attention
would be given. If God would not dwell there, He assured them that
"My name shall abide there" (1 Kings 8:29). The difference may
have been theologically important, but was too subtle to make an
impact on the people. Furthermore, Solomon received the Lord's
assurance that:

> I consecrate this House which you have built and I set
> My name there forever. My eyes and My heart shall ever
> be there. (1 Kings 9:3)

The connection between David and Jerusalem is often stressed in
verses such as 1 Kings 11:32:

> But one tribe shall remain his—for the sake of My ser-
> vant David and for the sake of Jerusalem, the city that I
> have chosen out of all the tribes of Israel.

Thus the chosen House of David, the chosen City of David, and
the chosen House of the Lord all combined to give Jerusalem a unique
status. It became the very heart and soul of the people of Israel.

However, David's conquest and fortification of Jerusalem did not

Jerusalem with Temple of Solomon, Liber Chronicorum, Nurenberg, 1493 (Collection of the National and University Library, Jerusalem; with permission)

make it safe from attack. The first such attack took place in 927 b.c.e. during the reign of Rehoboam, son of Solomon:

> In the fifth year of King Rehoboam, King Shishak of Egypt marched against Jerusalem and carried off the treasures of the House of the Lord and the treasures of the royal palace. (1 KINGS 14:25–26)

Another attack was made during the reign of King Joash (837–798 B.C.E.):

At that time, King Hazael of Aram came up and attacked Gath and captured it; and Hazael proceeded to march on Jerusalem. Thereupon King Joash of Judah took all the objects that had been consecrated by his fathers, King Jehoshaphat, Jehoram, and Ahaziah of Judah, and by himself, and all the gold that there was in the treasuries of the Temple of the Lord and in the royal palace, and he sent them to King Hazael of Aram, who then turned back from his march on Jerusalem. (2 KINGS 12:18–19)

Jerusalem was also attacked by its rival kingdom of Israel, which had split off in 933 B.C.E. during the reign of Solomon's son Rehoboam. Many years later, the city was plundered by King Jehoash of Israel (800–785 B.C.E.):

He marched on Jerusalem, and he made a breach of four hundred cubits in the wall of Jerusalem, from the Ephraim Gate to the Corner Gate. (2 KINGS 14:13)

Yet another attack came in 735 B.C.E. when Pekah, King of Israel, confederated with King Rezin of Aram to attack King Ahaz in Jerusalem, "but could not overcome [him]." (2 Kings 16:5). Ahaz saved himself, however, by sending the treasures of Jerusalem to King Tiglath-pileser of Assyria, who in turn captured Damascus and put Rezin to death (2 Kings 16:9).

The most serious attack, however, came in 701 during the reign of King Hezekiah. In a foretaste of what was to come, Sennacherib of Assyria attacked. The northern kingdom of Israel had already been captured and its ten tribes sent into exile. Hezekiah was anxious to avoid the same fate:

In the fourteenth year of King Hezekiah, King Sennacherib of Assyria marched against all the fortified towns of Judah and seized them. King Hezekiah sent this message to the king of Assyria at Lachish: "I have done wrong; withdraw from me; and I shall bear whatever you impose on me." So the king of Assyria imposed upon King Hezekiah of Judah a payment of three hundred talents of silver and thirty talents of gold. Hezekiah gave him all the silver that was on hand in the House of the Lord and in the treasuries of the palace. At that time Hezekiah cut down the doors and the doorposts of the Temple of the Lord, which King Hezekiah had overlaid [with gold], and gave them to the king of Assyria. But the king of Assyria sent the Tartan, the Rabsaris, and the Rabshakeh from Lachish with a large force to King Hezekiah in Jerusalem. They marched up to Jerusalem; and when they arrived, they took up a position near the conduit of the Upper Pool, by the road of the Fuller's Field. *(2 KINGS 18:13–17)*

Hezekiah was frightened by the demand of capitulation. The prophet Isaiah, however, assured him that God was not about to abandon the city He had chosen:

He shall not enter this city:

He shall not shoot an arrow at it,

Or advance upon it with a shield,

Or pile up a siege mound against it.

He shall go back

By the way he came;

He shall not enter this city

   —declares the Lord.

I will protect and save this city for My sake,

And for the sake of My servant David.

(2 KINGS 19:32–34)

That night the Assyrian camp was smitten by a plague, and the Assyrians were forced to retreat.

Isaiah's assurance of victory was based upon his belief in Jerusalem's special status as the city of God:

Fair Maiden Zion despises you,

She mocks at you;

Fair Jerusalem shakes

Her head at you.

Whom have your blasphemed and reviled?

Against whom made loud your voice

And haughtily raised your eyes?

Against the Holy One of Israel!

(2 KINGS 19:21–22)

David is the creator of Jerusalem, Solomon its builder, and Isaiah its prophet. It is he who personifies the city, raising it to almost mythological proportions, and proclaims its sanctity.

On the historical plane, it was Hezekiah who further improved the city. His main achievement was "how he made the pool and the conduit and brought the water into the city" (2 Kings 20:20).

The same Isaiah who assured Hezekiah that the city would be safe during his reign also predicted, however, the eventual destruction of Jerusalem by the Babylonians:

> A time is coming when everything in your palace which your ancestors have stored up to this day will be carried off to Babylon: nothing will remain behind, said the Lord.
> *(2 KINGS 20:17)*

The Silwan tunnel cut by Hezekiah. September 1967 (Israel Government Press Office; with permission)

The reason for this prophecy becomes clear during the reign of Hezekiah's son Manasseh (693–638 B.C.E.) who

> ... rebuilt the shrines that his father Hezekiah had destroyed; he erected altars for Baal and made a sacred post, as King Ahab of Israel had done. He bowed down to all the host of heaven and worshiped them, and he built al-

tars for them in the House of the Lord, of which the Lord
had said, "I will establish My name in Jerusalem." He
built altars for all the host of heaven in the two courts of
the House of the Lord. He consigned his son to the fire;
he practiced soothsaying and divination, and consulted
ghosts and familiar spirits; he did much that was displeas-
ing to the Lord, to vex Him. The scupltured image of
Asherah that he made he placed in the House concerning which the Lord had said to David and to his son
Solomon, "In this House and in Jerusalem, which I chose
out of all the tribes of Israel, I will establish My name
forever. . . ."

"Assuredly, thus said the Lord, the God of Israel: I am
going to bring such a disaster on Jerusalem and Judah
that both ears of everyone who hears it will tingle. I will
apply to Jerusalem the measuring line of Samaria and the
weights of the House of Ahab; I will wipe Jerusalem clean
as one wipes a dish and turns it upside down. . . ."

Moreover, Manasseh put so many innocent persons to
death that he filled Jerusalem [with blood] from end to
end. . . . (2 KINGS 21:3–7, 12–13, 16)

It was during the reign of Manasseh's son, the pious Josiah (638–609
b.c.e.), that Jerusalem reached it peak. In Josiah's work of restoring
the Temple, which had fallen into disrepair, a book was discovered
which scholars today identify with Deuteronomy. It predicted disaster, but it also made demands that were new in regard to the cen-
tralization of the cult. As a result, Josiah carried out a sweeping religious reform in Jerusalem and throughout the country:

Then the king ordered the high priest Hilkiah, the priests
of the second rank, and the guards of the threshold to
bring out of the Temple of the Lord all the objects for
Baal and Asherah and all the host of heaven. He burned

them outside Jerusalem in the fields of Kidron, and he removed the ashes to Bethel. . . . He also defiled Topheth, which is in the Valley of Ben-hinnom, so that no one might consign his son or daughter to the fire of Molech. He did away with the horses that the kings of Judah had dedicated to the sun at the entrance of the House of the Lord, near the chamber of the eunuch Nathan-melech, which was in the precincts. He burned the chariots of the sun. And the king tore down the altars made by the kings of Judah on the roof by the upper chamber of Ahaz, and the altars made by Manasseh in the two courts of the House of the Lord. He removed them quickly from there and scattered their rubble in the Kidron Valley. . . . (2 Kings 23:4–7; 10–12)

After the death of Josiah in a vain stand against Pharoah Neco, Jerusalem's independence was at an end. The kings who followed became vassals of Nebuchadnezzar. The beginning of the destruction occurred when Jehoiachin rebelled in 597 B.C.E.:

At that time the troops of King Nebuchadnezzar of Babylon marched against Jerusalem, and the city came under siege. King Nebuchadnezzar of Babylon advanced against the city while his troops were besieging it. Thereupon King Jehoiachin of Judah, along with his mother, and his courtiers, commanders, and officers, surrendered to the king of Babylon. The king of Babylon took him captive in the eighth year of his reign. He carried off from Jerusalem all the treasures of the House of the Lord and the treasures of the royal palace; he stripped off all the golden decorations in the Temple of the Lord—which King Solomon of Israel had made—as the Lord had warned. He exiled all of Jerusalem: all the commanders and all the warriors—ten thousand exiles—as well as all the craftsmen and smiths; only the poorest people in the land were left. *(2 KINGS 24:10–14)*

When his successor, Zedekiah, also rebelled, the final siege began:

On the tenth day of the tenth month, Nebuchadnezzar moved against Jerusalem with his whole army. He besieged it; and they built towers against it all around. The city continued in a state of siege until the eleventh year of King Zedekiah. By the ninth day [of the fourth month] the famine had become acute in the city; there was no food left for the common people.

Then [the wall of] the city was breached. All the soldiers [left the city] by night through the gate between the double walls, which is near the king's garden—the Chaldeans were all around the city; and [the king] set out for the Arabah. But the Chaldean troops pursued the king, and they overtook him in the steppes of Jericho as his entire force left him and scattered. They captured the king and brought him before the king of Babylon at Riblah; and they put him on trial. They slaughtered Zedekiah's sons before his eyes; then Zedekiah's eyes were put out. He was chained in bronze fetters and he was brought to Babylon.

On the seventh day of the fifth month—that was the nineteenth year of King Nebuchadnezzar of Babylon—Nebuzaradan, the chief of the guards, an officer of the king of Babylon, came to Jerusalem. He burned the House of the Lord, the king's palace, and all the houses of Jerusalem; he burned down the house of every notable person. The entire Chaldean force that was with the chief of the guard tore down the walls of Jerusalem on every side. The remnants of the people that was left in the city, the defectors who had gone over to the king of

> Babylon—and the remnant of the population—were
> taken into exile by Nebuzaradan, the chief of the guards.
> But some of the poorest in the land were left by the chief
> of the guards, to be vinedressers and field hands.
>
> The Chaldeans broke up the bronze columns of the
> House of the Lord, the stands, and the bronze tank that
> was in the House of the Lord; and they carried the bronze
> away to Babylon. They also took all the pails, scrapers,
> snuffers, ladles, and all the other bronze vessels used in
> the service. The chief of the guards took whatever was of
> gold and whatever was of silver: fire pans and sprinkling
> bowls. The two columns, the one tank, and the stands
> which Solomon provided for the House of the Lord—all
> these objects contained bronze beyond weighing. The one
> column was eighteen cubits high. It had a bronze capital
> above it; the height of the capital was three cubits, and
> there was a meshwork [decorated] with pomegranates
> about the capital, all made of bronze. And the like was
> true of the other column with its meshwork. *(2 KINGS
> 25:1–17)*

Thus was the Jerusalem of the First Temple period destroyed in 586
B.C.E.

The Biblical historical account of Jerusalem continues some seventy years later when Cyrus of Persia, now the ruler of Babylonia,
issues a decree permitting a return to Jerusalem:

> In the first year of King Cyrus of Persia, when the word of
> the Lord spoken by Jeremiah was fulfilled, the Lord
> roused the spirit of King Cyrus of Persia to issue a procla-
> mation throughout his realm by word of mouth and in
> writing as follows:
>
> "Thus said King Cyrus of Persia: The Lord God of
> Heaven has given me all the kingdoms of the earth and

The Broad Wall, built at the end of the First Temple period, uncovered in the Jewish Quarter; looking northeast (Ancient Jerusalem Revealed. Israel Exploration Society; with permission)

has charged me with building Him a house in Jerusalem, which is in Judah. Anyone of you of all His people—may his God be with him, and let him go up to Jerusalem that is in Judah and build the House of the Lord God of Israel, the God that is in Jerusalem; and all who stay behind,

wherever he may be living, let the people of his place assist him with silver, gold, goods, and livestock, beside the
freewill offering to the House of God that is in
Jerusalem." *(EZRA 1:1–3)*

Those who returned commenced the work of re-establishing
Jerusalem and its institutions:

When the seventh month arrived—the Israelites being
settled in their towns—the entire people assembled as
one man in Jerusalem. Then Jeshua son of Jozadak and
his brother priests, and Zerubbabel son of Shealtiel and
his brothers set to and built the altar of the God of Israel
to offer burnt offerings upon it as is written in the
Teaching of Moses, the man of God. They set up the altar
on its site because they were in fear of the peoples of the
land, and they offered burnt offerings on it to the Lord,
burnt offerings each morning and evening. Then they celebrated the festival of Tabernacles as is written. . . . From
the first day of the seventh month they began to make
burnt offerings to the Lord, though the foundation of the
Temple of the Lord had not been laid. . . .

When the builders had laid the foundation of the
Temple of the Lord, priests in their vestments with trumpets, and Levites sons of Asaph with cymbals were stationed to give praise to the Lord, as King David of Israel
had ordained. They sang songs extolling and praising the
Lord, "For He is good, His steadfast love for Israel is eternal." All the people raised a great shout extolling the
Lord because the foundation of the House of the Lord
had been laid. Many of the priests and Levites and the
chiefs of the clans, the old men who had seen the first
house, wept loudly at the sight of the founding of this
house. Many others shouted joyously at the top of their

voices. The people could not distinguish the shouts of joy from the people's weeping, for the people raised a great shout, the sound of which could be heard from afar. (EZRA 3:1–4, 6, 10–13)

After much tribulation, the house was finally finished—

> . . . on the third of the month of Adar in the sixth year of the reign of King Darius. The Israelites, the priests, and the Levites, and all the other exiles celebrated the dedication of the House of God with joy. (EZRA 6:15–16)

The condition of the city itself, however, remained poor:

> The narrative of Nehemiah son of Hacaliah:
> In the month of Kislev of the twentieth year, when I was in the fortress of Shushan, Hanani, one of my brothers, together with some men of Judah, arrived, and I asked them about the Jews, the remnant who had survived the captivity, and about Jerusalem. They replied, "The survivors who have survived the captivity there in the province are in dire trouble and disgrace; Jerusalem's wall is full of breaches, and its gates have been destroyed by fire." (NEH. 1:1–3)

Nehemiah, the king's cupbearer, appealed to Artaxerxes:

> I answered the king, "May the king live forever! How should I not look bad when the city of the graveyard of my ancestors lies in ruins, and its gates have been consumed by fire?" The king said to me, "What is your request?" With a prayer to the God of Heaven, I answered the king, "If it please the king, and if your servant has found favor with you, send me to Judah, to the city of my ancestors' graves, to rebuild it." (NEH.2:3–5)

Receiving permission, he left for Jerusalem:

> I arrived in Jerusalem. After I was there three days I got
> up at night, I and a few men with me, and telling no one
> what my God had put into my mind to do for Jerusalem,
> and taking no other beast than the one on which I was
> riding, I went out by the Valley Gate, at night, toward
> the Jackals' Spring and the Dung Gate; and I surveyed
> the walls of Jerusalem that were breached and its gates,
> consumed by fire. I proceeded to the Fountain Gate and
> to the King's Pool, where there was no room for the beast
> under me to continue. So I went up the wadi by night,
> surveying the wall, and, entering again by the Valley
> Gate, I returned. The prefects knew nothing of where I
> had gone or what I had done, since I had not yet di-
> vulged it to the Jews—the priests, the nobles, the pre-
> fects, or the rest of the officials.
>
> Then I said to them, "You see the bad state we are
> in—Jerusalem lying in ruins and its gates destroyed by
> fire. Come, let us rebuild the wall of Jerusalem and suffer
> no more disgrace." (NEH. 2:11–17)

Against active opposition from the Samaritans, the rebuilding of the
walls began:

> And they all conspired together to come and fight against
> Jerusalem and to throw it into confusion. Because of them
> we prayed to our God, and set up a watch over them day
> and night. . . .
>
> From that day on, half my servants did work and half
> held lances and shields, bows and armor. And the officers
> stood behind the whole house of Judah who were rebuild-
> ing the wall. The basket-carriers were burdened, doing
> work with one hand while the other held a weapon. As
> for the builders, each had his sword girded at his side as

he was building. The trumpeter stood beside me. I said to the nobles, the prefects, and the rest of the people, "There is much work and it is spread out; we are scattered over the wall, far from one another. When you hear a trumpet call, gather yourselves to me at that place; our God will fight for us!" And so we worked on, while half were holding lances, from the break of day until the stars appeared.

I further said to the people at that time, "Let every man with his servant lodge in Jerusalem, that we may use the night to stand guard and the day to work." Nor did I, my brothers, my servants, or the guards following me ever take off our clothes, [or] each his weapon, even at the water. . . .

When the wall was rebuilt and I had set up the doors, tasks were assigned to the gatekeepers, the singers, and the Levites. I put Hanani my brother and Hananiah, the captain of the fortress, in charge of Jerusalem, for he was a more trustworthy and God-fearing man than most. I said to them, "The gates of Jerusalem are not to be opened until the heat of the day, and before you leave your posts let the doors be closed and barred. And assign the inhabitants of Jerusalem to watches, each man to his watch, and each in front of his own house."

The city was broad and large, the people in it were few, and houses were not yet built. (NEH. 4:2–3, 10–17; 7:1–4)

The feelings of the time may best be gauged by the praise lauded upon those who chose to live there:

The officers of the people settled in Jerusalem; the rest of the people cast lots for one out of ten to come and settle in the holy city of Jerusalem, and the other nine-tenths

> to stay in the towns. The people gave their blessing to all
> the men who willingly settled in Jerusalem. *(NEH. 11:1–2)*

Beyond this point, the historical books of the Bible offer us no information about Jerusalem in the days of the Second Temple.

THE PROPHETS

The sacredness of Jerusalem is taken for granted by the prophets. As
a result, it is both held to a high standard of morality, and therefore
denounced for its failings, and lauded as the sacred city of God. As
the major city of the kingdom of Judah and as its religious center,
Jerusalem was often singled out for denunciation by the prophets
because of the lack of morality of its leaders and many of its inhabitants. The eighth-century prophet Micah saw how the doctrine of
God's dwelling in Jerusalem led to false assumptions concerning the
city's status and indestructibility:

Hear this, you rulers of the House of Jacob,

You chiefs of the House of Israel,

Who detest justice

And make crooked all that is straight,

Who build Zion with crime,

Jerusalem with iniquity!

Her rulers judge for gifts,

Her priests give rulings for a fee,

And her prophets divine for pay;

Yet they rely upon the Lord, saying,

"The Lord is in our midst;
No calamity shall overtake us."
Assuredly, because of you
Zion shall be plowed as a field,
And Jerusalem shall become heaps of ruins,
And the Temple Mount
A shrine in the woods.

(MICAH 3:9–12)

His contemporary, First Isaiah, spoke in a similar condemnatory vein, going so far as to compare Jerusalem with the cities that had come to represent total degredation:

Fair Zion is left
Like a booth in a vineyard,
Like a hut in a cucumber field,
Like a city beleaguered.
Had not the Lord of Hosts
Left us some survivors,
We should be like Sodom,
Another Gomorrah.

Hear the words of the Lord,
You chieftains of Sodom;
Give ear to our God's instruction,
You folk of Gomorrah!
"What need have I of all your sacrifices?"

Says the Lord.
I am sated with burnt offerings of rams,
And suet of fatlings,
And blood of bulls;
And I have no delight
In lambs and he-goats.
That you come to appear before Me—
Who asked that of you?
Trample My courts no more;
Bringing oblations is futile,
Incense is offensive to Me.
New moon and sabbath,
Proclaiming of solemnities,
Assemblies with iniquity,
I cannot abide.
Your new moons and fixed seasons
Fill Me with loathing;
They are become a burden to Me,
I cannot endure them.

(ISA. 1:8–14)

Alas, she has become a harlot,
The faithful city
That was filled with justice,
Where righteousness dwelt—
But now murderers.

Your silver has turned to dross;

Your wine is cut with water.

Your rulers are rogues

And cronies of thieves,

Every one avid for presents

And greedy for gifts;

They do not judge the case of the orphan,

And the widow's cause never reaches them.

(ISA. 1:21–23)

Using his poetic name for Jerusalem—Ariel, the lion of God—Isaiah predicts terrible war against the city:

"Ah, Ariel, Ariel,

City where David camped!

Add year to year,

Let festivals come in their cycles!

And I will harass Ariel,

And there shall be sorrow and sighing.

She shall be to Me like Ariel,

And I will camp against you round about;

I will lay siege to you with a mound,

And I will set up siegeworks against you.

And you shall speak from lower then the ground,

Your speech shall be humbler than the sod;

Your speech shall sound like a ghost's from the ground,
Your voice shall chirp from the sod.
And like fine dust shall be
The multitude of your strangers;
And like flying chaff,
The multitude of tyrants."

And suddenly, in an instant,
She shall be remembered of the Lord of Hosts
With roaring, and shaking, and deafening noise,
Storm, and tempest, and blaze of consuming fire.
Then, like a dream, a vision of the night,
Shall be the multitude of nations
That war upon Ariel,
And all her besiegers, and the siegeworks against her,
And those who harass her.
Like one who is hungry
And dreams he is eating,
But wakes to find himself empty;
And like one who is thirsty
And dreams he is drinking,
But wakes to find himself faint
And utterly parched—
So shall be all the multitude of nations
That war upon Mount Zion.

(ISA. 29:1–8)

Jeremiah, who began to prophecy in 625 B.C.E., some eighty years after Isaiah had begun his work, similarly denounced the wickedness of the city and called for repentance:

> For thus said the Lord to the men of Judah and to Jerusalem:

Break up the untilled ground,

And do not sow among the thorns.

Open your hearts to the Lord,

Remove the thickening about your hearts—

O men of Judah and inhabitants of Jerusalem—

Lest My wrath break forth like fire,

And burn, with none to quench it,

Because of your wicked acts.

Proclaim in Judah,

Announce in Jerusalem,

And say:

"Blow the horn in the land!"

Shout aloud and say:

"Assemble, and let us go

Into the fortified cities!"

Set up a signpost: To Zion.

Take refuge, do not delay!

For I bring evil from the north,

And great disaster.

(JER. 4:3–6)

Roam the streets of Jerusalem,

Search its squares,

Look about and take note:

You will not find a man,

There is none who acts justly,

Who seeks integrity—

That I should pardon her.

(JER. 5:1–2)

But what I see in the prophets of Jerusalem

Is something horrifying:

Adultery and false dealing.

They encourage evildoers,

So that no one turns back from his wickedness.

To me they are all like Sodom

And [all] its inhabitants like Gomorrah.

(JER. 23:14–15)

Unlike Isaiah, Jeremiah has no message of immediate salvation. Where Isaiah had predicted that a siege against Jerusalem would not succeed, Jeremiah proclaims its coming destruction. Only a complete change of heart could possibly avert disaster. See Jeremiah 6:1–2.

Even the Temple of the Lord, Jerusalem's glory, is to Jeremiah nothing more than a den of thieves. Standing at the very site, he delivers a scathing oration. See Jeremiah 7.

Ezekiel, who was with the exiles in Babylonia even before the destruction of Jerusalem in 586 b.c.e., also prophesied the ruin of Jerusalem, albeit in a very different style:

The word of the Lord came to me: Further, O mortal, arraign, arraign the city of bloodshed; declare to her all her
abhorrent deeds! Say: Thus said the Lord God: O city in
whose midst blood is shed, so that your hour is approaching; within which fetishes are made, so that you have become unclean! You stand guilty of the blood you have
shed, defiled by the fetishes you have made. You have
brought on your day; you have reached your year. Therefore I will make you the mockery of the nations and the
scorn of all the lands. Both the near and the far shall
scorn you, O besmirched of name, O laden with iniquity!
(EZEK. 22:1–5)

His extensive and elaborate parable of Jerusalem as an unfaithful
woman, which occupies the entire sixteenth chapter, is perhaps the
most devastating of all the prophetic denunciations:

I will inflict upon you the punishment of women who
commit adultery and murder, and I will direct bloody and
impassioned fury against you. I will deliver you into their
hands, and they shall tear down your eminence and level
your mounds; and they shall strip you of your clothing
and take away your dazzling jewels, leaving you naked and
bare. Then they shall assemble a mob against you to pelt
you with stones and pierce you with their swords. They
shall put your houses to the flames and execute punishment upon you in the sight of many women; thus I will
put a stop to your harlotry, and you shall pay no more
fees. When I have satisfied My fury upon you and My
rage has departed from you, then I will be tranquil; I will
be angry no more. (EZEK. 16:38–42)

See also Ezekiel 23.

These same prophets forsee a wonderful future for Jerusalem after it has been punished:

In the days to come,
The Mount of the Lord's House shall stand
Firm above the mountains;
And it shall tower above the hills.
The peoples shall gaze upon it with joy,
And many nations shall go and shall say:
"Come,
Let us go up to the Mount of the Lord,
To the House of the God of Jacob;
That He may instruct us in His ways,
And that we may walk in His paths."
For instruction shall come forth from Zion,
The word of the Lord from Jerusalem.
Thus He will judge among the many peoples,
And arbitrate for the multitude of nations,
However distant;
And they shall beat their swords into plowshares
And their spears into pruning hooks.
Nations shall not take up
Sword against nation;
They shall never again know war;
But every man shall sit
Under his grapevine or fig tree

With no one to disturb him.

For it was the Lord of Hosts who spoke.

(MICAH 4:1–4)

This prophecy is also found in First Isaiah, 2:2–4, who above all abounds in pictures of the glorious future of Jerusalem:

"I will restore your magistrates as of old,

And your counselors as of yore.

After that you shall be called

City of Righteousness, Faithful city."

Zion shall be saved by justice,

Her repentant ones, by righteousness.

(ISA. 1:26–27)

In the days to come,

The Mount of the Lord's House

Shall stand firm above the mountains

And tower above the hills;

And all the nations

Shall gaze on it with joy.

And the many peoples shall go and say:

"Come,

Let us go up to the Mount of the Lord,

To the House of the God of Jacob;

That He may instruct us in His ways,

And that we may walk in His paths."
For instruction shall come forth from Zion,
The word of the Lord from Jerusalem.
Thus He will judge among the nations
And arbitrate for the many peoples,
And they shall beat their swords into plowshares
And the spears into pruning hooks:
Nation shall not take up
Sword against nation;
They shall never again know war.

(ISA. 2:2–4)

And a highway shall appear there,
Which shall be called the Sacred Way.
No one unclean shall pass along it,
But it shall be for them.
No traveler, not even fools, shall go astray.
No lion shall be there,
No ferocious beast shall set foot on it—
These shall not be found there.
But the redeemed shall walk it;
And the ransomed of the Lord shall return,
And come with shouting to Zion,
Crowned with joy everlasting.

They shall attain joy and gladness,
While sorrow and sighing flee.

(ISA. 35:8–10)

Jeremiah and Ezekiel also forsaw an eventual restoration. Even those who had denounced so completely believed that after the destruction there would be an everlasting rebuilding:

For the day is coming when watchmen
Shall proclaim on the heights of Ephraim:
Come, let us go up to Zion,
To the Lord our God! . . .
For the Lord will ransom Jacob,
Redeem him from one too strong for him.
They shall come and shout on the heights of Zion,
Radiant over the bounty of the Lord—
Over new grain and wine and oil,
And over sheep and cattle.
They shall fare like a watered garden,
They shall never languish again.
Then shall maidens dance gaily,
Young men and old alike.
I will turn their mourning to joy,
I will comfort them and cheer them in their grief.
I will give the priests their fill of fatness,

And my people shall enjoy My full bounty

—declares the Lord.

(JER. 31:6, 12–14)

So, too, Ezekiel:

> Truly, thus said the Lord God: I will deal with you as you
> have dealt, for you have spurned the pact and violated
> the covenant. Nevertheless, I will remember the covevant
> I made with you in the days of your youth, and I will es-
> tablish it with you as an everlasting covenant. You shall
> remember your ways and feel ashamed, when you receive
> your older sisters and your younger sisters, and I give
> them to you as daughters, though they are not of your
> covenant. I will establish My covenant with you, and you
> shall know I am the Lord. Thus you shall remember and
> feel shame, and you shall be too abashed to open your
> mouth again, when I have forgiven you for all that you
> did—declares the Lord God. (EZEK. 16:59–63)

The prophet who wrote most extensively and exclusively in praise of
Jerusalem was the anonymous prophet whose work is found in the
book of Isaiah, beginning with chapter 40. Commonly referred to as
Second Isaiah, he lived in the Babylonian exile and mourned the
state of destruction and foresaw the coming restoration:

Comfort, oh comfort My people,

Says your God.

Speak tenderly to Jerusalem,

And declare to her

That her term of service of over,

That her iniquity is expiated;
For she has received at the hand of the Lord
Double for all her sins.

(ISA. 40:1–2)

Zion says,
"The Lord has forsaken me.
My Lord has forgotten me."
Can a woman forget her baby,
Or disown the child of her womb?
Though she might forget,
I never could forget you.
See, I have engraved you
On the palms of My hands,
Your walls are ever before Me.
Swiftly your children are coming;
Those who ravaged and ruined you shall leave you.
Look up all around you and see:
They are all assembled, are come to you!
As I live

—declared the Lord —

You shall don them all like jewels,
Deck yourself with them like a bride.
As for your ruins and desolate places
And your land laid waste—

You shall soon be crowded with settlers,
While destroyers stay far from you.
The children you thought you had lost
Shall yet say in your hearing,
"This place is too crowded for me;
Make room for me to settle."

> (ISA. 49:14–20)

Truly the Lord has comforted Zion,
Comforted all her ruins;
He has made her wilderness like Eden,
Her desert like the Garden of the Lord.
Gladness and joy shall abide there,
Thanksgiving and the sound of music.

> (ISA. 51:3)

So let the ransomed of the Lord return,
And come with shouting to Zion,
Crowned with joy everlasting.
Let them attain joy and gladness,
While sorrow and sighing flee.

> (ISA. 51:11)

Awake, awake, O Zion!
Clothe yourself in splendor;
Put on your robes of majesty,
Jerusalem, holy city!

> (ISA. 52:1)

Unhappy, storm-tossed one, uncomforted!
I will lay carbuncles as your building stones
And make your foundations of sapphires.
I will make your battlements of rubies,
Your gates of precious stones,
The whole encircling wall of gems.
And all your children shall be disciples of the Lord,
And great shall be the happiness of your children.
You shall be established through righteousness.
You shall be safe from oppression,
And shall have no fear;
From ruin, and it shall not come near you.

(ISA. 54:11–14)

For the sake of Zion I will not be silent,
For the sake of Jerusalem I will not be still,
Till her victory emerge resplendent
And her triumph like a flaming torch.
Nations shall see your victory,
And every king your majesty;
And you shall be called by a new name
Which the Lord Himself shall bestow.
You shall be a glorious crown
In the hand of the Lord,
And a royal diadem
In the palm of your God.

Nevermore shall you be called "Forsaken,"

Nor shall your land be called "Desolate";

But you shall be called "I delight in her,"

And your land "Espoused."

For the Lord takes delight in you,

And your land shall be espoused.

As a youth espouses a maiden

Your sons shall espouse you;

And as a bridegroom rejoices over his bride,

So will your God rejoice over you.

Upon your walls, O Jerusalem,

I have set watchmen,

Who shall never be silent

By day or by night.

O you, the Lord's remembrancers,

Take no rest

And give no rest to Him,

Until He establish Jerusalem

And make her renowned on earth.

(ISA. 62:1–7)

The post-exilic prophet Zechariah was concerned largely with the return of the exiles and the rebuilding of Jerusalem:

> Thus said the Lord of Hosts: I am very jealous for Zion, I am fiercely jealous for her. Thus said the Lord: I have returned to Zion, and I will dwell in Jerusalem. Jerusalem

will be called the City of Faithfulness, and the mount of
the Lord of Hosts the Holy Mount.

   Thus said the Lord of Hosts: There shall yet be old
men and women in the squares of Jerusalem, each with
staff in hand because of their great age. And the squares
of the city shall be crowded with boys and girls playing in
the squares. Thus said the Lord of Hosts: Though it will
seem impossible to the remnant of this people in those
days, shall it also be impossible to Me?—declares the Lord
of Hosts. Thus said the Lord of Hosts: I will rescue My
people from the lands of the east and from the lands of
the west, and will bring them home to dwell in Jerusalem.
They shall be My people, and I will be their God—in
truth and sincerity. (ZECH. 8:2–8)

Zechariah's vision is apocalyptic, with the eventual triumph coming
after much tribulation and resulting in Jerusalem's becoming the pilgrim site for the entire world:

   In that day, even the bells on the horses shall be inscribed "Holy to the Lord." The metal pots in the House
of the Lord shall be like the basins before the altar; indeed, every metal pot in Jerusalem and in Judah shall be
holy to the Lord of Hosts. And all those who sacrifice
shall come and take of these to boil [their sacrificial
meat] in; in that day there shall be no more traders in the
House of the Lord of Hosts. (ZECH. 14:20–21)

THE WRITINGS

Two books in the third section of the Bible, the Writings, contain
poetic material concerning Jerusalem: Psalms and Lamentations.

Jerusalem and its wonders are frequently the subject of the psalms. The most well known is Psalm 48:

The Lord is great and much acclaimed
  in the city of our God,
  His holy mountain—
  fair-crested, joy of all the earth,
  Mount Zion, summit of Zaphon,
  city of the great king.
Through its citadels, God has made Himself known as a haven,
See, the kings joined forces;
  they advanced together.
At the mere sight of it they were stunned,
  they were terrified, they panicked;
  they were seized there with a trembling,
  like a woman in the throes of labor,
  as the Tarshish fleet was wrecked
  in an easterly gale.
The like of what we heard we have now witnessed
  in the city of the Lord of Hosts,
  in the city of our God—
  may God preserve it forever!   *Selah.*

In Your temple, God,
  we meditate upon Your faithful care.
The praise of You, God, like Your name,
  reaches to the ends of the earth;

Your right hand is filled with beneficence.

Let Mount Zion rejoice!

Let the towns of Judah exult,

    because of Your judgments.

Walk around Zion,

    circle it;

    count its towers,

    take note of its ramparts;

    go through its citadels,

    that you may recount it to a future age.

For God—He is our God forever;

    He will lead us evermore.

Psalm 122 speaks specifically about the Temple and the city which contains it, Jerusalem. This is one of the psalms recited by pilgrims as they ascended the Temple Mount:

I rejoiced when they said to me,

    "We are going to the house of the Lord."

Our feet stood inside your gates, O Jerusalem,

    Jerusalem built up, a city knit together,

    to which tribes would make pilgrimage,

    the tribes of the Lord,

    —as was enjoined upon Israel—

    to praise the name of the Lord.

There the thrones of judgment stood,

    thrones of the house of David.

Map of Jerusalem at the end of the First Temple period. The dots represent excavated Israelite sites (Ancient Jerusalem Revealed. Israel Exploration Society; with permission)

Pray for the well-being of Jerusalem:

"May those who love you be at peace.

May there be well-being within your ramparts,

peace in your citadels."

For the sake of my kin and friends,

I pray for your well-being;

for the sake of the house of the Lord our God,

I seek your good.

Other psalms intended for pilgrims contain similar references:

May the Lord bless you from Zion;

may you share the prosperity of Jerusalem

all the days of your life,

and live to see your children's children.

May all be well with Israel!

(Pss. 128:5–6)

Some of the Jerusalem psalms reflect specific historic events:

By the waters of Babylon,

there we sat,

sat and wept,

as we thought of Zion.

There on the poplars

we hung up our lyres,

for our captors asked us there for songs,
our tormentors, for amusement,
"Sing us one of the songs of Zion."
How can we sing a song of the Lord
on alien soil?
If I forget you, O Jerusalem,
let my right hand wither;
let my tongue stick to my palate
if I cease to think of you,
if I do not keep Jerusalem in memory
even at my happiest hour.

Remember, O Lord, against the Edomites
the day of Jerusalem's fall;
how they cried, "Strip her, strip her
to her very foundations!"
Fair Babylon, you predator,
a blessing on him who repays you in kind
what you have inflicted on us;
a blessing on him who seizes your babies
and dashes them against the rocks!

(Pss. 137)

When the Lord restores the fortunes of Zion
—we see it as in a dream—
our mouths shall be filled with laughter,

our tongues, with songs of joy.
Then shall they say among the nations,
"The Lord has done great things for them!"
The Lord will do great things for us
and we shall rejoice.

Restore our fortunes, O Lord,
like watercourses in the Negeb.
They who sow in tears
shall reap with songs of joy.
Though he goes along weeping,
carrying the seed-bag,
he shall come back with songs of joy,
carrying his sheaves.

(PSS. 126)

The Book of Lamentations contains several chapters that are descriptions of Jerusalem at the time of the destruction:

Alas!
Lonely sits the city
Once great with people!
She that was great among nations
Is become like a widow;
The princess among states
Is become a thrall.
Bitterly she weeps in the night,

Her cheek wet with tears.
There is none to comfort her
Of all her friends.
All her allies have betrayed her;
They have become her foes.
Judah has gone into exile
Because of misery and harsh oppression;
When she settled among the nations,
She found no rest;
All her pursuers overtook her
In the narrow places.
Zion's roads are in mourning,
Empty of festival pilgrims;
All her gates are deserted.
Her priests sigh,
Her maidens are unhappy—
She is utterly disconsolate!
Her enemies are now the masters,
Her foes are at ease,
Because the Lord has afflicted her
For her many transgressions;
Her infants have gone into captivity
Before the enemy.
Gone from Fair Zion are all
That were her glory;

Her leaders were like stags
That found no pasture;
They could only walk feebly
Before the pursuer.

All the precious things she had
In the days of old
Jerusalem recalled
In her days of woe and sorrow,
When her people fell by enemy hands
With none to help her;
When enemies looked on and gloated
Over her downfall.
Jerusalem has greatly sinned,
Therefore she is become a mockery.
All who admired her despise her,
For they have seen her disgraced;
And she can only sigh
And shrink back.
Her uncleanness clings to her skirts.
She gave no thought to her future;
She has sunk appallingly,
With none to comfort her.—
See, O Lord, my misery;
How the enemy jeers!
The foe has laid hands

On everything dear to her.
She has seen her Sanctuary
Invaded by nations
Which You have denied admission
Into Your community.
All her inhabitants sigh
As they search for bread;
They have bartered their treasures for food,
To keep themselves alive.—
See, O Lord, and behold,
How abject I have become!

Zion spreads out her hands,
She has no one to comfort her;
The Lord has summoned against Jacob
His enemies all about him;
Jerusalem has become among them
A thing unclean.

(LAM. 1:1–11, 17)

They have ravished women in Zion,
Maidens in the towns of Judah.
Princes have been hanged by them;
No respect has been shown to elders.
Young men must carry millstones,
And youths stagger under loads of wood.

The old men are gone from the gate,
The young men from their music.
Gone is the joy of our hearts;
Our dancing is turned into mourning.
The crown has fallen from our head;
Woe to us that we have sinned!

Because of this our hearts are sick,
Because of these our eyes are dimmed:
Because of Mount Zion, which lies desolate;
Jackals prowl over it.

But You, O Lord, are enthroned forever,
Your throne endures through the ages.
Why have You forgotten us utterly,
Forsaken us for all time?
Take us back, O Lord, to Yourself,
And let us come back;
Renew our days as of old!
For truly, You have rejected us,
Bitterly raged against us.

(LAM. 5:11–22)

THE SECOND GATE

Jerusalem in Second Temple Literature

The Citadel of David, late 1960s

During the period of the Second Temple, from the return from the Babylonian Exile in the fifth century B.C.E. until the first century C.E., the writing of books in Biblical style continued. Apocalyptic writing also continued in the century following the destruction. These books were not accepted into the canon of Jewish scripture and were preserved in Greek translations by the Church. In addition there were other sacred works composed by the members of the Dead Sea sect which were totally unknown until the discovery of these scrolls in the 1940s. Other important works from this time are the philosophical writings of the Jewish philosopher from Alexandria, Philo, writing in the first century B.C.E., and the historical books by Josephus Flavius in the first century C.E.

☙ The Letter of Aristeas

There is disagreement about the dating of this work, written in Greek, probably in Alexandria. Many conjecture that it stems from the time of Antiochus Epiphanes, about 170 B.C.E., and was a defense of Judaism. Aristeas, a Jew in the court of Ptolemy II (285–246 B.C.E.) is sent to Jerusalem to bring scholars to translate the Bible into Greek. In a letter written to his brother, he describes his journey to Jerusalem. If it was indeed written in the second century B.C.E., it provides us with a rare description of the Second Temple and Jerusalem prior to its complete rebuilding by Herod. However, the lavishness of the description itself, as well as some of the details, which seem imaginary, have led scholars to believe that the description was written after the destruction of Herod's Temple and was based upon memories of that magnificent structure and not of the simple building constructed by the returnees from Babylon.

When we reached the region we beheld the city situated in the center of all Judaea upon a mountain which rises to a lofty height. Upon its crest stood the Temple in all its splendor; and there were three encompassing walls, above seventy cubits in height and of a breadth and length in keeping with the structure of the edifice. The whole was built with a lavishness and sumptuousness beyond all precedent. From the construction of the doorway and its fastenings to the door-posts and the solidity of the lintel it was obvious that no expense had been spared. The style of the curtain corresponded in every respect to the door; especially when the fabric was kept in unceasing motion by the current of wind beneath, since, the current being from below, the curtain bulged out from the bottom to its highest extent, the spectacle was highly agreeable and hard to tear oneself from. The altar was built in keeping with the size of the place and of the offer-ings consumed upon it by fire, and the ascent was on a similar scale. The ascent was gradual, from a proper regard for decency, and the ministering priests were swathed in "coats of fine linen" reaching to the ankles. The edifice looks toward the east, and its back to the west. The entire floor is paved with stones and sloped downward to the appropriate places, to admit of flushing with water in order to wash away the blood of the sacrifices; for many myriads of beasts are offered on the days of the festivals. The water supply is inexhaustible, for an abundant natural spring pours forth within the Temple area, and there are furthermore marvelous underground reservoirs passing description, to a distance of five stades, as was pointed out, round the foundations of the Temple; of these each had innumerable pipes, so that the various channels converged at the several reservoirs. The floors and sides of these reservoirs, they explained, were overlaid with lead, and above them a great mass of plaster was laid, everything being made secure. There are numerous outlets, they said, at the foot of the altar, invisible to all except those engaged in the ministration, so that the vast accumulation of sacrificial blood is cleansed away in the twinkling of an eye. I am myself convinced of the system of reser-voirs, and I shall show how my belief was confirmed. They took me more than four stades out of the city, and at a certain place bade me bend over and listen to the rushing noise of the meeting of the waters. Thus the size of the cisterns was made evident to me, as I have described them.

In its exhibition of strength and in its orderly and silent perfor-mance the ministration of the priests could in no way be sur-passed. . . . Complete silence prevails, so that one might suppose that not a person was present in the place, though those performing the service amount to some seven hundred—besides the great multitude

Herodian construction of large ashlars at the southernn wall of the Temple Mount (Ancient Jerusalem Revealed. Israel Exploration Society; with permission)

of persons bringing sacrifices to be offered—but everything is done with reverence and in a manner worthy of the great divinity. . . .

To obtain a thorough knowledge of everything we ascended the citadel of the city which lies hard by and looked about. It is situated on a very lofty spot and is fortified with a number of towers which are built of large blocks of stone right up to the very top, as a protection, so we were informed, for the precincts of the Temple, so that in case of any attack or revolution or enemy invasion no one could make his way into the walls which encompass the Temple. On the towers of the citadel are set artillery and various other engines of war, and their lofty eminence commands the aforesaid walls. The towers are guarded, furthermore, by the most loyal of men, who have given demonstrative proof of devotion to their country. These men had orders not to quit the citadel, except on festivals, and then only by turns, nor did they permit anyone to enter. Very scrupulous care was exercised even when they received an order from their leader to admit any visitors as sightseers, as happened in our case, for though we were unarmed and only two, they would barely admit us to study the arrangements for the sacrifices. They said they were pledged to such conduct by oaths: they had all sworn, and of necessity and religious scruple they fulfilled the stipulation of their oath, that though they were five hundred they would not admit more than five persons at the same time; for the citadel was the whole defense of the Temple, and he that founded it had thus secured its protection.

The extent of the city is moderate, its compass being about forty stades, as far as one may conjecture. In the position of its towers and of the thoroughfares, some of which appear above and some below, with the cross-streets cutting through them, it has the familiar aspects of a theater, for, the city being built upon a mountain, its parts rise one above another, and there are stairs to the thoroughfares. Some persons make their way at the higher level and some underneath, and they are careful to keep apart as they go, so that those in a state of purification may touch nothing improper. . . .

✑ The First Book of Maccabees

*Written in Hebrew, this book recounts in straight narrative the
history of the struggle between the Syrian Greeks and the Jews,
eventually under the leadership of the Maccabees, between 175
and 135 B.C.E. Because the book was not included in the canon,
the Hebrew was lost, and the text was preserved only in Greek.*

After smiting Egypt, in the one hundred and forty-third year [168
b.c.e.], Antiochus turned back, went up against Israel, and entered
Jerusalem with a great army. He entered the Temple in his arrogance,
and took the golden altar, the lamp for the light and all its equipment, the table of the show-bread, the cups, the bowls and the gold-
en censers, the curtain, the crowns; and the golden adornment on
the front of the sanctuary he stripped off entirely. He seized the silver, the gold, and the precious vessels; he also took the hidden treasures which he found. Taking them all, he carried them away to his
own country. He massacred people and spoke most arrogantly.

And great was the sadness in Israel, everywhere;

Both rulers and elders groaned;

Maidens and young men languished,

The beauty of the women was altered.

Every bridegroom took up lamentation,

And she that sat in a bridal-chamber mourned.

Shaken was the earth over those who dwelt therein,

And the whole house of Jacob was clothed with shame.

After two years, the king sent the officer of the Mysians to the cities of Judah, and entered Jerusalem with a strong force. He spoke peaceful words to them craftily, and they trusted him. Then he fell suddenly upon the city, and dealt it a great blow, destroying many people of Israel. He despoiled the city, burnt it with fire, razed its houses and its surrounding walls. They led the women and children captive, and took possession of the cattle. They fortified the city of David with a high and strong wall with mighty towers, and it became their citadel. They put sinful people therein, men who were transgressors against the Torah; and they entrenched themselves in it. They stored up arms and provisions, and after collecting together the spoils of Jerusalem, they laid them up there. They became a great menace, for it served them as an ambuscade against the sanctuary, an evil adversary against Israel continually.

They shed innocent blood around the altar,

And polluted the sanctuary.

Because of them the inhabitants of Jerusalem fled,

She became a dwelling place of foreigners,

And foreign she became to her own brood,

And her children forsook her.

Her sanctuary was laid waste like a wilderness,

Her feasts were turned into sadness,

Her sabbaths into a reproach,

Her honor into contempt.

As great as had been her glory,

By so much was her dishonor increased.

And her high renown was turned into sadness.

(1 MAC. 1:20–40)

On the twenty-fifth day of Kislev in the one hundred and forty-sixth year [168 b.c.e.], he erected an abomination of desolation upon the altar, and in the surrounding cities of Judah they erected altars. They burned incense also at the doors of the houses and in the streets. The books of the Torah which they found, they tore into pieces and burned. Wherever a book of the covenant was found in anyone's possession, or if anyone respected the Torah, the decree of the king imposed the sentence of death upon him. Month after month they dealt brutally with every Israelite who was found in the cities. On the twenty-fifth of the month they offered sacrifices upon the altar which was set on the altar of burnt-offering. (1 Mac. 1:54–59)

☙

At that time Mattathias, son of John, son of Simeon, a priest of the family of Joarib, moved away from Jerusalem and settled in Modin. . . . When he saw the blasphemous things that were taking place in Judah and Jerusalem, he said:

"Wretched am I, why was I born to behold,

The dissolution of my people and the destruction of the holy city,

To sit idly by while it is given into the hands of its enemies,

The sanctuary into the hand of foreigners?

Her people have become as a man without honor,

Her glorious treasures captured, taken away;

Her infants have been killed in her streets,

Her young men, by the sword of the enemy.

What nation has not shared,

And what kingdom has not seized her spoil?

All her adornment has been taken away.

Instead of a free woman, she has become a slave.

Yea, behold, our sanctuary and our beauty,

And our glory have been laid waste!

The heathen have profaned them.

Why then should life continue for us?"

(1 MAC. 2:1–13)

Judah and his brothers said, "Now that our enemies are crushed, let us go up to purify and dedicate the sanctuary."

The entire army gathered together and went up to Mount Zion. They saw the sanctuary desolated and the altar profaned, the gates burned up, the weeds growing in the courts as in a forest or as on one of the mountains, and the priests' chambers torn down. They tore their garments and made great lamentation, and put ashes on their heads, and fell on their faces on the ground, blew solemn blasts upon the trumpets, and cried out to Heaven. Judah appointed certain men to fight against the garrison in the citadel, until he could cleanse the sanctuary. He selected priests without blemish, whose delight was in the Torah, and they purified the sanctuary, carrying out the stones that had defiled it into an unclean place. They took counsel as to what they should do about the altar of burnt offering, which had been defiled. A good plan occurred to them, namely, to tear it down, lest it become a reproach to them, because the heathen had defiled it. So they pulled down the altar, and put away the stones in the Temple Mount, in a suitable place, until a prophet should come to decide what to do with them. They took whole stones, according to the Torah, and constructed a new altar like the former one. They built the sanctuary and the interior of the Temple, and hallowed the

A menorah and other objects incised on a plastered wall in the Jewish Quarter during the Herodian period (Ancient Jerusalem Revealed. Israel Exploration Society; with permission)

courts, and made new holy vessels, and brought the candlestick, the altar of incense, and the table into the Temple. They burned incense on the altar, and lit the lights on the candlestick so that they would shed light in the Temple. They put loaves of bread upon the table, hung up the curtains, and finished all the work which they had undertaken to do.

On the twenty-fifth day of the ninth month, that is the month of Kislev, in the one hundred and forty-ninth year [165 B.C.E.], they arose early and offered sacrifice according to the Torah upon the new altar of burnt offering which they had made. At the same time and on the same day on which the heathen had profaned it, on that very day it was consecrated with songs and harps and lutes and cymbals. All the people fell on their faces and prostrated themselves, and uttered praises to Heaven who had caused them to prosper. They celebrated the dedication of the altar for eight days, brought burnt offerings with joy, and offered a sacrifice of deliverance and praise. They μalso adorned the front of the Temple with golden crowns and small shields, and rededicated the gates and the priests' chambers, and fitted then with doors. Thus there was great joy among the people, and the reproach caused by the heathen was removed. Judah and his brothers and the entire congregation of Israel decreed that the days of dedication of the altar should be kept with gladness and joy at their due season, year after year, for eight days from the twenty-fifth of the month of Kislev. At that time they built high walls and strong towers around Mount Zion, so that the heathen could never again come and destroy them, as they had done before. (1 MAC. 4:36–60)

ॐ The Psalms of Solomon

This collection of psalms is ascribed to Solomon with no historical or literary justification. They are thought to have been compiled in the first century B.C.E. They were first published in the seventeenth century from a Greek manuscript. The historical references may refer to events in the time of Pompey (63 B.C.E.).

God is a righteous judge and he will not be impressed by appearances.

For the gentiles insulted Jerusalem, trampling [her] down;

> he dragged her beauty down from the throne of glory.

She put on sackcloth instead of beautiful clothes,

> a rope around her head instead of a crown.

She took off the wreath of glory which God had put on her;

> in dishonor her beauty was thrown to the ground.

And I saw and implored in the Lord's presence and said,

> "Let it be enough, Lord, to make your hand heavy on Jerusalem by bringing gentiles [upon her]."

For they ridiculed [her] and did not refrain in anger and vicious rage,

> and they will be finished unless you, Lord, censure them in your anger.

For they have not done it in zeal, but in emotional passion

> to pour out their anger against us in plunder.

(PSS. OF SOLOMON 2:19–24)

Sound in Zion the signal trumpet of the sanctuary;

announce in Jerusalem the voice of one bringing good news,

for God has been merciful to Israel in watching over them.

Stand on a high place, Jerusalem, and look at your children,

from the east and west assembled together by the Lord.

From the north they come in the joy of their God;

from distant islands God has assembled them.

He flattened high mountains into level ground for them;

the hills fled at their coming.

The forests shaded them as they passed by;

God made every fragrant tree to grow for them.

So that Israel might proceed under the supervision of the glory of their God.

Jerusalem, put on [the] clothes of your glory,

prepare the robe of your holiness,

for God has spoken well of Israel forevermore.

May the Lord do what he has spoken about Israel and Jerusalem;

may the Lord lift up Israel in the name of his glory.

May the mercy of the Lord be upon Israel forevermore.

(PSS. OF SOLOMON 11:1–9)

Noncanonical Psalms from Qumran

*Among the many nonbiblical works found in the Dead Sea Scrolls
were various psalms which feature the city of Jerusalem. The
dates of these psalms are unknown, but obviously precede the
destruction of the Temple in 70 C.E.*

Jerusalem [is the city] the Lord [chose],

From everlasting to (everlasting). . . .

[For the name] of the Lord is invoked upon it,

[And His glory] is seen upon Jerusalem [and] Zion.

Who can utter the name of the Lord,

And who can proclaim all [His] praise?

The Lord remembered him with His favor,

and visited him,

that He might show him the prosperity of His chosen ones

to make him rejoice [in the joy of His people.]

4Q380

APOSTROPHE TO ZION

I remember thee for blessing, O Zion:

with all my might have I loved thee.

May thy memory be blessed forever!

Great is thy hope, O Zion;

that peace and thy longed-for salvation will come.

Generation after generation will dwell in thee
and generations of saints will be thy splendor:
Those who yearn for the day of thy salvation
that they may rejoice in the greatness of thy glory.
On the abundance of thy glory they are nourished
and in thy splendid squares will they toddle.
The merits of thy prophets wilt thou remember,
and in the deeds of thy pious ones wilt thou glory.
Purge violence from thy midst:
falsehood and iniquity will be cut off from thee.
Thy sons will rejoice in thy midst
and thy precious ones will be united with thee.
How they have hoped for thy salvation,
thy pure one have mourned for thee.
Hope for thee does not perish, O Zion,
nor is hope in thee forgotten.
Who has ever perished [in] righteousness,
or who has ever survived in his iniquity?
Man is tested according to his way:
every man is requited according to his deeds;
all about are thine enemies cut off, O Zion,
and all thy foes have been scattered.
Praise of thee is pleasing, O Zion,
cherished through all the world.
Many times do I remember thee for blessing;

with all my heart I bless thee.

Mayest thou attain unto everlasting righteousness,

and blessings of the honorable mayst thou receive.

Accept a vision bespoken of thee,

and dreams of prophets sought for thee.

Be exalted, and spread wide, O Zion;

praise the Most High, thy saviour;

let my soul be glad to thy glory.

11QPs

ꙮ Second Baruch

*Sometimes known as the Apocalypse of Baruch, this book claims
to be the work of Jeremiah's scribe, Baruch. It is thought to have
been written after the destruction of the Second Temple, sometime
toward the end of the first century C.E. or the beginning of the
second. Many of the ideas found in it are also found in the
midrashic writings that originated at a similar period.*

And the Lord said to me:

This city will be delivered up for a time,

And the people will be chastened for a time,

And the world will not be forgotten.

Or do you think that this is the city of which I said: On the palms of
my hands I have carved you? (Isa. 49:16) It is not this building that
is in your midst now; it is that which will be revealed, with me, that
was already prepared from the moment that I decided to create
Paradise. And I showed it to Adam before he sinned. But when he
transgressed the commandment, it was taken away from him—as also
Paradise. After these things I showed it to my servant Abraham in
the night between the portions of the victims. And again I showed
it also to Moses on Mount Sinai when I showed him the likeness of
the tabernacle and all its vessels. Behold, now it is preserved with
me—as also Paradise. *(2 BAR. 4:1–6)*

ꙮ

And behold, suddenly a strong spirit lifted me and carried me above
the wall of Jerusalem. And I saw, and behold, there were standing

four angels at the four corners of the city, each of them with a burning torch in his hands. And another angel came down from heaven and said to them, "Hold your torches and do not light them before I say it to you. Because I was sent first to speak a word to the earth and then to deposit in it what the Lord, the Most High, has commanded me." And I saw that he descended in the Holy of Holies and that he took from there the veil, the holy ephod, the mercy seat, the two tables, the holy raiment of the priests, the altar of incense, the forty-eight precious stones with which the priests were clothed, and all the holy vessels of the tabernacle. And he said to the earth with a loud voice:

Earth, earth, earth, hear the word of the mighty God,

and receive the things which I commit to you,

and guard them until the last times,

so that you may restore them when you are ordered,

so that strangers may not get possession of them.

For the time has arrived when Jerusalem will also be delivered up for a time,

until the moment that it will be said that it will be restored forever.

And the earth opened its mouth and swallowed them up.

After these things I heard this angel saying to the angels who held the torches:

> Now destroy the walls and overthrow them to their foundations so that the enemies do not boast and say, "We have overthrown the wall of Zion and we have burnt down the place of the mighty God." (2 BAR. 6:3–7:1)

☙ Fourth Baruch

*Although this book has come down to us only in Christian
versions, it is based upon a Jewish work written after the
destruction of the Temple in 70 C.E. It purports to describe the
way in which Jeremiah hides the vessels of the Temple, the
destruction of the First Temple, and the way in which eventually
Jeremiah returns with the exiles to worship in the rebuilt Temple
at the behest of Baruch, who writes to him.*

But when the hour of night arrived, as the Lord had said to Jeremiah,
they went up together onto the walls of the city, Jeremiah and
Baruch. And behold, there was a sound of trumpets, and angels came
out of heaven holding torches in their hands, and they stood on the
walls of the city. And when Jeremiah and Baruch saw them, they
wept, saying, "Now we know that the word is true." And Jeremiah
pleaded with the angels, saying, "I implore you not to destroy the city
just yet, until I have a word with the Lord." And the Lord spoke to
the angels saying, "Don't destroy the city until I speak to my chosen
one, Jeremiah." Then Jeremiah spoke, saying, "Please Lord, let me
speak before you." And the Lord said, "Speak, my chosen one,
Jeremiah." And Jeremiah said, "Behold, Lord, we know now that you
are delivering the city into the hands of its enemies, and they will
carry the people off into Babylon. What do you want me to do with
the holy vessels of the [Temple] service?" And the Lord said to him,
"Take them and deliver them to the earth, saying, 'Hear, earth, the
voice of him who created you. . . . Guard the vessels of the [Temple]
service unto the coming of the beloved one.' "

. . . Jeremiah and Baruch went into the sanctuary and, gathering
up the vessels of the [Temple] service, they delivered them to the

earth, just as the Lord had instructed them. And immediately the earth swallowed them up. *(4 Bar. 3:1–11, 18–19)*

❧

And when it was morning, behold the host of the Chaldeans surrounded the city. And the great angel trumpeted, saying, "Come into the city, host of the Chaldeans; for behold the gate has been opened for you. Therefore, let the king come in with his multitude and take all the people captive." But Jeremiah, taking the keys of the Temple, went outside of the city and, facing the sun, he tossed them, saying, "I say to you, sun, take the keys of the Temple of God and keep them until the day in which the Lord will question you about them. Because we were not found worthy of keeping them, for we were false stewards." *(4 Bar. 4:1–5)*

ꥰ The Writings of Philo

*Philo Judaeus, also known as Philo of Alexandria, lived from ca.
20 B.C.E. to 50 C.E. A member of an aristocratic Jewish family,
he was well acquainted with the great works of classical antiquity
and wrote in a rich and classical Greek. We know little of his
life, however, and less of his background in Jewish knowledge. He
did make a trip to Jerusalem and extensively philosophized upon
its place in Judaism.*

THE EMBASSY TO GAIUS

*Philo recounts his mission to Rome to protest the erection of
statues to the emperor in synagogues and then in the Temple.*

We had travelled from Rome to Puteoli following Gaius, who had
come down to the sea side and was spending some time round the
bay passing from one to another of the numerous and expensively
furnished country houses which he owned. While we were anxiously
considering the statement of our case, there came to us one with a
troubled look in his bloodshot eyes and gasping convulsively. He
drew us a little way apart since there were some people standing near
and said, "Have you heard the new tidings?" and when he was going
to report it he was brought up short, as a flood of tears streamed from
his eyes. He began again and the second time stopped short and so
too a third time. When we saw this we were all in a flutter and bade
him tell us the matter which he said had brought him there. "For,"
we said, "you have not come just to have your weeping witnessed. If
the facts are worth tears do not be the only one to feel sorrow." He
managed with difficulty while sobbing and breathing spasmodically
to say, "Our temple is lost, Gaius has ordered a colossal statue to be

set up within the inner sanctuary dedicated to himself under the name of Zeus." *(XXIX 185–188)*

☙

[Agrippa] took a tablet and wrote to him [Gaius] as follows:

> ... All men, my emperor, have planted in them a pas-
> sionate love of their native land and a high esteem for
> their own laws; and on this there is no need to instruct
> you, who love your native city as ardently as you honour
> your own customs. ... I as you know am by birth a Jew,
> and my native city is Jerusalem in which is situated the
> sacred shrine of the most high God. ... As for the holy
> city, I must say what befits me to say. While she, as I
> have said, is my native city she is also the mother city
> not of one country Judaea but of most of the others in
> virtue of the colonies sent out at divers times to the
> neighbouring lands Egypt, Phoenicia, the part of Syria
> called the Hollow and the rest as well and the lands lying
> far apart, Pamphylia, Cilicia, most of Asia up to Bithynia
> and the corners of Pontus, similarly also into Europe,
> Thessaly, Boeotia, Macedonia, Aetolia, Attica, Argos,
> Corinth and most of the best parts of Peloponnese. And
> not only are the mainlands full of Jewish colonies but also
> the most highly esteemed of the islands Euboea, Cyprus,
> Crete. I say nothing of the countries beyond the Euphrates,
> for except for a small part they all, Babylon and of the
> other satrapies those where the land within their confines
> is highly fertile, have Jewish inhabitants. So that if my
> own home-city is granted a share of your goodwill the
> benefit extends not to one city but to myriads of the oth-
> ers situated in every region of the inhabited world. ... It
> was in Jerusalem, my emperor, that your much-prayed-for

succession was first announced, and from the holy city
the rumour travelled to the mainlands on both sides, and
for that reason it deserves to hold the premier place in
your esteem. . . . I come finally to my supplication for the
temple. This temple, my Lord Gaius, has never from the
first admitted any figure wrought by men's hands, because
it is the sanctuary of the true God. For the works of
painters and modellers are representations of gods perceived by sense but to paint or mould a likeness of the invisible was held by our ancestors to be against their religion. Your grandfather Agrippa visited and paid honour
to the temple, and so did Augustus by the letters in
which he ordered the first fruits to be sent from every
quarter and by instituting the perpetual sacrifice. Your
great-grandmother too. . . . Thus no one, Greek or non-
Greek, no satrap, no king, no mortal enemy, no faction,
no war, no storming or sacking of the city, nor any existing thing ever brought about so great a violation of the
temple as the setting up in it of an image or statue or any
hand-wrought object for worship. . . .

Your maternal grandfather M. Agrippa, being in Judaea
when Herod my grandfather was king of the country, saw fit
to come up from the coast to the capital situated in the
centre of the land. But when he surveyed the temple and
the rich array of the priests and the worship paid by the native population he was filled with wonder thinking that he
had seen something to be profoundly reverenced, something
greater than words could describe. His discourse to those of
his friends who were there with him consisted of nothing
else but praise of the sanctuary and all that pertained to it.
Thus throughout the days which he spent in the city out of
courtesy to Herod he resorted to the precinct, delighting
himself with the spectacle both of the ornate structure and
of the sacrifices and the ritual observed in the services and

the majestic aspect of the high priest when arrayed in the sacred vestments and conducting the holy rites. . . .

Now they say [the statue] is to be in the inmost part of the temple in the special sanctuary itself, into which the Grand Priest enters once a year only on the Fast as it is called, to offer incense and to pray according to ancestral practice for a full supply of blessings and prosperity and peace for all mankind. And if any priest, to say nothing of other Jews, and not merely one of the lowest priests but of those who are ranked directly below the chief, goes in either by himself or with the High Priest, and further even if the High Priest enters on two days of the year or thrice or four times on the same day death without appeal is his doom. So greatly careful was the law-giver to guard the inmost sanctuary, the one and only place which he wished to keep preserved untrodden and untouched. How many deaths think you would those who have been trained to holiness in these matters willingly endure if they should see the statue imported thither? I believe that they would slaughter their whole families, women and children alike, and finally immolate themselves upon the corpses of their kin. . . .

But what of your grandfather, the best of the emperors that ever were to this day, he who first received the title of Augustus for his virtue and good fortune, who disseminated peace everywhere over sea and land to the ends of the world? Did he not, hearing by report the story of the temple and that it had no work of man's hands, a visible effigy of an invisible being, erected in it, marvel and pay it honour? . . . He gave orders for a continuation of whole burnt offerings every day to the Most High God to be charged to his own purse. . . . Under such an instructor in piety your great-grandmother Julia Augusta adorned the temple with golden vials and libation bowls and a multitude of other sumptuous offerings.

Gaius received the letter and, as he read it, its every sentiment filled him with resentment at the ill-success of his project, yet at the same time he began to bend under the claims for justice coupled with supplication . . . and he ordered letters to be sent to Publius Petronius, governor of Syria, that he should forbear to take further steps to violate the tradition of the temple of the Jews. *(XXXVI 276–XLI 333)*

ON DREAMS

Now the city of God is called in the Hebrew Jerusalem and its name when translated is "vision of peace." Therefore do not seek for the city of the Existent among the regions of the earth, since it is not wrought of wood or stone, but in a soul, in which there is no warring, whose sight is keen, which has set before it as its aim to live in contemplation and peace. For what grander or holier house could we find for God in the whole range of existence than the vision-seeking mind, the mind which is eager to see all things and never even in its dreams has a wish for faction or turmoil? I hear once more the voice of the invisible spirit, the familiar secret tenant saying, "Friend, it would seem that there is a matter great and precious of which thou knowest nothing, and this I will ungrudgingly shew thee, for many other well-timed lessons have I given thee. Know then, good friend, that God alone is the real veritable peace, free from all illusion, but the whole substance of things created only to perish is one constant war. For God is a being of free-will; the world of things is Fatality. Whosoever then has the strength to forsake war and Fatality, creation and perishing, and cross over to the camp of the uncreated, of the imperishable, of free-will, of peace, may justly be called the dwelling-place and city of God." *(II 250–253)*

✑ The Writings of Josephus Flavius

Josephus was a military commander who participated in the Great Revolt against the Romans as commander of Galilee (66 C.E.) but surrendered to the Romans in 67 C.E. under suspicious circumstances. A prisoner of the Romans, he managed to ingratiate himself with them and became a favorite of Roman rulers and a citizen of Rome, where he settled. He became the historian of the war and also recounted all of Jewish history for the Roman world.

ANTIQUITIES OF THE JEWS

And now Herod, in the eighteenth year of his reign . . . undertook a very great work, that is, to build of himself the temple of God, and make it larger in compass, and to raise it to a most magnificent altitude, as esteeming it to be the most glorious of all his actions, as it really was, to bring it to perfection; and that this would be sufficient for an everlasting memorial of him; but as he knew the multitude were not ready nor willing to assist him in so vast a design, he thought to prepare them first by making a speech to them, and then set about the work itself; so he called them together, and spake thus to them: ". . . Our fathers, indeed, when they were returned from Babylon, built this temple to God Almighty, yet does it want sixty cubits of its largeness in altitude; for so much did that first temple which Solomon built exceed this temple; nor let anyone condemn our fathers for their negligence or want of piety herein, for it was not their fault that the temple was no higher; for they were Cyrus, and Darius the son of Hystaspes, who determined the measures for its rebuilding; and it hath been by reason of the subjection of those fathers of ours to them and to their posterity, and after them to the Macedonians, that they had not the opportunity to follow the original model of this pious edifice, nor could raise it to its ancient altitude; but since I am now, by God's will, your governor, and I have had peace a long time, and have gained great riches and large revenues, and, what is the principal thing of all, I am at amity with and well regarded by the Romans, who, if I may say so, are the rulers of the whole world, I will do my endeavour to correct that imperfection, which hath arisen from the necessity of our affairs, and the slavery we have been under formerly, and to make a thankful return, after the most pious manner, to God, for what blessings I have received from him, by giving me this kingdom, and that by rendering his temple as complete as I am able."

And this was the speech which Herod made to them; but still this speech affrighted many of the people, as being unexpected by them; and because it seemed incredible, it did not encourage them, but put a damp upon them, for they were afraid that he would pull down the whole edifice, and not be able to bring his intentions to perfection for its rebuilding; and this danger appeared to them to be very great, and the vastness of the undertaking to be such as could hardly be accomplished. But while they were in this disposition, the king encouraged them, and told them he would not pull down their temple till all things were gotten ready for building it up entirely again. And as he promised them this beforehand, so he did not break his word with them, but got ready a thousand wagons, that were to bring stones for the building, and chose out ten thousand of the most skillful workmen, and bought a thousand sacerdotal garments for as many of the priests, and had some of them taught the arts of stone-cutters, and others of carpenters, and then began to build; but this not till every thing was well prepared for the work.

So Herod took away the old foundations, and laid others, and erected the temple upon them, being in length a hundred cubits, and in height twenty additional cubits, which, upon the sinking of their foundations, fell down; and this part it was that we resolved to raise again in the days of Nero. Now the temple was built of stones that were white and strong, and each of their length was twenty-five cubits, their height was eight, and their breadth about twelve; and the whole structure, as also the structure of the royal cloister, was on each side much lower, but the middle was much higher, till they were visible to those that dwelt in the country for a great many furlongs, but chiefly to such as lived over against them, and those that approached to them. The temple had doors also at the entrance, and lintels over them, of the same height as the temple itself. They were adorned with embroidered veils, with their flowers of purple, and pillars interwoven; and over these, but under the crown-work, was spread out a golden vine, with its branches hanging down from a great height, the largeness and fine workmanship of which was a surprising sight to the spectators, to see what vast materials there were, and with what great skill the workmanship was done. He also encompassed the entire temple with very large cloisters, contriving them to be in a due proportion thereto; and he laid out larger sums of money upon them than had been done before him, till it seemed that no one else had so greatly adorned the temple as he had done. There was a large wall to both the cloisters, which wall was itself the most prodigious work that was ever heard of by man. The hill was a rocky ascent that declined by degrees toward the east parts of the city, till it came to an elevated level. This hill it was which Solomon, who was the first of our kings, by Divine revelation, encompassed with a wall; it was of excellent workmanship upwards, and round the top of it. He also built a wall below, beginning at the bottom, which was encompassed by a deep valley; and at the south side he laid rocks together, and bound them one to another with lead, and included some of the inner parts, till it proceeded to a great height, and till both the largeness of the square edifice and its altitude were immense, and till the vastness of the stones in the front were plainly visible on the outside, yet so that the inward parts were fastened together with iron, and preserved the joints immovable for all future times. When this work was done in this manner, and joined together as part of the hill itself to the very top of it, he wrought it all into one outward surface, and filled up the hollow places which were about the wall, and made it a level on the external upper surface, and a smooth level also. This hill was walled all around, and in compass four furlongs each angle containing in length a furlong: but within this wall, and on the very top of all, there ran another wall of stone also, having, on the east quarter, a double cloister, of the same length with the wall; in the midst of which was the temple itself. This cloister looked to the gates of the temple; and it had been adorned by many kings in former times; and round about the entire temple were fixed the spoils taken from barbarous nations; all these had been dedicated to the temple by Herod, with the addition of those he had taken from the Arabians.

Now on the north side was built a citadel, whose walls were square, and strong, and of extraordinary firmness. This citadel was built by the kings of the Asamonean race, who were also high priests before Herod, and they called it the Tower, in which were reposited the vestments of the high priest, which the high priest only put on at the time when he was to offer sacrifice. . . .

Now in the western quarters of the enclosure of the temple there were four gates; the first led to the king's palace, and went to a passage over the intermediate valley; two more led to the suburbs of the city; and the last led to the other city, where the road descended down into the valley by a great number of steps, and thence up again by the ascent; for the city lay over against the temple in the manner of a theatre, and was encompassed with a deep valley along the entire south quarter; but the fourth front of the temple, which was southward, had indeed itself gates in its middle, as also had the royal cloisters, with three walks, which reached in length from the east valley unto that on the west, for it was impossible it should reach any farther: and this cloister deserves to be mentioned better than any other under the sun; for while the valley was very deep, and its bottom could not be seen, if you looked from above into the depth, this further vastly high elevation of the cloister stood upon that height, insomuch that if any one looked down from the top of the battlements, or down both those altitudes, he would be giddy, while his sight could not reach to such an immense depth. This cloister had pillars that stood in four rows one over against the other all along. . . . the roofs were adorned with deep sculptures in wood, representing many sorts of figures. The middle was much higher than the rest, and the wall of the front was adorned with beams, resting upon pillars, that were interwoven into it, and that front was all of polished stone, insomuch that its fineness, to such as had not seen it, was incredible, and to such as had seen it, was greatly amazing. Thus was the first enclosure. In the midst of which, and not far from it, was the second, to be gone up to by a few steps: this was encompassed by a stone wall for a partition, with an inscription, which forbade any foreigner to go in under pain of death. Now this inner enclosure had on its southern and northern quarters three gates [equally] distant one from another; but on the east quarter, toward the sun-rising, there was one large gate, through which such as were pure came in, together with their wives; but the temple further inward in that gate was not allowed to the women; but still more inward was there a third [court of the] temple, whereinto it was not lawful for any but the priests alone to enter. The temple itself was within this; and before that temple was the altar, upon which we offer our sacrifices and burnt-offerings to God. Into none of these did king Herod enter, for he was forbidden, because he was not a priest. However, he took good care of the cloisters and the outer enclosures, and these he built in eight years.

But the temple itself was built by the priests in a year and six months; upon which all the people were full of joy; and presently they returned thanks, in the first place, to God; and in the next place, for the alacrity the king had showed. They feasted and celebrated this rebuilding of the temple: and for the king, he sacrificed three hundred oxen to God, as did the rest every one according to his ability; the number of which sacrifices is not possible to set down, for it cannot be that we should truly relate it; for at the same time with this celebration for the work about the temple fell also the day of the king's inauguration, which he kept of an old custom as a festival, and it now coincided with the other, which coincidence of them both made the festival most illustrious. . . .

It is also reported that during the time that the temple was building, it did not rain in the day time, but that the showers fell in the nights, so that the work was not hindered. (*BOOK XV, CHAP. XI, 1–7*)

WARS OF THE JEWS

THE DESTRUCTION OF THE TEMPLE AND THE CITY

And now two of the legions had completed their banks on the eighth day of the month Lous [Ab]. Whereupon Titus gave orders that the battering rams should be brought, and set over against the western edifice of the inner temple; for before these were brought, the firmest of all the other engines had battered the wall for six days together without ceasing, without making any impression upon it;

but the vast largeness and strong connexion of the stones were superior to that engine, and to the other battering rams also. Other Romans did indeed undermine the foundations of the northern gate, and after a world of pains removed the outermost stones, yet was the gate still upheld by the inner stones, and stood still unhurt; till the workmen, despairing of all such attempts by engines and crows, brought their ladders to the cloisters. Now the Jews did not interrupt them in so doing; but when they were gotten up, they fell upon them and fought with them; some of them they thrust down, and threw them backwards headlong; others of them they met and slew; they also beat many of those that went down the ladders again, and slew them with their swords before they could bring their shields to protect them; nay, some of the ladders they threw down from above when they were full of armed men; a great slaughter was made of the Jews also at the same time, while those that bore the ensigns fought hard for them, as deeming it a terrible thing, and what would tend to their great shame, if thµey permitted them to be stolen away. Yet did the Jews at length get possession of these engines, and destroyed those that had gone up the ladders, while the rest were so intimidated by what those suffered who were slain, that they retired; although none of the Romans died without having done good service before his death. Of the seditious, those that had fought bravely in the former battles did the like now, as besides them did Eleazar, the brother's son of Simon the tyrant. But when Titus perceived that his endeavours to spare a foreign temple were turned to the damage of his soldiers, and made them be killed, he gave order to set the gates on fire. . . .

So Titus retired into the tower of the Antonia, and resolved to storm the temple the next day, early in the morning, with his whole army, and to encamp round about the holy house. But as for that house, God had, for certain, long ago doomed it to the fire; and now that fatal day was come, according to the revolution of ages; it was the tenth day of the month Lous [Ab], upon which it was formerly burnt by the king of Babylon; although these flames took their rise from the Jews themselves and were occasioned by them; for upon Titus retiring, the seditious lay still for a little while, and then attacked the Romans again, when those that guarded the holy house fought with those that quenched the fire that was burning in the inner [court of the] temple; but these Romans put the Jews to flight, and proceeded as far as the holy house itself. At which time one of the soldiers, without staying for any orders, and without any concern or dread upon him at so great an undertaking, and being hurried on by a certain divine fury, snatched somewhat out of the materials that were on fire, and being lifted up by another soldier, he set fire to a golden window, through which there was a passage to the rooms that were round about the holy house, on the north side of it. As the flames went upward, the Jews made a great clamour, such as so mighty an affliction required, and ran together to prevent it; and now they spared not their lives any longer, nor suffered any thing to restrain their force, since that holy house was perishing, for whose sake it was that they kept such a guard about it.

And now a certain person came running to Titus, and told him of this fire, as he was resting himself in his tent after the last battle; whereupon he rose up in great haste, and, as he was, ran to the holy house, in order to have a stop put to the fire; after him followed all his commanders, and after them followed the several legions, in great astonishment; so there was a great clamour and tumult raised, as was natural upon the disorderly motion of so great an army. Then did Caesar, both by calling to the soldiers that were fighting, with a loud voice, and by giving a signal to them with his right hand, order them to quench the fire. But they did not hear what he said, though he spake so loud, having their ears already dinned by a greater noise

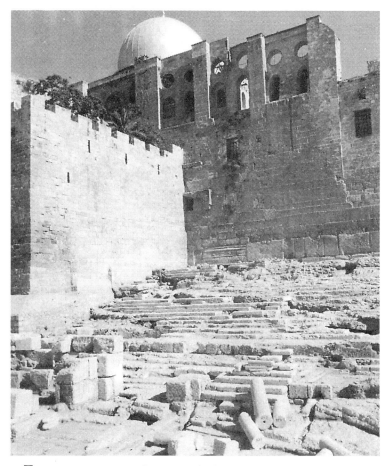

The Temple Mount and the monumental stairway at the Ophel along its southern wall; looking north (Ancient Jerusalem Revealed. Israel Exploration Society; with permission)

another way; nor did they attend to the signal he made with his hand neither, as still some of them were distracted with fighting, and others with passion. But as for the legions that came running thither, neither any persuasions nor any threatenings could restrain their violence, but each one's own passions was his commander at this time; and as they were crowding into the temple together, many of them were trampled on by one another, while a great number fell among the ruins of the cloisters, which were still hot and smoking, and were destroyed in the same miserable way with those whom they had conquered; and when they were come near the holy house, they made as if they did not so much as hear Caesar's orders to the contrary; but they encouraged those that were before them to set it on fire. As for the seditious, they were in too great distress already to afford their assistance; they were every where slain, and every where beaten; and as for a great part of the people, they were weak and without arms, and had their throats cut wherever they were caught. Now round about the altar lay dead bodies heaped one upon another, as at the steps going up to it ran a great quantity of their blood, whither also the dead bodies that were slain above [on the altar] fell down.

And now, since Caesar was no way able to restrain the enthusiastic fury of the soldiers, and the fire proceeded on more and more, he went into the holy place of the temple, with his commanders, and saw it, with what was in it, which he found to be far superior to what the relations of foreigners contained, and not inferior to what we ourselves boasted of and believed about it. But as the flame had not as yet reached to its inward parts, but was still consuming the rooms that were about the holy house, and Titus supposing what the fact was, that the house itself might yet be saved, he came in haste and endeavoured to persuade the soldiers to quench the fire, and gave order to Liberalius the centurion, and one of those spearmen that were about him, to beat the soldiers that were refractory with their staves, and to restrain them; yet were their passions too hard for the regards they had for Caesar, and the dread they had of him who forbade them, as was their hatred of the Jews, and a certain vehement inclination to fight them, too hard for them also. Moreover the hope of plunder induced many to go on, as having this opinion, that all the places within were full of money, and as seeing that all round about it was made of gold. And besides, one of those that went into the place prevented Caesar, when he ran so hastily out to restrain the soldiers, and threw the fire upon the hinges of the gate, in the dark; whereby the flame burst out from within the holy house itself immediately, when the commanders returned and Caesar with them, and when nobody any longer forbade those that were without to set fire to it. And thus was the holy house burnt down, without Caesar's approbation. . . .

While the holy house was on fire, everything was plundered that came to hand, and ten thousand of those that were caught were slain; nor was there a commiseration of any age, or any reverence of gravity, but children, and old men, and profane persons, and priests were all slain in the same manner. . . . The flame also was carried a long way, and made an echo, together with the groans of those that were slain; and because this hill was high, and the works at the temple were very great, one would have thought the whole city had been on fire. Nor can one imagine any thing either greater or more terrible than this noise; for there was at once a shout of the Roman legions, who were marching all together, and a sad clamour of the seditious, who were now surrounded with fire and sword . . . one would have thought that the hill itself, on which the temple stood, was seething hot, as full of fire on every part of it, that the blood was larger in quantity than the fire, and those that were slain more in number than those that slew them; for the ground did no where appear visible, for the dead bodies that lay on it; but the soldiers went over

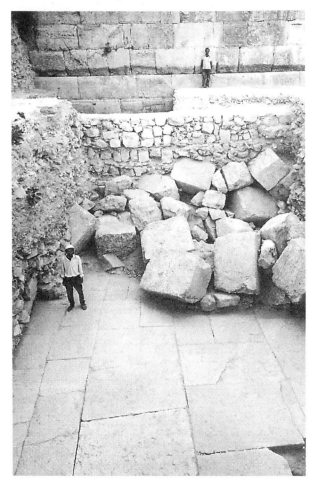

A *paved Herodian street at the foot of the Western Wall of the Temple Mount, north of Robinson's Arch; heaps of fallen stones from the wall cover the street (Ancient Jerusalem Revealed. Israel Exploration Society; with permission)*

heaps of those bodies, as they ran upon such as fled from them. . . . As for the priests, some of them plucked up from the holy house the spikes that were upon it, with their bases, which were made of lead, and shot them at the Romans instead of darts. . . .

And now the Romans, judging that it was in vain to spare what was round about the holy house, burnt all those places, as also the remains of the cloisters and the gates, two excepted; the one on the east side, and the other on the south; both which, however, they burnt afterward. They also burnt down the treasury chambers. . . .

Now as soon as the army had no more people to slay or to plunder, because there remained none to be the objects of their fury (for they would not have spared any, had there remained any other work to be done), Caesar gave orders that they should now demolish the entire city and temple, but should leave as many of the towers standing as were of the greatest eminency; that is, Phasaelus, and Hippicus, and Mariamne; and so much of the wall as enclosed the city on the west side. This wall was spared, in order to afford a camp for such as were to lie in garrison, as were the towers also spared, in order to demonstrate to posterity what kind of city it was, and how well fortified, which the Roman valour had subdued; but for the rest of the wall, it was so thoroughly laid even with the ground by those that dug it up to the foundation, that there was left nothing to make those that came thither believe it had even been inhabited. This was the end which Jerusalem came to by the madness of those that were for innovations; a city otherwise of great magnificence, and of mighty fame among all mankind. (*BOOK VI, CHAP. IV, 1–2, 5–7; CHAP. V, 1; BOOK VII, CHAP. I, 1.*)

THE THIRD GATE

Jerusalem in Rabbinic Literature

The Damascus Gate at night, July 1968 (Israel Government Press Office; with permission)

Rabbinic literature is a very wide category that encompasses works from the time of the Mishna (200 C.E.) through various midrashic collections compiled in the Middle Ages. Much of this later material, however, either stems from earlier works or is a later adaptation of it. All of it reflects the values of the pharisaic sages and their heirs, the rabbis. It contains interpretations of scriptural verses, saying of the sages, laws and legends concerning Jerusalem. The selection below is but a part of the vast material to be found in rabbinic works but reflects the basic rabbinic concepts connected to Jerusalem.

❧ Jerusalem—the Chosen

Abraham called the place "yireh" as it is said: "And Abraham named that site Adonai-yireh, whence the present saying, 'On the mount of the Lord there is vision'" (Gen. 22:14). Shem called it "shalem" as it is said: "And Melchizedek, king of Shalem" (Gen. 14:18). Said the Holy One, "If I call it 'yireh' as Abraham did, Shem, that righteous man, will complain. If I call it 'shalem' as Shem did, Abraham, that righteous man, will complain. Therefore I will use both names and call it Yirushalayim [Jerusalem]—'yireh-shalem.'" (GEN. RABBA 56:14)

❧

The world is like a human eye. The white is like the ocean which surrounds the earth. The pupil is like the earth. The opening in the pupil is like Jerusalem. The reflection in the opening is like the Temple—may it be built speedily in our days and in the days of all Israel! (DERECH ERETZ ZUTA 9)

❧

The Land of Israel is the center of the world. Jerusalem is the center of the Land of Israel. The Temple is the center of Jerusalem. The heichal [the Temple Hall] is the center of the Temple. The Ark is the center of the heichal. The rock of the foundation is in front of the Ark, and upon it the entire world is founded. (TANHUMA KEDOSHIM 10)

❧

113

Rabbi Joshua ben Levi interprets the words: Jerusalem built up, a city knit [*hubru*] together (Pss. 122:3)—a city that makes all Israel one fellowship [*haverim*]. (YER. HAGIGAH 3:6)

❧

Rabbi Simeon bar Yochai expounded: "He stands and measures the earth; He glances and makes nations tremble" (Hab. 3:6). The Holy One measured all the nations and found none worthy to receive the Torah except Israel. The Holy One measured all the generations and found none worthy to receive the Torah except the generation of the wilderness. The Holy One measured all the nations and found none worthy of having His Presence rest thereon except Mount Moriah. The Holy One measured all cities and found none worthy of having the Holy Temple built therein except Jerusalem. The Holy One measured all the mountains and found none worthy of having the Torah given upon it except Sinai. The Holy One measured all the lands and found none worthy of Israel except the Land of Israel. That is the meaning of the verse: "He stands and measures the earth; He glances and makes nations tremble" (Hab. 3:6). (LEV. RABBA 13:2)

❧

A place which is higher than other places is better than they. The Land of Israel is higher and therefore better than other places [as it is said]: "Let us go up and we shall gain possession of it" (Num. 13:30). . . . The Temple is higher and therefore better than all other temples [as it is said]: ". . . and the many peoples shall go and shall say: Come, let us go up to the mount of the Lord, to the house of the God of Jacob" (Isa. 2:3). (SIFRE DEUT. 37)

❧

There is no beauty like the beauty of Jerusalem. (*AVOT DE RABBI NATAN 28*)

🔊

Praying in Jerusalem is like praying before the Throne of Glory. The gate to heaven is there and it is open so that the Lord may hear. (*PIRKE DE RABBI ELIEZER 35*)

🔊

There was a stone [in the Holy of Holies] from the time of the early prophets called "Shetiyah" . . . because from it the world was founded [*hushtat*]. . . . The creation of the world began from Zion, as it is said: "A psalm of Asaph. God, the Lord God, spoke and summoned the world from east to west" (Pss. 50:1). And it continues: "From Zion, perfect in beauty" (Pss. 50:2). (*YOMA 53B–54B*)

🔊

"The Lord loves the gates of Zion" (Pss. 87:2). In every city the king has a palace. Which one does he love the most? The palace which is in his own city. Said the Holy One: I love synagogues and houses of study. But what do I love even more than they? The gates of Zion, for that is My own palace. (*YALKUT SHIMONI PSS. 836*)

🔊

"He [Noah] offered burnt offerings on the altar" (Gen. 8:20). Rabbi Eliezer ben Jacob said: This was on the great altar which is in Jerusalem, for there primal Adam had offered his offering as well. (*GEN. RABBA 34:20*)

🔊

Jerusalem is the light of the world, as it is said: "And nations shall walk by your light" (Isa. 60:3). Who is the light of Jerusalem? The Holy One, as it is said: "For the Lord shall be your light everlasting." (Isa. 60:19). (*GEN. RABBA 60:19*)

☙ Jerusalem—the Unique

There are ten portions of beauty in the world. Nine are in Jerusalem, one in the rest of the world.

There are ten portions of suffering in the world. Nine in Jerusalem, one in the rest of the world.

There are ten portions of wisdom in the world. Nine in Jerusalem, one in the rest of the world.

There are ten portions of godlessness in the world. Nine in Jerusalem, one in the rest of the world.

There are ten portions of Torah in the world. Nine in Jerusalem, one in the rest of the world. (AVOT DE RABBI NATAN B 48)

☙

Whoever has not seen Herod's Temple has never seen a beautiful building. Of what did he build it? Rabba said: yellow and white marble. Others say: blue, yellow and white marble. Alternate rows projected out in order to leave room for cement. He intended to cover it with gold but the Rabbis told him not to since it was more beautiful as it was, resembling the waves of the ocean. (BABA BATRA 4A)

☙

"All streams flow into the sea, yet the sea is never full" (Eccl. 1:7). All Israel enters Jerusalem three times each year at the festivals. "Yet the sea is never full"—Jerusalem is never filled up. (KOHELET RABBA 1)

☙

There were 480 synagogues in Jerusalem, each one with its own school and academy, a school for teaching Scripture, an academy for teaching Mishna. All of them, as well as the Temple, were destroyed by Vespasian. *(Y. Megilla 3:1)*

❧

All the trees of Jerusalem were made of cinnamon. When they kindled their wood, their perfume would spread throughout the entire Land of Israel. When the Temple was destroyed, they were hidden away and only a trifle remained. *(Shabbat 63a)*

❧

If one prays in Jerusalem it is as if one were praying before the Throne of Glory, for the very gate of heaven is located there, as it is said: "that is the gateway to heaven" (Gen. 28:17). *(Midrash Pss. 91:7)*

❧

There were twenty-four plazas in Jerusalem. Each plaza had twenty-four alleys. Each alley had twenty-four streets. Each street had twenty-four courts. Each court had twenty-four inner courts. Each inner court had twenty-four houses. The population of each inner court was double the number of those who left Egypt in the Exodus. *(Lam. Rabba 1:2)*

❧

Because of the fragrance of the incense, brides in Jerusalem did not have to perfume themselves. *(Yoma 39b)*

❧

"Fair-crested, joy of all the earth" (Pss. 48:3). . . . Everyone says of her: "Is this the city which is called perfect in beauty, joy of all the earth?" (Lam. 2:15). . . . In what way is she "joy of all the earth"? She makes the entire land rejoice. If a man had transgressed, his heart would trouble him. He would then go up to Jerusalem, bring a sacrifice, and attain atonement; His heart would then rejoice, and he would leave feeling happy. Therefore it is said: "joy of all the earth." (MIDRASH PSS. 48:2)

🔊

Ten miracles were done for our ancestors in Jerusalem [only eight are listed—ed.]:

No woman ever miscarried because of the smell of the sacrifices;

No man was ever attacked [by demons] in Jerusalem;

No man ever met with an accident in Jerusalem;

No fire ever broke out in Jerusalem;

No buildings ever collapsed in Jerusalem;

No man ever said to another, "I cannot find an oven in Jerusalem in which to roast the passover sacrifices";

No man ever said to another, "I have not found a bed to sleep in in Jerusalem";

No man ever said to another, "There is no place for me to lodge in Jerusalem." (AVOT DE RABBI NATAN 35)

🔊

All good things and blessings which the Holy One will bestow upon Israel in the future will come exclusively from Zion.

Deliverance is from Zion: "O that deliverance of Israel might come from Zion!" (Pss. 14:7).

Might is from Zion: "The Lord will stretch forth from Zion your mighty scepter" (Pss. 110:2).

Blessing is from Zion: "Blessed is the Lord from Zion, He who dwells in Jerusalem. Halleluya" (Pss. 135:21).

The shofar is from Zion: "Blow the shofar in Zion!" (Joel 2:1).

Dew, blessing, and life are from Zion: "Like the dew of Hermon that falls upon the mountains of Zion. There the Lord ordained blessing, everlasting life" (Pss. 133:3).

Torah is from Zion: "For Torah shall come forth from Zion, the world of the Lord from Jerusalem" (Isa. 2:3).

Help and sustenance are from Zion: "May He send you help from the sanctuary, and sustain you from Zion" (Pss. 20:3). *(LEV. RABBA 24:4)*

❧

Our rabbis taught: During the forty years before the destruction of the Temple the lot ["For the Lord"] never came up in the right hand, nor did the scarlet strap turn white [on Yom Kippur], nor did the westernmost light shine. The doors of the *heichal* [Temple] would open by themselves. Rabban Yohanan ben Zakkai rebuked them saying: "*Heichal, heichal*, why will you sound your own warning? I know that you will be destroyed, for Zechariah ben Ido has already prophesied about you: 'Throw open your gates, O Lebanon, and let fire consume your cedars!' " (Zech. 11:1).

Rabbi Isaac ben Tabai said: Why is it [the Temple] called Lebanon? Because it whitens [*malbin*] the sins of Israel. Rabbi Zutra ben Tobiah said: Why is it called "forest," as it is written: "Lebanon Forest House" (1 Kings 10:21)? To teach us that just as a forest produces shoots, so does the Temple. As Rabbi Hosea said: When Solomon built the Temple, he planted all kinds of precious golden trees which produced fruit in season. When the wind blew against them, the fruit would fall, as it is said: "May his fruit rustle like Lebanon" (Pss. 72:16). They were a source of income for the priests, but as soon as idolaters entered the Temple, they dried up, as it is said: "And the blossoms of Lebanon wither" (Nahum 1:4). But the Holy One, blessed is He, will restore it to us, as it is said: "It shall blossom abundantly, it shall also exult and shout. It shall receive the glory of Lebanon, the splendor of Carmel and Sharon" (Isa.35:2). (YOMA 39B)

🕮

When Nicanor went to Alexandria of Egypt to fetch doors [for the gate to the Temple], a storm arose at sea upon his return to drown him. They took one of the doors and threw it into the sea, but the sea would not cease its rage. When they tried to take the other to cast it into the sea, he clung to it and said, "Throw me in with it!" The sea immediately became calm. He was upset about the other door, but when he arrived at Acco harbor, it broke through and came up from under the boat. . . . Therefore, all the gates of the Temple were replaced by golden ones except for the gates of Nicanor, because of the miracles associated with them. Some say: because the bronze of which they were made shone like gold. (YOMA 38A)

🕮

There were five gates to the Temple Mount—the two gates of Hulda on the south, used both for entrance and exit, the gate of Kiponus on the west, used both for entrance and exit, the gate of Taddai on the north, not used [by the public] at all, the eastern gate which had a representation of the palace of Susa over it and through which the

High Priest and those who assisted him in the burning of the red heifer would go to the Mount of Olives. (*MIDDOTH 1:3*)

❧

There was a place one cubit square on which was a slab of marble. In it was fixed a ring with a chain on which were hung the keys. When closing time came, the priest would raise the slab by the ring and take the keys from the chain. Then the priest would lock up. . . . when he had finished, he would replace the keys on the chain and the slab in its place, lay his garment on it, and sleep there. . . . (*MIDDOTH 1:9*)

❧

The Temple Mount was five hundred cubits by five hundred. . . . All who entered the Temple Mount entered by the right and went around that way. They exited by the left. If, however, something had happened, the person would enter and go around to the left. "Why do you go round to the left?" "Because I am a mourner." "May He who dwells in this House comfort you. . . ." (*MIDDOTH 2:1–2*)

❧

When the Ark was there, the High Priest could enter and exit by its light. Once it was taken away, he would have to grope in the dark. (*Y. YOMA 5:3*)

☞ The Destruction of Jerusalem

Because of Kamza and Bar Kamza Jerusalem was destroyed. There was a man who had a friend named Kamza and an enemy named Bar Kamza. He was making a banquet and told his servant, "Go and bring Kamza." He went and brought Bar Kamza. When the host saw him seated there he said to him, "You are always slandering me—what are you doing here? Get out!" [Bar Kamza] said, "Since I am already here, let me stay. I will pay the cost of my food and drink." He said to him, "No." [Bar Kamza] said, "I will pay for the cost of half of the banquet." He said to him, "No." [Bar Kamza] said, "I will pay the cost of the entire banquet." He said to him, "No." He took him by the hand and dragged him out. [Bar Kamza] said, "Since the rabbis were sitting there and did not protest it must mean that they agreed with him. I will go to the government and inform against them." He went and told the Emperor, "The Jews are rebelling against you." He said to him, "How can I be certain of that?" He said to him, "Send them a sacrifice and see if they offer it or not." [The Emperor] sent a fine calf with him, but he made a blemish on its upper lip—some say in the white of the eye—in a place which we [Jews] consider as rendering it unfit, but they [the Romans] do not.

The rabbis were of the opinion that it should be offered in order to maintain good relationships with the government, but Rabbi Zechariah ben Abkulas said, "People will say that blemished animals are being offered on the altar." They thought that they should kill [Bar Kamza] in order to prevent him from informing on them, but Rabbi Zechariah said, "Is one executed for causing a blemish to consecrated animals?!" Said Rabbi Yohanan, "Because of the scruples of Rabbi Zechariah ben Abkulas our Temple was destroyed, our Sanctuary was burned and we were exiled from our land!" . . . We learn from this how serious it is to shame another person, for the Holy One aided Bar Kamza, destroyed His Temple and burnt His Sanctuary. (*GITTEN 55B*)

◐

Jerusalem was destroyed because they went according to the strict laws of the Torah and did not go beyond the requirements of law. (*BABA MEZIA 30B*)

◐

Rabbi Yohanan ben Torta said: Why was Shilo destroyed? Because they did not respect the sacred offerings there. Why was the first Temple of Jerusalem destroyed? Because of the idolatry, sexual immorality, and bloodshed that was in Jerusalem. But what of the latter Temple? We know that the people labored in the Torah and were careful to observe tithes. Why were they exiled? Because they loved money and hated one another, thus teaching you that hatred of one's fellow is more weighty before God than idolatry, sexual immorality, and bloodshed. But the last building that will be built in the future—in our lifetimes and in our days!—what is said of it? "In the days to come the mount of the Lord's house shall stand firm above the mountains and tower above the hills; and all the nations shall gaze upon it with joy. And the many peoples shall go and shall say: 'Come, let us go up to the Mount of the Lord, to the House of the God of Jacob; that He may instruct us in His ways, and that we may walk in His paths' " (Isa. 2:3). (*TOS. MENAHOT 13:22–23*)

◐

Vespasian came and besieged Jerusalem for three years. There were three very wealthy men there, Nakdimon ben Gurion, Ben Kalba

Shabua and Ben Zizit Hakeshet. . . . One of them said to them, "I will supply them with wheat and barley." Another said to them, "I will supply wine, oil and salt." The third said to them, "I will supply wood."

The Zealots were then in the city. The rabbis said to them, "Let us go and make peace with [the Romans]," but they would not permit it. Rather they said, "Let us go and make war against them." The rabbis said to them, "It will not succeed." [The Zealots] then went and burnt the stores of wheat and barley so that there was a famine. . . .

Abba Sikra, the son of Rabbi Yohanan ben Zakkai's sister, was the leader of the Zealots in Jerusalem. He sent him a message, "Come to me secretly." When he came, [Rabban Yohanan] said to him, "How long do you intend to continue this way? You will slay everyone through famine!" [Abba Sikra] said, "What can I do? If I say anything they will kill me at once." [Rabban Yohanan] said to him, "Find some way so that at least something can be saved!" He said to him, "Pretend to be ill so that people will come and ask about your health. Put something that smells bad nearby so that everyone will say that you are dead. Then let your disciples and no one else bear your litter so that someone will not notice that you are light, since the living are lighter than the dead." He did so. Rabbi Eleazar took one side and Rabbi Joshua the other. When they reached the door, some [Zealots] wanted to pierce [the body with a spear] but they said, "Do you want [the Romans] to say that they pierced their master?" They wanted to push it. They said to them, "Do you want them to say they pushed their master?" They opened the gate of the city and he got out.

When he arrived [at the Roman camp] he said, "Greetings unto you, O King!" [Vespasian] said to him, "You are doubly condemned to die. Once for calling me king when I am not king and again because if I am king, why did you not come to me before this?" He said to him, "As to what you said about not being a king, you will be king. . . . As to why I did not come sooner, the Zealots would not let me. . . ."

A messenger then came from Rome and said, "Arise! Caesar is dead and the notables of Rome wish to appoint you the leader!" . . . (Vespasian) said, "I am going now. Someone else will be sent here. But you can ask a favor of me and I will grant it." He said to him, "Grant me Yavneh and its sages, [spare] the dynasty of Rabban Gamliel. . . ." (*GITTIN* 56B)

❧

When the Temple was destroyed for the second time, large numbers in Israel became ascetics, binding themselves to neither eat meat nor drink wine. Rabbi Joshua spoke to them and said: "My sons, why do you not eat meat nor drink wine?" They replied: "Shall we eat flesh which used to be brought as an offering on the altar now that the altar no longer exists? Shall we drink wine which used to be poured as a libation on the altar but is no longer?" He said to them: "If that is so, we should not eat bread because the meal offerings have ceased." They said: "True. We can manage with fruit." He said: "We should not eat fruit either since there is no longer an offering of first fruits." They said: "Then we can manage with other fruits [that were not brought]." He said: "But we should not drink water either because there is no longer the ceremony of pouring water." To this they could find no answer, so he said to them: "My sons, come and listen to me. Not to mourn at all is impossible because the disaster has occurred. To mourn overmuch is also impossible. The sages have therefore ordained that a man may stucco his house, but he should leave a little bare. A man may prepare a full banquet, but he should leave out an item or two. A woman may put on all her ornaments,

*H*ebrew inscription from the southwestern corner of the Temple Mount: "to the house of the trumpeting to pr[oclaim]" (Ancient Jerusalem Revealed. Israel Exploration Society; with permission)

but leave off one or two . . . for it says: 'If I forget you, O Jerusalem, let my right hand wither; let my tongue stick to my palate if I cease to think of you, if I do not keep Jerusalem in memory even at my happiest hour' " (Pss. 137:5–6). What is meant by "my happiest hour"? Rabbi Isaac said: This is symbolized by putting ashes on the head of a bridegroom. (BABA BATRA 60B)

〆

Rabbi Jose said: It once happened that I was walking along and entered one of the ruins of Jerusalem in order to pray. Elijah—of blessed memory—came and guarded me at the entrance and waited until I finished my prayer. When I finished he said to me, "Peace unto you, my master." I said to him, "Peace unto you, my master and my teacher." He said to me, "My son, why did you enter this ruin?" I said to him, "In order to pray." He said to me, "You should have prayed along the road." I said to him, "I was afraid lest passers-by stop me." He said to me, "You should have prayed a short version. . . . My son, what sound did you hear in this ruin?" I said to him, "I heard a

Model of the Second Temple, Jerusalem, at Holyland Hotel, 1967 (Central Zionist Archives; with permission)

Bat Kol [a heavenly voice] like the keening of a dove, and it said: 'Woe to the children because of whose sins I have destroyed My House, burnt My Temple, and exiled them among the nations!' " He said to me, "By your life and your head! It is not only now but every day—three times—that it speaks so. Not only that, but whenever Israel enters synagogues and houses of study and says; 'May His great Name be blessed!' the Holy One, Blessed is He, shakes His head and says, 'Happy is the King who is praised so in His house! Desolate is the Father who has exiled His children and desolate the children who have been exiled from their Father's table!' " (*BERACHOT 3A*)

✥ The Western Wall

"There He stands behind our wall" (Songs 2:9)—behind the Western Wall of the Temple. Why? Because the Holy One swore that it would never be destroyed. (SONGS RABBA 2:22)

✥

"The Lord is in His holy place" (Pss. 11:4). As long as the Holy Temple existed, God's Presence dwelt therein. Once our sins caused it to be destroyed, God's Presence removed itself to heaven, as it is said: "His throne is in heaven" (ibid). Said Rabbi Eleazar ben Pedat: God's Presence did not depart from there—destroyed or not!—as it is said: "The Lord *is* in His holy place." Even though His throne is in heaven, His Presence is in the Holy Temple, as it is said: "My eyes and My heart shall forever be there" (1 Kings 9:3). And thus it says: "He answers me from His holy mountain" (Pss. 3:5). Even though it is only a ruined mountain, it retains its sanctity.

Rabbi Eleazar ben Pedat says: Consider what Cyrus said: "Let him go up to Jerusalem that is in Judah and build the house of the Lord God of Israel, the God that is in Jerusalem" (Ezra 1:3). Even though it is destroyed, God Himself has not departed from there. . . .

Said Rabbi Aha: The Presence of God will never depart from the Western Wall, as it is said: "There He stands behind our wall" (Songs 2:9). (MIDRASH PSS. 11:3)

☙ Heavenly Jerusalem

"Said Rabbi Simeon ben Yohai: The Temple on high is only eighteen *mil* above the Temple below. How do we know? It says "and that is the gateway to heaven" (Gen. 28:17). The numerical value of the word *v'zeh* ["and that is"] is eighteen.

Another interpretation: The Holy One showed Jacob the Temple when it was standing and when it had been destroyed and yet again when it was rebuilt. "He said: How awesome is this place" (Gen. 28:17). This refers to the Temple when it was standing, as in the verse "You are awesome, O God, in Your holy places" (Pss. 68:36); "and that is" refers to it when destroyed, as in the verse "Because of that our hearts are sick—because of Mount Zion, which lies desolate" (Lam. 5:17–18); "This is none other than the house of God and that is the gateway to heaven" refers to it when rebuilt and beautified in the future, as in the verse "For He made the bars of your gates strong" (Pss. 147:13). (GEN. RABBA 69:17)

☙

Said the Holy One, "I will not enter heavenly Jerusalem until I enter earthly Jerusalem." Is there a "heavenly Jerusalem"? Yes, as it is said: "Jerusalem built up, a city knit together [*hubra*]" (Pss. 122:3). Rabbi Joshua ben Levi said, "It means a city which makes all Israel into one fellowship [*haverim*]." (MIDRASH PSS. 122:4; TAANIT 5A)

☙

One should direct one's heart in prayer toward the Holy of Holies. Rabbi Hiyya said: Toward the heavenly Holy of Holies. Rabbi Simeon ben Halafta said: Toward the earthly Holy of Holies. Rabbi

*Arrival of the Messiah in Jerusalem and Return of the Jews; woodcut from
an Italian Passover Haggada; Venice, early 1600s*

Pinhas said: There is no disagreement here. The earthly Holy of
Holies is directly opposite the heavenly Holy of Holies. This is the
meaning of the phrase: "The place You made Your abode" [*machon
leshivtecha*] (Exod. 15:17)—"directed toward [*mechaven*] Your abode."
(*YER. BER. 4:5*)

🕉

Elijah said, "I see a great and beautiful city which descends from
heaven fully built, as it is said: 'Jerusalem built up, a city knit together' (Pss. 122:3). Built up and refined, its people sitting within it
. . . and I see houses and gates of pearl and doorposts of precious jewels. The treasures of the Temple are spread out at the entrance,
among them Torah and peace, as it is said: 'And all your children
shall be learned of the Lord and great shall be the peace of your children' " (Isa. 54:13). (*NISTAROT ELIYAHU, BET HAMIDRASH 3, p. 67f.*)

ॐ Jerusalem—in the Future

Once Rabban Gamliel, Rabbi Eleazar ben Azaria, Rabbi Joshua, and Rabbi Akiba were going up to Jerusalem. When they came to Mount Scopus they rent their garments. When they came to the Temple Mount they saw a fox going out of the Holy of Holies. They began to weep, except for Rabbi Akiba, who laughed. They said to him, "Why are you laughing?" He said to them, "Why are you weeping?" They said to him, "The place of which it is written: 'any outsider who encroaches shall be put to death' (Num. 1:51)—now foxes roam in it! Should we not weep?" He said to them, "That is exactly why I am laughing. It is written: 'I shall call reliable witnesses, the priest Uriah and Zechariah' (Isa. 8:2). What is the connection between these two? Uriah lived at the time of the First Temple, Zechariah, at the time of the Second Temple. Scripture is making Zechariah's prophecy dependent upon that of Uriah. Uriah wrote: 'Zion shall be plowed as a field, and Jerusalem shall become heaps of ruins, and the Temple Mount a shrine in the woods' (Jer. 26:18, 20). Zechariah wrote: 'There shall yet be old men and women in the squares of Jerusalem' (Zech. 8:4). Before the first prophecy came true, I was afraid that the second would not be realized. Now that the first has come true, I am certain that the second will come to pass." Thus did they say to him, "Akiba, you have comforted us, Akiba you have comforted us." (MAKKOT 24B; SIFRE DEUTERONOMY 43)

ॐ

Rabbi Yohanan says: Whoever mourns for Jerusalem will merit seeing it at its time of rejoicing, as it is said: "Rejoice for Jerusalem and be glad for her, all you who love her! Join in her jubilation, all you who mourned over her" (Isa. 66:10). But whoever did not mourn for Jerusalem will not see it at its time of rejoicing. *(YALKUT SHIMONI LAM. 998)*

𑁍

"Daughters of Jerusalem" (Songs 1:5). Said Rabbi Yohanan: In the future Jerusalem will become a metropolis for all the nations and will draw people unto herself as a stream to do her honor. This [is the meaning of "daughters"] as we see in the verses: "Ashdod, its daughters [i.e., dependencies] and its villages—Gaza, its daughters and its villages (Josh. 15:47). *(SONGS RABBA 1:5)*

𑁍

"I will make . . . your gates of precious stones" (Isa. 54:12). There will be one great gate in Jerusalem and two wickets made of one great stone. In the future the Holy One will bring jewels and pearls hollowed out ten cubits by twenty and make them the gates of Jerusalem. *(MIDRASH PSS. 87:2)*

𑁍

Jerusalem will be redeemed only through justice as it is said: "Zion will be redeemed through justice and her repentant ones through righteousness (Isa. 1:27)." *(SHABBAT 139A)*

𑁍

In the future the Holy One will enlarge Jerusalem so that it will occupy the space a horse could cover running from morning until midday. *(PESACHIM 50A)*

𑁍

In the future the Holy One will bring the mountains of Sinai, Tabor, and Carmel together and build the Temple upon their peak. This is the meaning of the verse: "In the days to come, the Mount of the Lord's House shall stand firm above the mountains" (Isa. 2:2). . . . Furthermore, the Temple will sing aloud and the mountains will answer the song. . . . In the future Jerusalem will become a beacon to the nations of the world and they will walk in her light, as it is said: "And nations shall walk by your light" (Isa. 60:3). (PESIKTA DE RAV KAHANA 21:4)

Great is peace, for the Holy One announces the redemption of Jerusalem only with peace, as it is said: "How welcome on the mountain are the footsteps of the herald announcing peace . . . telling Zion, 'Your God is King!' " (Isa. 52:7). (DEUT. RABBA 5:15)

Jerusalem will not be rebuilt until all the exiles have been brought back. If someone says to you that all the exiles have been brought back but Jerusalem has not been rebuilt, do not believe him. Why? For it is written: "The Lord rebuilds Jerusalem" (Pss. 147:2) and then: "He gathers in the exiles of Israel" (ibid). Israel said to the Holy One, "Master of the universe, was not Jerusalem rebuilt once only to be destroyed again?" He said to them, "Because of your sins was Jerusalem destroyed and you were exiled from it, but in the time-to-come I will build it and never destroy it again, as it is said: 'For the Lord has built Zion; He has appeared in all His glory' " (Pss. 102:17). (TANHUMA NOAH 11)

In the future Jerusalem will be raised up until it reaches the Throne of Glory, as it says: "The place is too crowded for me; make room for me to settle" (Isa. 49:20). Yet you do not yet know the full praise of Jerusalem until you see what is written: "And I Myself—declares the Lord—will be a wall of fire all around it, and I will be a glory inside it" (Zech. 2:9). That indicates the praise of Jerusalem! (PESIKTA DE RAV KAHANA 20:7)

〰

And thus you find that in the world-to-come the Holy One will expand Jerusalem, as it is said: "the structure became wider from story to story" (Ezek. 41:7)—until it will reach the heavens. . . . Once it reaches the heavens, it will say, "My place is too small." What will the Holy One do? He will bring clouds and raise it from one heaven to the next. Said Rabbi Eliezer: Eventually it will reach the Heavenly Throne itself! (TANH. TZAV 12)

〰

Indeed, it shall be said of Zion, "Every man was born there" (Pss. 87:5). One who desires [to see Zion] is the same as one who was born there. [Both are children of Zion.] (KETUBOT 75A)

〰

Says the Holy One: In the time to-come when Zion is rebuilt I shall be a wall unto her, as it is said: "And I Myself—declares the Lord—will be a wall of fire around it, and I will be a glory inside it" (Zech. 2:9). (EXODUS RABBA 40)

〰

Rabban Simeon ben Gamliel says: All nations and kingdoms will be gathered unto Jerusalem in the future, as it is said: "All nations shall assemble there, in the name of the Lord, in Jerusalem" (Jer. 3:17). (AVOT DE RABBI NATAN A 35)

☙

"Blessed shall you be in the city" (Deut. 28:3). This refers to Jerusalem, which is called "the city," as it is said: "Is this the city that was called perfect in beauty?" (Lam. 2:15). "And blessed shall you be in the field" (Deut. 28:3). This refers to Zion, as it is said: "Zion shall be plowed as a field" (Jer. 26:18). And when will the Holy One bring this blessing upon Israel? When Jerusalem will be rebuilt and the exiles restored to her midst, as it is said: "Like the dew of Hermon that falls upon the mountains of Zion. There the Lord ordained the blessing, everlasting life" (Pss. 133:3). May this happen speedily in our days! Amen. (TANHUMAH TAVO 4)

☙

Jerusalem is the light of the world, as it is said: "And nations shall walk by your light" (Isa. 60:3). And who is the light of Jerusalem? The Holy One Blessed is He, as it is said: "For the Lord shall be your light everlasting" (Isa. 60:19). (YALKUT SHIMONI ISA. 501)

☙

Said the Holy One to Israel: By your lives, I burnt it and I shall rebuild it, as it is said: "I will build you firmly again, O Maiden Israel!" (Jer. 31:3). (PESIKTA RABATI 31)

☙ Laws Concerning Jerusalem

"The Lord rebuilds Jerusalem" (Pss. 147:2). Whoever does not mention a good and spacious land, the covenant, and Torah [in the Blessing after Meals], and the kingship of David in the blessing "Who rebuilds Jerusalem," has not fulfilled his obligation.... One begins with the words, "For Jerusalem Your city," and concludes with "Who rebuilds Jerusalem" because of this verse: "The Lord rebuilds Jerusalem" (Pss. 147:2). (*YALKUT MECHIRI, PSS. 147*)

☙

Additions may not be made to the city [of Jerusalem] or to the courts of the Temple except by a king, prophet, urim and tummim (Exod. 28:30), a Sanhedrin of seventy-one members, two loaves of thanksgiving, song, and the court walking after them accompanied by the two loaves of thanksgiving, and all Israel following behind them. (*SHEBUOT 14A*)

☙

A man may compel all [his household] to go up [with him] to the Land of Israel, but none may be forced to leave it. They may be compelled to go up to Jerusalem, but none may be forced to leave it.... Our rabbis taught: If [a husband] wishes to go up [to the Land or to Jerusalem] and his wife refuses, she may be pressed to do so, but if she does not she may be divorced without [being paid what is due from] her *ketubah*. If she wishes to go up and he docs not, he may be pressed to do so and if he does not, he must divorce her and pay her *ketubah*. (*KETUBOT 110B*)

☙

One who sees the cities of Judah in their ruined state recites the verse, "Your holy cities have become a desert: Zion has become a desert, Jerusalem a desolation" (Isa. 64:9) and tears his garment. One who sees Jerusalem in its ruined state recites the verse, "Our Holy Temple, our pride, where our fathers praised You, has been consumed by fire: all that was dear to us in ruined" (Isa. 64:10) and tears his garment.

As soon as he reaches Mount Scopus he tears his garment; he tears its separately for the Temple and separately for Jerusalem. (MOED KATAN 26A)

❧

Our rabbis taught: One tears one's garment . . . [when seeing] the Holy Temple or Jerusalem. One tears first for the Temple and then enlarges it for Jerusalem. . . .

[Seeing] Jerusalem in its destruction one says: "Our holy Temple, our pride, where our fathers praised You, has been consumed by fire: and all that was dear to us is ruined" (Isa. 64:10).

As soon as one reaches Scopus, one tears the garment, and he tears it separately for the Holy Temple and separately for Jerusalem. (MOAD KATAN 26A-B)

❧

When a man plasters his house, he should leave a small space unfinished in remembrance of Jerusalem. When a woman adorns herself with jewels, she should leave something off in remembrance of Jerusalem, as it is said: "If I forget you, O Jerusalem, let my right hand forget its cunning" (Pss. 137:5). (MIDRASH PSS. 137:6)

❧

Outside of the Land of Israel those who pray should direct their hearts toward the Land of Israel, as it is said: "and pray in the direction of their land" (2 Chron. 6:38).

In the Land of Israel those who pray should direct their hearts toward Jerusalem, as it is said: "and they pray to You in the direction of the city You have chosen" (2 Chron. 6:34).

In Jerusalem those who pray should direct their hearts toward the Holy Temple, as it is said: "if he comes to pray toward this House" (2 Chron. 6:32).

In the Holy Temple those who pray should direct their hearts toward the Holy of Holies, as it is said: "the supplications which Your servant and Your people offer toward this place" (1 Kings 8:30).

Those in the north face the south, those in the south face the north, those in the east face the west and those in the west face the east so that all Israel prays toward one place. (*TOSEFTA BERACHOT 3:16*)

☙

One prays constantly for Jerusalem. In the Blessing after Meals: "Builder of Jerusalem." In the Amida: "God of David and Builder of Jerusalem." In the blessings of the Shema: "Who spreads His tabernacle of peace over us, over all Israel and over Jerusalem." (*Y. BERACHOT 4:5*)

THE FOURTH GATE

Jerusalem in the Literature
of the Geonic Period

Jaffa Gate to the Old City, late nineteenth century (Photograph by La Maison Bonfils). The Museum of Photography at Tel-Hai Industrial Park; with permission

The period from the end of the sixth century C.E. *until the twelfth century is commonly termed the "geonic period" because of the Geonim, who headed the great academies of Talmudic learning that flourished in Babylonia. The Geonim themselves created a literature that was different from previous Jewish writings. Whereas the writers of the apocalyptic books had disguised themselves as ancient historical figures, and whereas the rabbis has abstained from writing, so that all their traditions were transmitted orally and only later written down, the Geonim did not hesitate to write long letters, responsa, and complete philosophical books. For the first time, the Geonim also issued prayerbooks containing their versions of the liturgy. During this time, however, other forms of literature continued as well— liturgical poetry, mystical writings, and historical accounts of events of the day.*

୬୬ Redemption

Saadia Gaon

> *Saadia ben Joseph (882–942) was the head of the Sura
> academy. The following is taken from his great philosophical
> work,* The Book of Beliefs and Opinions.

Any Israelite, again, who will remain in the desert or who will have
no one of the nations to bring him to Jerusalem, will be brought so
speedily by our Lord as though a cloud had lifted him up and carried
him, as it is stated by Scripture: *Who are these that fly as a cloud, and
as the doves to their cotes?* (Isa. 60:8). Or it would seem as though the
winds had borne him, as it is said by Scripture: *I will say to the north-
wind: Give "up," and to the south-wind: "Keep not back, bring my sons
from far,"* etc. (Isa. 43:6).

When, then, those [of the nations of the world] who are alive
unite with the living among the Jewish believers, as I have described,
the resurrection of the dead will take place. . . . Then, too, will our
Lord, magnified and exalted be He, restore His sanctuary, as has been
described for us: *When the Lord hath built up Zion, When He hath
appeared in His glory* (Pss. 102:17).

The structure [of the city] and the Temple will be of the form
explained by Ezekiel: *In the five and twentieth year of our captivity, etc.*
(Ezek. 40:1). They will be studded with jewels and precious stones,
as Isaiah said: *And I will make thy pinnacles of rubies, and thy gates of
carbuncles* (Isa. 54:12). The entire land will be inhabited, as it is said
in Scripture: *And the parched land shall become a pool, and the thirsty
ground springs of water* (Isa. 35:7).

Then the light of [God's] *Presence* will appear shining upon the
Temple with such brilliance that all lights will become faint or dim

143

in comparison with it. . . . So brilliant will that light be that anyone who does not know the road to the Temple will be able to travel by its brightness, for it will extend from heaven to earth, as it has been said: *And nations shall walk at thy light, and kings at the brightness of thy rising* (Isa. 60:3).

ꙮ Heavenly Jerusalem
Midreshei Geulah

> *Building upon the concept of the "heavenly Jerusalem," this mystic text describes an encounter between Moses and the Messiah where this heavenly building and its implications are discussed.*

Moses asked the Messiah son of David: The Holy One told me that He will build a Temple on earth, the Temple for Israel but I see that He builds a Temple in heaven by His own hand!

The Messiah said to Moses: Moses! Your father Jacob saw the House that will be built on earth and he also saw the House which the Holy One will build by His own hand in heaven, and he understood completely that the House which the Holy One will build in heaven by His own hand out of precious stones and pearls and the splendour of His Presence—that is the House which will endure for Israel for ever and ever until the end of all generations. That is what Jacob said on the night when he slept on a stone and saw Jerusalem built up on the earth and Jerusalem built up in heaven. . . . And when Jacob saw one Jerusalem on earth and one in heaven he said, "This is none other than the House of God!" (Gen. 28:17).—This is not the House that will endure for my children through all the generations but rather the House of God which He builds with His own hands. And if you say: The Holy One will build Himself a Temple in heaven with His own hands, so will He build it on earth with His own hands, as it is said: "The sanctuary, O Lord, which Your hands established" (Exod. 15:17).

When Moses our teacher—peace be upon him!—heard these things from the Messiah son of David he rejoiced greatly, turned again toward the Holy One and said to Him: Master of the universe! When will this Jerusalem which has been built descend to earth? The Holy One said: I have not revealed the time to anyone, neither the first nor the last ones, and shall I tell it to you? He said to Him: Master of the universe! Give me some hint! The Holy One said to him: I shall scatter Israel throughout the gates of the earth and disperse them to the four corners of the world among all the nations and the verse shall be fulfilled which says: "Even if your outcasts are at the ends of the world, from there the Lord your God will gather you, from there He will fetch you" (Deut. 30:4). And yet again I will gather those who have gone into exile with Yohanan ben Kareach to Pathros and those who will be in the land of Shinar and in Hamath and Elam and Kush—as it is said: "In that day, My Lord will apply His hand again to redeeming the other part of His people from Assyria—as also from Egypt, Pathros, Nubia, Elam, Shinar, Hamath, and the coastlands" (Isa. 11:11). Moses then descended from heaven contented.

꩜ The Jews Return to Jerusalem

This letter of unknown date from the Adat HaRabbanim in Jerusalem, which was found in the Cairo Geniza, describes the return of Jews to Jerusalem under the calif 'Umar I (Omar) in the seventh century and their participation in the cleaning of the Temple Mount upon which the El Aksa Mosque and Dome of the Rock were to be built.

This was the doing of our God, who granted us favor before the kingdom of Ishmael, which has now gained control of the Holy Land from Edom. When they came to Jerusalem they brought with them Israelites who could show them the site of the Temple and who then dwelt with them until this day. And they made an agreement with them that they would honor the Temple and not desecrate it and would pray at its gates, and they would not prevent this.

All the Muslims in the city and surrounding came, together with a group of Jews. Then they were ordered to sweep the site of the Temple and to clean it. Omar was in charge of their work. Whenever they uncovered another layer, he would ask the Elders of the Jews if this was the stone known as the Foundation Stone. One of the Sages explained the various sections of the place until it was uncovered. Then he ordered that the wall of the sanctuary be built and a dome be erected over the stone and overlaid with gold. Afterward the Jews sent messages to all the parts of the Land of Israel to inform them of the way in which Omar had assisted them. And they inquired of them, "How many people will be coming to Jerusalem?" They gathered before Omar and said to him, "How many of the Community of Jews will the Emir of the Believers command to come to this city?" Omar replied, "What will your enemies say? Speak to them and then

I will bring an end to the controversy between you." He then summoned the Patriarch and his friends and said to them, "Behold, these Jews have taken over all. . . . How many of them do you say shall come?" The Patriarch said, "Let the number be fifty households, including women and children." The Jews replied, "Let us be less than two hundred households." The controversy raged between them until Omar decreed that seventy households should come. They agreed to that. After that he asked, "Where do you wish to live within the city?" They replied, "In the southern sector of the city, which is the market of the Jews." Their request was to enable them to be near the site of the Temple and its gates, as well as to the water of Shiloah, which could be used for immersion. This was granted them by the Emir of the Believers. So seventy households including women and children moved from Tiberias and established settlements in buildings whose foundations had stood many generations.

ꙮ No Jerusalem

(A liturgical poem used in Seder Avodah of Yom Kippur)

No fire and no guilt offering,
  No garments and no oil,
No lots and no coals of fire
  No court and no fine incense,
No Temple and no sprinkling,
  No confession and no fat offering,
No immersion and no purification,
  No Jerusalem and no forest of Lebanon,
No basin and no foundation,
  No Levonah and no shewbread,
No altar and no meal offering,
  No pleasant fragrance and no libation,
No flour offering and no spices,
  No wood and no burnt offering,
No curtain and no sin offering,
  No Zion and no frontlet of gold,
No incense offering and no sacrifice,
  No blending of spice and no fragrant odor,
No gifts and no peace-offerings,
  No thank-offerings and no daily offering—
For through our sins and the sins of our ancestors, all of this has been taken from us.

ॐ Burial Kaddish Prayer for Jerusalem

Exalted and sanctified be His great Name in the world which He is to create anew in the future, when He will revive the dead and bring them to life everlasting. He will rebuild the city of Jerusalem and restore the Temple in its midst, uproot idolatry from the Land and restore the worship of Heaven to its site.

THE FIFTH GATE

Jerusalem in Writings of
the Middle Ages

*Temple of Solomon, Liber Chronicorum, Nurenberg, 1493 (Collection of
the National and University Library, Jerusalem; with permission)*

☙ Travelers' Accounts of Jerusalem

During the Middle Ages Jews were dispersed throughout the world, and many of them undertook the difficult and sometimes dangerous trip to see the remnants of Jerusalem. They left behind them letters and diaries that describe the condition of Jerusalem during those years.

JACOB HACOHEN

Rabbi Jacob ben Rabbi Nathaniel HaCohen visited Jerusalem sometime before its conquest by Saladin in 1187.

In Jerusalem are the Tower of David and the Temple and the Sanctuary, and the Western Wall (but its upper stones are new), and King Solomon's quarries, and the Gates of Mercy, and the well in which the priests washed, and the Monument of Absalom, and below Mount Olivet, opposite the tower, is a tower upon a tower and it is (?) cubits high, and no road passes it, and the waters of Siloam are over against Mount Zion and Jerusalem. Between Zion and Jerusalem there is nothing but one wall. These things are known and none knows more. I also saw the Valley of Jehoshaphat into which they throw stones, and every day at least one hundred die and their bodies are brought from Benjamin's Gate down between the monument and the waters of Siloam, a great descent, until they come to Mount Olivet. Three big cisterns are there, and I asked how it is that these cisterns are not full, and they answered that the waters run away and it is not known where the water goes. Then said I, Jacob, to the Rabbis, "This is what our lord the prophet Isaiah said, 'His fire is in Zion and his furnace in Jerusalem' " (Isa. 30:9).

Ayyubid tower (or gate) beneath the inner side of the southern wall of the Old City, uncovered in the Jewish Quarter (Ancient Jerusalem Revealed. Israel Exploration Society; with permission)

RABBI BENJAMIN OF TUDELA

The most famous of Jewish travelers, Benjamin traveled for many years, beginning around 1160 and returning to Spain in 1172/73. His journeys took him throughout the Mediterranean world and included an extensive trip through the Land of Israel, which was then under the control of the Crusaders. He recounted his adventures in his Book of Travels, first published in 1543.

From thence it is three parsangs to Jerusalem, a small city strongly fortified with three walls. It is full of people whom the Mohammedans call Jacobites, Armenians, Greeks, Georgians, Franks, and indeed people of all tongues. The dyeing house is rented by the year, and exclusive privilege of dyeing is purchased from the king by the Jews of Jerusalem, two hundred of whom dwell in one corner of the city, under the Tower of David. The lower portion of the wall of the Tower of David, to the extent of about ten cubits, is part of the ancient foundation constructed by our ancestors; the remaining part was added by the Mohammedans. The city contains no building stronger than the tower of David. There are at Jerusalem two buildings, from one of which—the hospital—there issue forth four hundred knights, and therein all the sick who come hither are lodged and cared for in life and in death. The other building is called the Temple of Solomon, being the palace originally built by King Solomon. Three hundred knights are quartered there, and issue therefrom every day for military exercise, besides those knights who come from the land of the Franks and other parts of Christendom, having taken a vow upon themselves to serve there a year or two until their vow is fulfilled. In Jerusalem is a large church called the Sepulchre, and here is the sepulchre of that man, unto which the Christians make pilgrimages.

Jerusalem has four gates, called the gates of Abraham, David, Zion, and Gushpat, which is called the gate of Jehoshaphat, facing our ancient Temple, now called Templum Domini. Upon the site of the sanctuary Omar ben al-Khatab erected an edifice with a large and magnificent cupola, into which the Gentiles do not bring any image or effigy, but they merely come there to pray. In front of this place is the Western Wall, which is one of the walls of the Holy of Holies. This is called the Gate of Mercy, and thither come all the Jews to pray before the wall of the court of the Temple. At Jerusalem you also see the stables erected by Solomon, which formed part of his palace, forming a very substantial structure, composed of large stones, and the like of it is not to be seen anywhere in the world. There is also visible to this day the pool used by the priests before offering their sacrifices, and the Jews coming thither write their names upon the wall. The gate of Jehoshaphat leads to the valley of Jehoshaphat, which is the gathering place of nations. Here is the pillar called Absalom's hand and the sepulchre of King Uzziah.

In the neighborhood is also a great spring called the waters of Siloam, connected with the brook of Kidron. Over this spring is a large structure dating from the times of our ancestors. Very little water is found at Jerusalem; the people for the most part drink rain water, which they collect in cisterns in their houses. . . .

In front of Jerusalem is Mount Zion, on which there is no building except a place of worship belonging to the Christians. Facing Jerusalem for a distance of three miles are the cemeteries belonging to the Israelites, who in the days of old buried their dead in caves, and upon each sepulchre is a dated inscription, but the Christians destroy the sepulchres, employing the stones thereof in building their houses. These sepulchres reach as far as Zelzah in the territory of Benjamin. Around Jerusalem are high mountains.

On Mount Zion are the sepulchres of the House of David, and the sepulchres of the kings that ruled after him. The exact place cannot be identified, inasmuch as fifteen years ago a wall of the church of Mount Zion fell in. The Patriarch commanded the overseer to take the stones of the old walls and restore therewith the church. He did so, and hired workmen at fixed wages; and there were twenty men who brought the stones from the base of the wall of Zion. Among these men there were two who were sworn friends. On a certain day the one entertained the other; after their meal they returned to their work, when the overseer said to them, "Why have you tarried today?" They answered, "Why need you complain? When our fellow workmen go to their meal we will do our work." When the dinnertime arrived, and the other workmen had gone to their meal, they examined the stones, and raised a certain stone which formed the entrance to a cave. Thereupon one said to the other, "Let us go in and see if any money is to be found there." They entered the cave, and reached a large chamber resting upon pillars of marble overlaid with silver and gold. In front was a table of gold and a sceptre and crown. This was the sepulchre of King David. On the left thereof in like fashion was the sepulchre of King Solomon; then followed the sepulchres of all the kings of Judah that were buried there. Closed coffers were also there, the contents of which no man knows. The two men essayed to enter the chamber, when a fierce wind came forth from the entrance of the cave and smote them, and they fell to the ground like dead men, and there they lay until evening. And there came forth a wind like a man's voice, crying out: "Arise and go forth from this place!" So the men rushed forth in terror, and they came unto the Patriarch, and related these things to him. Thereupon the Patriarch sent for Rabbi Abraham el Constantini, the pious recluse, who was one of the mourners of Jerusalem, and to him he related all these things according to the report of the two men who had come forth. Then Rabbi Abraham replied, "These are the sepulchres of the House of David; they belong to the kings of Judah, and on the morrow let me enter, I and you and these men, and find out what is there." And on the morrow they sent for the two men, and found each of them lying on his bed in terror, and the men said: "We will not enter there, for the Lord doth not desire to show it to any man." Then the Patriarch gave orders that the place should be closed up and hidden from the sight of man unto this day.

RABBI MOSHE BEN NAHMAN

> *Also known as the Ramban and Nahmanides, Moshe ben Nahman (1194–1270) was one of the greatest scholars of Spain. Born in Gerona, he functioned in Catalonia until going*

*to the Land of Israel in 1267. In Jerusalem, he organized the
community and founded a synagogue and a yeshiva. From
1268 until his death he served as the rabbi of Acre. When he
arrived in Jerusalem in Elul 1267, he wrote a letter to his son
describing the situation there.*

I write you this missive in Jerusalem, the Holy City. All praise and
thanksgiving to the Rock of my salvation, for I have been privileged
to arrive in peace on the ninth day of the month of Elul. There I
stayed in peace until the day after Yom Kippur, when I set out to go
to Hebron, the city in which our Fathers are entombed, so that I
could bow down before them and arrange for my own resting place in
that holy city. What shall I tell you about the Land? How terrible is
its abandonment and its desolation. The sum of it is that the holier
the place, the worse the destruction. Jerusalem is more desolate than
the rest of the Land, Judah more than the Galilee. Yet for all its
destruction, it is wonderful. It has nearly two thousand inhabitants,
about three hundred Christians who escaped from the Sultan. There
are no Israelites among them, for when the Tatar hordes invaded, they
fled from there and many were slain by the sword. There are only two
dyers who purchase dyes from the government, unto whom a minyan
gathers for prayers in their house on the Sabbath. I encouraged them
and we found an abandoned building with marble pillars and a lovely
arch which we converted into a synagogue, for the city is wide open,
and anyone who wishes to take possession of an abandoned building
can do so. People have contributed to the refurbishing of the building, and we have already sent to the city of Shechem for Torah scrolls
that had been sent there for safekeeping from Jerusalem when the
Tatar hordes invaded. And now we have a synagogue in which we can
pray. For there are many who come to Jerusalem, men and women
from Damascus, Tzova [Aleppo] and other places in order to see the
Temple and to weep over it. Who ever is privileged to see it in its

destruction will be privileged to see it rebuilt and repaired when the Divine Presence returns unto it. You, my son, your brothers and all your father's household will be privileged to behold the welfare of Jerusalem and the comfort of Zion.

COMMENTARY TO THE TORAH

A mournful sight I have perceived in thee, Jerusalem. Only one Jew is here, a dyer, persecuted, oppressed, and despised. At his house gather great and small when they can get a minyan. They are wretched folk, without occupation and trade, consisting of a few pilgrims and beggars, though the fruit of the land is still magnificent and the harvests rich. Indeed it is still a blessed country, flowing with milk and honey. . . .

Oh! I am a man who has seen affliction. I am banished from my table, removed far away from friend and kinsman, and too long is the distance for me to meet them again. . . . I left my family. I forsook my house. And there with my sons and daughters, and with the sweet and dear children whom I have brought up on my knees, I left also my soul. My heart and my eyes will dwell with them forever. . . . But the loss of all this and of every other glory my eyes saw is compensated by having now the joy of being a day in thy courts, O Jerusalem, visiting the ruins of the Temple, and crying over the desolate sanctuary; where I am permitted to caress thy stones, to fondle thy dust, and to weep over thy ruins. I wept bitterly, but I found joy in my tears. I tore my garments, but I felt relieved by it.

ISAAC CHELO

> *Isaac ben Joseph ibn Chelo (or Hilo) lived in the fourteenth century and provides the following account of his visit in Jerusalem in 1334.*

Alas, by reason of our sins, where the sacred building (the Temple) once stood, its place is taken today by a profane temple, built by the King of the Ishmaelites when he conquered Palestine and Jerusalem from the uncircumcised. The history of that event was in this wise:

The king, who had made a vow to build up again the ruins of the sacred edifice, if God put the holy city into his power, demanded of the Jews that they should make known those ruins to him. For the uncircumcised, in their hate against the people of God, had heaped rubbish and filth over the spot, so that no one knew exactly where the ruins stood. Now there was an old man then living who said: "If the King will take an oath to preserve the western wall, I will discover to him the place where the ruins of the holy temple are." So the king straightway placed his hand on the thigh of the old man and swore by oath to do what he demanded. When the old man had shown him the ruins of the temple under a mound of defilements, the King had the ruins cleared and cleansed, taking part in the cleansing himself, until they were all fair and clean. After that he had them all set up again, with the exception of the western wall, and made of them a very beautiful temple, which he consecrated to his God.

It is this western wall which stands before the temple of Omar ibn al Khattab, and which is called the Gate of Mercy. The Jews resort thither to say their prayers, as Rabbi Benjamin has already related. Today, this wall is one of the seven wonders of the Holy City, of which the names are: the Tower of David, Solomon's Palace, the tomb of Huldah the prophetess, the Sepulchres of the Kings, the Palace of Queen Helena, the Gate of Mercy, and the Western Wall.

The first of these is the Tower of David mentioned above, near the gate of that name. It is of very ancient and very solid construction, and in the oldern times, the Jews used to dwell about it. Today there are no habitations in the vicinity but, instead, so many fortifications, as to make this ancient stronghold quite impregnable in our time.

The second is an ancient building called Solomon's Palace. In former days, when the uncircumcised were in possession, this building was appointed to receive the sick of the holy city; today a market of considerable importance is held there.

The third is the tomb of the prophetess Huldah. . . . as was narrated by the great author in the following words: "They allowed no sepulchre in Jerusalem except the tombs of the House of David and that of Huldah, which have been there from the days of the earliest prophets." [Avot de Rabbi Natan 35A]

The tomb of Huldah the prophetess, on the summit of the Mount of Olives, is very beautifully built. But the sepulchres of the House of David which were on Mount Zion are no longer known today either to Jews or Mussulmans; for they are not the Tombs of the Kings about which we are now going to speak.

These latter sepulchres are the fourth of the wonders of the Holy City. They are, as we have already said, near the cave of Ben Sirah. They are of ancient and massive construction, in form a masterpiece of sculpture. All the strangers who come to visit the Holy City say they have never seen anything so beautiful.

The fifth of the curiosities to be seen is the Palace of Queen Helena, who came to Jerusalem with King Monbaz and was adopted into the Jewish religion there. This palace is a fine building inhabited today by the Cadi and his councillors.

The sixth is the Gate of Mercy, near the Temple. Formerly there were two gates, the one for wedding parties, the other for mourners, as we are told in the Chapters of Rabbi Eliezer the Great, the German Kabbalist, blessed by his memory! These two gates have been buried in the earth for the fulfilment of the Scriptures.

Finally, the last remarkable thing in the Holy City is the Western Wall, of which we spoke above.

The Jewish community in Jerusalem, God be gracious to her! is

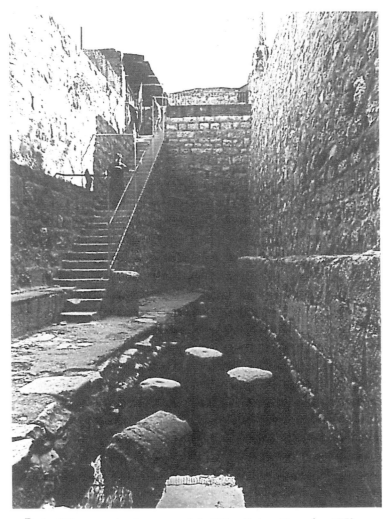

Pool of Silwan storing the waters of the Gihon Spring, December 1978 (Israel Government Press Office; with permission)

quite numerous. It is composed of fathers of families from all parts of the world, principally from France. The leading men of the community, as well as the principal rabbis, come from the latter kingdom—among others Rabbi Chaim and Rabbi Joseph. They live there in happiness and tranquility, each according to his condition and fortune, for the royal authority is just and great. May God re-establish her and raise her to the highest prosperity!

Among the different members of the holy congregation at Jerusalem are many who are engaged in handicrafts such as dyers, tailors, shoemakers, etc. Others carry on a rich commerce in all sorts of things, and have fine shops. Some are devoted to science, as medicine, astronomy, and mathematics. But the greater number of their learned men are working day and night at the study of the Holy Law and of the true wisdom, which is the Kabbalah. These are maintained out of the coffers of the community, because the study of the law is their only calling. There are also at Jerusalem excellent calligraphists and the copies are sought for by strangers who carry then away to their own countries.

I have seen a Pentateuch written with so much art that several peoples at once wanted to acquire it, and it was only for an excessively high price that the Chief of the Synagogues of Babylon carried it off with him to Bagdad.

Obadiah Da Bertinoro

This famous Italian rabbi was born ca. 1450 and died sometime before 1516. In 1485 he left Italy and traveled; in 1488 he reached the Land of Israel, where he served as rabbi. He was buried on the Mount of Olives. His letters from Jerusalem describe the situation when he arrived.

About three-quarters of a mile from Jerusalem, at a place where the mountain is ascended by steps, we beheld the famous city of our delight, and here we rent our garments, as was our duty. A little further on, the sanctuary, the desolate house of our splendour, became visible, and at the sight of it we again made rents in our garments. We came as far as the gates of Jerusalem, and on the 13th of Nissan, 5248, at noon, our feet stood within the gates of the city. . . . Jerusalem is for the most part desolate and in ruins. I need not repeat that it is not surrounded by walls. Its inhabitants, I am told, number about four thousand families. As for Jews, about seventy families of the poorest class have remained; there is scarcely a family that is not in want of the commonest necessaries; one who has bread for a year is called rich. Among the Jewish population there are many aged, forsaken widows from Germany, Spain, Portugal, and other countries, so that there are seven women to one man. . . .

The Jews are not persecuted by the Arabs in these parts. I have travelled through the country in its length and breadth, and none of them has put an obstacle in my way. They are very kind to strangers. . . .

The Synagogue here is built on columns; it is long, narrow, and dark, the light entering only by the door. There is a fountain in the middle of it. In the court of the Synagogue, quite close to it, stands a mosque. The court of the Synagogue is very large and contains many houses, all of them buildings devoted by the Ashkenazim to charitable purposes and inhabited by Ashkenazi widows. There were formerly many courts in the Jewish streets belonging to these buildings, but the Elders sold them, so that not a single one remained. They could not, however, sell the buildings of the Ashkenazim, and no other poor had a right to them. The Jews' street and the houses are very large; some of them dwell also on Zion. At one time they had more houses, but these are now heaps of rubbish and cannot be rebuilt, for the law of the land is that a Jew may not rebuild his ruined house without permission, and the permission often costs more than the whole house is worth. The houses of Jerusalem are of stone, none of wood or plaster. . . .

Jerusalem, notwithstanding its destruction, still contains four very beautiful, long bazaars, such as I have never before seen, at the foot of Zion. They have all dome-shaped roofs, and contain wares of every kind. They are divided into different departments, the merchant bazaar, the spice bazaar, the vegetable market, and one in which cooked food and bread are sold. When I came to Jerusalem there was a dreadful famine in the land. . . . Many Jews died of hunger; they had been seen a day or two before asking for bread, which nobody could give them, and the next day they were found dead in their houses. Many live on grass, going out like stags to look for pasture. At present there is only one German Rabbi here, who was educated in Jerusalem. I have never seen his equal for humility and the fear of God; he weaves night and day when he is not occupied with his studies, and for six months he tasted no bread between Sabbath and Sabbath, his food consisting of raw turnips and the remains of St. John's bread, which is very plentiful here, after the sugar has been taken out of it. . . .

Now, the wheat-harvest being over, the famine is at an end, and there is once more plenty, praise be to God. Here, in Jerusalem, I have seen several kinds of fruit which are not to be found in our country. There is one tree with long leaves, which grows higher than a man's stature, and bears fruit only once; it then withers, and from its roots there rises another similar one which again bears fruit the next year, and the same thing is continually repeated. The grapes are larger than in our country. . . . All the necessaries of life, such as meat, wine, olives, and sesame-oil, can be very cheap. The soil is excellent; but it is not possible to gain a living by any branch of industry, unless it be that of a shoe-maker, weaver, or goldsmith. . . .

Persons of various nationalities are always to be found in Jerusalem from Christian countries, and from Babylonia and Abyssinia. The Arabs come frequently to offer up prayers at the temple, for they hold it in great veneration. . . . No Jew may enter the enclosure of the temple. Although sometimes the Arabs are anxious to admit carpenters and goldsmiths to perform work there, nobody will go in, for we have all been defiled [by touching bodies of the dead]. I do not know whether the Arabs enter the Holy of Holies or not. I also made enquiries relative to the Eben Shethiah where the Ark of the Covenant was placed, and am told that it is under a high and beautiful dome built by the Arabs in the court of the Temple. It is enclosed in this building, and no one may enter. There is great wealth in the enclosure of the temple. We hear that the monarchs build chambers there inlaid with gold, and the king now reigning is said to have erected a building, more splendid than any ever before built, adorned with gold and precious stones.

The temple enclosure has still twelve gates. Those which are called the gates of mercy are of iron, and are two in number; they look towards the east of the temple and are always closed. They only reach half-way above the ground; the other half is sunk in the earth. It is said that the Arabs often tried to raise them up but were not able to do so.

The western wall, part of which is still standing, is composed of large, thick stones, such as I have never before seen in an old building, either in Rome or in any other country. At the north-east corner is a tower of very large stones. I entered it and found a vast edifice supported by massive and lofty pillars; there are so many pillars that it wearied me to go to the end of the building. Everything is filled with earth which has been thrown there from the ruins of the temple. The temple-building stands on these columns, and in each of them is a hole through which a cord may be drawn. It is said that the bulls and rams for sacrifice were bound here. Throughout the whole region of Jerusalem, in fields as well as vineyards, there are large caves connected with one another.

The Mount of Olives is lofty and barren; scarcely an olive tree is to be found on it. From the top, Sodom and Gomorrah may be seen in the distance; they now form a salt sea. . . . On the Mount of Olives are the graves of the Prophet Haggai and Huldah the Prophetess and more than ten caves, one leading out of the other. The sepulchre of the seventy Elders, which lies about two thousand cubits from Jerusalem, is splendid, especially that of Simon the Just. . . .

At the foot of the slope of the temple mountain are Jewish graves; the new ones are at the foot of the Mount of Olives, and the valley runs between the grave-yards. Not far from here are the monuments of Absalom and of the Prophet Zachariah; at the latter place, prayers are offered up on fast days; and on the 9th of Ab lamentations are repeated.

I have taken a house here close to the Synagogue. The upper chamber of my dwelling is even in the wall of the Synagogue. In the court where my house is there are five inhabitants, all of them women. There is only one blind man living here, and his wife attends on me. . . . Most of those who come to Jerusalem from foreign countries fall ill, owing to climatic changes and the sudden variations of the wind, now cold, now warm. All possible winds blow in Jerusalem. It is said that every wind before going where it listeth, comes to Jerusalem to prostrate itself before the Lord, Blessed be He that knoweth truth. . . .

🌙

Finished in haste in Jerusalem, the Holy City. May it soon be rebuilt in our days. On the 8th Elul, 5248.

MOSES BEN ISRAEL NAPHTALI PORGES PRAEGER

> *Moses Praeger of Prague wrote* Ways of Zion, *from which this excerpt is taken, in 1650 as a guide to those who would travel to the Land of Israel. He describes the routes to the land and the life of Jerusalem at the time.*

Listen, all you men and you women as well,
to what Moses Praeger the scribe has to tell.
This book did I with God's aid indite
through many a day and night.
May His Name be our guide,
and let whoever would do the right
read this book with careful eye,
whether by day or by night.
That no harm may him befall
and he secure himself against all
when he forsakes his land for good and all.
For I did see what me befell
because I did not consider well
the things that I ought to have left behind,
and so lost money and peace of mind.
To Jerusalem many a thing I brought
that there I might full well have bought.
While what in Prague I rushed to sell,
I might have used there full well.
This I saw and a great deal more,
which for all men was in store

who wished to go to Jerusalem.
It never occurred to them
how they would live once they were there.
So it came about they were not aware
that in Jerusalem they would cry and swear.
Why do we wish to take this turn?
We would so gladly home return.
Therefore I thought in mine heart
that none ought to come to loss and smart.
Let each one bethink him in his heart,
from food and from drink he can never part.
As for money and worldly worth,
Jerusalem has great dearth
though she stands at the very center of the earth.
Nor let anybody think
that commerce can him profit bring,
since Ladino, Arabic and Turkish
he has to know before everything.
Best the Jerusalem community to lend,
for now they pay at twelve per cent.
After let each man follow his bent.
But he who can make large buttons of silk
may laugh full well with all of his ilk.
He makes a good living on what he can sell
and God grant other folk do as well. . . .

The only bedding to take along is that which is to be used on the way. Feathers can be obtained cheaply at Jerusalem from the German community. You can never bring along a sufficient quantity of sheets, shirts, veils, tablecloths, handkerchiefs, and all other kinds of linen, for in Jerusalem these things are expensive and not very good. Each person should also take along a pair of good shoes as well as woolen winter stockings, for such clothing is not very good in Jerusalem. Apart from this, winter is cold in Jerusalem, even though it does not freeze. Men's clothing should not be brought along in quantity, for they are not expensive here. In Ofen let each man buy something to wrap around his head after the fashion of the Turks, and if the cloth is quite white you should sew a few colored threads into it, but none of green. It is very dangerous to wear anything of green. Sometimes the borders of the prayer shawl are also green, and this must be changed in advance. Green, the color of the Prophet, is forbidden to Jews in the whole of Turkey and Jerusalem.

In Jerusalem many copper vessels are used and they are very expensive here. Let every man bring along his copper kneading basin, for bread is baked at home and the laundry is also washed there. One should bring copper pots, large and small, which have a tin lining inside. Also an iron tripod on which the pots are placed for cooking, likewise a pan for seething fish and a copper kettle for drawing water out of the cistern in each house. Also a basin which is taken along to the baths. The baths, thank God, are very good and heathful. Do not take much silver and gold along, even if you are rich, for that only attracts attention. But it is good to bring iron padlocks in order to lock up your rooms and boxes.

Books are not expensive in Jerusalem, so you should not burden yourself with them on account of the expense of transportation. Let each person take with him only a thick prayer book, a Pentateuch with commentaries, a Penitential Prayer Book, the Mishnah, Rabbi

Mordecai Jaffe's Levush, a Shomrim la-Boker, a Festival Prayer Book according to the Prague usage, a Midrash, En Yaakov, the Shulhan Arukh, and the Yalkut. The women-folk take with them a Teutsch Humash, Festival Prayer Book, and Tehinnah; also other Teutsch books.

The prayer books should be small, for there is no lectern in the synagogues and the books must be held in the hand. A good house-wife will also take Spanish sewing needles with her, also pins large and small, such as are needed and used at home.

All kinds of spices are to be found and very cheap; but muscat blossoms are rarely seen. Most foodstuffs are sold in Jerusalem by weight, and naturally other things as well. There is no beef, but now and again there is buffalo meat, which does not taste so good. Geese, ducks, chickens, and doves are found in plenty and cheap. There are two kinds of oil; one called Siridj is very cheap, better than goosefat or butter, and is made of seed. The other oil is sweet oil, cheaper than Siridj but not so good and also not good for burning. Young radishes, all kinds of onions, and parsley root, are all very cheap and can be had all the year round. Large citrons for preserving, oranges, and lemons, appear in the market all the winter. Sometimes oranges go eight for a kreutzer, and sometimes even more cheaply. They are used to make lemonade, and folk keep the juice fresh in glasses by adding a little olive oil on top. Mushrooms or German chanterelles are very cheap. In winter there is fresh fish, both large and small, but different kinds from those to be found abroad. The fish are caught in the sea and brought here in a day and a half. That is why there is no fresh fish in summer; for it can go bad on the way.

For a large living room an annual rent of eight lion thalers is paid; for a smaller, five or six. Folk who dwell in the Synagogue Court, where the Loeb synagogue and the two Houses of Study are, live cramped and often lack water. But on the other hand they can go to the synagogue very early in the morning every day. For the synagogue is locked in the evening as soon as the Evening Prayer is over, and not opened again until the break of day. To go through the streets at night is dangerous. Anyone who does not dwell in the Synagogue Court has ample room and also more water at home. The water is good and healthful. He who so desires can drink it with liquorice at twenty kreutzer the rotl. There are some who drink it with lemonade. The water is only rain water and not well water. Every house has a large, very well whitewashed cistern under the ground, and up above there is a little hole, where the water runs in and is drawn up. In years when there is little water it must be bought from Turks, who bring it into the house in leather sacks.

Let each provide him well, I say,
ere from his home he goes away,
and then no grief he'll need to know,
as at first I strove to show.
And young folk, do not venture here,
you'll only growl and roar, I fear.
The bridegroom his dowry will have to give,
else in Jerusalem he never can live.
Whether he be rich or poor,
he must seek his own kind,
and whether he knows nothing or a great deal,
he'll find only many thistles and thorns.
Therefore let young folks stay in their own land
and the old folk come with money in hand.
A young man will find no sustenance here

though he dwell in Jerusalem a full hundred year.
And since he will have to leave the City,
to come here at all would be a great pity.
So let them not lose their youthful years,
and come to suffer pain and tears.
If a man is rich then let him be sure
to bring here enough for a three years' store.
For sometimes a long time is spent
till things from his own land are sent.

And know this every man always,
though the Land of Israel is waste these days
and in ruins by reason of our sins,
yet in every mood it is always good,
as our great Master the learned Ramban
showed in the letter to his son.

ᦉᐟ Jerusalem in Mystical Literature

*During the Middle Ages, Jewish mystical speculation, which had
its origins in early rabbinic times, flourished. The most famous
mystical work of the period was the Zohar (The Book of
Splendor), which purports to be the work of the Tanna Rabbi
Simeon bar Yohai. Scholarly investigation has proved conclusively,
however, that it is the composition of the Spanish kabbalist Moses
ben Shem Tov de Leon, who died in 1305.*

ZION AND JERUSALEM

Rabbi Judah began by quoting, "The Lord thundered in the heavens,
and the Most High gave forth His voice; hailstones and coals of fire"
(Pss. 18:14). Come and see. When the Holy One, blessed by He, created the world, He prepared for it seven pillars upon which it was to stand,
and these pillars all rest upon one single pillar, and they have already
explained it, for it is written, "Wisdom has built her house; she has hewn
out her seven pillars" (Prov. 9:1), and they all stand at one level, called
"the righteous, foundation [*yesod*] of the world" (Prov. 10:25). When the
world was created, it was created from the single point of the world, and
the center of all. And what is it? Zion, as it is written, "A Psalm of
Asaph. God, God, the Lord has spoken, and called the earth, from the
rising of the sun to its setting" (Pss. 50:1). From which place? From Zion,
as it is written, "Out of Zion, the perfection of beauty, has God shined
forth" (Pss. 50:2), from the place that is the limit of the perfection of
complete faith, as it should be. Zion is the strength and the point of the
whole world, and from that place the whole world was made and completed, and from it the whole world is nourished.

Come and see. "The Lord thundered in the heavens, and the

Most High gave forth His voice. . . ." Since it says, "The Lord thundered in the heavens," what need has it to say "and the Most High gave forth His voice"? But here we have a mystery of faith. When I say that Zion is the perfection and beauty of the world, and the world is nourished by it, there are really two levels, namely, Zion and Jerusalem. One is Judgment and one is Mercy, and both are one, Judgment on one side, Mercy on the other. (ZOHAR I, 186A)

THE FOUNDATION STONE

[Rabbi Judah] began by quoting: "Beautiful in elevation, the joy of the whole earth, Mount Zion, the uttermost parts of the north, the city of a great king" (Pss. 48:3). Come and see. When the Holy One, blessed be He, created the world, He threw down a precious stone from beneath the throne of His glory, and it sank into the deeps, and another in the realms above. And there was another edge, a supernal one, a single point, which is in the middle of the world, and the world expanded from there, to the right and to the left, and upon all sides, and it is sustained by this central point. This stone is called *shetiyah* [foundation], because from it the world was founded [*ashtil*] on all sides. Moreover *shetiyah* [may be read] *shat yah* ["the Lord placed"]. The Holy One, blessed be He, placed it so that it might be the foundation of the world, and the foundation of all.

The earth expanded in three circles around this point. In the first expansion around this point there existed all the clarity and purity of the world, and it was situated above, over the whole earth, around this point. The second expansion around the first expansion did not have the clarity and purity of the first, but it was fine and clear, with the greatest clarity that dust can have. The third expansion was darkness and the coarsest type of dust. And around this were the waters of the oceanic sea, which encompass the whole world.

Consequently, this point stands in the center, and all the circles of the world's expansion go around it.

The first expansion is the Temple, with all the palaces and courts, the whole array, and Jerusalem, the entire city within the wall. The second expansion is the land of Israel, which is hallowed in sanctity. The third expansion are the other lands, the abode of the other peoples. And the oceanic sea encompasses all. And they have already taught that this mystery is [contained in] the colors in the eye that surround the central point of the eye, which mirrors the whole eye, like the central point, which we have mentioned, that mirrors all. There the Holy of Holies stands, the ark and the ark-covering, which mirror all. Therefore this point mirrors the whole world. And so it is written, "Beautiful in elevation, the joy of the whole earth, Mount Zion. . . ." "Beautiful"—beautiful is this mirror and a joy to all. "Elevation"—the elevation of the tree that is the beauty of all. (ZOHAR II, 222A–222B)

THE TEMPLE ABOVE

Rabbi Jose thereupon began to speak on the words: "The song of songs which is Solomon's" (Songs 1:1). Said he: "This song King Solomon poured forth when the Temple was erected and all worlds, above and below, had reached their perfect consummation. And although concerning the exact time of its singing there is some difference of opinion among the members of the Fellowship, we may be certain that it was not sung until that time of absolute completion, when the Moon—the *Shekhinah*—came to her fulness and was revealed in the full perfection of her radiance, and when the Temple had been erected in the likeness of the Temple that is above. The Holy One, blessed be He, then experienced such joy as He had not known since the creation of the world. . . ." (ZOHAR, TERUMAH)

The Foundation Stone within the Dome of the Rock, 1898 (Central Zionist Archives; with permission)

FOR HER SAKE

Now, when the Holy One created the world, He divided it into two parts: one part that should be habitable and the other a desert, the former on one side and the latter at the other. Then He redivided the habitable part in such a manner that it formed a circle, the centre of which is the Holy Land. The centre of the Holy Land is Jerusalem, and, again, the centre of Jerusalem is the Holy of Holies. . . . The domain of the mystery of the Faith is that very central point of the Holy Land which is in the Holy of Holies, the place where the *Shekhinah* dwelt, and even though She dwells there no longer, and the Holy of Holies exists no more, yet for Her sake the whole world is still supplied with food, and nourishment and satisfaction ever stream forth, emanating from thence to all the inhabited regions of the world. (*ZOHAR, TERUMAH*)

☙ Customs Relating to Jerusalem

RABBI JOSEPH KARO

> *In his authoritative code of Jewish Law, the* Shulhan Aruch,
> *Rabbi Joseph Karo (1488–1575), who moved to Sefad from
> Turkey in 1563, recorded the following laws regarding
> remembering Jerusalem.*

A bridegroom puts ashes on his head where *tefillin* are worn in order
to remember Jerusalem. There are places where the custom is to
break a glass at the time of the wedding ceremony or to place a black
cloth or other sign of mourning on the head of the groom. (*SHULHAN
ARUCH, ORAH HAIM 560*)

MAIMONIDES

> *Moshe ben Maimon—Maimonides—was the greatest
> philosopher and legalist of the Middle Ages. Born in Cordova
> in 1135, he died either in Egypt or in the Land of Israel in
> 1204. In his legal code* Mishneh Torah *he recounts customs
> concerning mourning for the Temple.*

When the Temple was destroyed, the sages decreed that one should
not build buildings that are plastered and cemented as kingly buildings are. Rather one plasters and whitewashes but leaves a space one
ama square opposite the entrance unwhitewashed. However, if one
acquired a place alreaded plastered and cemented, one is not
required to remove the finish from the walls. They also decreed that

178

if one makes a banquet, one should leave something out and leave a place vacant with no setting. When a woman makes silver or gold jewelry such as are currently in use, she should leave something out so that it will not be a perfect set. When a groom takes a bride, he should take some ash and put it on his forehead where the tefillin is placed. All of this is done in order to remember Jerusalem, as it is said, "If I forget you, O Jerusalem. . ." (Pss. 137:5). They also decreed that instruments should not be played and songs not sung. . . . Then they decreed that grooms should not wear crowns on their heads, nor any sort of adornment on the head . . . and that brides should not wear crowns of silver or gold. Brides may, however, wear cloth crowns. *(MISHNEH TORAH, LAWS OF FASTS 5:12–15)*

ᗑᗑ Jerusalem in Medieval Poetry

*From the sixth through the fifteenth centuries, there was a great
flourishing of Hebrew poetry, ranging from the early
payytanim—writers of liturgical poetry—of whom we know
little, through the highly personal and sophisticated Spanish poets.
Jerusalem is a major theme of these poets, both as a cause of
mourning for its destruction and as a symbol of hope for the
restoration of Israel.*

JOY OF THE WHOLE WORLD

Yose ben Yose
(LAND OF ISRAEL; CA. 600)

Through Zion make for yourself an awesome name,

Endow it, as in the past, with a royal throne;

Bring back to life the city which is the joy of the whole world

And establish your throne in the royal city;

As bright as the sun display the glories of the metropolis to the
people

And manifest in our time the honor of your reign.

(TRANSLATED BY ZALMAN DIMITROVSKY)

I REMEMBER

Amittai ben Shephatiah
(ORIA, SOUTH ITALY; LATE NINTH CENTURY)

I remember, O God, and I am vexed

When I behold the flourishing cities of the world

While the city of God is cast down to the depths of Sheol—
Nevertheless we turn toward Yah, our eyes are toward Yah!

May it be Your will, O He who attends the sound of weeping—
To gather our tears in Your cup
And save us from all cruel decrees
For we look to You alone!

(TRANSLATED BY REUVEN HAMMER)

MY HEART SEETHES

Shmuel Hanagid
(CORDOVA, SPAIN; 993–1055 OR 1056)

My heart seethes: the halls of our youth are stripped bare;
    Urim and Tummim light the exiles' feet.
  I dwell outside Zion, foul as a corpse,
    shamed as one slain, angel-struck.
Can strayed Israel return, walk God's streets again,
    can the proud meet their day?
  What store can we put in tradition's store—
    the loosing of chains,
      the slavers brought down,
        the righteous uplifted, redeemed?
  Shall song spill from my lips and my sons'
    from the altar steps;
  Shall I yet see the sons of the Living God
    wing to Zion like doves?

As God lives: I shall so!
  —nor say, I serve princes and kings,
    mine splendor and might;
Nor open my ear to the Tempter's voice—
    You loom over men like a god!
What gain yours in your people's return?
    What return in the exiles' redemption?
Far best for my soul that I stand in God's courts
    than rule worlds:
  Ambrosia on unclean soil
    I hold lees.

Lord. send forth your rays,
    raise Zion, raise Zion's dear sons;
Restore our lost youth with your love,
    turn us eagles again.
Glut your lamb, lion-torn, with foe's blood
    that my flame lick your altar,
      thick laden with rams.

  (TRANSLATED BY DAVID SIMHA SEGAL)

EARTH'S BEAUTY
Judah Halevi
(SPAIN; CA. 1075–1141)

Earth's beauty and joy
  and Great King's seat—

For you my soul yearns
  from the ends of the west.

My pity moans, mounts
  when I recall you, East—
Your glory exiled
  and your dwelling waste.

Oh, who might set me
  upon eagles' wings
That I might drench your dust
  with tears?

I seek you, though your king be gone;
  and though I find
For Gilead's balm,
  adder and snake—

Shall I not pity, shall I not
  kiss your stones—
  your earth beyond honey
  sweet upon my lips?
  (TRANSLATED BY DAVID SIMHA SEGAL)

MY HEART'S IN THE EAST
Judah Halevi

My heart's in the east and I languish on the margins
of the west. How taste or savor what I eat?

How fulfil my vows and pledges while Sion
is shackled to Edom and I am fettered to Arabia?
I'd gladly give up all the luxuries of Spain
if only to see the dust and rubble of the Shrine.

(TRANSLATED BY GABRIEL LEVIN)

ODE TO SION
Judah Halevi

Will you not ask, Sion, of your captives' well-being,
   they who diligently quest
      after your welfare and are the remnant
   of your flock? From west
to east, north to south, Peace from the near
   and far off, from all sides
      round about you, Greetings,
   from a captive of desire,
who sheds tears like the dew of Hermon and longs
   for them to streak your slopes.
      Weeping of your afflictions
   I am a jackal, dreaming the return
of your fortunes, a lute for your songs.

How I yearn for Bethel and Penuel, for Mahanaim
   and all the saintly meeting
      grounds. The Shechina dwelled
   among you there, and your Maker

flung open your gates to face the gates of heaven.

   The glory of Adonai your only light,

      neither sun, moon or stars

   shone over you. I would pour out

my life on the very site where the spirit

   of Elohim once drenched

      your chosen ones. Royal city,

   throne of the Lord, though

slaves have long dethroned your princes.

If only I could roam the grounds

   where Elohim was revealed

      to your seers and heralds.

   Who will give me wings to flee far off,

bearing the shreds of my torn heart

   to your cleft mountains? Falling on my knees,

      I would delight in your stones

   and be stirred to pity

by your dust. I would weep by the tombs

   of my fathers and stand

      bewildered in Hebron

   facing the pick of graves.

Crossing your woods and fields, I would stop

in Gilead to marvel at Mount Abarim—Abarim and Hor,

   where rest the two great beacons

      who guided and gave you light.

The air of your land quickens
the very life of the soul, the grains
   of your dust are oozing myrrh,
      and your streams
   are honey from the comb.
How I would delight to walk naked and barefoot
   among the rubble
      where your shrines once stood:
   here is the site where your ark was hidden away,
and here is the innermost chamber

where your cherubim once dwelled.
   I will raze my crown of hair,
      and curse Time that defiled
   your crowned ones in a polluted land.
How can I enjoy food and drink
   when I see dogs tearing into your young lions?
      How can daylight soothe
   my eyes while I behold the eagle's mangled body
dangling from the Raven's beak.
   Gently, cup of sorrow, be still,
      body and soul are filled with your bitterness.
   I drink your wrath remembering Oholah,
and recalling Oholibah drain your dregs.*

* See Ezek. 23. The two women represent Samaria and Jerusalem (ed.).

Love, grace, the very life of your companions
    are bound fast to you, Sion, paragon
      of beauty: they delight in your well-being,
    and weep forlorn at your desolation and ruin;
they long for you even from the pit
    of captivity; they bow, each in his place,
      toward your gates. The flock
    of your people—exiled, scattered,
from mountain range to hillside—have not forgotten
    your borders; they cling to the edge
      of your cloak and strive
    to climb up into your palm
to grasp its fronds. Were Shinar and Patros
ever equal to you in their greatness, can all
    their empty divination
      compare with your Urim and Tummim?
    Who is equal to your anointed
and prophets, who to your Levites and singers?
    Petty kingdoms will perish,
      but your strength is everlasting,
    your crown endures from one
generation to another. God yearns
    to dwell with you: happy the man
      determined to set

out and settle on your sovereign

grounds; happy is he who waits

   and lives to behold your lights rising as dawn

      breaks over him, and he sees

   your chosen prospering, and thrills

at your joy, when you regain the vigor of youth.

                   (TRANSLATED BY GABRIEL LEVIN)

LAMENT FOR ZION
Author Unknown

We approached to ask our mother's well-being,
We stood at her door and wept.
The guards found us, they beat us, they wounded us—
"Away, unclean!" they cried to us.

Again we came, but approached not.
Upon a distant mount we stood.
She who dwells alone came out to greet us,
Gazing from her prison she faced us.

We raised our eyes to see her,
But so wasted was she that we knew her not.
Her shape and form were gone,
Bound in chains and burdened with fetters.

We raised our voice in weeping
For the desecration of Mount Moriah,

For our impoverished mother,
With nothing to sustain her.

Our cries rose in her ears
And she joined in our complaint.
She cried in supplication and lamented:
"Behold I dwell as a widow.

My sons have gone into captivity,
My sanctuary is devastated,
I am left naked and exposed—
For this do I weep."

(TRANSLATED BY REUVEN HAMMER)

SHALOM TO THE CITY SHALEM
Judah Alharizi
(SPAIN; 1170–1235)

Stripped of her fabled beauty;
Oh, Where has it vanished?
Ask those who behold her.

I plead for her dust day by day,
She is the sickness of my soul and its dispair;
When my eyes will behold her radiance once again
Clouds of tears will shroud them no more.

O God—who desired her as His dwelling—
Witness her dispair, annul her captivity;
She laments her Beloved's departure.

Upon His return unto her
He will wipe the tears from her cheeks!
(*TRANSLATED BY REUVEN HAMMER*)

CRY, O ZION
(from the Tisha b'Av Liturgy)
Author Unknown

Cry, O Zion and her cities—
Like a woman in travail—
Like a mourning widow
Lamenting the husband of her youth!

For the desolate Temple,
Destroyed because of the sins of her flock;
For the entry of the enemies of God
Into the sanctum of her Shrine . . .

For the exile of the servants of God
Those who sweetly sang her songs;
For their blood freely shed
Like waters of her streams . . .

For the children of her kings
Her nobles from David's house;
For their beauty now vanished
When her crowns were captured . . .

For God's Glory exiled
When her Temple was destroyed;

For the oppression of the foe
Clothing her in sack-cloth . . .

For Your Name desecrated
By those who beseiged her;
For the cries imploring You—
O listen and heed her pleas!

Cry, O Zion and her cities—
Like a woman in travail—
Like a mourning widow
Lamenting the husband of her youth!

(TRANSLATED BY REUVEN HAMMER)

THE SIXTH GATE

Jerusalem in the Literature of the Turkish and Mandatory Periods

Zion Gate to the Old City, ca. 1898 (Central Zionist Archives; with permission)

The material in this section spans a little over two centuries, a period of time in which Jewish settlement increased in the Land of Israel, at first through the actions of individuals, small groups, and philanthropists and then through the more conscious efforts of the newly formed Zionist movement, which began a political program to create a Jewish State. Jerusalem is seen here both as a holy city and as a real place that requires rebuilding and serves as a center of political activity and cultural renewal, and as a focal point of Jewish–Arab tension.

LIFE IN JERUSALEM (1834–1863)

Avraham Yaari

> *In his book* The Goodly Heritage, *Avraham Yaari collected stories about life in early Jerusalem, quoting from diaries and other writings of the time.*

Yehoshua Yellin . . . describes in the following pages Jewish life in Jerusalem during his early years. . . .

When my late father came to Jerusalem [1834—ed.] he found the city neglected and deserted. . . . Most of its houses and courtyards were in ruins, and those that remained whole were small, low and dark. Their tiny windows were covered with grilles to hide the women from the gaze of passers-by. The shops were in a similar case. Only a few were occupied by vendors of the rough, black pottery made in Gaza and Hebron, or by leather-workers and cobblers. . . . There were but few shopkeepers. Houses and shops could be bought for next to nothing; but the Jews did not interest themselves in purchasing them, as they did not see any possibility of gaining a worthwhile living from them. They were more concerned with obtaining tenancy rights. . . .

My late father, who was always profoundly attached to the Land of Israel, had always wanted to own some property. But as the houses within the walls were old and cramped, and the air within them was foul owing to the narrow, tortuous and filthy streets, he would have none of them, and decided instead to buy a plot outside the walls for all that there was no vestige of human habitation there— only some Christian monks and merchants had acquired plots outside the wall—and despite the fact that the City gates were closed at nightfall by order of the authorities and remained shut all night. Before sunset a soldier would go out and announce that the gates were about to be closed, and all those without hurried inside. Any who tarried had to spend the night in the open.

David Yellin began to negotiate for a stretch of land some distance from the City wall (it is known today as the Russian Compound, in the heart of the modern city). But the parties differed concerning the width of a path that was to run through the land, and the deal fell through. . . .

Though in less affluent circumstances than before, the elder Yellin did not give up his idea of becoming the owner of a piece of land. He therefore joined forces with Yehoshua's brother-in-law, Shaul, who was of a like mind. The two scraped together some money and were offered a stretch of land at the village of Kolnia, about seven kilometers west of Jerusalem. . . . The village lay alongside the Jaffa–Jerusalem highway, and it had the merit of being the site of a place mentioned in the Bible—Motza, by which name it is now known. So charmed were the prospective purchasers by the beauty of the spot, that they decided to acquire it. Foreign nationals, however, were not permitted to buy land outside the City unless by a special dispensation of the Sultan, and so Yellin and his partner consulted James Finn (the British Consul), who suggested a somewhat involved way of getting round the difficulty. . . .

The Consul was held in great awe by the Pasha and other high Government officials. During the time he held office, he had several Pashas removed by complaining of them to the British Ambassador in Istambul; for at the time Britain wielded more influence there than any other country. Even the great sheikh, Haj Mustapha abu-Ghosh, who held sway over all the villages on the northern side of Jerusalem, kept aloof from us and did not interfere. . . .

The sudden death of David Yellin (in 1863) prevented the execution of the scheme.

A Narrative of a Forty Days' Sojourn in the Holy Land

Sir Moses Montefiore

At five o'clock in the morning we were already saluted by friends who had anticipated our approach, and, half an hour afterwards, we halted at the spot whence a full view might be had of the Holy City. There we performed the ceremony of Keriah [tearing one's garment as a sign of mourning—ed.] and pronouncing the customary blessing, surrounded by an increasing number of people from all directions.

As we continued moving toward Jerusalem, I had nothing but to look right and left and see the number of new houses; some of them very large buildings, and the mouths of friends did not rest from telling us, "This is a house belonging to one of us"; "That piece of ground has been bought by N.N., one of our Community"; and as we still further proceeded, there was no necessity any more to inform us of the name of any proprietor, as the whole family of the occupants came out of their houses, and I had the happiness of myself seeing hundred of our brethren, lining the fronts of their dwellings. Presently my attention was directed to the presence of my much-esteemed friend, the Rev. Samuel Salant, a gentleman who had been introduced to me, when in Constantinople, by the late Rev. Moses Rivlin, in the year 5601 (1840), and who has been one of my correspondents on matters connected with the Holy Land for the last thirty-five years. His countenance was radiant with joy when he saw me, and he pronounced the blessing of "Shehekheyanoo" [thanks-giving for having lived to experience a special event—ed.]. I was delighted to find him looking so well, appearing almost as young as when I saw him nine years ago. Proceeding a little farther on the road, a new Synagogue was shown to me, in the place called

"Nakhalat Shibeah"; it was surrounded by a number of houses, occupied, I was told, by fifty families. Again, a plot of ground was pointed
out to me as belonging to a party intending to build thereon sixty
houses. And, when coming near the Upper Gikhon pool, not far
from the windmill which I caused to be built on the Estate "Kerem
Moshe Ve-Yehoodit," eighteen years ago, my attention was directed
to two other windmills recently built, which, I was told, gave a good
profit to the Greeks who owned them.

Great was my delight when I considered that but a few years had
passed since the time when not one Jewish family was living outside
the gate of Jerusalem—not a single house to be seen; and now I
beheld almost a new Jerusalem springing up, withbuildings, some of
them as fine as any in Europe. "Surely," I exclaimed, "we are
approaching the time to witness the realization of God's hallowed
promises unto Zion! 'I will make thee an eternal excellency, a joy of
many generations.'—Is. lx.15."

When my carriage reached the Jaffa gate I was obliged to alight.
Neither the streets nor the pavements in Jerusalem, the driver
observed, are yet prepared for carriages.

◖◗

In the evening I received an invitation from the Building
Committee of the little Colony called "Meah Shearim" to lay the
foundation stone of a new row of houses. "The Company," they said,
"on whose behalf we crave the honour of your presence, numbers
now 120 members, under the direction of Mr. Salmon Beharan,
assisted by the Treasurer, Mr. Ben Zion Lion, and the Secretary, Mr.
Jesaias Ornstein. The object is to build every year not less than ten
houses, which, on completion, are to be allotted to ten members.
The Company was established but two years ago, and there are

Bucharian Jew in Jerusalem, Date unknown (Central Zionist Archives; with permission)

already twenty houses built and inhabited.

"There will be a Synagogue, College, and School; likewise a Public Bath in the centre of the square, and a very large cistern for the supply of water."

On my enquiry whether they were the only Building Society in Jerusalem, they replied, "No, there are two others. . . ." So that altogether there will be 235 of our Brethren, in a few years, proprietors of most comfortable houses in a very salubrious locality, outside the city, which they secured unto themselves by their own exertions, by their own money.

Friday (13th August) I proceeded to the Western Wall to offer up the customary prayers. The road leading to that hallowed spot, and the houses in its vicinity, are still in a state of ruin, causing man and horse to stumble over detached fragments of ancient structures, and remind the pilgrim that a great deal of work has yet to be done before the paths of Zion will be even and smooth. When I visited Jerusalem, in the year 1866, I exerted myself very much to have an awning made in front of the Western Wall. I had already made an agreement for the execution of the work, but unexpectedly some obstacle occurred, which could not be surmounted, and the matter dropped. A gentleman recently tried to place there some seats for the accommodation of the numerous visitors arriving daily at that spot, and not succeeding in his endeavours, he asked permission to have at least a number of large square marble stones placed there, and was allowed to do so. But they did not remain long in the place assigned to them; first one stone was removed, then another, until at last all of them disappeared. . . .

The Haham Bashi [Chief Rabbi—ed.] having requested me to receive a special deputation, I appointed the afternoon for an interview, though I felt greatly the fatigue from this morning's exertions, and was obliged to retire to my chamber. About two o'clock p.m., Haham Shalom Moshe Khay Gagin, principal of the Yesheebat Toledoth Yitzhak, and Signor Yitzkhak Kalamaro, the Treasurer of the Synagogue "Bethel," entered. They communicated to me their intentions of securing land for the building of 80 houses, a Synagogue, Beth Hamidrash, and a Public Bath. They had already, they said, decided to purchase for that purpose a plot of ground near the City wall, measuring 26,000 builders' yards, at the price of 900 Napoleons, toward which amount the Gurgistan Congregation was ready to contribute 650 Napoleons; but unfortunately the expenses necessary for the purpose of securing the purchase by a proper contract, proved to be so great that they had to relinquish it.

The deputation made to me certain proposals on that subject, which I promised them to take into consideration.

They also communed with me on matters referring to the Kerem Moshe ve-Yehoodit, and I gave them full instructions how to act, so as to secure the object in view.

Doorway to the School for Sewing at the Schneller Woods, date unknown; labeled as "the second house outside the city walls" (Central Zionist Archives; with permission)

COMING TO JERUSALEM

Eliezer Ben Yehudah

> *Famous for his pioneering work to revive the Hebrew*
> *language, Eliezer Ben Yehudah (1858–1922) was born in*
> *Lithuania and left Europe for the Land of Israel in 1881.*

The next morning, when the coach stood near the square before Jaffa Gate, two men came up to me and called in Hebrew, "Shalom Aleichem" (Welcome). They had been sent by Reb Yisrael-Dov, the owner of "HaHavatzelet" [a Hebrew periodical—ed.] to greet me and bring me and my wife to our house. . . .

Anyone familiar with Jerusalem today would find it difficult to even imagine the desolation in those days of that square before Jaffa Gate. All the beautiful buildings which you can now see on both sides of the square and above it as you come to "Hamoskovia" [the Russian Compound—ed.] had not yet been built. All that existed was only a few dark, squat, miserable huts on either side, befitting the ruined state of the entire city. As you came to the city there was a long, low, impoverished-looking building on the left containing some dark and dingy stores with low and narrow entrances. As we neared the stores I noticed that in some of them the entrances had been broken down and workers were rebuilding them, raising the entrances, widening them and in general giving the stores a more pleasant appearance. I asked my companions, "Who owns these stores and who is repairing and improving them?" They told me that this was the property of the Armenian Patriarchate which had begun of late to build houses and stores in a European style. I was upset to hear that strangers were building Jerusalem and I sadly voiced my feelings to my wife, but the men sent by Reb Yisrael Dov comforted me by saying: It doesn't matter! They are building for us. When the

Redeemer comes—speedily in our days!—all of these buildings will be ours.

These words were uttered with such simplicity and sincerity that there could be no doubting that they believed what they were saying to me completely. And I must say that such belief was held strongly by all the Jewish residents of the Land of Israel at that time. Some years later, when Yemenite Jews began to come to Jerusalem, I heard the same simple, certain convictions from them: They are building and building—everything will be ours when the victorious Messiah comes.

Because of this perfect faith the Jewish inhabitants of the Land of Israel were not bothered by the fact that Jerusalem and the other cities of the Land were being built by strangers. Now that we have been worthy to witness the beginning of redemption, I see that this simple faith of our brothers of the Land of Israel of that generation was not so foolish after all. But at that time, when I has just arrived in the Land of our Fathers, the fact that our mother city was being built by strangers and that the inhabitants were not troubled by it upset me very much, so much so that I could pay attention to nothing else.

It was in that despondent mood that I went through Jaffa Gate into the holy city within the wall—the ruined, desolate city of David King of Israel, cast down to the depths of Sheol. No special feeling was aroused within me. Even the words, "the Citadel of David"—which my companions spoke to me when we passed by the tower to the right of Jaffa Gate—made no particular impression upon me. Had someone told me in advance that my entrance into Jerusalem would be so trivial, so unable to stir my blood or arouse any emotions within me, I would certainly have reprimanded such a person. But I must admit that that is exactly how it was. I was completely apathetic, as if I were walking in the streets of any one of the world's cities. Thus did I go the entire way from Jaffa Gate to the site of the Temple.

A "Moshav Zekenim" (Home for the Elderly) in Jerusalem, date unknown
(Central Zionist Archives; with permission)

TRUTH FROM THE LAND OF ISRAEL

Ahad HaAm

> Asher Hirsch Ginsberg (1856–1927), known best by his pen
> name Ahad HaAm ("one of the people"), was a great essayist
> and Zionist leader. His first visit to the Land of Israel took place
> in 1891, and he wrote his impressions in this famous essay.

I came to Jerusalem for Passover eve to pour out my thoughts and my
anger before the "sticks and stones," the ancient remnants of our
most precious places. Obviously my first stop was the Wall. There I

"*The Help of the Needy*"—a settlement built at the foot of Mount Zion ⟶
"*with sixty houses to house sixty needy families who will be chosen by a lottery
to be held every three years,*" date unknown (Collection of the National and
University Library, Jerusalem; with permission)

found crowds of our brothers, dwellers of Jerusalem, standing and praying in loud voices. Their thin faces, their strange motions and their odd dress seemed to fit the terrible state of the Wall. As I stood and contemplated them and the Wall one thought filled my mind: these stones are witnesses to the destruction of our land; these men—to the destruction of our people. Which destruction is greater? For which should we lament more bitterly? If the land is destroyed but the people remains full of life and strength, a Zerrubabel, Ezra and Nehemiah can arise and the nation will follow them, return and rebuild. But if the people is destroyed, who can restore it and when whence will its help arise? (*21 Iyar 5651*)

My Memoirs

Yosef Yoel Rivlin

> *The Rivlin family settled in the Land of Israel in the early 1800s and participated in the building of settlements outside the walls of the Old City and in the establishment of Jewish life and institutions in Jerusalem. Yosef Yoel Rivlin (1889–1971) was an educator and scholar and wrote these accounts of life in Jerusalem during his youth.*

Every neighborhood had its own synagogue, next to which could be found the "oven"—the only public buildings, even though only a few steps and a narrow path separated one neighborhood from another: Mazkeret Moshe from Mishkanot Yisrael, Mishkanot Yisrael from Even Yisrael. In the more developed neighborhoods, which became the centers for surrounding areas, there was also a Talmud Torah with a few classes for beginners. Strangely enough, Sukkat Shalom, that row of houses which stretched from Mishkanot Yisrael to Even Yisrael, a neighborhood of wealthy old Russians, where most of the homes had two rooms or even two and a half with a balcony enclosed by iron railings, had no synagogue of its own. Those prominent, wealthy men who were known by the city of their origins—I remember "the honorable man from Velkovisk"; Reb Tzvi Mondshein, "the man of Warsaw"—had to pray either in the Mazkeret Moshe synagogue or the Mishkanot Yisrael synagogue.

A narrow path was all that divided Ohel Moshe from Mazkeret Moshe, and the windows of each neighborhood faced those of the other, but only their backs faced each other. The doors and entrances of each neighborhood faced inward, toward the other row of houses within the neighborhood, with a public garden between the two rows. The rectangle of the neighborhood was closed off by short rows of houses in the other directions. That was the plan of all the early neighborhoods.

Ohel Moshe and Mazkeret Moshe were two totally separate worlds, two different entities. In Mazkeret Moshe they spoke Yiddish, pure Lithuanian Yiddish, while Ladino was the language of Ohel Moshe, as spoken by the Jews of Turkey and the Balkans. When the Yemenites came and settled in a group of houses south of Mishkanot Yisrael and east of Mazkeret Moshe, the Hebrew language, in the special accent of Yemenite Jewry, began to compete with the two "official" languages, Yiddish and Ladino.

Only a few Sephardim managed to make their way into the Ashkenazic neighborhood, either to live there or to purchase their own homes. Even fewer Ashkenazim penetrated the Sephardi neighborhood. . . .

The bath-houses played an important part in my life. I think that when I was a child there were two "steam-baths" in Jerusalem. One was on a wide street, Batrik Street, not far from the path leading to the sepulcher of Jesus. The other, which was fancier, was near the Temple Mount and was called "The Hot Bath of Al-harem." Hasidim and very observant people had nothing to do with it. They said that

The Misgav Ladach Hospital in the Old City, year unknown (Central Zionist Archives; with permission)

it was within the borders of the Temple Mount, which was forbidden to Jews so long as there were no "ashes of the red heifer" which could be used for purification. When I was young many people said that some fanatics had proclaimed a "herem" against Moses Montefiore himself because he had entered the courtyard of the Temple Mount. He was probably misled by his secretary, Eliezer Loewe, who cited the lenient ruling of the Ravad that the rule of the holiness of the Sanctuary is not operative at this time, thus leading to a Jerusalem scandal. Father and his friends permitted themselves to go to that bath-house. . . .

Those sweat-baths were among the few pleasures of this world which a Jerusalmite could enjoy at that time. One would enter a large room—directly from the street. In the center was a fountain, in some of which there were little fish or floating lemons, or even flowering plants around it. There were high ledges around the walls, with steps leading up to them on which were padded sofas covered with silk from Damascus. One would sit for a few moments to recover from the walk. Then one of the attendants of the bath-house would come and bring you sheets. You would undress garment after garment and wrap yourself in the sheets—like a thick, wide towel—around your hips and going as far as the knees. You would take off your shirt and he would put a beautiful, colorful silk scarf on your shoulders which covered half your body from the hips upward: he would bring you wooden sandals which were on the steps and then you would pass into an empty inner hallway—it had nothing but a bench in it—which led to the baths themselves. . . .

Early in the morning the day before Yom Kippur we would go to the Western Wall. That was the time when it was most crowded there, for people from all the different groups would assemble there. There were many who prayed the morning service in groups before the Wall, Sephardim, Ashkenazim, Yemenites and Bucharians. At first there was no partition separating men from women at the Wall; the early Sephardim and Perushim did not think of it. But when the number of Hasidim grew and the group of "guardians of modesty" sprang up, they erected one in the northern corner of the Wall on the day before Yom Kippur when there was a large crowd.

RAISE A BANNER TO ZION

Saul Tschernichovsky

> *One of the greatest poets of the period of the revival of Hebrew,*
> *Tschernichovsky (1875–1943) settled in the Land of Israel in*

1931, living first in Tel Aviv and then in Jerusalem. This poem,
however, was written in Odessa in 1897.

Raise a banner to Zion! Raise a banner to Zion!

Take courage and go up—the dedicated of the people.

Until the last breath our hands will not weaken,

So long as blood flows in our veins.

Young and old—unsheathe the sword.

Who is afraid or faint of heart?

Our wives, our children go to the gate,

We the pioneers go out to battle.

On this day we are brothers in arms.

From Ashdot of Lebanon till the isles of the sea

From the far reaches of the north coming to Damaskas—

For life or death—pride of Jacob—arise!

Raise a banner to Zion and found the kingdom!

It is the temple of Jacob's God

A fortress for the young.

Our hands shall seize the holy task—dagger in hand.

Raise the banner to Zion—heros of Judah!

Ours is a God of strength, my brothers.

We have no fortress, no wall—

We ourselves are the stronghold

Our bodies—the towers of seige

Our hearts—the barricade.

(*TRANSLATED BY REUVEN HAMMER*)

IN PALESTINE

Theodore Herzl

> *Theodore Herzl (1860–1904), the father of modern political*
> *Zionism, was born in Budapest and lived in Europe his entire life.*
> *He did visit Palestine in 1898 in order to meet with the Kaiser on*
> *November 2 in Jerusalem. In his diary, he describes this visit.*

We then took the train in the frightful heat to Jerusalem. It took an
hour merely to leave Jaffa station. Sitting in the cramped, crowded,
burning-hot compartment was pure torture. While crossing the dismal and desolate countryside I began to develop a fever, and grew
more feverish and weaker as we rode further into the Sabbath. For,
because of the delay in our departure, and to Wolffsohn's positive
despair, we found ourselves traveling on the Sabbath. We arrived at
Jerusalem under a full moon. I would have gladly driven the half-
hour's distance from the station to our hotel; but the gentlemen
made such sour faces that I had to resign myself, down with fever as
I was, to walking to the city. I literally tottered along on my cane,
while with the other hand I braced myself alternately on Wolffsohn's
or Schub's arm.

In spite of my weariness, Jerusalem and its grand moonlit contours
made a deep impression on me. The silhouette of the fortress of Zion,
the citadel of David—magnificent!

The streets were alive with Jews sauntering in the moonlight.

I felt very sick before going to sleep. I took quinine and vomited
after it. Then Schnirer rubbed me with spirits of amphor, and slept
that night in my little narrow room. Wolffsohn was quite beside himself; perhaps he had given me up.

In the morning I awoke relieved. But I am still very feeble. It is
now evening, and I have not stirred from the house. All I can do is

A 1950 picture of the house in which Herzl stayed in Jerusalem during his visit in 1898 (Central Zionist Archives; with permission)

look out of the window and conclude that Jerusalem is magnificently situated. Even in its present decay it is a beautiful city; and, if we get in here, can become one of the finest in the world.

From my hotel window, this afternoon, I saw the Kaiser pass through the triumphal arches—first the Jewish and then the Turkish. He is said to have stopped a little longer at the Jewish.

I was not among those at the Jewish arch, for there are two factions here. One wanted me to deliver a communal address to the Emperor; the other apparently wished to keep me away altogether— me and my Zionism. Since, as I was informed, the Haham Bashi

(Chief Rabbi) at Constantinople has proposed to his colleagues here that I be laid under the great ban, I preferred on the whole not to go near these niggling Oriental protesters.

➤

Jerusalem, October 31 [1898]

When I remember thee in days to come, O Jerusalem, it will not be with delight.

The musty deposits of two thousand years of inhumanity, intolerance, and foulness lie in reeking alleys. The one man who has been present here all this while, the lovable dreamer of Nazareth, has done nothing but help increase the hate.

If Jerusalem is ever ours, and if I were still able to do anything about it, I would begin by cleaning it up.

I would clear out everything that is not sacred, set up workers' houses beyond the city, empty and tear down the filthy rat-holes, burn all the non-sacred ruins, and put the bazaars elsewhere. Then, retaining as much of the old architectural style as possible, I would build an airy, comfortable, properly sewered, brand-new city around the Holy Places.

➤

We have been to the Wailing Wall. Any deep emotion is rendered impossible by the hideous, miserable, scrambling beggary pervading the place. At least such was the case, yesterday evening and this morning, when we were there.

➤

Yesterday evening we visited the Tower of David. As we went in, I said to my friends, "It would be a neat idea on the Sultan's part if he held me prisoner here."

The views from the crumbling pinnacles seizes the imagination as the city melts away in the evening mists.

Earlier we had walked—rather quickly—through the Via Dolorosa, a route the Jews shun as something maleficent. Seidner, who once lived in Jerusalem, flatly refused to accompany me. I should have considered it cowardice not to go, and despite him went along to the street of the Holy Sepulchre. My friends restrained me from entering the Church itself. It is also forbidden to set foot in the Mosque of Omar and the Temple area, under pain of excommunication by the rabbis—as Sir Moses Montefiore discovered to his cost.

What superstition and fanaticism on every side! Still, I have no fear of any or all of these fanatics.

❧

We inspected a Jewish hospital today. Misery and squalor. Never-the-less I was obliged, for appearance's sake, to testify in the visitors book to its cleanliness. This is how lies originate.

From the gallery of an ancient synagogue, we enjoyed a view in the morning sunshine of the Temple area, the Mount of Olives and the whole storied landscape.

I am firmly convinced that a splendid New Jerusalem can be build outside the old city walls. The old Jerusalem would still remain Lourdes and Mecca and Yerushalayim. A very lovely beautiful town could arise at its side.

October 31 [1898]

The Kaiser is consecrating the Church of the Redeemer today. While touring the city I avoided his procession. At Mikveh Israel it was good, here it would be bad, to stand in his path.

❧

In the afternoon we ascended the Mount of Olives.

Thrilling moments. What couldn't be made of this place! A city like Rome—and the Mount of Olives furnishing a panorama like the Giancolo.

I would cordon off the old city with its relics, and keep out all ordinary traffic; only places of worship and philanthropic institutions would be allowed to remain inside the old ramparts. And on the ring of encircling hillsides, which our labor would clothe with greenery, there would gradually rise a glorious New Jerusalem. The élite from every part of the world would travel the road up to the Mount of Olives. Loving care can turn Jerusalem into a jewel. Everything holy enshrined within the old walls, everything new spreading round about it.

We climbed the Russian ("Belvedere") Tower—myself only as far as the first balcony, for I began to feel giddy, but the others to the very top. Incomparable views over the Jordan valley with its precipitous slopes, the Dead Sea, the mountains of Moab, the eternal city of Jerusalem.

A man needs leisure and a tranquil mind to elaborate all of these impressions.

ᘒ

On our drive back we visited the rock-hewn Tombs of the Kings. They were formerly in the possession of a French Jew, Pereire, who presented them to the French government. So inconceivable it seemed that the Jews themselves should ever own anything.

ᘒ

November 2 [1898]
. . . Eight minutes past one o'clock. We are already back from the audience. That brief reception will live on forever in Jewish history,

The Tomb of the Kings, date unknown (Central Zionist Archives; with permission)

and possibly entail world consequences. But how droll were the details of the whole business.

We had finished our sketchy lunch by 11:30. I kept my gentlemen on short rations, so as to have them in good trim.

By noon we were all dressed. Bodenheimer had a grotesque top-hat, and cuffs so big that his shirt-sleeves kept wriggling into view. At the last moment we had to hunt him up another pair. I put on (for the first time) my miserable little Medjidie decoration. . . . We drove in the white dust and burning noonday heat to the encampment. A few Jews in the streets looked up as we passed. Pond ducks, when the wild ducks are flying overhead.

The Turkish sentries hesitated to let Schnirer and myself go beyond the railings which enclosed the camp. Then a noncommissioned officer turned up and let us pass.

Once within the enclosure, Count von Kessel, in colonial uniform, met us and directed us to a reception tent. We stood inside for about ten minutes, surveying the little salon with its furniture and richly colored carpets.

Then we were summoned to the Imperial tent. The Kaiser awaited us there, in gray colonial uniform, veiled helmet on his head, brown gloves, and holding—oddly enough—a riding crop in his right hand. I halted a few paces before the entrance and bowed. The Kaiser held out his hand to me very affably as I came in. Somewhat to one side stood Bülow in a dusty, gray lounge-suit, holding my corrected draft in his hand. The four others entered the spacious tent after me. I asked if I might present them; the Kaiser nodded, and I did so. As each name was pronounced he raised his hand to the visor of his helmet.

Then, after exchanging a glance with Bülow, I took the paper and read it aloud, at first in a low and somewhat tremulous voice, but gradually *très à mon aise*. From time to time I glanced up from the paper and looked into the Emperor's eyes, which he kept leveled on me in a steady gaze.

When I had done, he spoke—and said more or less the following: "I thank you for these communications, which have deeply interested me. The matter certainly calls for further study and discussion." Then he expressed some views on the present colonization: "The land needs, above all, water and shade." He made use of several technical terms connected with agriculture and forestry. His personal observations convinced him that the soil was arable. . . .

The Kaiser said: "We have hit the hottest time of the year. That day we met was the worst. We took the temperature at Ramleh: 88 in the shade, 106 in the sun."

The Kaiser's procession near Jaffa Road in 1898 (Central Zionist Archives; with permission)

Bülow said in dulcet tones: "As His Majesty the Emperor was graciously pleased to observe, water is the main need. Dr. Herzl will know better than I what the Greek poet says: 'Water is the best thing' " (Pindar).

I rejoined: "We can supply the country with it. It will cost millions, but it will produce millions."

"Well, you have plenty of money," the Kaiser exclaimed jovially, and tapped his boot with his riding crop, "more than all of us."

Bülow *abondait dans ce sens*: "Yes, the money which is such a problem for us, you have in abundance."

I pointed out what could be done with the water power of the Jordan and drew Seidener, as an engineer, into the discussion. . .

I managed to allude to my idea of restricting the old city to humanitarian institutions, cleaning it up, and building a New Jerusalem which could be viewed from the Mount of Olives as Rome from the Giancolo.

I was not able to bring in Wolffsohn and Bodenheimer, for the Kaiser closed the audience by again giving me his hand. I went out first, casting a quick glance behind me. The Kaiser stood sidewise, facing Bülow and talking to him, and looking as though he wished to give himself a *contenance*.

As we went away Count von Kessel asked, "Already over, the audience?" He was less obliging than at Constantinople and I inferred that our stock had somewhat depreciated.

Upon leaving, I said to Schnirer: "*Il n'a dit ni oui ni non.*"

Again there was some reluctance over letting us pass the barriers. But outside stood the secret-service agent and self-styled Zionist Mendel Kramer, who has followed us ever since Jaffa—by order, I fancy, of the Turkish government—and made them open the way for us.

He said neither yes nor no. Evidently a good deal has been happening behind the scenes. . . .

❧

Jaffa, November 4 [1898]

After the audience, day before yesterday, we drove back to the Marx house. A few persons who had seen us leave and return obtruded themselves in the guise of visitors. It took some trouble to clear out the drawing-room.

At half past three I drove in company with Wolffsohn, Bodenheimer, and the settler Broza to the beautifully situated but still terribly poor colony of Motza, where that sturdy young fellow started four or five years ago to cultivate the then nameless and infertile acres. He has now begun to see and reap the fruits of his stubborn industry. The drive along the picturesque mountain road from Jerusalem to Motza—somewhat reminiscent of the Pyrenees—passed quickly enough while the colonist Broza told about the hardships of the first years. Once, when the vines were just about to sprout, a roe wandered through in the night and ate all the shoots. Thereafter, he camped out with a rifle for three nights and didn't sleep a wink for fear of marauding hyenas, with which the region is infested. Was ever a soil more heroically conquered?

A house in Motza, 1903 (Central Zionist Archives; with permission)

Herzl's remains lying in state in the courtyard of the Jewish Agency building in Jerusalem prior to his burial on Mount Herzl; August 16, 1949 (Photograph by P. Shlezinger. Central Zionist Archives; with permission)

I planted a young cedar on Broza's holding at Motza, down the sheltered slope which faces away from St. Jean (Ain Karim). Wolffsohn planted a young date-palm. Several Arabs helped us, besides Broza and Katz.

We returned to Jerusalem after dusk.

So as not to call attention to our departure, I asked my friends to defer packing until after night-fall. I got up at two in the morning to pack my own things.

We took the early train yesterday from Jerusalem to Jaffa. I wanted to get out of the port and the country then and there, and hastened to the harbor. I took a skiff and had the boatmen row me out to a Lloyd steamer which was on the the point of sailing. . . .

LAND OF DELIGHT

A. S. Hirschberg

> *In his book* Eretz Hemdah, *Hirschberg describes his visit to the wall in 1901.*

On the day after I arrived, I went with one of my young friends to the Western Wall, the place to which every Jew who visits Jerusalem turns first. It was a warm clear day, like one of the days at the beginning of summer in our home country; and here it was the month of Kislev—winter! We came to the vegetable market and from there we passed through narrow, crooked streets, some climbing and some descending, and through alleys, some of which were open and most of which had stone walls on both sides (for the Arabs build their houses inside the courtyards) until we came to a small, narrow alley. One side of this was the Western Wall and the other side was a solid wall of one of the hovels of the Magreb Quarter.

When I arrived, there were only two men standing in front of the wall praying and a few Sephardi beggars asking for alms. Some of the beggars were standing and some were sitting on the ground or on boxes that they had brought with them. The Sephardi beadle came over to me and made a tear in the side of my coat and gave me a little prayerbook from which to recite the special prayer for one's first visit to the Wall. I began to mumble the prayer and suddenly I started to weep as I never had until that day, and I was not able to control myself.

I was in shock. The walk through the squalid streets and filthy alleys, the appearance of the Arabs with their dirty children dressed in rags and barefoot, had depressed me so much that nothing I saw could impress me. When I came to the Wall, I did feel that I was standing in a holy place, but my senses were dulled and my heart laid waste. Then came this prayer touching on all ills man is heir to, replaying all aches in the inner heart and the dam broke! All my private troubles mingled with our nation's misfortune to form a torrent. Here I was standing before the Wall, this silent witness to Israel's glory of ancient times and against it I saw all those places and all those times of suffering and torture throughout the whole world and all history! The inquisitions and the pogroms that have been visited on our pitiful nation passed before my eyes—and these stones do not move. . . . Tears blind me and the letters in the prayerbook dance before my eyes. My nerves jangle and my innermost emotions are totally shaken and sweep over me so that I am almost faint. . . . I turned to escape like a fugitive from this Wall without finishing the prayer I had started, but the beadle held me and gave me a wick to kindle in the small, inferior oil lamp that stood at the end of the Wall. For me it was as though he had given me a memorial candle to kindle for the soul of our people dying there in exile.

For the six months of my stay in Jerusalem it was the Wall that attracted me most because it is the one and only memorial to our ancient greatness that is authenticated both by our tradition and by scholarly research. The Jews of Jerusalem flock there regularly for prayers, particularly for the afternoon and evening services on the eve of the Sabbath and festivals and for the additional services on those days themselves. Other favorite times are the eve of the Passover festival to read the account of the preparation of the paschal lamb and the night of the fast of the ninth of Av to mourn the destruction of the Temple. They stand before the Wall in groups, and the recitation of the holy prayers never ceases. All kinds of Jews are there. Thin, scrawny, sharp-nosed Yemenites dressed in poor, worn Arab robes recite the prayers in their unique pronunciation. A quorum of rich, fat, elegantly clad Sephardim, in their black coats and tarbooshes on their well-groomed heads, say the prayers solemnly and with great dignity. At their side is a group of Perushim, dressed in a weird mixture of east and west with medieval Polish fur hats on their heads; honoured old men and earnest, pale young men screw up their faces to achieve the concentration fitting for prayer to God. And there are groups of Hasidim, in their kaftans of red, gold or sky-blue silk and velvet, who shake themselves violently until their sidelocks flail, as they respond, 'Holy, holy, holy is the Lord of Hosts' in great ecstasy. And the women! The Ashkenazi women stand a way off and jump little jumps as they respond to every Kedushah prayer they hear. The Sephardi ladies love the Wall with a special love and most of them come to it enveloped in white sheets.

Those who cannot read the texts of the prayers make modest prayerful signs to the Wall. All, when they leave, kiss each stone individually and back away as though they were leaving the royal presence, stretching out their fingers toward it with eyes raised on high.

The square stones of the Wall, arranged one on top of the other, joined together with no sign of cement; these stones which, scratched and cracked though they be, are not consumed in the teeth of time, are a symbol to the people that stands before them in prayer. . . . How can they fail to excite and exalt the heart of every Jew who comes for the first time to the Wall?!

A VISIT TO JERUSALEM IN 1907

Chaim Weizmann

> *Chaim Weizmann (1874–1952) was born in Motol in Russia, lived in England, and became a world-famous scientist. As a young man he became a Zionist and eventually president of the Zionist Organization and then the first President of the State of Israel. His life and his visits to Jerusalem are described in his book* Trial and Error.

My most unhappy experience during the three-weeks tour of the country . . . was Jerusalem. I went up from Jaffa, not without misgivings. Jaffa already had the small beginnings of a new life, and the promise of a new society; Jerusalem was the city of the *Challukkah*, a city living on charity, on begging letters, on collections. Here the reality turned out as bad as the anticipation. From the Jewish point of view it was a miserable ghetto, derelict and without dignity. All

The Wall in 1917 with Austrian soldiers and Jews in attendance (Central Zionist Archives; with permission)

the grand places belonged to others. There were innumerable churches, of every sect and nationality. We had not a decent building of our own. All the world had a foothold in Jerusalem—except the Jews. The hotel to which we were directed was a dilapidated and verminous ruin, with nondescript people pouring in and out all day long, and all of them engaged apparently in wasting their own and each other's time. It depressed me beyond words, and I left the city before nightfall. I remained prejudiced against the city for many years, and even now I still feel ill at ease in it, preferring Rehovoth to the capital.

But I was struck, as everyone must be, by the glorious surroundings of Jerusalem; and I thought then that there was only one place where, in time to come, we might erect some building worthy of the Jewish community; there was one hill still uncrowned by monastery or Church—the Scopus, on which stood then only the small villa of Lady Grey Hill, and on which now stands the Hebrew University.

HOW THE GLORIOUS DAY OF DELIVERANCE CAME TO JERUSALEM

Hemda Ben Yehuda

> *Hemda Ben Yehuda (1873–1951), came to Jerusalem in 1892 to become the second wife of Eliezer Ben Yehuda. She was a writer and editor who, in addition to aiding her husband, wrote several books and articles. Oddly enough, the following article which she wrote appeared in a book issued by Christian fundamentalists in America discussing the future of the city of Jerusalem.*

Gaza was taken by the English and recovered by the Turks, remaining in their hands seven months. In June, 1917, General Allenby captured Beersheba and then Gaza. Ludd surrendered, Ramleh fell; on November 16, Jaffa was captured. Victorious English troops then marched upon Jerusalem.

For three years the Holy City had suffered privations and sorrows. It was as if the plague had raged within the walls. Most of the houses were closed because the inhabitants were dead, or deported, exiled or in prison. Deserted were the streets. One dreaded to be seen outdoors for fear of falling victim to the rage of the Turks.

People hid themselves in cellars and subterranean passages, where life continued underground by the light of olive oil lamps.

The musicians composed music, the poets composed verses, the professors meditated upon the pupils whom they hoped to receive in the coming hour of deliverance.

The women kept house underground; but there was little food to prepare. They had forgotten the appearance of a loaf of bread. The babies died for lack of milk.

Even in these hiding places, one heard the roar of Turkish cannon, which was directed against the "Nebi Samuel" (the Tomb of Samuel), where the English had fortified themselves. One passionate desire filled the hearts of Jews and Christians alike as they waited for the hour of deliverance. Their confidence in the victorious strength of the English failed not. The devout souls were uplifted in ardent prayer. Pious vows were pronounced. They prayed that the Lord God would deliver them by a miracle, and show His hand as in former days.

But now it seemed as if the Arm of the Lord was turned against the Jews and deliverance seemed far off. Their fervent prayers were rudely interrupted by the intrusion of Turkish soldiers. The gendarmerie entered and penetrated down to the cellars and arrested the defenceless Hebrews. They tore the husbands from the arms of their wives, and separated the children from their parents. They beat their prisoners and loaded them with chains and drove them outdoors into the mud and rain. The storm lashed the helpless prisoners as they were driven forth without coats and without bread. The soldiers goaded them forward like cattle to the assembly places where those who were to be deported were gathered together. The wives and the young women threw themselves upon the necks of their husbands and fathers and brothers, insisting that they should share the horrors of this terrible forced journey. The victims were taken away in the direction of Jericho.

❧

Austrians in Jerusalem were maltreated and deported. Then the vials of wrath were poured upon the American Jews also. They were arrested on the streets and in the houses and beaten and dragged away and forced to march on foot, exposed to mud and rain, all the way to Damascus. Those who were sick were carried on litters. One American discovered concealed in a cellar was sent laden with chains to Damascus.

In the meanwhile the Turkish cannon was destroying the Tomb of Samuel, and the English were making a movement whose object was to encircle Jerusalem. The Turks and Germans commanded that the city should be defended and they sent for re-inforcements from Damascus. The garrison was not sufficiently strong in numbers or in morale to sustain the attack without aid. When the reinforcements failed to arrive, the Turks perceived that they would be obliged to evacuate.

In great haste, they arrested everyone whom they caught on the streets, including the Dutch consul and a distinguished Austrian physician, a member of the Board of Health.

Djemal Pasha had already left for Damascus. Soon after, an edict was issued commanding the deportation of all the Christian and all the Jewish inhabitants of Jerusalem.

The governor did the favor to the Dutch consul and two other distinguished prisoners to allow them a respite of three days in which to prepare for their journey. The Turkish authorities were themselves embarrassed as to the means of executing this last great act of deportation, which included the great mass of the population of Jerusalem. It was expected that the Germans would be of assistance in enforcing the edict, but the Germans were occupied in saving themselves. After the flights, the exiles, the deportations, executions and imprisonments, it was estimated that over thirty thousand Jews and Christians still remained in the city.

In vain the Jews implored Zaki Bey to save them. He replied that nothing could save them! They must prepare for the deportation. Then a bitter suspicion entered the hearts of the Jews. They suspected that even their friend, Zaki Bey himself, was an accomplice of the Turks. It was observed that all of the families with whom Zaki Bey was chiefly associated were the special objects of persecution. The Jews surmised that he had abused their confidence and betrayed them.

In these terrible days in Jerusalem, Jews and Christians fasted and prayed. Their common sorrow and desolation drew them nearer to one another. They sought concealment in the darkest cellars and deepest subterranean passages. Jews and Christians found refuge together.

It was in this darkness and dread that the Jews awaited the coming of their great festival of light and gladness, Hannucca, the Feast of Deliverance in former days, and now approaching as the day of destruction! The women, weeping, prepared the oil for the sacred lights, and even the men wept, saying that this would be the last time they should keep the feast in Jerusalem! They strained their ears to hear the horses' hoofs and the tread of the soldiers coming to arrest them and drive them forth. The women pressed their children to their breasts crying: "They are coming to take us!—the persecutors, the assassins!"

Then, suddenly, other women came rushing from outside down into the depths, crying:

"Hosanna! Hosanna! The English!—the English have arrived!"

Weeping and shouting for joy, Jews and Christians, trembling and stumbling over one another, emerged and rushed forth from the caverns and holes and underground passages.

With loud cries, with outstretched hands, they blessed the company of their deliverers, who advanced in a glory of light, for all Jerusalem was illuminated by the crimson light of the setting sun!

With the victors, entered Justice and Peace, into the city so long ruled by Terror and Pain.

Pious Jews uttered thanksgivings to the Lord God of Hosts who had wrought deliverance in this great historic day, in the very hour of the beginning of "Hannucca," the Feast of the Miracle of Lights.

On the previous day the Turkish troops had evacuated, driving before them numbers of unfortunate prisoners, the last victims of their rule of force. For the last time on leaving, the hated Turkish soldiers had entered the houses to rob and spoil, to carry off everything they could lay hands on.

On the next day after the beginning of Hannucca, the troop of English conquerors entered and shared their own bread with the famished populace, and offered the support of their hands to the feeble and the aged. On the following day, when the great English army entered the city, the women threw themselves on the necks of the soldiers, calling for the benediction of heaven upon them. Young women kissed the hems of their garments, and children threw flowers on their path. It was the time of the early flowers in Palestine— the first flowers which announce the resurrection of Nature after the burning heat of summer is past.

How simple and modest was the entry of General Allenby into the Holy City!

He came with the members of his staff, marching on foot, and passed between the ranks of soldiers who lined the streets on either side and presented arms.

How solemn and imposing was the reception of the hero by the heads of three great religions—the Jewish Rabbis, the Mufti and sheiks, and the Christian priests!

How impressive, and with what relief to waiting hearts, was the proclamation that all the shrines and sacred places of the three religions should be equally respected. These are the words of the proclamation:

> Lest any of you be alarmed by reason of your experiences at the hands of the enemy who has retired, I hereby inform you that it is my desire that every person should pursue his lawful business without fear of interruption. Furthermore, since your city is regarded with affection by the adherents of three of the great religions of mankind, and its soil has been consecrated by the prayers and pilgrimages of multitudes of devout people of these three religions for many centuries, therefore I make it known to you that every sacred building, monument, holy spot, shrine, traditional site, endowment, pious bequest or customary place of prayer of whatsoever form of the three religions will be maintained according to the existing customs and beliefs of those to whose faith they are sacred. . . .

Then life revived in the city which had been ravaged by death. The new rulers distributed medicine and hospital supplies for the recovery of the sick. The soldiers shared their rations with the famished population. As soon as possible, food was procured from Egypt. Seed was given to the peasants and army horses and mules were bestowed to plow the neglected fields.

General Allenby entering Jerusalem on foot near the Jaffa Gate (Central Zionist Archives; with permission)

THE RENAISSANCE OF THE JEWISH SOUL

Chaim Weizmann

> *The following is taken from the address given by Weizmann when
> the foundation stone for the Hebrew University was laid on
> Mount Scopus, July 24, 1918.*

We have to-day laid the foundation stone of the first Jewish university, which is to be erected on this hill, overlooking the city of
Jerusalem. Many of us will have had our thoughts cast back to the great
historic scenes associated with Jerusalem, scenes that have become a
part of the heritage of mankind. It is not too fanciful to picture the souls
of those who have made our history here with us to-day, inspiring us,
urging us onward, to greater and ever greater tasks. . . .

What is the significance of a Hebrew University? What are going
to be its functions? Whence will it draw its students? What language
will it speak? It seems at first paradoxical that in a land with so sparse
a population, in a land where everything still remains to be done, in
a land crying for such simple things as ploughs, roads and harbours,
we should begin by creating a centre of spiritual and intellectual
development. But it is no paradox for those who know the soul of the
Jew. It is true that great social and political problems still face us and
demand their solution from us. We Jews know that when the mind is
given fullest play, when we have a centre for the development of
Jewish consciousness, then coincidentally we shall attain the fulfilment of our material needs. In the darkest ages of our existence we
found protection and shelter within the walls of our schools and col-
leges, and in the devoted study of Jewish science the tormented Jew
found relief and consolation . . . amid all the sordid squalor of the
Ghetto there stood schools of learning, where numbers of young Jews
sat at the feet of our rabbis and teachers. . . .

The cornerstone ceremony of the Hebrew University, July 24, 1918, with Chaim Weizmann in front of the canopy (Collection of the National and University Library, Jerusalem; with permission)

A Hebrew University? I do not suppose that there is any one here who can conceive of a university in Jerusalem being other than a Hebrew one. The claim that the University should be a Hebrew one rests on the values the Jews have transmitted to the world from this land. Here in the presence of adherents of the three great religions of the world, which amid many diversities built their faith upon the Lord who made himself known unto Moses, before this world which has founded itself on Jewish law, paid reverence to Jewish seers, has acknowledged the great mental and spiritual values the Jewish people have given it, the question is answered. . . . By a strange error people have regarded Hebrew as one of the dead languages, but for thousands of my people Hebrew is and always has been the sacred tongue, and in the streets of Tel Aviv, on the farms of Hulda and Ben Shemen, it has already become the mother-tongue. Here in Palestine, amid a babel of languages, Hebrew stands out as the one language in which every Jew communicates with every other Jew. . . .

Our university, formed by Jewish learning and Jewish energy, will mould itself into an integral part of our national structure which is in the process of erection. It will have a centripetal force, attracting all that is noblest in Jewry throughout the world; a unifying centre for our scattered elements. There will go forth, too, inspiration and strength, that shall revivify the powers now latent in our scattered communities. Here the wandering soul of Israel shall reach its haven, its strength no longer consumed in restless and vain wanderings. Israel shall at last remain at peace with itself and with the world. There is a Talmudic legend which tells of the Jewish soul deprived of its body, hovering between heaven and earth. Such is our soul to-day; to-morrow it shall come to rest, in this our sanctuary. That is our faith.

POGROM IN JERUSALEM

Chaim Weizmann

March 1920

We arrived [in Jerusalem] to find Herbert Samuel already in Palestine. Allenby and Bols (the latter was then Military Governor of Palestine) had invited him in as adviser to the administration. Everyone was relieved to have Samuel there, for General Allenby's premonition had been only too sound: we all felt that things were not going well, that there was tension in the country. There was a great deal of open agitation in Arab circles, and there was no evidence that local administrators were making any effort to avert trouble; on the contrary, there were members of the official hierarchy who were encouraging the troublemakers. I am not alarmist by nature, and I was inclined at first to be sceptical about the reports. But they persisted, and some of our young people who were close to Arab circles were convinced that "the day" was set for Passover, which that year coincided with both Easter and Nebi-Musa—an Arab festival on which the inhabitants of the neighboring villages assemble in Jerusalem to march in procession to the reputed grave of the Prophet Moses on a near-by hill. Galilee, too, was in ferment owing to its nearness to Syria, whence Feisal was being edged out, and where friction between the English and the French was growing daily. Lawless bands prowled and raided on our northern hills, and as is usual in such cases banditry took on an aspect of patriotism. A month before my arrival Joseph Trumbeldor, one of the earliest and greatest of the chalutz leaders, had gone up with some companions to the defense of Tel Hai, an infant colony near the Syrian border; and there he and five companions, two of them women, were killed by marauders. The tragedy had plunged the whole Yishuv into mourning.

As Passover approached the tension grew more marked, and by that time some of the more friendly of the British officals—for instance Meinertzhagen (now the Palestine administration's political officer)—were apprehensive. Before leaving Jerusalem to spend Passover with my mother, I called on General Allenby, who was then in the city. I found him with General Bols and Herbert Samuel at Government House, still located in the old German hospice on the Mount of Olives. My representations regarding impending trouble made little impression on them. Bols said: "There *can* be no trouble; the town is stiff with troops!" I replied that I had some experience with the atmosphere which precedes pogroms; I knew also that troops usually proved useless at the last moment, because the whole paroxysm was liable to be over before they could be rushed to the field of action. There would be half an hour or an hour of murder and looting and by the time the troops got there everything would be in order and there would be nothing for them to do but pick up the pieces. However, I could see that I was wasting my breath. I was advised not to worry, and go home to my family for the Passover as arranged. I could feel assured that everything would go off quietly in Jerusalem.

Against my better judgment I went home, though what I could have done after this if I had stayed on in Jerusalem it is difficult to say. Passover in Haifa came and went; and the next morning there was no disturbing news from Jerusalem—no news at all, in fact. I felt uneasy. I tried to telephone, but could get no connection, which naturally increased my anxiety. So I decided—greatly to my mother's disappointment—to go up to Jerusalem and to take Benjy with me. The journey was uneventful as far as Nablus, but there I found a police escort. The Governor of Nablus, who supplied it, dropped a vague hint or two, and I became more and more convinced that "something" really had happened.

Jerusalem, when we got there, looked deserted. A curfew had been imposed, and there was little movement in the streets except for the police and military patrols. We made straight for Dr. Eder's flat in the center of the city, and found him deeply disturbed. The story he had to tell was one that has since become all to familiar: Arabs assembling at the Mosque of Omar, listening to speeches of violent incitement, forming a procession fired with fanatic zeal, marching through the streets attacking any Jews they happened to meet. In spite of all the rumors which preceded the attack, the Jews seem to have been caught completely unawares, and practically no resistance was offered. When one small group of young men, under Captain Jabotinsky, had come out to defend their quarter, they had been promptly arrested. The troops had, of course, arrived when all was over, and quiet now reigned in the city. The situation was "well in hand."

In the trials which followed before a military court, Jabotinsky received the savage sentence of fifteen years' hard labor. He was later amnestied (by Herbert Samuel when he became High Commissioner), but rejected the amnesty with scorn, because it included Aref el Aref, the main instigator of the pogrom, Amin el Husseini (the notorious Grand Mufti of later years) and one or two others of the same type. He insisted on making his appeal, and the sentence was in due course quashed. . . .

All of us felt that this pogrom might have been averted had proper steps been taken in time to check the agitation, had the attitude of the administration been different. The bitterness and incitement had been allowed to grow until they found their natural expression in riot and murder. . . . It might seem, to a dispassionate British observer, that we were making too much of this pogrom. (Only six Jews were killed, though there were many serious injuries.) But it is almost impossible to convey to the outside world the sense of horror and bewilderment which it aroused in our people, both in Palestine and outside. Pogroms in Russia had excited horror and pity, but little surprise; they were "seasonal disturbances," more or less to be expected round about Easter and Passover festivals. That such a thing could happen in Palestine, two years after the Balfour Declaration, under British rule ("the town is stiff with troops!") was incomprehensible to the Jews, and dreadful beyond belief. For those whose facile optimism had led them to believe that all political problems were safely out of the way, and that all we had to do was get on with the "practical" work, this was—or should have been—the writing on the wall.

A JERUSALEM DIARY

Simon Greenberg

> *Simon Greenberg (1901–1993) was Vice Chancellor of the Jewish Theological Seminary. A committed Zionist, he attended the Hebrew University and graduated in its first class. In his diary, he described his life in Jerusalem at that time.*

Thursday, January 15, 1925

I am surpassingly happy, this evening reaching a state approaching unbounding ecstasy. [Judah] Magnes, [Max] Margolis, Is[adore

Dedication ceremony of the Hebrew University Campus on Mount Scopus being addressed by the Earl of Balfour (Collection of the National and University Library, Jerusalem; with permission)

Hoffman] and I walked from the University through the fields back to town. Darkness had already enveloped the city, but not completely. The last rays of the sun reddened the borders of the clouds on the horizon and brightened those higher in the heavens. They appeared like vast mountains of richly colored glass, rising directly behind the city. To this expanse of physical territory before us, was added the wide scope and unbounded hopes which filled all our hearts for the future of the University and of our work here. Time and again Magnes kept asking us as students and Margolis as a lecturer, "Did you ever anywhere else in the world, feel the significance of the subject matter as much as you do here, when it is delivered in Hebrew, before an audience that understands?" "Did you ever think that the form in which a subject is delivered, should influence the content, so profoundly?"

And the student body, how they sit and drink in every word spoken by the professor. What a thirst there was here for some word of the Lord, for knowledge of a higher and profounder type.

And what joy it is for me to be here, and feel part of it all. Such days can never be repeated again, at least not in my life.

SOUND THE SHOFAR!

Moshe Segal

> *The following is an excerpt from* The Diary of Moshe Segal *in which he describes the situation of Jews in regard to the Western Wall in 1929.*

. . . Some time ago I had decided to pray on Yom Kippur at the remnant of our ancient Temple, the Western Wall. This is the Wall that our enemies and those who manipulate them have started to desecrate in recent years, in order to abuse our deepest feelings; abuse which signifies the beginning of an attempt to deprive us of our rights in our land. In the month of Av, 1929, we all swore an oath at this Wall to guard and protect it, and so it is the duty of us all, of every Jewish boy, to visit it whenever possible and to participate in the traditional prayers there, particularly on our people's most holy day. I went up to Jerusalem. Because of the difficulties of the journey from the Galilee, I said the evening prayers in the Hebron Yeshivah, which I love because of its wonderful atmosphere. . . . The following morning I went to pray at the Western Wall.

Notwithstanding the fast, very many people visit the Wall on this day and a great number stay there the whole day to pray, without leaving it at all. This year, the British policemen guarded the place properly; they accompanied the Mugrabis [Arabs] whenever they crossed the area, necessarily or otherwise, with trays laden with steaming cups of coffee and various sweetmeats, to aggravate the thirst of the fasting Jews. The cantor, a very old man, led all the day's prayers. . . . When he came to the prayer, "Close the mouths of our adversaries and accusers! Rid us of pestilence, the sword, captivity and destruction! Raise up the glory of Israel, Your people!" he put special meaning into his mighty voice which stirred the worshipers greatly. The sun began to set. The *Ne'ilah* prayer, in which our fate is sealed until next Yom Kippur, is full of warmth and emotion and exalted ethical meaning and stretches out its hand to welcome penitents. You forget all the intrigues and conspiracies around the Wall. There is only one feeling: the eyes of all Jews, wherever they are, are turned towards these stones; all Jewish hearts are praying this sublime prayer together with you, and you are confessing, "The Lord is God!" and in honour of His majesty the shofar is sounded every year. And then, suddenly you remember: sounding the shofar is forbidden! . . . Who forbade it? The evil government under whose auspices innocent blood is shed. Do we have to accept the yoke of this government? And with all the emotion in your heart you want to grasp the shofar and sound it with all your strength to acknowledge that the Lord of Israel is God and there is none other. . . . the innermost thought of your heart drives you to action. . . .

A hand, by force of its orders, arrested me. . . . Darkness in the hearts of the surprised worshipers; a darkness which spread in the hearts of all our brethren in their exiles. How long will gentiles defile our holy sanctuary?

TO S. Z. SCHOCKEN AFTER THE 1929 RIOTS
S. Y. Agnon

> *Shmuel Yosef Agnon (1888–1970) was the greatest of modern Hebrew writers. Born in Galicia, he came to the Land of Israel in 1907. From 1924 on he settled permanently in Jerusalem, the setting of many of his stories. In 1966 he was awarded the Nobel Prize for Literature. Agnon had an extensive correspondance with his friend and patron, the famous publisher Shneur Zalman Schocken. In this letter he describes his experiences during the 1929 riots in the Jerusalem neighborhood of Talpiot, where he lived.*

On Friday morning the Talpiot Neighborhood Secretary came to me and asked if I would go out to guard the neighborhood, because all the guards were exhausted. I stared at him in astonishment. The whole thing seemed to me like a kind of joke, and I found it hard to give up even one hour of my work time. When I left my room I saw some Arabs walking armed in the streets and one of them shook his sword at Jerusalem. But still I did not see any cause for fear. I expected that the Arabs and the Jews in the Old City would come to blows, but I was not really afraid. In the afternoon things took a different turn. Everyone who had a shop in the town came home, one complaining that he had been forced to close his shop and another saying that Arab dignitaries had come to plead with him to persuade the Jewish shopkeepers not to close their shops. In the meantime the people of Talpiot were forming little groups. People who did not know each other began to speak with one voice. Suddenly there was a rumour that a band of Arabs had attacked the Women Workers' Farm which is next to Talpiot and destroyed it. The Arabs had also attacked the Workers' Brigade, just a fifteen-minute walk from Talpiot and wounded one of the workers (he died of his wounds). Among the people of Talpiot were many optimists who said the Arabs would never come to Talpiot; after all, many of them earned their living there. There were also some who boasted that they had pistols and in the event of an attack they could defend Talpiot. All this time we were asking the Governor for help, and in the end an armoured car came with three or four English soldiers and an Arab policeman and a Jewish policeman. On the face of the Englishman I saw a hidden sneer at the Jews crowding together and in his voice there was a kind of bravado. As if to say, you don't have to be afraid as long as I am here. In the meantime the sun set and I went into the synagogue. I said to myself: Today there will surely not be many worshippers and this place must not be without prayer. When I came there I found only four old men who clung to the hem of my coat and wanted me to tell them what would happen. I stood and prayed by myself and made haste to leave the synagogue and go home to say grace. When I had finished my meal I went to my neighbour's house where the defence guards were gathered. When I saw that they did not need me I went home and brought them something hot to drink and then I went back again and sat in my doorway with two or three neighbours and we spoke about the events of the day. Close to eleven o'clock some people came and said, leave your houses and go to Gordon's. The maid and I set out (for my wife and children, may they live long, were then at Dr. Brin's in Bat Galim). We had to go to the home of Gordon, the director of the Anglo-Palestine Company, for all the people of our street were gathering there. I went to Gordon's house. There were about forty people there, men, women and children. They had locked all the doors and placed armed guards at the gates. I sat in the room for about an hour and went out to stand with the guards. Finally, when nothing was heard from the Arabs some of our people decided that we could go home. I went back home and got undressed and lay down on my bed, but sleep did not come to me. I kept going out to hear if there was anything new. Suddenly two or three neighbours knocked on the door and said, Come out! I was vexed at all this muddle and replied, what do you want of me? Once again we went to Gordon's. I felt no fear but a great languor such as I had never felt before. I kept thinking how good it would be to be asleep in my own bed. Close to sunrise I decided to go home. I woke our maid too and said: Get up, you silly girl and go to sleep in your own bed. You can sleep until noon. She went and I too was about to go but I was delayed on the way by a man who told me different things. Suddenly a foul, mouldy smell reached my nose. I looked and saw that a man was sitting on a stone and one of his feet was shod in a half-torn felt shoe and the other was tied up in a rag. I asked, what does it mean? And they told me that he was from the *Haganah* and had not taken off his shoes or socks for five days and five nights and now his feet were swollen. At that moment I no longer felt the smell at all, as if there was no smell. When I was standing there we heard shots that shook the air. We ran into Gordon's house. All the time I kept on thinking that our maid was also alone in the house and wondering if she was safe. I spoke to X and to Y but they did not listen and those who did answer me out of respect said that nothing would happen to her. I imagined how the girl would hide and how she would save herself. I said, at a time like this she will put her curiosity aside and sit quietly in a corner. And thanks to this I held out for about half an hour. Before our maid went home three young girls went to Dr. Klausner's house (one was their maid and two others went along with her). She went to tidy the house before the Klausners woke up (they were sleeping in a neighbour's house). Suddenly we heard a dreadful cry: Help! Save me! I'm dying! We peeped out and saw a young girl bleeding. Immediately two of our men crawled out: Mr. Saltzman, the owner of the electric shop in Talpiot, and a Yemenite called Sha'altiel, and they brought back two young girls covered in blood. Klausner's maid was badly wounded in the arm and kept on screaming: I'm a poor girl, I have to work for my living, if I have no arm how can I work? I shall die of hunger, Oh mother, mother. In the meantime the third girl was still in Dr. Klausner's house and our own maid was in my house. I stood there helplessly without knowing what to do; they would not let me go out and there was no one to fetch her. The armed men stood guard and the cowards stood and trembled in every limb at the sound of the firing. Suddenly there was a lot of smoke. The Workers' Brigade house was on fire. One shot followed the other and Gordon's house shook beneath the feet of terrified men and women and the children cried without stopping. I who was not armed took first one baby and then another to calm them, but how could I calm others when I myself was full of fear for the fate of the young girl in my house? Between one shot and the next X and Y came up to me and said: you should be grateful that your wife and children aren't here. But I as usual was not sensible of my good fortune but only of my great sorrow, for possibly at that very moment that same young girl was, God forbid, being killed in my house. At last I found two people who had come in an automobile from the city and I said to them: Come with me to save a Jewish soul, and my voice made such an impression on them that they went and brought her to Gordon's house, and two others joined them and brought the third girl from Klausner's house too. The young girl who worked as a maid in our house was called Haya. And when the young men brought her I cried aloud: Haya! And they said it's not Haya, for they had brought the young girl from Klausner's house. At long last the two young men came with Haya and I saw that it really was Haya. At that moment my heart was eased and from then on I did not feel our terrible and dangerous situation. Even when a bullet passed over the heart of our neighbor Mrs. Kornberg while she was nursing her son I felt nothing. All the time I was full of the feeling that this young girl had been saved and her fate would now be the same as my fate and the fate of all the other people there with me. Then someone came and told us that a young man from Talpiot had been badly wounded. In the meantime the Arabs stopped shooting and my neighbor, the architect Kornberg, went to see his house and came back and said that it was on fire. I sat with him on the ground, because of the bullets which might be fired into the house, and my heart was empty of pity. All that time I saw before my eyes the Klausners' little maid with her hurt dead arm and I thought what was all a man's property worth in comparison to that dead arm? In the meantime silence fell on Talpiot. But the silence was worse than the shooting. After the silence had lasted for a while we began to breathe again. Then I said: I'll go to my house and see what's happening there. I went and my maid went with me. I filled two small bags, one bag with my manuscripts about which I shall tell you another time. The girl wanted to take silverware and I scolded her. All the time I had the Klausners' maid before my eyes. After a few minutes we returned to Gordon's. In the meantime the rest of the residents of Talpiot had gathered there, ready to depart for the city. Professor Klausner and his wife came. Professor Klausner said with great pathos that if only they had given his wife a bed he would have remained in Talpiot, and told us about his state and feelings. He also complained bitterly about how his wife was not well and how they had not allowed the doctor to go to her (the doctor was with us to take care of the wounded). It was a heartrending sight when Kornberg took his two children and his wife took the baby and they set out from Talpiot leaving nothing behind them but a plot with a charred house. These poor people who had worked all their lives from five in the morning to late at night left without complaining about their situation.

Toward evening the Oxford people came. I gave them something to eat and they treated us with respect and sympathy. One of them showed me a big knife made by a fine craftsman which he had removed from the hands of an Arab. Not knowing English I let others speak to them while I myself stood and served them. After eating and drinking they announced that we had to leave Gordon's because they wanted to fortify themselves in the house. They said the women must leave for the city and only those men able to defend themselves could remain. We went to a neighboring house and lay down on the floor. It passed through my mind: the owner of this house has already managed to hide his carpets away. It was more comfortable at Gordon's. In the meantime they phoned the Governor and City Council to send us help and also put out all the candles so that we would not, God forbid, be a target for the Arab bullets. There were some residents of Talpiot who demanded categorically that we all leave Talpiot and stop exposing ourselves to danger. As against these there were some who said that they would not leave for the sake of the honour of the neighborhood. I, who all these years had not had a good opinion of Talpiot, suddenly felt an attachment to the place and I too said that I would not leave, and thus we lay (those of us who were unarmed) on the floor while those who were armed stood

The smashed door of a home in Talpiot damaged during the riots of 1929 (Central Zionist Archives; with permission)

by the windows. At nine o'clock a volley of loud shots was fired. I was lying there when suddenly I was called to the telephone. My wife was phoning from Haifa. I could not understand what she was asking and she could not hear what I was saying. Suddenly we were cut off. To me it seemed that my wife had fainted and I started thinking about her more and more all the time. I imagined her in a critically dangerous situation. Thus we lay, about twenty people in a closed room, with a young man armed with a revolver at every window. At nine o'clock loud shots were fired one after the other. Suddenly a sweet voice said: When I count to three, fire. And someone said: Close your eyes. I closed my eyes and heard one, two, three—and suddenly I saw flames and I was almost blinded. I thought what a good thing that my wife is not here, that my children are not here, and suddenly another thought came into my head: what was happening to them there in Bat Galim?

There were shots coming from both sides of the house. Between the shots I heard a voice in Arabic saying *hawaja*, which means Sir. Were the Arabs so close to the house? The shots grew louder. I touched my ears, trying to see if my hearing had been damaged. Suddenly the alarming thought came to me that we were alone in Talpiot with no one to defend us, for there was no response to the Arab shots from the English. Had the English deceived us?

For four hours we were without any defence and our only arms were the little pistols and one broken gun. All the events of the day passed before my eyes. I thought about the wounded girl from Klausner's house and remembered that I had made a vow to give her a pound, and I thought, God grant me the chance, that I will be able to keep the vow. And then I thought about how I had the biggest archive in the world on the history of *Eretz Yisrael* and how much labour I had invested in arranging it and now it would all be lost. Perhaps I should have said to the Oxfordians: I am ready to give you one-tenth of the whole archive for Oxford if only you will save it. But as long as the archives belonged to me I had no right to place it above anything else at a time when the whole community was in great danger. But why should I dwell on such matters when the firing was getting louder and louder?

At three o'clock the residents of Talpiot agreed to leave the quarter. A big convoy came from the city to take us. Once twenty and twice twenty men. I wanted to take the two bags of manuscripts that I had brought with me and I could not find them. In all the commotion they had been lost and I could not on any account remember where they were. And I was forbidden to light a candle here, lest we betray our refuge to our enemies. In the meantime the people were being urged to get onto the bus. And I thought that I would have to leave my manuscripts behind and rely on the grace of God, for it was impossible that all these suffering people should stand and wait for me. In the meantime the Neighbourhood Secretary came and lit a candle and found my manuscripts.

We left the house and boarded the bus. One soldier stood and counted us twice and then another soldier came and counted us again. The bus started off. There were two or three shots. The soldiers among us hid their heads.

One man buried his head between my knees and by so doing he forced me to sit up very straight. I thought that he had succeeded in finding a good hiding place for himself and perhaps because of this hiding place he would be saved from all the bullets and they would hit me, God forbid. I don't remember if it was out of pity for the man or in an act of thoughtlessness that I spread my hands on my knees too, so that if a bullet came it would on no account enter that man's head. Thus we drove very fast until we reached the Russian Compound, where the army was stationed. There they took us off the bus and the bus went back to Talpiot to take the rest of the peo-

Interior of a home in Talpiot damaged during the riots of 1929 (Central Zionist Archives; with permission)

ple who had remained behind. Then they brought us to the City Council building. The Council building was full of refugees from all around Jerusalem, some mute with fear, some crying with misery for themselves and for their brothers, and some sitting and drinking tea. I went to B.A., the head of the *Haganah*. He lay on the balustrade and asked me for news of Talpiot. I told him about the boy from Talpiot who had been badly wounded and he replied that he had buried him. An hour ago he had returned from the Mount of Olives, where he had buried all who had been killed in Jerusalem. Many people who knew me asked me if I had saved my manuscripts. I answered: I have saved them, but the archive is still in my house, the archive on the history of *Eretz Yisrael*. They started telephoning all the "top people" to tell them to send a convoy and save the unique archive. One was not at home and a second found some excuse and a third was busy with some other matter. Suddenly Broza [Makleff] arrived from Motza weeping bitterly. I left the Council building with my two bags in my hand and slippers on my feet and I did not know where to turn. One moment I thought I must have a cup of tea, and the next I thought first I must put my manuscripts away in a vault for safekeeping. Why hadn't I had a cup of tea at the City Council? Since Saturday night I had had nothing hot to eat or drink. All around me I saw hundreds of eyes looking at me with astonishment and tears, for in the meantime they had heard about all what had passed in Talpiot. Someone came to ask me to go with him to Rabbi Kook, for the rabbi had inquired after my health. But I did not go to the rabbi. I knew that he had other worries. At last I found an acquaintance who took upon himself the responsibility for my manuscripts and I gave them to him for safekeeping. And another acquaintance, a shopkeeper, found me and took me by the hand and led me to his house and gave me water to wash my hands and face and also a cup of tea, and he also opened his shop despite the danger and sold me a pair of shoes. I recovered my spirits a little and set off to find out what was happening in Talpiot. But some old men from Talpiot dogged me every step and would not let me be. They said that they wanted to stay with me. I knew that I should give them comfort and that it was not right to abandon them in the streets of Jerusalem, but their own inquisitiveness saved me from them, for upon finding some acquaintances of theirs they stopped to talk to them and thus I was rid of them and went on my way.

Where to? It was impossible to take a single step. Here I was held up by people asking questions, there by the sounds of the weeping of the plundered, and there by my new shoes. In the meantime the sun rose and I who had left my house dressed in woolen clothes was sweating like a wax candle in the light of the sun. Suddenly I saw one of the drivers of Talpiot driving a car. I climbed in next to him and heard that he was going to X in Talpiot to collect some things from his house. I said that I would go with them. I went with him to ask a soldier to accompany us. In the meantime, other people came and took our car. While I was standing there I saw Mr. Krishevsky, who used to be the Deputy Commissioner of Jerusalem. I approached him and told him about my archives and two or three people who were standing next to him laughed bitterly at the man who came at a time of such trouble to talk about some old books. But Krishevsky said that such an archive was as precious as human lives. He told me to wait twenty minutes for him and then we would see what to do. He went off and I stood there and different soldiers kept coming and chasing me away from my place, there was hardly a square foot of the Russian Compound from which I was not banished. In the meantime I met the milkman from Mekor Baruch and he lamented his four cows which he had left behind there. At last Krishevsky came, bringing with him two other Jewish soldiers, and we went to Talpiot. Krishevsky spoke to the soldiers on guard. They fired a few shots to find out if there were any Arabs there. There were no shots from the Arab side. Nevertheless they ordered us to be very careful and to wait another ten minutes and then to crawl slowly to the house. At last I reached the house. The doors were open and inside everything was in ruins. I did not know what to do first. The archives were scattered all over the house and on the balustrade and in the yard, what should I take first and what last, and Krishevsky telling me all the time to hurry, we only had permission to stay for ten minutes and we had already wasted as much outside. I removed some manuscripts which I had left behind on Saturday from my writing desk and then I took a manuscript of *Yalkut Teman* which is the only one of its kind in the world, and also a manuscript commentary on the *Sayings of the Fathers* written four hundred years ago by a pupil of Rabbi Asher, of blessed memory, and a manuscript of the *Saragossa Scroll*, and I also took some manuscripts from the archive. And Mr. K did the same, taking whatever he found, and we returned to the city. On the way we met some Arabs; from their faces we could see they had come to loot. [Someone] asked if we should kill them. Krishevsky said No! We all knew that if it had been the other way around they would have done the opposite. At last I returned to the city with a handful of manuscripts and the clear knowledge of what had been done in my house and the houses of my neighbours. Afterwards I went to send a telegram to my wife telling her that we were alive.

Afterwards we met an acquaintance who was staying in a hotel and he drew me unwillingly into his room and offered me his bed. I thought that I would fall asleep at once, after all I had not slept for two days and two nights, but thinking is one thing and doing is another. So I got up and sent my acquaintance with a telegram to you, my esteemed friend, *Manuscripta und Leben gerettet* [Manuscripts and life safe] and he told me afterwards that he had corrected the telegram and added the word "*nur*" [only]. I suppose that he meant well.

From then on nothing of importance happened to me. Except that for three days I remained without any word from my wife and children and to make things worse, on that same day (that is, Sunday) whenever people asked me, where are the wife and children? I would sometimes reply in Talpiot, when I should have replied in Bat Galim. And the eyes of all those who heard my answer filled with tears. When I saw their tears I was afraid and asked: "Why, is there still danger?" and people turned away from me weeping. Before evening I sat down to rest and everyone who passed me shook their heads and pointed at me. Indeed, those hours were very hard. . . .

*T*orn and desecrated books in a home in Talpiot following the riots of 1929
(Central Zionist Archives; with permission)

The terrible impression made by the upheaval in my house cannot be described in words. Three thousands books (many of which I
inherited from my late father-in-law) overturned and scattered and
torn, and among them an ancient illuminated *Haggadah* with its big
shining letters crying out from the page: And we shall cry out to the
Lord, God of our fathers, and He shall see our affliction.

Much more have I to tell you, my noble friend, and God grant
that I live to tell you these things in a time of gladness and rejoicing.
And now I have no more words. May the Lord give strength to His
people and may He bless His people with peace.

THE SEVENTH GATE

Jerusalem in Modern Nonfiction

The Lions' Gate, ca. 1989 (Central Zionist Archives; with permission)

In the period from the establishment of the State of Israel until today, writing about Jerusalem has proliferated as never before. This reflects both the conditions of modern life in general and the special place that Jerusalem has played and continues to play in the historical events surrounding the founding of Israel. This section and the two that follow it are all devoted to this period of some fifty years. This section contains material from diaries and other personal accounts and reflections about Jerusalem written by those who participated in the great events of our time.

JERUSALEM IS CALLED LIBERTY

Walter Lever

> *Walter Lever, who taught English literature at Manchester University in England, was invited by the Hebrew University to teach a course there in the Spring of 1947. Thus he and his wife Anita lived through the days of the birth of the State in Jerusalem.*

The mandatory government had cut the city up into "zones" and prohibited areas. Barbed wire fences, dragons' teeth fortification and great screens shut off the view in every direction. A hundred yards on from Zion Square was the "central zone" round the post office and the main shopping streets. Half of Rehaviah was requisitioned and forbidden to all civilians without a special pass. The broad open vistas of southern Jerusalem were available only to the soldiers and police. As for the Old City which I so much wanted to visit, I was warned on the first night under no circumstances to go except in a conducted party, since no police protection could be counted on in case of trouble.

From the hour of my arrival I could sense the political tension in the city. When I took the bus for the first time, it was stopped suddenly by steel-helmeted soldiers who pushed their way between the seats with their loaded sten-guns at the ready, and curtly demanded to see each passenger's identity card. On another occasion it took their fancy to order us all out of the bus, line us up in the street, and paw our clothes for illicit weapons. A shot or explosion in any outlying quarter set the sirens wailing as if an air-raid was in progress, and all traffic throughout the city had to stop in its tracks for anything between twenty minutes and two hours, until the all-clear sounded. I do not remember that these elephant-and-flea tactics resulted in a single terrorist being caught during my stay, and suspect that their real purpose was an assault upon mass psychology, an attempt to overawe the populace by a constant exhibition of armed force. . . .

"Town" for the Jerusalem Jew consisted in those days of the triangle formed by Jaffa Road, Ben Yehudah Street and King George Avenue, reaching past the municipal gardens to the Jewish Agency Building and the approach to Rehaviah. Beyond stretched the British zones and the Arab quarters. The whole distance could be walked, at a sauntering pace, in less than twenty minutes. Within these bounds, urban life was necessarily simple, and had an agreeable quality of intimacy. Few people had a surplus of spending money, and amusements were mainly self-created. One visited friends at their homes, attended an occasional concert of chamber music or a lecture, walked out to the open country around Beth Hakerem or Bait Vegan on a Sabbath morning. The young generation's notion of a good time consisted principally of an evening stroll under the pines of King George Avenue refreshed by coffee and ices at Café Allenby or Marcus, with friends round the table and acquaintances to hail from the open windows. Girls wore neat, gaily embroidered blouses and eschewed the more elaborate kinds of make-up; the boys were sufficiently dressed for any occasion in shorts and open-necked white shirts—or, for a touch of dandyism, in Russian-style linen tunics with high, embroidered collars. In the mild air, with older people sitting at their balconies and the street lamps making a golden glow, Jerusalem seemed like the home of one large family.

∾

The news of what happened on the Scopus road that afternoon was announced on the evening radio and appeared in the press the next

The British compound—"Bevingrad"—on Princess Mary Street prior to the proclamation of the State in 1948 (Central Zionist Archives; with permission)

morning. I relate the story as it was told me by S., an American neighbour holding a position in one of the university offices, when I visited him the following day. At 4:15 in the afternoon . . . two buses packed with students, lecturers and staff workers left the university for the city. "Near Sheikh Jarrah," said my neighbour, "the first bus slowed down to go round the bend. I was sitting at the front, near the driver. Suddenly I saw the glass of the windscreen splinter. It's odd, but I don't recollect hearing shots fired. The driver must have braked in time, for the bus came to a halt. I didn't know anyone was hit till I saw the driver's head sink slowly down on the wheel. It was a queer movement, just as if he'd nodded off to sleep. I remember staring at him, then realizing in a flash that in a few seconds the next bus would catch up, not able to pass, and we'd all be trapped on the road. Shots were already coming through the side windows: I got up and began tugging at the driver to see if I could budge him from his seat. He was a stout, heavily built man and a dead-weight now that he was unconscious. I tugged away like hell until I had got him out and set myself in his place, then I put my foot down on the accelerator and thank God, we started to move. The bullets came in over my head and behind me I could now hear the moans of those who had been wounded. There was a girl with a splinter of glass in her eye, who kept screaming that she was blind. I've never driven a bus before in my life, but I stuck it out, keeping my foot on the accelerator and sounding the horn like a madman all the way, while people shouted directions and tried to guide me. The journey seemed as if it would never end, but at long last we were back in the city. I drove across to the Hadassah City Clinic and there we stopped and took in the wounded for treatment."

That was the last time that lectures were held on Mount Scopus. For some weeks the university was closed and the buses ceased to run.

❧

May 14th, 1948

Or day one, year one of the apocalypse. . . There's no world left except this city, cut off in space, ringed round with enemies. There's no month of May, no year 1948: only day and night, with chances changing every hour and tomorrow as arbitrary as the particles of the quantum theory. . . .

The new era began early this morning. There was a ring at the door just as I was waking up. B. from our *emdah* [position—ed.] stood on the step telling me that I was to go at once to Bait Vegan and report for duty. . . .

At the road-block outside Bait Vegan, which marks our front line on this sector, they gave me a pickaxe and directed me toward the wadi below the quarry. It reaches all round the southern outskirts as far as the Bethlehem road. I climbed down the rough slope. It was a morning of matchless beauty; the hills radiant; every wild flower between the rocks gemlike and unearthly. Over to the left was the long white skyline of Jerusalem. A terrific battle was raging there. I could hear the ceaseless rattle of automatic gunfire and the perpetual crash of bombs. The din mounted in an infernal crescendo; it seemed that the city could stand no more; that at any moment it would break into fragments.

Down in the wadi the air was hot and still. Stripped to the waist, a number of men were hacking out a deep trench to serve as a tank trap . . . I fell into line with them and copied their stroke. . . . We worked on steadily. . . . An argument started up between Shelomo, a chubby, lively boy of twenty from our quarter, and a man from Bait Vegan, lean and grave, with a fair beard and the black skullcap of the orthodox. He remarked quietly, as he laid his pickaxe down:

"Now we shall see the miracle in our day, when God stretches out His arm to save His people."

Shelomo, who had become an atheist in his last school year, retorted:

"If anyone saves them, it'll be us of the Haganah."

The man stared at him with blue, scornful eyes.

"Perhaps you have not read in the Torah how the Red Sea was divided, and the people passed between?"

"Natural causes," grinned Shelomo provocatively. "It is also written in the book of Amos that God brought up other peoples from bondage: the Philistines from Caphtor and the Syrians from Kir. What if He now helps the Arabs, or even the British?"

"You will see the answer with your own eyes," said the other man calmly. And he began to quote, also from Amos, how the Lord would regather His people, and raise up the fallen tabernacle of David.

In the midst of this battle of texts, came someone running down the hill-slope, waving his arms wildly and yelling:

"Cheers! Cheers! The Police Headquarters—and the Central Post Office—and Barclay's Bank—with all Rehaviah and Talbieh— in our hands, boys! Long live Hebrew Jerusalem!"

He had come from town with dispatches, and breathlessly told us the news. The great central zone of "Bevingrad" was occupied by the Haganah at the very moment the British were departing. They penetrated it from the side approach and nullified all the elaborate fortifications. From there they stormed down Princess Mary Avenue, past the Arab road-blocks, and on as far as Allenby Square, a hundred yards from the Old City. At the same time Zone B in Rehaviah and Talbieh was peacefully occupied, and the fighters fanned out down Mamillah Road and to the bottom of King George Avenue. Everywhere the Arabs were in flight; it could only be a matter of hours before the Old City fell.

I came home toward evening. . . . I threw myself back in a chair and tried to get the news on the radio. But the electric current was too feeble, so I got up again and went across to the house of S. our neighbours. Their radio was just audible and we caught the Haganah broadcast from Tel Aviv. Ben Gurion's speech to the Provisional Council was being relayed, proclaiming the independent "State of Israel." . . . On tiptoe Mrs. S. crept over, handing us each a little glass of *rishon* wine. Fainter still, we heard the strains of Hatikvah: now our national anthem. Rather solemnly we stood up, raised our glasses and drank to the future of Israel. Before the anthem was played to an end, the current failed completely, and the radio went dead.

THE FAITHFUL CITY

Dov Joseph

> *Dov Joseph (1899–1980) came to Jerusalem from Canada in 1921 after serving in Palestine in the Jewish Legion. In April 1948 he became military governor of Jerusalem and later served in the Knesset.*

Disorders in the Old City began with an Arab demonstration on December 1, accompanied by the stoning of Jewish homes and firing at Jewish buses. The next day three Jews were shot through a break in the concrete wall separating the Arab and Jewish quarters. On December 8 two Jews were stabbed to death and an attempt was made to break into a synagogue, and three days later Arabs set fire to a Jewish house and tried to mob the quarter. Sniping by now had become regular. Shops were forced to close, schools did not open, sanitary services stopped functioning. The Arab attacks were designed to drive the Jews out of the Old City and physically to destroy the Jewish quarter.

After one night of violence and terror, the Armenian and Christian communities, which had lived in friendship with the Jews, broke off contact with them. This cut the Jews off from their chief intermediaries with the Arab venders of vegetables. Food could now reach them only by convoy through Arab districts. The British supplied guards for the evacuation of Arabs from their homes in the New City. Those Jews who left said they did so because their livelihood was outside the Old City and they did not wish to eat the bread of charity.

The technique of the Arab attacks on the Jewish quarter, in fact the technique of fighting in the Old City in general, had not changed much since the days of the Romans. The revolver and the submachine gun replaced the bow and arrow, and the mortar the ballista. The struggle remained one of fighting from house to house, from window to window and from roof to roof. Each battle, of the hundreds fought by day and by night during the six months the siege of the Old City lasted, was identical in principle and resembled the battles which had taken place throughout the centuries in such Eastern cities.

The Hagana command now made its preparations for the defense of the quarter. It was divided into two main sections; one comprised all the part eastward of the Street of the Jews and the other all the area sloping upward to the west of it.

The enemy consisted of members of Arab gangs. They took control of the Armenian quarter and used their mosques for military purposes. Later they were helped by the Arab Legion, which seized positions on Mount Zion and sniped over Zion Gate. British secret-service men could be seen moving about among the Arabs. Ten British policemen were stationed permanently in an Arab mill just opposite our Kahana position.

In general the Armenians remained neutral. They did, however, provide a number of spies for the Arabs. They walked about the Jewish quarter photographing our positions. The Assyrians, who lived mostly in the Armenian quarter, maintained strict neutrality.

The immediate Hagana problem was to increase its force inside the Old City from eighteen to at least 120 men. By private arrangement with a few British guards, two buses and three taxis entered the Jewish quarter on December 10 and their passengers quickly scattered to their positions. This was the only substantial reinforcement that was to arrive. The occasional bribing of another British guard or the introduction of personnel disguised as teachers or religious functionaries added only a handful more. The total number of armed defenders never exceeded 150 and eventually, by the attrition of war, fell far below that figure. The Arabs, of course, entered the Old City at their will without being searched.

Hagana arms were mainly revolvers, Sten guns and hand grenades. There were one two-inch mortar with very few shells, one Lewis machine gun, about a dozen rifles, some explosives, wireless equipment and medical supplies. The Hadassah Medical Organization maintained a medical unit inside the quarter throughout the siege.

Some ammunition had been hidden in the Old City in advance. One of the chief caches, which included ten tommy guns, was a "slick" held by the Etzel, who obstinately refused to reveal its whereabouts to the defenders. This dissident organization at first refused to take orders from the Hagana commanders. They could not be utilized rationally. They often left positions that we thought were standing firm, without informing us beforehand. We were thus exposed unnecessarily to the danger of enemy infiltration. The conduct of all the members of the dissident organizations in the Old City highlighted the profound difference which exists between the organization of acts of terrorism and the steady, trained action required to defend or carry out the planned operations of a nation at war. . . .

We never solved the problem of supplying the Old City. At the end of December the Arabs set up roadblocks, manned by armed men, to stop all Jewish traffic into the Jewish quarter. The British authorities were responsible for these roadblocks, since their police stood by as the Arabs enforced their control of entry. It took the most agonizing negotiations to arrange for a British convoy to escort our trucks past these roadblocks. This was no military matter, but a straightforward political act: the British wanted the Jews out of the Old City and were prepared, if necessary, to starve them into leaving.

The distance the convoys had to travel was only a few hundred yards, and an operation would normally take from twenty to thirty minutes. The trucks, already loaded, were inspected by British police and Army. Three armored cars and a strong escort would convoy them to the Zion Gate, which was the gate the Arabs insisted be used for such convoys. The police inspector would unlock the gate from the inside and send a patrol to remove the bars the Arabs had set up outside. Then the trucks would back to the gate one by one and be unloaded very rapidly by some forty Jewish porters, who carried the goods another 150 yards to some of the houses where they were stored.

In the first five days of January, not an ounce of food entered the Old City. There was an acute shortage of kerosene for cooking and no milk whatsoever for the children. An official of the Jewish Agency who was inside the Old City reported that while the inhabitants of the Jewish quarter were not starving, they were completely isolated and contact had to be re-established. Jewish dead in the Old City had been unburied for five days. On the fifth of the month the matter was twice raised with the authorities. The government was asked to see that convoys went through at all costs, or they would have to be sent through under Jewish armed escort. The regular answer received from the British was that the matter was "delicate."

It was while these negotiations were going on that the Etzel decided to plant a bomb at the Arab National Guard outpost at the Jaffa Gate entrance to the Old City, which was blocking food convoys to the Jewish quarter. It killed fourteen Arabs and wounded forty others. While retreating, three of the Jews were shot dead by police and soldiers. This happened on January 7, which was the day the British had finally promised that a convoy would go through. Naturally, it did not pass that day. Negotiations continued without result. Finally our spokesman announced, "If you hear a loud explosion from the direction of the Old City, you can take it that we have blown a hole in the wall." It would have been no mean undertaking to make a hole in the Old City wall, which was some four yards thick at the top and about ten yards thick at ground level. But the announcement, made without histrionics, in cold, level terms, had its effect. The British promised to see to it that convoys passed through.

❧

We had two objectives inside Jerusalem which we wanted desperately, for old and tangled reasons: the recapture of the Old City, the citadel of our Biblical dreams and the symbol of so many ancient forces which had helped to make us a nation, and the capture of Sheikh Jarrah, the vital link which would re-establish contact for us with the Hebrew University and the Hadassah Hospital on Mount Scopus, two great symbols of the reborn strength of the Jewish people. We failed in both. This was because we chose deliberately to concentrate what strength we had on another objective: the clearing of a safe road from new Jerusalem to the sea. In this we succeeded. A hundred years from now historians may say that our choice, which assured the inclusion of Jerusalem in the State of Israel, was a major turning point in the history of the Middle East. . . . At the Jerusalem end of the road, it was imperative that we take the villages of Malha and Ein Karem. The first was captured on July 13 by a youth unit of Hagana troops; it was one of the points from which the Arab Legion had bombarded Jerusalem and it closed the ring we were drawing tight around Ein Karem. This large village fell four days later. Most of the Arab Legion and the Egyptian troops which held it managed to escape before the end; the rest had no choice but to surrender. This same operation won for us the heights now known as Mount

Herzl, where the national military cemetery of Israel is located and where my younger daughter, killed in action in the Negev, is buried.

◎〉〉

The Old City had not been demilitarized, and we had made as careful preparations to capture it as our supply and manpower position permitted. But the first week of the renewed fighting had seen our forces concentrated on widening the corridor to the sea, and although our demolition squads broke through the Jaffa Gate twice and blew up snipers' buildings, it was not until Friday, July 16, that we could mount an attack on the scale necessary to have any chance against the new defenses organized by the Arab Legion. Even this was hurried; that same afternoon I had received instructions from Tel Aviv that we were to cease fire at 5:45 the next morning if the Arabs agreed to accept a new demand by the United Nations for a truce inside Jerusalem three days before the second truce became operative throughout the country.

So we had roughly five and a half hours. Shaltiel decided to make the try anyway, even though he was not completely ready and the time was too short. In this he was obviously right. We attacked at two points. Our troops broke into the Old City at the New Gate and established a bridgehead within the walls. We tried unsuccessfully to breach the wall near the Zion Gate with an unusually large charge of explosives, and our attacking unit had to withdraw. But this was as far as we could go in Operation *Kedem*, or Antiquity, which was the last Jewish attempt to recapture the Old City.

An unavoidable hitch had delayed the preliminary softening-up bombardment in this operation, which was a combined one, Hagana forces co-operating with Irgun Zvai Leumi and Lehi units. The enemy was expecting the attack and had concentrated large forces.

The Arabs opened a violent bombardment along the whole length of the walls, since they did not know precisely where our attack would develop. At 3 A.M. New Gate was blown open by explosives, and our forces advanced 150 yards and seized ten buildings, which they held in expectation of a second wave of attack. This reinforcement did not materialize due to some failure in planning. Finally, at 5:45 A.M., the general order was given to all our troops to cease fire and break off the action, and those in the Old City were ordered to withdraw. One of the accidents which had delayed the commencement of the action and so conditioned the subsequent withdrawal was that an Arab shell scored a lucky hit on an ammunition vehicle which was in one of the rear bases of the Etzel detachment. Thousands of bullets were destroyed and two men were killed. The other incident was at the New Gate. There the Arabs had built a roadblock of wood and shavings. This was ignited by a shell, and it took twenty minutes before the blaze could be extinguished and our men could move forward. These were irrevocable, precious moments and it is on such flickers of fortune's eyelash that one can say the fate of the Old City was determined.

THE SIEGE OF JERUSALEM

Pauline Rose

> *Pauline Rose was invited to come to Jerusalem in 1945 by her sister. She made a trip in March 1946 and returned to England in June. She came again in Feburary of 1948, settled there, eventually on Mount Zion, and wrote two books recounting her experiences during the War of Independence and then the Six Day War.*

THE OLD CITY

A Sabbath morning! The Old City is in flames! Smoke is rising from the burning synagogues within its walls!

Driven out of their burning homes, after months of attack, hunger and thirst, those brave Jewish people: men, women and children—a mere handful in comparison with the numbers of the enemy—have been forced to surrender. For many months they had defended their homes, their synagogue, their lives. With little ammunition, cut off from all supplies of arms and food, from all communication with their brethren outside the walls, their power to hold out so long cannot be explained in terms of this world.

☽

My friend Malla, the Rabbi's daughter, came in, looking very pale and distressed. She shook my hand.

"The women and children are being escorted out of the Old City to-day," she said. "Come with me to help in receiving them."

It was only ten minutes walk to Kiryath Shmuel, the suburb where many beautiful houses had been abandoned by the Arabs after battles during the previous weeks. In these empty houses the refugees were being lodged. Crowded together, sitting on the floor, all earthly possessions tied in a bundle beside them, were old men and women; rabbis who had spent their lives in the now smouldering synagogues of the Old City; women who knew nothing of the world beyond the homes in which they had served their husbands and families. Their primitive lives, lived in the tradition of centuries, were expressed in their faces.

They were now uprooted from their world, unable to grasp the meaning of the calamity that had befallen them. Some wept in despair; others were resigned—praying silently whilst a few shouted

hysterically in anger and bitterness. Then there were the younger
women, and the sad faces of children with fear in their eyes and thin
half-starved bodies. Young mothers held babies in their arms. Signs
of suffering were on all faces. In the streets more were arriving—old
men and women. The young men were held prisoners by the Arabs.

It was a very hot day. The refugees carried their tins, begging for
a drink. There was no water.

*The Stambuli Synagogue in the Old City after the liberation in
1967 (David Harris; with permission)*

An old woman saw Malla and fell at her feet weeping. She had been a neighbour of theirs in the Old City. Words were difficult between them.

"Everything has gone," the woman muttered between her sobs. "At first they came into our houses and shot at us. Then, as they set fire to our homes, we retreated. We hid for days in cellars and kept alive with a little food we had stored. When they came to burn the last houses, we had to surrender."

"And our home?" asked Malla, her last hope dying. For a moment the old woman could not answer. Then she cried: "I saw it burning with my own eyes."

I remembered again the portrait of Malla's sister, who had died in Poland—her mother's most precious possession; the old Rabbi's *Tenach* which he valued above all things, and which even the Nazis had permitted him to take with him. I remembered the different things that had been collected together to make that home in the Old City. What the Nazis had permitted them to take out of their Polish home the Arabs had destroyed in their home in Jerusalem!

I looked at Malla. She was very pale and very brave.

"They can destroy our possessions and burn our houses," she said. "But we will build new ones. They cannot take our land from us. We are in Israel."

There were shouts and people were running to the end of the dusty road—the water-cart had arrived! Each one received a small ration of water. Later the bread arrived and was cut into measured chunks. There was nothing else that day. The next day there was hot soup, a little margarine, and some black olives.

Smoke was still rising from the burning synagogues and homes in the Old City. The flames had done their work.

༄

15th May, 1948

The pre-natal pains are over! Amidst bloodshed, suffering and anguish, in an atmosphere of hostility, the Jewish State is born. It is named: "The State of Israel" and is destined to withstand all its enemies. It is born a partitioned land, not yet receiving the full bloodstream from its throbbing heart—Jerusalem!

The frustrated world is compelled to accept the partitioned State—the body. But Jerusalem —the heart, the soul—is the seat of the battle.

On this momentous day of birth—the Sabbath day—I write from the city of Jerusalem, the Jewish city, the Holy City. The palpitating heartbeats, throbbing with life's destiny, can be felt in all people, in all places, at all times.

In the morning the hushed silence continued, charged with suppressed excitement, fearful expectancy, anxiety-veiled joy. The streets are emptier than usual. Small groups of people gather anxiously and curiously at corners near the entrance to "Bevingrad," the evacuated British security zone. Later the Jewish flag is hoisted on the "Generale Building," which had housed the British police. Only an occasional shot is heard in the distance.

The silence is tense; the people wait for the proclamation of birth. No newspapers! No electricity! No radio broadcast! Undercurrents of suppressed joy and fear flow through the city in alternate waves.

What is happening to the new-born life? Will it be allowed to take breath? Will the world accept it? Are the enemies' fingers round its throat intending to strangle it?

The heartbeats are loud and fast in the Jewish city of Jerusalem.

Before long the silence is broken; the awe of birth is over. The guns, silenced momentarily by the powers turning the page of destiny, open fire and volleys of shots are poured into the throbbing heart of Israel's city.

Moslems, aided by "Christians," are attacking the Jews from Mount Zion. . . .

◈

18th May, 1948

It is two days since the birth of the State of Israel. An aftermath of pain, anguish, fear and bloodshed; of courage, sacrifice and faith; of chained freedom and obscured joy.

The enemy surrounds us—is on our doorstep! Terrible battles are in progress. All sections of the Jewish city are being shelled. Heavy explosions continually rend the air, leaving behind a trail of destruction, death, pain and shattered nerves. Helpless men, women and children are being injured and killed. Shops are closed, streets are cleared. Jerusalem is a desolate city: no food, no water supply, no lighting, no news broadcasts. All able men and women are called up for full-time service. The enemy is pushing at the door. . . .

Jerusalem is like a city under sentence of death, bearing within it the certainty of life. The heart of Israel cannot be destroyed. Death in the Holy City can only mean resurrection—new life.

◈

20th May, 1948

A deathly pallor still rests on the face of Jerusalem. From midnight to dawn the cannons roared, shells exploded, machine guns rattled, and every other type of gun added to the infernal noise which penetrated every house in the city. The sleepless, helpless inhabitants listened in tense silence and darkness to the battle of life and death.

With the first rays of dawn, the birds made a brave effort to counteract the nerve-racking sounds of continuous battle. The light of day brought with it the relief of abated shooting and shelling, followed by a period of comparative quiet.

Rockets firing over Mount Zion in June of 1948 (photograph by Werner Braun; with permission)

I went out to get some news. The *Palestine Post*—for the first time in its history—could not be printed. We received a few stenciled pages. News passed from mouth to mouth.

"Mount Zion is in Jewish hands!"

"Our flag flies on the Tower of David!"

"The Haganah have joined up with the defenders within the Old City!"

Fifteen hundred Jews had held their positions for many days against thirty thousand Arabs within the walls of the Old City! Last night a handful of Jews penetrated the massive ramparts surrounding the city, and brought relief to the brave defenders within.

News items continued to be passed on.

"Reinforcements of troops, guns and tanks are pouring in for the Arab Legion."

"Amongst the captured Arab prisoners are British officers. . . ."

As I write bullets and shells whiz past overhead, exploding at all distances, near and far. Women and children strained with fear, anxiety, lack of food and water, and many sleepless terrifying night, seek safe places of shelter.

Darkness is now awaiting the departure of the sun. It is symbolic that Jerusalem is at this time without light. In the utter darkness of this life and death struggle, the light of prayer is making a trail in the heart of mankind. There is much prayer opening the way to God in this tormented city. It will need more prayer and dependence upon the God of Israel, before the State of Israel can come into its full inheritance.

The struggle for the new life continues, the shadows are darkening. What has this night is store for us?

GOING INTO CAPTIVITY

Aharon Liron

> *Aharon Liron fought in the War of Independence and was one of the defenders of the Old City of Jerusalem. Afterwards, he felt it a duty to tell the entire story of the seige of the Old City and the battles surrounding it in a comprehensive book in Hebrew titled* The Old City of Jerusalem in Siege and Battle.

More than once history records that the leaders and commanders of Jerusalem met in fateful sessions to debate the future of their city. Thus King Zedekiah and his ministers convened in the days of the First Temple. Thus too the leaders of the revolt in Second Temple times met, and thus did the leaders of the Jews and the Arabs meet in the days of the Crusades. And now so too did the commanders, heads of the community and the representative of the military (Mr. Ben-Shemesh) convene for the distressing, fateful and historic meeting that Friday. May 28, 1948, at 13:00 hours in one of the rooms of Batei Mahse.

Mr. Mordechai Weingarten and Commander Shaul Tawil gave a report of their mission:

> We proposed a cease-fire so that the wounded could be evacuated and the dead removed from the Quarter, but Abdullah Bek al-Tel refused to accept this proposal. He contended that in a previous incident (in the Katamon neighborhood) the Jews had taken advantage of the lull in fighting to reorganize and afterwards conquered the entire area of Katamon. "Therefore," he contended, "this is war. I have casualties and you have casualties. I do not evacuate mine, and you do not evacuate yours." He proposed instead that we surrender according to the terms he proposed, and the delegates accepted his idea.

At the conclusion of the meeting an open, individual vote was taken. Everyone there was asked if he was for or against surrender. One after the other, they all voted for surrender, with the exception of Issar, who abstained.

Mr. Weingarten and Commander Tawil left in order to formulate the final terms. The leaders of the Legion wanted Moshe Rusnak to personally sign the document of surrender, and in the end he went out and joined the talks in which the document was being formulated. According to the recollection of those who participated in formulating it the document went as follows:

> Since the Jews requested a cease-fire, the representative of His Majesty Abdul-lah, Abdullah Bek al-Tel, presented

the following terms, which the Jews have accepted, and these are they:

1. All armaments, weapons and military equipment will be surrendered.

2. All males capable of carrying arms will be taken into captivity. It has been verbally agreed that the captives will be taken to Amman under the supervision of the United Nations commander for Jerusalem, Dr. Pablo de Azcarate.

3. All inhabitants, women and children, wounded and fighters, will be evacuated from the Jewish Quarter and taken outside the Old City under the supervision of the representative of the United Nations. Inhabitants who so wish may remain in the Quarter under the protection of the Legion and will enjoy the same rights as all other inhabitants of the Old City.

4. The signatory to this agreement on behalf of King Abdullah is responsible, in his name and in the name of his fellow officers and commanders, for the well-being of all the inhabitants taken captive and all the wounded until they arrive at their destination.

5. The conquest of the Jewish Quarter by the armies of the Arab Legion is complete.

"At approximately 14:00 hours, in the headquarters of Abdullah Bek El-Tel, I signed two copies of this document—one in Arabic and one in English," relates the military commander of the Quarter, Moshe Rusnak. "Abdullah Bek al-Tel and Dr. Azcarate also signed. Azcarate was the representative of the United Nations. I had several run-ins with him. Tel had agreed to several of my additional demands, such as the presence of a representative of the Red Cross, and I took it upon myself to invite him to come from the city, but solely because of Azcarate no representative of the Red Cross was actually present. Mr. Weingarten also wanted to sign the document. Abdullah Tel said that the signature of the commander of the Haganah was sufficient for him. Weingarten insisted and Abdullah Tel agreed. Tel took one copy and gave me the other. We returned with Abdullah Tel to the Jewish Quarter in order to execute the agreement. Since I wanted our organizations to receive the copy I had—so that they could demand that the agreement be carried out properly and could retain the historic document—I turned it over to Mr. Weingarten, while we were returning to the Quarter. I assumed that he would not be a captive, but the document did not reach its intended destination."

The first few moments after we received the news of the decision to surrender, we did not know how to react.

"You are going to Jerusalem," we said to the women enviously.

They were sad. They looked at us encouraging but with pity, "And you are journeying to Rabbat-Ammon."

The group at Batei Mahse grew larger. The inhabitants came out of their hiding places and filled the square and the courtyards, talking with one another about the terms of surrender.

Those stationed at the various posts came running to ask what their instructions were. At first the commanders themselves did not know what should be done.

When the initial confusion had passed, runners were sent to all the posts with Motke Pincas' message: "All arms are to be collected and put into the yard at Batei Mahse. Lose yourselves among the inhabitants."

When the messenger came to the position at Batei Mahse he found the guys discussing whose turn it was to clean the weapons. . . .

A few of them amused themselves with target practice. For the first time they wanted a taste of not having to conserve ammunition. . . .

Many of us washed our feet for the first time in two weeks. Those who had spare clothes, changed their garments.

Judith Jaran came into the hospital in a panic: "What's to be done? Some Arabs recognized me. They are pointing at me and whispering."

We calmed her down and found a solution: we cut her hair, put her in a nurse's uniform and she went to tend the wounded.

We were surprised by the first Arab officer who entered the hospital accompanied by two sergeants. His manner was restrained and his look was pleasant. He sat down to drink some coffee and said, "Those are the fortunes of war."

Mother saw Haim and approached him, her head bowed. Haim lifted up her face with his finger upon her chin. "Mother, I want you to laugh," he said. She smiled a moment, then tears welled up in her eyes and she began to sob.

"Don't worry," Haim comforted her. "You have other sons. Tell Yosef to take revenge upon them as much as possible. . . . I hope those outside will continue the fight."

Many of the troops who had been sent as reinforcements, mainly the older ones and the heads of families, removed their garments in the room where I was, and put on civilian clothes, especially Hassidic garments. Some went to various families in order to leave with them as family members. One succeeded.

When I left that room I suddenly met Albert, the only British soldier to have joined us on the thirteenth of May.

"What will happen to you?" I asked him.

"I spoke with the British commander of the Arab Legion," he replied, "and requested to be taken captive with you. We will go together."

At exactly 17:00 hours, when Legionnaires were already walking around the nearby rooms, the last message concerning the surrender was broadcast by wireless to Jerusalem: "We have surrendered according to the terms of evacuation. Tell Mount Zion to be prepared to receive us. Tell the hospital to prepare places. It is not clear if they intend to take captives. They are liable to take the fighters. In the meantime, it is probable that the place will be evacuated." After the departure, the office was destroyed, to the distress of Yael, the teacher, who had sat there for weeks on end, night and day, red-eyed, and Uri Golani, who had been in charge of the technical areas.

Afterwards, all the papers belonging to the Haganah and to Etzel were destroyed.

In the late afternoon hours the orders were given: "Everyone is to assemble in the yard of Batei Mahse. The wounded are to go into the hospital immediately."

A group of Legionnaires entered the Quarter in order to carry out the surrender agreement.

Abdullah Bek al-Tel, the military commander of Arab Jerusalem on behalf of the Legion, personally directed the action, in the presence of Moshe Rusnak, the commander of the Haganah in the Jewish Quarter. He looked over the group and then called out, "All the soldiers are to be separated out."

To the consternation of the entire group, the first to come forth was Reb Moshe Yitzhak, an elderly man of seventy-eight, bent over, leaning on his cane, who stepped forward very slowly. An old man like that—and a resident yet! Among the residents, especially the Ashkenazic ones, we had seen many who were not particularly positive toward us.

What he did made such a strong impression that the young men who had thought to try to sneak into Jerusalem as residents stepped forward from the group—almost all of them—some thirty-five. Motke Pincas lined them up. When the Arab commander saw the number of fighters who had stood up to his entire army he was terribly ashamed: "That is all the soldiers?" he asked. "Thirty-five men killed more than two hundred of our soldiers? Had I known that before, I would have sent in my men armed with batons."

And here he was going to have to display his captives all along the route—in the villages of Jerusalem, in Jericho, in Shuna, in A-Salt, in Amman, in Zarka and in Mifrak. What is he going to display? Thirty-five men? He will become a laughing stock. No indeed! The victory must make a strong impression in the Arab world. He commanded his troops to take every man they could see. The old, the sick, youngsters, children were all taken. When Moshe Rusnak protested, Abdullah Tel replied that he would sort them properly later.

The men were lined up and proceeded under guard.

Before the evacuation of the residents to the area outside the wall, we were asked to send someone out to the Jewish forces on Mount Zion to make contact with them. Commander Nissan Zeldas, who was appointed for that task, was summoned to Abdullah Tel and assured him that he would return. He went out with Hava Kirshenbaum, carrying a white flag. They left through Zion Gate and contacted the members of the Palmach. The next morning Nissan and Hava Kirshenbaum returned, as promised, in order to maintain the honor of the Jewish soldier.

A group of Legionnaires entered the hospital with orders to take out anyone who appeared healthy. They took any wounded man who could walk around and sent them to the group of residents who were still gathered in the yard. We sat crowded on both sides of the wide porch on piles of mattresses. Inside the wounded lay on beds or on the ground.

The row of buildings opposite hid the yard and all that happened there from our view. From afar arose a loud sound of voices which gradually became quieter until it disappeared in the distance. A strange quiet reigned. Our ears were accustomed to constant noise— to the sound of shooting, to echoes of explosions, to the explosion of shells, and now all sound disappeared and it was as if our ears were deprived of something. We seemed to continue to hear those sounds. The noise of shooting and the explosion of bullets still echoed in our ears.

Fighters from the Legionnaires and other armed groups passed between the rows of mattresses. The Arab fighters who knew the people who lived here, approached, shook hands and joked with one another. Conversations were started. The Arabs expressed their surprise, even disbelief, at the small quantity of our weapons and the small number of our soldiers.

Our people answered sharply: "It's not such a big thing to conquer a small area like ours when you have so much ammunition and so many soldiers. If we had had your arms, you wouldn't be here now."

Everything was murky. The red color of the roof opposite us was dim and mixed little by little with the yellow-rose wall. Everything was dull and gray. The windows became dark stains and the shadows of the columns and their arches stood out on the facade of the building opposite.

A red light which illuminated the wall of the next building drew my attention.

"They have lit a bonfire in the yard," someone said as if talking to himself.

Our guards sat down on chairs, leaned their rifles against the wall and looked around indolently. There was a slight breeze. Talk was frozen, only silence emerged from the depth of our hearts, memories, pictures, experiences and feelings; we were disturbed, full of questions, wanting answers, wanting to understand why and how this had ended thus. It was a time of soul searching.

An experience full of hope and pain is coming to an end. Difficulties, gratefulness, shame and glory. Yes, glory. Many of us will remember with thanks the doctors, the nurses, the medics, the women and the girls who cooked, washed and performed all kinds of services. Last but not least—the children. The doctors who tended at least four hundred cases, operated well into the night by the light of kerosene lamps, and only at dawn managed to get some sleep on the operating room floor; those who washed garments for the hospital during all the days of fighting; those who cooked, supplying three meals a day and hot drinks twenty-four hours a day! Sixteen-year-old Sarah who obtained all the needed supplies for the kitchen; the baker who managed to make pitta for us even when it was dangerous; the children, from eight to sixteen, who brought food and ammunition to the various positions and conveyed orders and information, even in the most dangerous times—tremendous work done with courage and heroism such as one sees only occasionally even among soldiers. Children—messengers—wounded and even killed. Glory to all of them!

A Generation's Dream Is Realized

Uzi Narkiss

> *General Uzi Narkiss, born in Jerusalem, served in the army for twenty-seven years and was the commanding officer of Central Command during the Six Day War; he was responsible for the battle that liberated the Old City.*

At 9:00 came Motta's [Motta Gur—ed.] message that Augusta Victoria had been captured and everyone at Binyanei Ha'ooma was seized with its impact. The time has come. We were upon the walls.

"Shall we move?" I murmured impatiently.

We moved.

The forward H.Q. group—two half-tracks and two jeeps—were waiting and in we climbed, with Didi Menussi and Raffi Amie, a Kol Israel man, whom Didi had graciously invited for "the experience of your life." We drove toward the Mandelbaum Gate, still blocked because of the mines, and therefore switched direction to the P.Ag.I. houses, taking the paratroops' assault axis to the police school. I wanted to get to the Rockefeller Museum to see Motta, since I'd had no contact with him after he announced the occupation of Augusta Victoria. We passed the East Jerusalem Y.M.C.A., whose smashed windows and besmirched walls gave bleak evidence of battle. The American Consulate on the right was also battle-scarred; a destroyed gas station stood next to the temporary memorial erected by the paratroopers to their fallen comrades. We sped by, passing an undamaged mosque and the bullet-riddled buildings in an alley, called "the Alley of Death" by paratroopers, for the fallen who had attempted to rescue their comrades.

Suddenly the [city] wall rose before us, and the battlements of Nablus Gate. The Gate was not yet ours; Legionnaires guarded the parapet and we turned back to Salah e-Din Street, where broken windows, burned automobiles, and derelict electric wires spoke of war. Opposite the Rivoli Hotel was a damaged Egged bus and several paratroopers. I asked what they were doing.

"Wounded evacuation point," one replied.

"Are there wounded?"

"Two, not seriously."

"And what's ahead?"

"Don't know. Shooting."

Another group of paratroopers halted our advance, warning about shooting at the end of the road, where Salah e-Din Street meets

The Mandelbaum Gate passage between new and old Jerusalem, 1968 (Central Zionist Archives; with permission)

Herod's Gate and the Old City walls. We could travel on it no farther and turned around, Haim Bar-Lev taking the wheel. Back on Nablus Road, we encountered all the terrible and pathetic remnants of war: death and destruction and chaos. Nothing stirred.

"I think they've all run away," I said to Bar-Lev.

The next day proved me wrong. The residents of East Jerusalem had simply hidden in their cellars, to emerge when the shooting stopped.

By 09:45 we were on Mount Scopus, gazing at the town below, which seemed idle and empty. All at once I saw smoke rising inside the Old City, behind the walls, and contacted Arik. "Are the paratroopers shelling the Old City?" When he said that they were, I ordered him to stop immediately, and at the same moment, I heard the paratroop G-Branch officer commanding his mortar units to stop shooting.

"We're going in," he cried.

"Where are you?" I called.

"At the Lions' Gate," and before the last word had been uttered we were back in our vehicles, racing down the mountain, our hearts as loud as the motors. We were going into the Old City!

Nineteen years earlier we had broken through the Zion Gate and entered the Jewish Quarter, only to leave it again in despair and bitter disappointment.

"Let us not go in if it's just to go out another time," I breathed.

"We shall never leave again," said Haim Bar-Lev.

Our convoy was on the slope of the hill below Rockefeller, where the road branches towards Gethsemane. From the corner position on the wall opposite, shots were still coming, and beneath, on the traffic island, was a silent Sherman tank and the sunshade of the policeman who was not on duty to use it.

The intermittent shots of the snipers could be heard from the walls. I threw a smoke-grenade, under cover of which we crossed to the abandoned tank, which had been hit the night before during the "Battle on the Bridge."

Snipers fired on a column of paratroopers, who marched on without changing pace, like men fatigued to the point of trance. One fell, and then another, but forward tramped the rest.

Next to the damaged tank, completely exposed, a paratrooper with a bazooka stood, legs apart, fighting a private duel with the snipers on the walls. He silenced the corner position.

We went back to the cars, abandoning the slow-moving half-tracks, and sped off in the jeeps. Ahead, on the road from the valley to the Lions' Gate, was a column of paratroopers, led by General Rabbi Shlomo Goren, Chief Army Chaplain, a *sefer Torah* under his arm, a shofar in his left hand, his beard bristling like the point of a spear, and his face bathed in perspiration. He was panting.

"Rabbi," I called out, "come aboard. We're going to the same place."

"No," he replied, "to the Temple Mount one goes on foot."

"Then we'll meet there." The jeep sprang forward. On the move I contacted Motta to find out where he was.

"The Temple Mount is ours!"

I couldn't believe it.

"I repeat," said Motta. "The Temple Mount is ours. I'm standing near the Mosque el-Omar right now. The Western Wall is a minute away."

Now was the time for the jeep to sprout wings, but at the moment it lacked not just wings but one of its wheels. Bang, and the jeep veered so sharply that only with all my strength could I stop it before it tumbled off the road. The tire was in shreds. We had no time or inclination to change. We crowded into the second jeep, leaving Yoel Herzl with the radio, thus cutting ourselves off from contact and the possibility of finding out what was going on. But, more important, we drove up the narrow road toward Lions' Gate. On the square in front of it an Arab bus was steadily burning. Electric cables were down. Legionnaires' bodies lay all around; a section of the gate had been torn from its hinges; the second section was flung open, and the arch above the Gate had been hit, so that its loose masonry threatened the heads of passers-by. But the carved lions were undamaged.

We drove through, along the road to the Gate of the Tribes and the Temple Mount, and down the Via Dolorosa to the second arch. It was blocked by the lead tank of the paratroopers. We climbed over it and continued on foot.

Yoel, behind us, picked off a sniper shooting at us from one of the houses. Except for that, the Via Dolorosa was cool and silent, the windows shuttered, the streets empty. Had our men been through here, I wondered. Beyond the second arch lay King Feisal Street, a brief, narrow, covered, tunnel-like lane, closed at the far end by a wide gate with a small wicket where pedestrians entered. This, too, was closed, but the bolt was not locked. We stepped through, and the breath caught in our throats.

We beheld the huge paved courtyard, crowned, against the blue sky of June 7th, 1967 (the 28th of the month of Iyar in the year 5727), by the golden cupola of the Dome of the Rock, gleaming, glistening, taking its gold from the sun.

A spectacle of legend.

We ran toward Motta Gur, standing on the Mount, where the flag of Israel flew. We were joined first by Moshe Stempel, Motta's deputy, and then by Rabbi Goren. We embraced and the Rabbi prostrated himself and genuflected toward the Holy of Holies. In a resonant voice he recited the ancient Prayer to Battle (Deut. 20:3–4):

> Hear, O Israel, ye approach this day into battle against
> your enemies; let not your hearts faint, fear not, and do
> not tremble, neither be ye terrified because of them; for
> the Lord your God is he that goeth with you, to fight for
> you against your enemies, to save you!

Hastily, I visited the Mosque and was delighted to find no damage, except to a glass door from the brief battle in the courtyard. There had apparently been resistance from inside. As the cleaning up continued, I told Motta once again to make sure that no holy places or shrines were touched.

We made our excited way through the streets to the Mugrabis' Gate, along a dim alley, turned right down a slight of steps, impatiently faced another right turn—and there it was. The Western Wall. I quivered with memory. Tall and awesome and glorious, with the same ferns creeping between the great stones, some of them inscribed.

Silently I bowed my head. In the narrow space were paratroopers, begrimed, fatigued, overburdened with weapons. And they wept. They were not "wailing at the Western Wall," not lamenting in the fashion familiar during the Wall's millennia of being. These were tears of joy, of love, of passion, of an undreamed first reunion with the ancient monument to devotion and to prayer. They clung to its stones, kissed them, these rough, battle-weary paratroopers, their lips framing the *Shema*. Returned, it seemed to the Temple. . . .

But more exalted, prouder than all of them, was Rabbi Goren. Wrapped in a *Tallit* (prayer shawl), blowing the ram's horn, and roaring like a lion: "Blessed be the Lord God, Comforter of Zion and Builder of Jerusalem, Amen!" Suddenly he saw me, embraced me, and planted a ringing kiss on my cheek, a signal to everyone to hug and kiss and join hands. The Rabbi, like one who had waited all his life for this moment, intoned the *Kaddish*, the *El moleh Rahamim* (O God, full of mercy . . .), in memory of those who had fallen in the name of the Lord to liberate the Temple, the Temple Mount and Jerusalem the City of the Lord: "May they find their peace in Heaven . . . and let us say Amen."

The restrained weeping became sobs, full-throated, an uncurbed emotional outburst. Sorrow, fervor, happiness and pain combined to produce this mass of grieving and joyous men, their cheeks wet, their voices unsteady. Again the *shofar* was blown: *tekiya* (a short, but unbroken sound), followed by the *shevarim* (a short but tremolo sound). And Rabbi Goren intoned, like a herald: "This year, at this hour, in Jerusalem!" (*le-shana hazot, be-sha'a hazot, beYerushalayim.*)

Until that moment I had thought I was immune to anything. Even the stones responded. "We shall stand at attention and salute!

Attention!" I shouted. "And sing *Hatikva*," came the choked voice
of Haim Bar-Lev. We started to sing. To our voices were added those
of the paratroopers, hoarse and indistinct. Sobbing and singing, it
was as though, through the *Hatikva*, we could unburden our hearts of
their fullness and our spirits of their emotion.

We spent ten minutes in front of the Western Wall and at 10:55
were on our way back to the basement of Binyanei Ha'ooma. There
was plenty of work to be done. The Old City had not yet been
cleared of snipers, and the West Bank had not yet been taken.

Meanwhile, we learned, the Jerusalem Brigade had at the last
minute made an improvised entry into the Old City through the Dung
Gate. Amos, the G-Branch officer, having heard the 55th Brigade's
announcement that Augusta Victoria had been taken, realized that
the paratroops would immediately break into the Old City and determined that Zahal's Jerusalem Brigade, which for nineteen years had
defended the divided city, must participate in that historic entry. Two
companies of the battalion which took Abu-Tor were assembled at
Mount Zion and moved along the Walls to the Silwan stream to enter
through the Dung Gate. They reached the Temple Mount shortly after
10 A.M. and from there turned westwards. . . .

At Binyanei Ha'ooma an Order-of-the-Day was born:

> We are standing on your threshold, Jerusalem. Today we
> entered your gates. Jerusalem, city of David and Solomon,
> is in our hands.
>
> This morning, in the shadow of the Western Wall, we
> sang *Hatikva*, we mourned our dead, fallen in the battle for
> the city.
>
> Troops of the Command, brave fighters, devoted war-
> riors, this day and your valor shall be in our hearts forever.
> —Major General Uzi Narkiss

REDEEMING THE VOW

Rabbi Shlomo Goren

> *Shlomo Goren (1917–1994) was born in Poland and came to the Land of Israel with his family in 1925. After studying at Hebron Yeshiva, he joined the Hagana in 1936 and became a chaplain during the War of Independence. He later served as Chief Ashkenazi Rabbi of Israel.*

Soldiers of Israel, beloved of your people, crowned with valor and victory!

God be with you, valiant warriors!

I am speaking to you from the Western Wall, remnant of our Holy Temple.

"Comfort, oh comfort My people, says your God" (Isa. 40:1).

This is the day for which we have hoped, let us be glad and rejoice in His salvation.

The dream of all the generations has been fulfilled before our eyes. The City of God, the Temple site, the Temple Mount, and the Western Wall—symbol of the Jewish People's Messianic Redemption—have been delivered this day by you, heroes of the Israel Defense Forces.

This day you have redeemed the vow of the generations: "If I forget you, O Jerusalem, let my right hand wither" (Pss. 137:5). We did not forget you, Jerusalem, our Holy City, home of our glory. And it is Your right hand, the right hand of God, that has wrought this historic deliverance.

Whose is the heart that will not exult at hearing those tidings of redemption? Henceforth the gates of Zion and of Old Jerusalem, and the paths to the Western Wall, are open for the prayers of their children, their builders and their liberators in the Land of Israel, and to the Jews of the Dispersion who may now come there to pray.

Rabbi Shlomo Goren, then Chief Chaplain of the Army, blowing the shofar at the Wall, June 1967 (Israel Government Press Office; with permission)

The Divine Presence, which has never forsaken the Western Wall, is now marching in the van of the legions of Israel in a pillar of fire to illuminate our path to victory, and is emblazoning us with clouds of glory before the Jewish people of the entire world. Happy are we that we have been privileged to earn this, the most exalted hour in the history of our people.

To the nations of the world we declare: we shall respectfully protect the holy places of all faiths, and their doors shall be open to all.

Beloved soldiers, dear sons of your people! To you has befallen the greatest privilege of Jewish history. There is now being fulfilled the prayer of the ages and the vision of the prophets: "For You, O God, didst destroy her in fire, and You will surely build her up again in fire, as it is written: 'And I Myself—declares the Lord—will be a wall of fire all around it, and I will be a glory inside it' (Zech. 2:9). Blessed are You, O Lord, consoler of Zion and builder of Jerusalem."

And to Zion and to the remnant of our Temple we say: Your children have returned to their borders, our feet now stand within your gates, Jerusalem: city bounded together once more with New Jerusalem; city that is "perfect of beauty and joy of the whole earth," capital city of the eternal State of Israel.

In the name of the entire community of Jewry in Israel and in the diaspora, and with joy sublime, I herewith pronounce the blessing: "Blessed are You, O Lord our God, King of the Universe, who has kept us alive and sustained us and brought us to this day."

Next year in rebuilt Jerusalem!

June 7, 1967

THE SEVENTH DAY

After the Six Day War a remarkable book was compiled by Kibbutz members, consisting of conversations with soldiers who expressed their feelings concerning the overwhelming events in which they had participated. The Hebrew name of the volume was Siach Lohamim—"Soldiers' Talk." The following excerpts were taken from the English version of that book.

LIKE A PSALM OF PRAISE

A LETTER BY ELIEZER

I was lucky that I served with the paratroop brigade that liberated Jerusalem. I believe that the hand of God was in my participation in the battle for the liberation of and reunion of Jerusalem. I see in it the hand of God, for ever since I reached maturity, and especially since I joined the army thirteen years ago, I've had a constant desire to take part in a war for the liberation of Jerusalem. On the other hand, this contradicted my social and political belief in the need for a dialogue with the Arabs as a basis for peace. But my yearnings to fight for the liberation of Jerusalem were above and beyond my political ideas.

Fears, natural in the face of possible death, were replaced by a great pride. I felt jubilant, here I was about to fight—and perhaps to die—for Jerusalem. Do you know the significance of Jerusalem for a religious man who prays three times a day: "And return speedily to Jerusalem, Thy city, in mercy, and dwell within it as Thou hast spoken"? . . . The Western Wall was never an archaeological site as far as I was concerned, not even a "holy place" as it's officially called. My education, my prayers and my longings transform Jerusalem in its entirety into an organic part of my very being, of my whole life. . . .

I felt as if I had been granted the great privilege of acting as an agent of God, of Jewish history. Because of all the great tension and turmoil of the war, I didn't at first have the time to think about the experiences and feelings of the other soldiers. But the atmosphere was full of a sense of greatness and holiness. We were in the Rockefeller Museum, just before we took the Temple Mount, and I asked a fellow soldier, a man born in Kibbutz Sha'ar Ha'amakim, what he thought of it all. He answered me with a verse from the

Bible: "I was glad when they said unto me, let us go unto the house of the Lord. Our feet shall stand within Thy gates, O Jerusalem. Jerusalem is builded as a city that is compact together." He smiled as he spoke, perhaps because it's not "fitting" for a member of HaShomer Hatzair [an extremely left-wing, secular group—ed.] to talk this way. But I saw his eyes, and I knew that that was how he really felt.

When we broke into the Old City and I went up to the Temple Mount and later to the Western Wall, I looked searchingly at the officers and the other soldiers. I saw their tears, their wordless prayers, and I knew they felt as I did: a deep feeling for the Temple Mount where the Temple once stood, and love for the Wall on whose stones so many generations have wept. I understood that it wasn't only I and my religious friends who sensed its greatness and sanctity; the others felt it too, no less deeply and strongly. It was easier for me to define my feelings, because I had my *tefillin* in my pack (perhaps King Solomon wore ones just like these when he built the Temple) and in my pocket there was the book of psalms written by David, the King of Jerusalem.

As I stood weeping by the Wall, there wept with me my father, my grandfather and my great-grandfather, all of them born in a Land of Israel where they needed Abdulla's permission to pray at the Wall. As I caressed its stones, I felt the warmth of those Jewish hearts which had warmed them with a warmth that will for ever endure.

I saw my friends, kibbutz-educated toward an attitude of scorn for traditional religious values, now overwhelmed by a feeling of holiness, and as elated and moved as I was. Then I saw the proof of what I had previously assumed, that there is in all of us, religious and non-religious alike, in the entire Jewish people, an intense quality of Jewishness that is neither destroyed by education nor blurred by foreign ideologies and values. The morning after the battle I said my morning prayers on the Temple Mount, and as the sun rose over liberated Jerusalem I lingered over the verse, "And may a new light dawn over Zion and may we speedily merit its radiance."

TONIGHT WE'RE MAKING HISTORY: A DISCUSSION

MICHA: I'm not a very emotional person about this sort of business. But I do remember how this whole question of Jerusalem gripped us. We certainly saw it as something special. I can truly say that I remember thinking that we were about to do something of real importance, of historical significance. That's how we put it to one another, "Tonight we're going into the Old City and it's . . ."

DANI: "Tonight we're making history. . . ."

MICHA: Yes. Without question. Apart from the fact that the whole war was something of historic significance, Jerusalem was extra special. . . . Look, I don't want to destroy any legends, but it wasn't as earth-shaking as it looked from the evening papers that day. It's true that some people were very moved; that for some of them it was something special. Lots of boys who hadn't had much to do with Judaism and weren't at all religious said that this war had made them feel that the Jewish people is something special. They appreciated the meaning of the verse: "Thou hast chosen us." I heard a lot of people say that. But I also heard lots of them say that it didn't mean anything to them. To them it was merely the climax of a specific assignment, without any Jewish significance. Historical significance, yes; but not something specifically Jewish.

I remember that one of the things I thought about later on, something that really affected me, was the business of Giora, our company commander. He was killed right next to me, near the Wall. One evening, we'd had a big 'do' in the amphitheatre on Mount Scopus. We sang "Jerusalem of Iron," and there were some professional artists. It was all very impressive, the moment itself, the background, the place and all that—and that was when I thought about Giora. Why wasn't he here with us? It's what one generally thinks at these moments. I really was very moved then. But in the middle of the fighting—when it happened, I remember that my only thought was that now I had to carry on and continue to advance, without saying a word to any of the men. Just not tell any of them—only tell them when it's all over. Some of them were completely broken up by the news.

DANI: If you were to ask me what day the Old City was taken on, I wouldn't be able to tell you. We'd crossed the border without a single radio, so we didn't hear about it immediately. But when we did find out, there was a truly spontaneous reaction. Most of the men began dancing around, jumping on and off the vehicles, under them, hugging one another. It was like being in exile and suddenly hearing that Jerusalem was ours. I had very mixed feelings about it. On the one hand, it didn't mean anything to me; on the other hand, it showed we'd given them a beating. I knew that one was supposed to feel pleased about it. But I wasn't specially happy about taking Port Tawafik. I wasn't even specially happy that Jerusalem had been taken in this fantastic way. I didn't feel particularly excited. . . . They asked me, "Is it true about the Wall?" And I said, "Okay, so what? We've taken Port Tawafik too!" I'll tell you something: holy or not, it left me cold.

MICHA: Morning prayers at the Wall were very awe-inspiring. All the time I kept thinking that the Wall symbolized the Jewish people's yearning for unity, its deep roots in the country; that we represented a whole people, a whole history. It meant a lot to me. I can't say that I felt any deep spiritual link with the stones themselves. It isn't like that. People don't realize that Judaism doesn't attach any sanctity to places as such. For example, the Bible says about Moses' burial place, "And no one knew where he was buried." For the same reason,

there's nothing holy about the Wall. But for us, the Wall's really—
what I saw before me was the realization of our people's unity, of their
longing, of the whole Jewish people. Not that particular place, but
what it means to the whole Jewish people. . . .

THE LIONS' GATE

> *The following selections are taken from another book compiled
> after the Six Day War,* The Lion's Gate *(Hebrew), edited by
> Yisrael Harel, consisting of reminiscences by members of the
> Parachute Brigade who conquered the Wall.*

FEAR AND TREMBLING

MOSHE AMIRAV

It is with a smile that I remember how we looked for the Wall. We
ran there, a group of panting soldiers, lost on the plaza of the Temple
Mount, searching for a giant stone wall. We did not stop to look at
the Mosque of Omar even though this was the first time we had seen
it close up. Forward! Forward! Hurriedly, we pushed our way through
the Magreb Gate and suddenly we stopped, thunderstruck. There it
was before our eyes! Gray and massive, silent and restrained. The
Western Wall! I remember that I had such a feeling only once before
in my life; it had been when I was a child when my father brought
me near to the Holy Ark in the synagogue. I, a little infant, had been
afraid that something would come out of the Ark, something big and
terrible from another world. . . .

Slowly, slowly I began to approach the Wall in fear and trembling
like a pious cantor going to the lectern to lead the prayers. I
approached it as the messenger of my father and my grandfather, of
my great-grandfather and of all generations in all the exiles who had

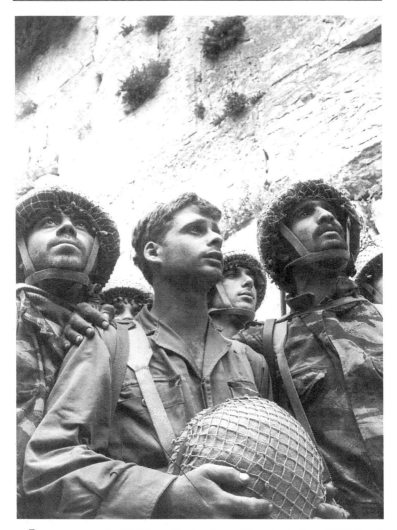

Paratroopers at the Wall immediately after its liberation in June 1967 (Israel Government Press Office; with permission)

never merited seeing it and so they had sent me to represent them. Somebody recited the festive blessing: "Blessed are You, O Lord our God, King of the universe who has kept me alive, and maintained us and brought us to this time," but I could not answer "Amen." I put my hand on the stone and the tears that started to flow were not my tears—they were the tears of all Israel, tears of hope and prayer, tears of hasidic tunes, tears of Jewish dances, tears which scorched and burned the heavy gray stone.

AT THE WESTERN WALL

Elie Wiesel

> *Nobel Prize winning author Elie Wiesel was born in Romania in 1928 and was imprisoned in various concentration camps. After the war he lived first in Paris and then in New York. His feelings about the events of the Six Day War led to the writing of his novel* Beggar in Jerusalem. *The following is a personal account he wrote of his visit to Jerusalem at the end of that war.*

They tell me this is the Wall.

No, I don't believe it. I am not able—I am afraid to believe it. Deep down, of course, I realize that they are right, that indeed it is the very Wall—which Jew cannot recognize it instantly! Yet I cannot believe that it is I—I who now stands before it, gazing as if in a dream, breathlessly confronting it as though it were a living being, ominipotent, all knowing, master of the secrets of the universe . . . above time, a being that bears me to a strange and distant world, where each stone has its own will, fate and memory. . . . I cannot believe that it is I who has conceived such stormy fantasies, that it is I who now trembles like a wisp of the wind!

I feel a weird sensation. . . . This is the first time that I am here,

Crowds coming from the Wall soon after the end of the Six Day War in 1967; note the tractors and bulldozers used to clear the plaza area (Central Zionist Archives; with permission)

yet I feel that I was at this very spot before. I have already seen these Jews, have heard their prayers. Every shape seems familiar, every sound as though it has arisen from the depths of my own past. But there is a difference. Before there were no young men and women milling about in uniforms. . . . What are they doing here? And why are they crying? I do not know. They themselves neither know nor say. They see nothing—except the Wall before them. But it is theirs, for it is they who bore it on their shoulders year after year and generation after generation. And their tears—their tears are the Wall's.

Indeed, the coverage of this war should be handled not only by newspaper columnists and military experts but by poets and kabbalists as well—for what has happened cannot be described in neat, logical terms.

Even if we knew every last detail of the war, we would still not understand what happened; even if all the military and political secrets were suddenly disclosed, we could not measure the great mystery in which we are encloaked as if by the command of the Almighty Himself.

There are those who speak of *Hasgacha Elyona*, Divine Providence and of the merit of our forefathers which protected us. And there are the rationalists who are willing to consider just the possibility of miracles. But there is no officer I've met who has not agreed that there are aspects to what has happened that dry intellect alone will never grasp.

Even the "freethinkers" interpret the experience as organically a religious one—it has compelled each Jew to confront his people, his past and his God.

To borrow the language of the rabbis: the enemy prophesied, but didn't understand his own prophecy. It was total, for he was defeated not only by the soldiers and officers of an army—he was defeated by the totality of Jewish history itself! Two thousand years of suffering, longing and hope were mobilized for the battle, just as the millions of martyrs of the holocaust were enlisted to the ranks. Like the biblical pillars of fire they came and shielded their spiritual heirs. What enemy could ever conquer them?

The words and phrases our enemy used caused the memory of the holocaust to defeat him. He did not realize that there are words which are forbidden to be uttered, not in our generation, not in regard to the Jewish people. . . . He didn't realize that a person can bring destruction on himself not only in one moment, as our rabbis of old tell us, but with one word!

He was too quick, too fast to threaten the destruction of Israel, and this was a monumental blunder.

True, the world community was not moved very much by his threats, but the Jewish nation throughout the globe shuddered and rose like one alongside the Jewish State, which for two weeks lay under heavy siege. A few words by Nasser was enough to make the situation a fight for survival of the whole Jewish people.

This time the soldiers of Israel felt they were not alone. Behind them were organized hundreds of wealthy and dedicated communities.

University students flooded embassies to enlist for the fight; the Hassidim of Williamsburg declared days of fasts and prayer; youngsters from assimilated homes organized fund raising drives and joined in protests; millionaires cast aside their businesses and took off for Jerusalem; community leaders went sleepless night after night because of the great efforts and profound anxiety. Never was the Jewish people so united, never so moved and anxious, never so ready and prepared to offer and sacrifice everything it had, its "might, heart and soul."

I know oldsters who withdrew their last savings from the bank and donated them to Israel; I know young students who cast away their studies and tests and joined in the fight; I know men who had stood "outside the Jewish camp," who had drifted from their people but now returned to it: more than one apostate took upon himself the yoke of Judaism anew because he now wanted to identify with his people. The miracle which took place among our people throughout their vast dispersion was as great as the miracle within the land itself.

Thus, it is only justice that mystics and poets have a hand in writing the history of our deeds. . . .

I try to understand, to believe—I succeed a bit . . . but the truth is, I still don't understand. The more the professional experts try to explain—the less I understand. It all seems like an ancient legend; as though we had all gone far, far back to the past. Perhaps that's why I have an almost palpable feeling of victory—we have conquered time itself! And my generation is not privileged to boast many such victories.

However, let's not fool ourselves. The world already envies our victory. Already we can hear the strident voices. . . . Israel is being extreme with its "hard" stance, some declare. Israel should show special patience, forgiveness and magnanimity towards her enemies, suggest others. There will be pressures, attempts to squeeze out of us this or that compromise. Even our "friends" are not likely to forgive that we were victorious—that it was such an impolite, swift victory, so complete, so magnificent. It is understandable. We have suddenly stripped them of the chance to pity us or even help us.

No, the war is continuing and will continue a long, long time. Except that now it will be fought with words. Let Israel's spokesmen, who must deal with the diplomats, ministers and heads of state, make certain not to surrender to the fine rules of "logic." The events that took place have finally freed Israel from the paralyzing chains of "logic." Let the world know: two plus two equals two thousand years when the subject is the Wall and its stones. Even the Almighty cannot allow what has happened to become as though it had not happened.

STRANGE CITY

Amos Oz

> *One of Israel's best-known writers and peace activists, Amos Oz was born in Jerusalem in 1939. Although from the age of fourteen he made his home in Kibbutz Hulda, he often chooses Jerusalem as a setting for his fiction. This piece, however, is a reflection about the city that appeared in* The Seventh Day.

I was born in Jerusalem and lived there throughout my childhood; when I was nine I lived through the days when Jerusalem was besieged and shelled. It was then that I first saw a dead man: a shell fired from the Arab Legion's gun batteries on Nebi Samuel hit a pious Jew and tore his stomach apart. I saw him lying in the street. He was a small man whose chin sprouted a meagre beard. His face, as he lay there dead, was white and amazed. It was July 1948. For many days afterwards I hated that man because he kept appearing in my dreams and frightening me. I knew that Jerusalem was surrounded by forces whose only desire was the city's death and mine, too.

Later I moved away from Jerusalem. I still loved her with a stubborn love as one might love a woman who holds aloof. Sometimes on my free days I would go to Jerusalem to pay court to her. Her alleyways knew me well though they affected not to.

I loved Jerusalem because she was journey's end, a city one arrived at but could never pass beyond; and also because she was never really a true part of the State of Israel; with the exception of a few roads Jerusalem has always held herself aloof, as if she had consciously chosen to turn her back on all the flat white commercial cities: Tel Aviv, Holon, Herzlia and Nethanya.

Jerusalem was different. She was the absolute negation of towns made up of cube-like blocks of flats, all painted white. She was different from the flat stretches of citrus groves, the gardens surrounded by hedges, the red roofs and irrigation pipes shining in the sun. Even the blue of her summer skies was different. Not for her the dusty white heavens of the coastal plain and the Sharon valley. An enclosed city. Wintry. Even in the summer it was always a wintry city. Rusty iron railings. Grey stone, sometimes imperceptibly shading into pale blue, sometimes into a reddish hue. Tumbledown fences. Rocky hillsides. Walled courtyards, closed in as if in anger.

And its citizens: a silent people, bitter as if for ever overcoming some inner fear. Observant Jews. Ashkenazi Jews in their fur *streimels* and old Sephardim in their striped robes. Soft-stepping scholars wandering through the streets, as if at a loss. Dreamy-eyed girls. Blind beggars, dumb or cursing. Madmen abroad with the divine spark in their eyes.

For twenty years Jerusalem turned her stubborn back on the stream of modern life. A slow-moving town in a country of feverish activity. An old, neglected mountainous suburb whose few flat stretches, crammed with buildings, burst at the seams with overflowing energy. The sad capital city of an exultant state. And the stranglehold. There were mutilated streets descending to blocked alleys. Barricades of concrete and rusty barbed wire. A city which is all border. A city not of gold but of tin sheeting, bent and full of holes. A city surrounded at night by the sound of foreign bells, foreign odours, distant views. A ring of hostile villages surrounded the city on three sides: Sha'afat, Wadi Jos, Issawia, Silwan, Azaria, Tsur Bachr, Bet Tsafafa. It seemed as if they had only to clench their hand and Jerusalem would be crushed within their fist. On a winter night you could sense the evil intent that flowed from them toward the city.

There was fear too in Jerusalem. An inner fear that must never be expressed in words, never called by name. It grew, solidified and crystallized in the twisting alleyways and the desolate lanes.

The city fathers, the heads of government, the housing estates, the newly planted trees, the traffic lights, all tried to tempt Jerusalem into a union with the State of Israel; and she, with the exception of some few streets, refused that union. Twenty years. Jerusalem continued to preserve a faded, obstinate Mandatory character. She remained sad.

Not within the State of Israel, but alongside it; Jerusalem as opposed to Israel.

I loved this town, because I was born there and because people who stand aloof tend to love towns which hold aloof.

This was a love which was received without mercy: Jerusalem was often the background for nightmares and dreams of terror. I no longer live in Jerusalem, but in my dreams I am hers and she does not relinquish her hold on me. I would see us both surrounded by enemies. The enemy in my dreams came not only from east, north and south, but completely surrounded us. I saw Jerusalem falling into the hands of her enemies. Destroyed, pillaged and burned, as in the stories of my childhood, as in the Bible, as in the tales of the destruction of the Temple. And I too, with no way of escape, with no place to hide, was trapped in the Jerusalem of my dreams.

Many were the stories I was told as a child of Jerusalem under siege. Jewish children always died in these stories. They died heroically, or were slaughtered, but the stories always ended with the town burning and the children dying. Sennacherib, Titus, the Crusaders. Riots, terrorists. Military rule. The High Commissioner, searches, curfew. Abdullah, the desert king. The guns of the Arab Legion. The convoy to Mount Scopus. The convoy to the Etzion bloc. An incited rabble. Inflamed mobs. Blood-thirsty ruffians. Brutal armed irregulars. All forever aimed at me. I always belonged to the minority, to the besieged, to those whose fate was sealed, who lived a life hovering on the brink of disaster.

So this time too, the city will be attacked. We shall die there like that little pious Jew who lay in the street, his face pale and amazed, as if he had suffered some grave insult. And more.

After the siege was lifted, a border was drawn though the heart of the city. All my childhood was passed in dead-end alleyways, facing streets one was forbidden to enter. The scar of destruction, no-man's-land, mine fields, wasteland, ruined, blackened buildings. Twisted, despairing iron girders rising starkly out of her ruined houses. And ever opposite: the other Jerusalem. The city surrounding my city. Foreign sounds and smells emanated from it, pale lights flickered there by night, and the cry of the muezzin at dawn. Atlantis. The lost continent. A city which was forever the focus of one's most insubstantial visions. I had blurred memories dating from my earliest childhood, the memory of colourful alleyways in the Old City, the narrow arched street leading to the Wall, Mandatory Arab policemen, street-vendors' stalls, tamarind, a riot of colour, an ever-present sense of lurking danger.

From over there, from beyond the border, an angry threat has been directed at me throughout most of my life. I remember wandering down the streets of Musrara at dusk, to the edge of no-man's-land. A glimpse of Schneller Woods from afar. Forbidden views seen from the observation point at Abu Tor. The shattered square of Notre Dame. The towers of Bethlehem opposite the woods of Ramat Rachel. Desert hillsides falling away from the suburb of Talpiyot. The Dead Sea glittering in the distance like a mirage. Rocky valleys at dawn.

On Sunday, 11 June 1967, I went to see the Jerusalem that lay beyond the border. I came to places which with dreams and the years had become petrified symbols within my heart, and lo and behold—people lived there—houses, shops, stalls, signposts.

And I was thunderstruck, as if my whole inner world had collapsed. The dreams were a deception. The world of terrible tales became a mockery. The perpetual threat was nothing but a cruel, twisted joke. Everything was burst asunder. Laid wide open. My Jerusalem, beloved and feared, was dead.

Now the town was different. Long-forgotten, neglected corners had come to life again. Bulldozers pushed new roads through heaps of rubble which I had imagined would be there for all eternity. Districts which had been utterly forgotten were filled with feverish activity. Hosts of pious Jews, soldiers in battledress, amazed tourists, smartly dressed women from Tel Aviv and Haifa, all streamed eastward. The tide flowed strongly to Jerusalem. The rest of the country poured into the open city. Everything within her orbit took an air of festivity. And I along with it.

These things cannot be expressed in words. Again I say that I loved Jerusalem in its entirety, but what does it mean? It is like a love affair, a contradictory, tortuous force: she is mine and yet strange to me, conquered but hostile, devoted yet inaccessible.

I could disregard all this. The skies are the same skies and the Jerusalem stone is the same throughout. Sheikh Jarrah is almost like Katamon.

But the city is inhabited. People live within her streets, and they are strangers. I do not understand their language; they are there—in their homes—and I am the stranger who comes from without. Courteous people, courteous to the point of offense, as if they have reached the very peak of happiness in having merited the honour of selling me postcards or Jordanian stamps. Welcome, we are brothers, it is just for you alone that we have waited all these years, just so that we could embrace you. And their eyes hate me, wish me dead. The accursed stranger. It grieves me, but I cannot order my words in a rational way.

I was in East Jerusalem three days after the conquest of the city. I arrived there straight from El Arish, in Sinai, wearing uniform and carrying a sub-machine gun. I was not born to sound the trumpet or liberate lands from foreign yokes. The lament of an enslaved people finds an echo in my ears, but I am deaf to the lament of "enslaved territory."

In my childhood dreams it was the Arabs who wore uniforms and carried machine-guns. Arabs who came to my street in Jerusalem to kill me. Twenty-two years ago, a slogan painted in red appeared on a courtyard wall not far from our house: "Judah fell in blood and fire;

by blood and fire will Judah rise again." One of the underground had written these words at night in burning red. I don't know how to write about blood and fire. If ever I write anything about this war, it will be about pus, sweat and vomit and not about blood and fire. With all my soul, I desired to feel in Jerusalem as a man who has dispossesed his enemies and returned to the patrimony of his ancestors. The Bible came to life for me: the Prophets, the Kings, Temple Mount, Absolom's Pillar, the Mount of Olives. The Jerusalem of Abraham Mapu and Agnon. I wanted to be part of it all, I wanted to belong.

Were it not for the people. I saw enmity and rebelliousness, sycophany, amazement, fear, insult and trickery. I passed through the streets of East Jerusalem like a man breaking into some forbidden place. Depression filled my soul.

City of my birth. City of my dreams. City of my ancestors' and my peoples' yearnings. And I was condemned to walk through its streets armed with a sub-machine gun like one of the characters from my childhood nightmares. To be a stranger in a very strange city.

Jerusalem of My Childhood

Muki Tzur

> *Born in Jerusalem, Muki Tzur is a member of Kibbutz Ein Gev. A prominent writer and educator, he served as the Secretary of the United Kibbutz Movement.*

The nocturne of Jerusalem which accompanied my childhood sounds again in my ears in these post-war days. Again I hear the whistle of the wind blown through the thousands of pine needles. Again I see the grey stone, the cramped alleyways which sought not breadth but only height, the narrow strip of sky high above, the heavy iron balconies, the bridges, the water tanks, the laundry blowing pennant-like in the backyards.

The days of the siege which filled my childhood come back again to me. Father helping us to fill sacks of earth to barricade the window-sill. Running off to school to see the Palmach soldiers; the sound of their evening sing-songs before they went out on duty. The onions which all the children planted in the gardens in an attempt to stave off the hunger of the siege. The refugees from the Old City who fled to the stone Arab houses of Katamon.

I remember a time when I cried: the tears I shed over the fall of the Etzion bloc. I couldn't grasp how it could possibly have been taken by the Arabs. "But they're heroes," I wept in despair. So my father explained that knowing how to face defeat was part of the process of war. Many are the faces that flash before me now: the soft-drink vendor and his shiny steel barrel, the old lady who would bring a basket of strawberries or figs to the corner of the road and weigh them up with stone weights.

Yes, these days have brought back many a picture of the city, of the far-off days of explosions and tears and happiness, homesickness and many dormant question-marks. Sometime I still hear my father's voice, in other words, but with the same tone, "In a war, my child, you have to know how to be victorious."

JERUSALEM—A CHARISMATIC CITY

Abraham Joshua Heschel

> *One of the great spiritual leaders of American Jewry, Abraham Joshua Heschel (1907–1972) came to America in 1940. He wrote numerous volumes on Jewish life and philosophy and taught at the Jewish Theological Seminary. Immediately after the Six Day*

War he visited Israel and wrote his impressions in the book from which this excerpt is taken, Israel: An Echo of Eternity.

In our own days the miracle has occurred. Jerusalem has proclaimed loudly: "My beloved is mine, and I am his!"

What happened on June 7, 1967? God's compassion has prevailed. So many devastations. Thousands of communities wiped out. Synagogues burned, people asphyxiated. No tombstones, no graves, all monuments meaningless.

In its solitude the Wall was forced into the role of an unreachable tombstone for the nameless dead. Suddenly the Wall, tired of tears and lamentations, became homesick for song. "O come, let us sing to the Lord, let us chant in joy to the rock of our salvation!" (Pss. 95:1). It will be called the Rejoicing Wall.

THE WALL

The Wall . . . At first I am stunned. Then I see: a Wall of frozen tears, a cloud of sighs.

Palimpsests, hiding books, secret names. The stones are seals.

The Wall . . . The old mother crying for all of us. Stubborn, loving, waiting for redemption. The ground on which I stand is Amen. My words become echoes. All of our history is waiting here.

No comeliness to be acclaimed, no beauty to be relished. But a heart and an ear. Its very being is compassion. You stand still and hear: stones of sorrow, acquaintance with grief. We all hide our faces from agony, shun the afflicted. The Wall is compassion, its face is open only to those smitten with grief.

So tough, so strong, so tenacious. How she survived the contempt of ages! For centuries while garbage was heaped in her front to cover her face, she remained impervious to desecration, mighty, of mysterious majesty in the midst of scorn.

So many different rulers held sway over the city, so many cataclysmic changes, so many upheavals, so many eruptions of passion came to pass—the Wall kept a silent watch. ". . . A thousand years in thy sight are but as yesterday when it is past, or as a watch in the night" (Pss. 90:4).

"Behold, I made him a witness to the peoples" (Isa. 55:4). These stones have a heart, a heart for all men. The Wall has a soul that radiates a presence.

When Jerusalem was destroyed, we were driven out and like sheep have gone astray; we have turned every one to his own way. The Wall alone stayed on.

What is the Wall? The unceasing marvel. Expectation. The Wall will not perish. The redeemer will come.

Silence. I hug the stones; I pray. O, Rock of Israel, make our faith strong and Your words luminous in our hearts and minds. No image. Pour holiness into our moments.

The Wall is silent? For an instant I am her tongue. Then I hear: I am a man of unclean lips. . . . O God, cleanse my lips, make me worthy to be her tongue. . . .

Suddenly ancient anticipations are resurrected in me. Centuries went and came. Then a moment arrived and stood still, facing me.

Once you have lived a moment at the Wall, you never go away.

NEXT YEAR IN JERUSALEM!

Anatoly Shcharansky

> *Anatoly Shcharansky, one of the most famous of all Jewish refuseniks, spoke movingly of Jerusalem when he was sentenced by a Soviet court after being accused of treason in 1977.*

Five years ago, I submitted my application for exit to Israel. Now I am further than ever from my dream. It would seem to be cause for regret. But it is absolutely otherwise. I am happy. I am happy that I lived honestly, in peace with my conscience. I never compromised my soul, even under the threat of death.

I am happy that I helped people. I am proud that I knew and worked with such honest, brave and courageous people as Sakharov, Orlov, Ginsburg, who are carrying on the traditions of Russian intelligentsia. I am fortunate to have been witness to the process of the liberation of Russia's Jews.

I hope that the absurd accusation against me and the entire Jewish emigration movement will not hinder the liberation of my people. My near ones and friends know how I wanted to exchange activity in the emigration movement for a life with my wife, Avital, in Israel.

For more than two thousand years the Jewish people, my people, have been dispersed. But wherever they are, wherever Jews are found, every year they have repeated, "Next year in Jerusalem." Now, when I am further than ever from my people, from Avital, facing many arduous years of imprisonment, I say, turning to my people, my Avital: Next year in Jerusalem.

THE EIGHTH GATE

Jerusalem in Modern Fiction

*View of the Jewish Quarter of the Old City, probably ca. 1937
(Central Zionist Archives; with permission)*

Jerusalem is the setting of so many modern works of fiction that the most that this anthology can do is present a small sample of the novels and short stories that feature Jerusalem as their background. The selections that appear here are for the most part selections from longer works and were chosen not so much for the stories they tell as for the descriptions of Jerusalem and life in Jerusalem at various periods of time which they convey.

CITY OF MANY DAYS

Shulamith Hareven

> CACHEZ-VOUS, CACHEZ-VOUS!
> GARDEZ-VOUS, GARDEZ-VOUS!

A game of hide-and-seek in the alley. Colorful voices slip like busy birds through the window bars of the houses, bearing news of summer on the large stones. A boy plays; a man walks; a woman does the wash. No need to prove anything. Growing up in Jerusalem is an identity all one's own.

❧

The school: named after its philanthropic founder, a German nobleman; a luxuriant caper plant, its flowers wedding-white, blooming spectacularly on its high wall.

❧

She grew and grew as though soaring toward some limitless height. She became bossy. Neither family, school, nor street claimed her allegiance anymore. She couldn't wait to be independent of them all. Meanwhile, she took to pitying at random, in sudden awakenings that came and went, frightening her as they did. On Jaffa Road a shop had been opened for orthopedic shoes with a manikin in the window: its dark hair neatly combed, its face agonizingly contorted, it sat there holding its aching foot while a hidden machine swung its head back and forth with an expression of eternal pain. Sara could never pass by the window without getting tears in her eyes. It wasn't the suffering itself that overwhelmed her, it was the fact that it never stopped. Day and night, while the rest of the world ate, slept, enjoyed itself, and went about its business, the poor manikin sat suffering in the window, on and on. Even when it was dark out. Even when nobody saw it, and the last bus, cart, donkey, and man had ceased moving down Jaffa Road, it kept shaking its head from the pain, unable to utter a sound because the mechanic who gave it its twisted, rather English face, its neatly combed hair and very red mouth, hadn't given it the power to cry. Somehow, for Sara, this was the height of indecency. She was sure that if only the manikin could whimper, someone in the shop would remember to shut off the machine that propelled it, at least for the night, so that it might get a little rest.

۞

Meanwhile, she remained in her tower. She read a lot. A closed garden.

I am a rose of Jerusalem and my halo is dust, a lily of the Valley of the Cross strewn with garbage, a queen in weary Zion reeking of cabbage breathing the breath of stones.

All words are dirty, impossible. Only the stone before dawn is clean and clear. Absolute.

Who didn't try to civilize them. Once their class was visited by a delegation of religious old ladies from England, most of them hobbling on canes because of the gout, who came to see how they studied the Scriptures. They were in the middle of Ezekiel that day, and the blushing teacher quickly skipped the chapter of the two whoring sisters, Oholah and Oholibah, so as not to embarrass the ladies. There were visits from American philanthropists, too, who came to see them doing exercises in the small yard, their baggy sweatshirts making them look like the inmates of an institution for pregnant orphans. One bitter winter day, when heavy gusts of wind trod visibly in the pale lemon-and-black light through the thistly field nearby, a guest of honor arrived from the Foundation of French Culture, or perhaps it was of French Friendship. A short man with ugly, glittering eyes, he wore an immaculate suit and spoke French with a carefully cultivated voice that was perhaps the one attractive thing about him. He stood before them with the look of a man who has eavesdropped on life and not liked what he has heard. Their principal, rubbing his hands, introduced him as Monsieur Gaston. In a French like rattling peas, the Culture Director, or perhaps it was the Friendship Director, proceeded to deliver a speech about the greatness of the Encyclopédistes, whom he, Monsieur Gaston, would now tell them about in Jerusalem. *Grandeur. Gloire*. The light of human reason. Enlightenment. The kerosene heater was on the blink that day and they were all nearly poisoned by the smoke. The girls sat looking gloomily at the fists of rain hammering on the melancholy windowpane, until a dark hail began to fall and drown out the speaker entirely. Monsieur Gaston whipped out a giant umbrella and disappeared like an evil dwarf.

Even their French teacher, fat old Monsieur Schnur of the Francofied Schnur family, disapproved of the lecturer. Perhaps Monsieur Gaston of Paris had slighted old Schnur, the patient torchbearer of the Encyclopédistes in the Holy City, but a few lessons afterward he declaimed to them in a sarcastic simper:

"In Paris, the city of light, the center of the great French culture, of which I, Monsieur Schnur, am about to tell you in Jerusalem, there is a museum. The name of the museum is le Louvre. And in the museum of le Louvre in the city of light stands a statue. The statue is nude. Do any of you know why this statue is nude? The statue is nude because the sculptor who made it was poor and had no money to buy it any clothes."

All the old man's chins trembled with laughter. The girls liked him. He had deserted the Friendship Director and gone over to them.

They were being civilized with penmanship, embroidery, and prayer. No longer did they pray for the health of Sultan Abd-el-

Hamid, but they still thanked the Lord for their souls every morning.
In music class they sang:

In valley deep and mountainside
God His bounty doth provide.

They were quizzed in science too.
    "Amarillo, how does light travel from place to place?"
    "On the waves of ether."
    "Saporta, what is the smallest part of matter which is indivisible?"
    "The atom."
    "Laniado, why does water go up a siphon?"
    "Because it's scared of the vacuum."
    The city kept growing on them. The British built a thousand and
one wonders: the YMCA, its tower resembling a tall erection, its

*The dormitory of the Alliance School in Jerusalem in 1908 (Central Zionist
Archives; with permission)*

interior decorated with Persian carpets, inlaid Damascus tables, Hellenistic mosaics, and English hunting scenes. They built the massive post office to look like one of Queen Victoria's railway stations, done up inside in strange, imported green marble. Dirt paths and wagon trails turned into paved roads, by the sides of which cypresses stood straight as sentries, drawing back from the dust of the horses. The Jews and the Arabs went on building as they always had, with flesh-colored Jerusalem stone and red roof tiles from Motsa. They draped grapevines on trellises, sat in courtyards under fig trees, and cured olives in soldered tin cans. The more educated among them went to browse in the British libraries. When Sara grew older, she began to borrow books from the YMCA. Once she went there on His Majesty's birthday and found it closed. The doorman, a black Sudanese dressed in a shiny white robe, a shiny red fez, and sneakers on his sockless feet, didn't open the heavy, European-wood door for her as usual. Instead he jigged up and down with joyous abandon:

"No mees, no mees, no libarry, no libarry, beeg day for you, beeg day for me, long leev de Keeng."

The air in the neighborhood: vibrant, familiar, smelling of stone that is lived in, used. She fell asleep at night to the high voices of the cistern cleaners returning from work, cradled by the sharp metallic bang of the shutter bolts, which Grandfather Amarillo always inspected shutter by shutter in case of thieves. Then came the cranking of the pulley-chain of the grandfather clock, which he set every evening. Cats rustling and yowling among the wild olive shoots. The kitchen clock chiming slowly. It was half a tone lower and then seconds faster than the other: soon the grandfather clock would chime too. A long, starry, oboelike breeze.

Early in the morning she was brought back to the light by the braying of Mahmousm Shabu's donkey, and the gurgly clink of the bottles of red wine from Mr. Hamkes's store that blistered in the

sacks on his back. A pinkering light in the stone. A window yawn-
ing open. *I thank Thee my God, King everlasting, Who restoreth to me
my soul*, all washed and shiny. Followed by the litany of the vegetable
man from Bet Sahur who arrived every morning with dawn: *Yallah*,
orranges! *Yallah*, frresh orranges! Tomat, tomat, tomat! The muezzin
from the mosque. the church bells and the goat bells. White para-
chutes of shivering sheep cluster cold on the fog-snagged hill. Back
to work come the cistern cleaners in their clothes that stink to high
heaven so that the waters of Jerusalem might be clean.

The sounds of a small city. As small as a man's palm.

۵»

The arched transoms of the Amarillos' windows are made of stained
glass, so that at any given hour of the day the light plays somewhere
on the floor tiles of the house in red, green, blue, violet, or an
ochrous lion-yellow like the hills of the Judaean wilderness at dusk.
Only one side of the house never gets any sun, not only because of
its northern exposure, but because it faces out on a high, blind wall
of Sa'ada's whorehouse. Sa'ada's girls wear heavy makeup and have
red purses that swing at their sides. She has procurers working for her
too, sallow, stupid young men whose job it is to shout, "Hello,
George, hello, George" at every passing man. Once, when Zaki
Amarillo was still a proper husband and father, a sudden gust of wind
blew some sheets that were drying on the Amarillo's roof into
Sa'ada's courtyard. It happened to be a day when Bukas was off. The
family debated who could be sent to fetch them. Not Gracia, who
mustn't be seen in the courtyard; not Zaki either, because there
might be gossip; Elder Amarillo was certainly out of the question;
while Sara, when she volunteered out of pure curiosity, got a spank-
ing for her pains.

"Couldn't you get along without them?" Zaki asked Gracia.

But Gracia refused.

"The plain ones, I don't care about, but the *broderie anglaise* ones, I got them from my grandmother."

The whole family went below and called, "Sa'ada. Sa'ada," in a chorus. Sa'ada didn't hear them, but the whole neighborhood did and laughed. So did Sa'ada's young panderers, who stood there shouting in high falsetto: "Sa'ada. Sa'ada. Where are you, *ya* Sa'ada?"

In the end Tia Victoria came to the rescue. "Why the hell should I care," she said.

She went over to Sa'ada's, a cigarette in the corner of her mouth, and came out a while later with the pile of sheets in her arms.

"Bravo, Victoria!" the curiosity-seekers congratulated her.

"What's the matter with you?" answered Victoria with a look of disdain. "She's all right, that Sa'ada. She would have brought the sheets over herself in another minute if she didn't feel so embarrassed."

ᴑ᷂

The city still squats on its haunches . . . a ripple of red roofs draped with a shimmering halo of heat like a clean muslin net that softens its colors and lines. Jerusalem is a veiled lady on a still, torrid day, feminine, forlorn, softly dreaming, self-absorbed, sucking time sweetly like an old sugar candy, her sons gathered under the many folds of her robe, picking rockrose and herbs. Other days she is a man, fierce, dry, and ancient, smelling of thyme and wild goat, his head covered with a sack against the wind, bare feet viny-veined, brusque-voiced and ornery, sniffing the slippery scent of sin in abandoned alleys, the odor of prophecy in public squares. The city lives without mirrors, each of its dwellers the key to an ancient, ironlike place, lattice-faced, wall-chested, sandaled feet skipping lightly over crooked, anonymous cobblestones, through openings, endless doors. Always an unsolved remainder, footprints belonging to no one, improbable clues, a taste of permanent mystery. A veiny, living tension from street to street, house to house. Each solemn girl in a courtyard is more girl than anywhere else, each baby wrapped in a shawl the only baby on earth, each single person the leaven of life. The city tenses its muscles under your feet. Put your hand on a wall and you feel the stone pulse. The very light percolates through it with each breath of the desert heat. Every house is itself. Alive. Alive.

❧

The Barzels stroll slowly through the twilight. Slowly, because Bimbi still has pains and a cough in his chest, and Hulda is pregnant. The child is large; Hulda smiles whenever it kicks her moonlike body, now taut as a drum. She calls it Goliath. They are out for their evening walk, like good Jerusalemites. It is almost autumn and the nights are getting cold. The young trees of Rehavia are growing up. New buildings are going up all around.

"Every true native of Jerusalem," says Professor Barzel, "is always hungry for the absolute. Even if he reaches it, he goes on pining for it. That's what Jerusalem is about"

"The problem is," says Hulda sadly, "that everyone has his own absolute. Look at the sky, Bibmi, how the blue behind those scaffolds is so much deeper than the blue in front of them."

He stops to rest for a minute: "They're building too much. It's changing the whole character of the city. Jerusalem shouldn't be so crowded or so square-angled. And those water tanks are an error."

"When I was a girl in Bet Hakerem, there was once an old stone-mason working down the street. One day Amatsia asked to be shown how to lay stones. There's nothing to it, the old man said. Just lay the stone however it wants to be laid."

A spasm of pain comes and goes as he smiles.

"Hulda, what will become of us? You'll have an old wreck for a husband."

"I'll have a Bimbi for a husband and a Goliath for a child."

In order to help pass the time, Professor Barzel conducts a study of the names of Jerusalem's neighborhoods, about which he writes to a friend in Germany:

The question of nomenclature is most interesting. Some neighborhoods here have names like prayers for succor and strength that never seem to come. As the present is always bad, the Jews have learned to live in a future that is always sure to be better. Romema, "Uplifted." Ruhama, "The Pitied One." Ezrat Yisra'el, "The Aid of Israel." Ge'ula, "Redemption." Talpiot, "Great Heights." Yemin Moshe, "The Right Hand of Moses"—perhaps this last refers to Sir Moses Montefiore who built it, and perhaps to Moses the Prophet, who held both hands aloft while the Israelites prevailed. Some live in Mekor Hayyim, "Life's Source," while others dream of Sha'arei Hesed, "Mercy's Gates"; still others who never planted a seed in their lives named their quarter Me'ah She'arim, "The Hundredfold Crop." And there are more modest, more secular names too: Nahalat Ahim, "The Brothers' Estate," Nahalat Shiv'a, "The Place of the Seven," Yegia Kappayim, "The Laborer's Lot," Kerem Avraham, "Abraham's Vineyard," Bayit ve-Gan, "House-and-Garden."

The Arabs, on the other hand, are more concerned with illustrious figures from their past. They have a quarter named after Sheikh Jarrah, a healer in Salladin's camp; they have an Omariyyah after Omar the Great, and Talbiyyah after Taleb. Ahmed Abu-Tor, a warrior of Salladin's who used to ride on an ox, gave his name to the neighborhood of Abu-Tor, "The Master of the Ox." The name Abu Dis derives from a forgotten Greek monk, Batabudission. The houses by the Saint-Simon Monastery were once called in Greek *kata monis*, "by the monastery," and the name Katamon has stuck to this day. A section of the city that was covered with sharp pebbles, *sarrar* in Arabic, became known as Musrara, Pebbletown. And imagine, among the filth and caved-in ruins of an Arab slum, coming across the glorious street name of Gottfried de Bouillion! Thus we live, my friend, caught between a forgotten Crusader past and a yearned-for biblical future, with nothing to hold onto but the present, this damnably difficult here and now.

❧

A light-and-shade-struck city of light-and-shade-struck people. A narrow, arched passageway, gravid-shaped, wide enough for a small donkey; the soft light behind it incandescing not on the man but on the red flap of his clothes, his dark patch of a head barely brushing the moss growing out of the wall. A burro slowly climbs the narrow steps. Around the corner the aquamarine mosaic of the Dome of the Rock, a sudden treasure to look at, a prismatic jewel in a setting of stone.

❧

A city you long for the more you are in it; in which you are most yourself and most miss yourself; in which whatever you find, you will want again from afar. A dichotomous city in which everything is its own looking glass, forever mirroring, always the same sky reflecting domed rock cut from sky, always the same broad evening light casting back in reverse the red roofs of the houses. People draw near and recede as in mirrors. A few last gilded roofs. Still the spires of the minarets. Evening comes with an avalanche of longing, and you walk slowly through Zion Square as the first lights go on and buy a coal-hot order of stemmed *hamleh m'lan* from the scarfaced Sudanese vendor, eating it as though there will never be food in the world and no you, only this one perfect hunger that must be shared with a friend because everything is in it, this entire evening, and that is more than one person can bear.

☙

A city on the desert's edge, its populace holding on with bare nails, high-strung, quarrelsome, haggling, wrangling, cupidous. The weaver weaves and hawks his wares; he sells his wares; the buyer buys. None turn to look at the desert from which their forefathers had come, scaling the heights from below to conquer this place.

And yet on certain nights, when a dry sirocco wind that has assembled its forces on the Plain of the Jordan, that has marshaled them again on the Mount of Qarantal, that has gathered reinforcements in the ascent of the Edomites, bursts through the streets of the city like the footfalls of an invisible invader, the desert overruns Jerusalem again. There is a groan, a stillness, a wound. And then silence once more. The broken tablets of the Law. Until morning.

☙

On the subject of reincarnation, Elias was sure that he had lived in Jerusalem in Herod's time and had been trampled to death there by a horse-drawn chariot in a narrow alley. In his nightmares he saw the horse bearing wildly down on him and the frightened eyes of the charioteer, he felt the wall against him, sudden and hard, and knew he could back off no farther. The dream kept recurring.

The Hebrew University Campus on Mount Scopus, ca. 1928 (Central Zionist Archives; with permission)

He felt at home, so he said, in the Herodian remnants of Jerusalem, in the ruined towers of Phasael and Antonia with their margined, finely dressed stones. A toga would have befit his tall frame. His sad, knowledgeable mouth could have spoken all the tongues of that complicated city without tripping. Greek sounded well on Elias. Not the Greek of Madame Savvidopoulos, but the blunt, wise, stinging Greek of those times.

No city lives closer to the almost invisible ghosts of past lives than Jerusalem; no city is better at blind, secret love. Hermetic, ironic, a sink of cold tempests, the city stands upright on the mountain against the cold night, most strong and most vulnerable, something in it never falling asleep. All placed outside of it are like a somehow undeserved vacation. Or is there any place at all outside of Jerusalem?

                                        ॐ

Sara stepped out of the building on Mount Scopus in which she taught, a silent presence, the whole city spread at her feet, and looked at the soft fleecy light out over the mountains, over the houses drowning in radiance, as if once this city, long, long ago, soon after Creation, had burst from some great rock, its truth flown molten and shiny over the hills. She could feel the moment to the quick. Now this is me, she told herself, now this is me, here on this hill, with this feeling of great peace that will never last, or standing in the street, people know me, I have three sons and so little time. Now this is me in this moment of hers. Tomorrow I'll be gone and the street will be gone, or another street and another time. And always, forever, this fleecy pile of light, that rock tumbled halfway down the hill to a lonely stop, a terraced alley, a dripping cypress tree, a caper plant in a wall. A place to walk slowly. A place to touch the sky: now it is close. To breathe in mountain and light. Now.

(*TRANSLATED BY HILLEL HALKIN WITH THE AUTHOR*)

TEHILA: THE PRAISE OF JERUSALEM

S. Y. Agnon

At the eve of new moon I walked to the Western Wall, as we in Jerusalem are accustomed to do, praying at the Western Wall at the rising of each moon.

Already most of the winter had passed, and spring blossoms had begin to appear. Up above, the heavens were pure, and the earth had put off her grief. The sun smiled in the sky; the City shone in its light. And we too rejoiced, despite the troubles that beset us; for these troubles were many and evil, and before we had reckoned with one, yet another came in its wake.

From Jaffa Gate as far as the Western Wall, men and women from all the communities of Jerusalem moved in a steady stream, together with those newcomers whom The Place [God—ed.] had restored to their place, albeit their place had not yet been found. But in the open space before the Wall, at the booth of the Mandatory Police, sat the police of the Mandate whose function was to see that no one guarded the worshippers save only they. Those who had come to pray were herded together and driven to seek shelter close up against the stones of the Wall, some weeping and some as if dazed. And still we say, How Long, O Lord? How long?—For we have trodden the lowest stair of degredation, yet you tarry to redeem us.

I found a place for myself at the Wall, standing at times amongst the bewildered bystanders. I was amazed at the people of the world: as if it were not sufficient that they oppressed us in all lands, yet they must also oppress us in our home. As I stood there I was driven from my place by one of the police who carried a baton. This man was in a great rage, on account of some ailing old woman who had brought a stool with her to the Wall. The policeman took a flying kick, throwing the woman to the ground, and confiscated the stool: for she had infringed the law enacted by the legislators, which forbade worshippers to bring seats to the wall. And those who had come to pray saw this, yet held their peace: for how can right dispute against might? Then came forward that same old woman whom I knew, and looked the policeman straight in the eye. And the policeman averted his glance, and returned the stool to its owner.

I went up to her and said, "Your eyes have more effect than all the pledges of England. For England, which gave us the Balfour Declaration, sends her officer to annul it; while you only looked upon that wicked one, and frustrated his evil intent."

She replied, "Do not speak of him so, for he is a good gentile, who saw that I was grieved and gave back her stool to that poor woman. . . . But have you said your afternoon prayer? I ask because, if you are free, I can put in your way the *mitzvah* of visiting the sick.

The *rabbanit* is now really and truly ill. If you wish, come with me and I shall take you by a short route." I joined her and we went together.

From alley to alley, from courtyard to courtyard, we made our way down, and at each step she took she would pause to give a piece of candy to a child, or a coin to a beggar, or to ask the health of a man's wife or, if it were a woman, the health of her husband. . . .

〜

". . . how is it that we keep walking and walking, yet we have still not come to the house of the *rabbanit*?"

She said, "You still have in mind those courtyards we used to take for a short cut. But now that most of the Old City has been settled by the Arabs, we must go by a roundabout way."

We approached one of these courtyards. She said, "Do you see this courtyard? Forty families of Israel once lived here, and here were two synagogues, and here in the daytime and nighttime there were study and prayer. But they left this place, and Arabs came and occupied it."

We approached a tumble-down house. She said, "Do you see this house? Here was a great academy where the scholars of the Torah lived and studied. But they left this house, and Arabs came and occupied it."

We came to the asses' stalls. She said, "Do you see these stalls? Here stood a soup-kitchen, and the virtuous poor would enter hungry and go forth satisfied. But they abandoned this place, and Arabs came and occupied it. Houses from which prayer and charity and study of Torah never ceased, now belong to the Arabs and their asses. . . . My son, we have reached the courtyard of the *rabbanit*'s house. Go in, and I shall follow you later. This unhappy woman, because of the seeming good she has known abroad, does not see the true good at home."

"What is the true good?" I asked.

She laughed. saying, "My son, you should not need to ask. Have you not read the verse, 'Happy the man thou choosest to dwell in thy courtyards?' For these same courtyards are the royal courts of the Holy One, the courts of our God, in the midst of Jerusalem. When men say 'Jerusalem,' their way is to add the words, 'Holy City.' But when I say 'Jerusalem,' I add nothing more, since the holiness is contained in the name; yes, in the very name itself. . . . Go up. my son, and do not trip on the stairs. Many a time have I said to the keeper of the community funds that these stairs are in need of repair; and what answer did he give me? That this building is old and due to be demolished, therefore it is not worth while spending a penny on its upkeep. So the houses of Israel fall into disuse until they are abandoned, and the sons of Ishmael enter and take possession. Houses that were built with the tears of their fathers—and now they abandon them. But again I have become a chatterer, and hasten my end."

☙

Tilli entered the room. She was carrying a bowl of soup, and seeing me she said:

"Ah, you are still here! But stay, my friend, stay. It is a great *mitzvah* to visit the sick. *Rabbanit*, how much better you look! Truly, salvation comes in the wink of an eye; for the Name is healing you every minute. I have brought a little soup to moisten your lips, now, my dear, raise your head and I shall prop up your pillow. There, my dear, that's better. My son, I am sorry that you do not live in the City, for then you would see for yourself how the *rabbanit*'s health is improving day by day."

"And do I not live in Jerusalem?" I said. "Surely Nachalat Shivah is Jerusalem?"

"It is indeed," answered Tilli. "God forbid that it should be otherwise. Rather may the day come when Jerusalem extends as far as

Damascus, and in every direction. But the eye that has seen all Jerusalem enclosed within her walls cannot accustom itself to viewing what is built beyond the walls as the City itself. It is true that all the Land of Israel is holy and, I need hardly say, the surroundings of Jerusalem: yet the holiness that is within the walls of the City surpasses all else. My son, there is nothing I have said which you do not know better than I. Why then have I said it? Only that I might speak the praise of Jerusalem."

I could read in the eyes of the *rabbanit* a certain resentment, because Tilli was speaking to me rather than to her. So I took my leave and went away.

Various preoccupations kept me for a while from going to the Old City; and after that came the nuisance of the tourists. How well we know these tourists, who descend upon us and upon the land, all because the Place has made a little space for us here! They come now to see what has happened; and having come, they regard us as if we were created solely to serve them. Yet one good thing may be said for the tourists: in showing them "the sights," we see them ourselves. Once or twice, having brought them to the City to show them the Western Wall, I met Tilli there. It seemed to me that a change had come over her. Although she had always walked without support, I noticed that she now leaned on a stick. Because of the visitors, I was unable to linger. For they had come to spy out the whole land, not to spend time upon an old woman not even mentioned in their itineraries.

When the tourists had left Jerusalem, I felt restless in myself. After trying without success to resume work, I bestirred myself and walked to the City, where I visited of my own accord all the places I had shown to the visitors. How can I describe what I saw? He who in His goodness daily renews the works of creation, perpetually renews His own City. New houses may not have been built, nor new trees planted; yet Jerusalem herself is ever new. I cannot explain the secret of her infinite variety. We must wait, all of us for those great sages who will one day enlighten us.

I came upon a man of learning, and he drew me to his house, where he set before me all his recent findings. We sat together in deep contentment, while I asked my questions, and he replied; or spoke of problems, which he resolved; or mentioned cloudy matters, which he made clear. How good it is, how satisfying, to sit at the feet of one of the learned men of Jerusalem, and to learn the Law from his lips! His home is simple, his furnishings austere, yet his wisdom ranges far, like the great hill ranges of Jerusalem which are seen from the windows. Bare are the hills of Jerusalem; no temples or palaces crown them. Since the time of our exile, nation after nation has come and laid them waste. But the hills spread their glory like banners to the sky; they are resplendent in everchanging hues; and not least in glory is the Mount of Olives, which bears no forest of trees, but a forest of tombs of the righteous, who in life and in death gave their thoughts to the Land.

(TRANSLATED BY WALTER LEVER)

THE DEBT OF BLOOD

Elisha Porat

In the army, I was lying and reading in my tent. It was the rare soldier who succeeded in reading a book in the army in those days: newspapers and light magazines were as much as most people could manage. My favorite poet at that time was Avraham Ben Yitzhak. In the one slim volume containing all his poems I found a hidden treasure of beauty. I would shut myself off from abrasive surroundings and contemplate his poems. Between one poem and the next, I would look wonderingly about me and soar on the wings of my thoughts far from the army camp which so oppressed my spirits. Once I was reading "The hills joined together around my town" when a soldier pushed past my bed. He stopped and bent down to see what I was reading that so absorbed my attention. When he saw the book his eyes widened. His eyes softened and he sat down on my bed. We introduced ourselves. Something stronger than we were drew us to each other, and we became friends. True, bosom friends. He had the body of a farmer and the soul of a poet.

From our posts in Jerusalem we would phone each other on the urban line, like a pair of lovers.

"Listen, I want to read you something, something great," he would tempt me.

"I'm listening, I'm listening."

And over the telephone on the local line, he would read me wonderful pages from Yizhar's *Tziklag Days* until the switchboard operator would interrupt us with typical military narrow-mindedness: "What's all this then—official business?"

"Yes," my friend would yell, "very important business." I pressed the receiver to my ear. I couldn't get enough of S. Yizhar's beautiful words. Nobody had ever read Yizhar to me like this before. Later, years later, when I read the book myself something strange happened to me. The eyes skimming the printed pages were mine, but the voice which I heard reading the words in my ears was his. I laid the book down and closed my eyes tightly. The autumn wind of Jerusalem blew through the leaves on the fig-trees and the flowers on the caper bushes shone like little torches. On our nocturnal walks he would show me the distant stars, the silhouettes of towers, and all the hills encircling Jerusalem.

"Even on the darkest night," he would boast, "I can identify every dome, every valley, every mountain range."

It was as if he had been born in Jerusalem, as if he had never seen another town in his life. I would remind him of the beginning of our friendship. Of the hills joined together around our town. And he would smile wordlessly. We would spend our leaves together, wandering about the town. Walking and talking. It was clear to him that we had some special destiny to fulfill. He was sure that he had something important to say, and that people would have to listen to him. He loved the Land of Israel with a burning passion. He would laugh at the various experts who knew the country by its flora and fauna, its geological formations, its history.

"With me, it's in my blood," he laughed. "You can put me down anywhere in the country and I'll know where I am by sticking out my tongue and sniffing the air."

Once we were walking in an orthodox quarter on a Friday evening. The façades of the houses were already steeped in a Sabbath peace, but on the back verandahs, facing the border, men sat playing cards with an absorption that looked as if it would last all night long. The sight of these men sitting in their undershirts and playing cards made him furious.

"Is that what we came to this country for?"

"Is that what we joined the army for?"

"Is that worth paying the price for?"

That night something cracked in him. He told me things about himself which he had never dared to speak of before. He was very agitated, and his voice shook strangely. He told me about a letter he had written to his girl. About the words he had written her in reply to certain fears she had confessed to him.

"The debt of blood, you understand? The debt of blood, that's what I believe in!"

He seized my hand, my shirt, he came very close to me.

"Don't you see, it's impossible to live in this country without some hugh debt. A terrible debt we have to pay so that we can go on living here." How strange his voice sounded in that orthodox quarter in Jerusalem on the Sabbath Eve. If I had compared him then to some prophet it would have been ridiculous. But his words tore something apart in my soul. From that night on I saw him differently. You could even say that I was a little jealous of him. I thought that he had outstripped the rest of us in some mysterious way. That perhaps he had already begun to grasp things which were deeper, truer, that were perhaps the beginnings of a dimension which I too was seeking then. And seeking with all my soul. I probed his words to find something which would make sense of the things we had done, some justification—you might also say, some opening to a new, different faith.

"And you," he asked me, "do you feel that you owe a debt?"

"Perhaps," I said, "I don't know."

And afterwards I had a bad feeling, as if I had missed an opportunity which might never return to me again. I could never speak about my private beliefs to anyone else. It seemed to me like something crude, revolting, almost indecent. As if we had come as close as possible to each other without risking collision. And then continued moving apart. Each one on his own course, moving inevitably, endlessly further away. Years later, in an army camp we had conquered from the Arab Legion, east of Nablus, I remembered him again. In the newspapers coming out after the week of war, the names of the fallen began to appear. I read his name slowly, stammering, joining the syllables together one by one as if I was beginning to read my first words all over again. I was sorry then that I had ever learnt to read. In that orthodox quarter of Jerusalem under those same balconies, he had fallen. For a moment I seemed to hear his voice at my side, to feel his trembling hand clutching my shirt.

"Is that what we came to this country for? Is that worth paying the price for?"

A monument to the soldiers of the Israel Defence
Forces who fell in the 1967 War; photograph taken in
1968 (Central Zionist Archives; with permission)

In the hills which had joined together around this town, something had been orphaned. And I seemed to grow a few years older at
once. Sometimes, although I know it's cheating, I continue my con-
versation with him. From the point at which I had been afraid of
exposing myself then.

"Yes," I answer him from the distance of the years. "Yes, I feel that I owe a debt."

"The debt of blood we spoke of then?"

"Any debt you like," I shout at him from my groaning heart.

Happy are they who sow and do not reap, happy are they who set forth and do not return.

In the first year after the war, when I was approaching the middle of my life, I learnt to read Hebrew on tombstones. I learnt fast. Within the space of a few days I could read the names, the dates. After a week or two I could draw a map of gravestones. And after a month I had already covered the whole country in monuments to the fallen. At first I would read the names aloud, in a slightly hesitant voice, syllable by syllable. Afterwards I pronounced them silently, only my lips moving. And today I already know how to read them to myself, in my head, or as some say: in my heart. I myself don't know.

(TRANSLATED BY DALIA BILU)

A JOURNEY THROUGH THE LAND OF ISRAEL

Pinchas Sadeh

MOUNT ZION

After many years I ascended Mount Zion again. The old dirt track was overgrown with weeds, and I took the stairs instead. Various signs greeted me, some with verses from the Bible, others announcing institutions and shops. A guard stopped me at the entrance to King David's tomb and lent me a skullcap. Four men were reciting psalms by the catafalque. Tourists of both sexes circulated through the dark interior beneath massive Gothic vaults. I climbed the minaret outside. A wind was blowing. Across from me, its tombstones gleaming whitely, was the Mount of Olives, and beyond it the mountains of Moab, screened by blue haze. When I looked at the nearby church steeple I saw that the holes from the shells that had hit it during the 1948 war, when I was first here, were still visible. Doves of peace were roosting in them now.

I climbed back down. I had time on my hands, and so I lingered for a while in the crypt beneath the vaults. Next to me sat a man behind a small table, selling certificates in testimony that the bearers thereof had trod in this holy place.

There was nothing to make me feel that this was really David's grave—nor had there been anything back then, during the war. At the time, it was true, I hadn't known that the tradition was a late one, originating apparently with the medieval traveler Benjamin of Tudela. The biblical City of David, in a corner of which the king no doubt lies, was hundreds of meters northeast of here. The Christian tradition that the Last Supper took place on this site, where the Church of the Dormition now stands, is undoubtedly much older, for the writings of Saint Epiphanus and, after him, of Saint Cyril date it back to as far as the third century. Then, though, I knew nothing about this either. No one had told me about it, nor had I encountered it in any book.

Throughout those days and nights, however, I had sensed something primeval, dark, about the place.

The wall of the Old City had loomed grayly before me by day, blackly at night. An Arab sniper lurked behind its apertures. No one dared set foot in the narrow lane between the church and the wall. It was enchanted ground. Whoever infringed on it paid with his life.

I used to stare at the wall from our firing positions in the church as though bewitched. Only a few dozen paces lay between me and it, yet they led through the gates of death.

Sometimes, at night, I would sit by one of the windows in the

Haganah soldiers on King David Street, 1948 (Central Zionist Archives; with permission)

church and send long bursts of fire from my machine gun at the wall, like a jackal howling at the moon. Invisible in the darkness, the mouths of the wall lit up in return each time the hidden machine gun opposite me flashed quickly back. The sound of my own gun, though deafening, was like a musical drumroll, and I liked the smell of the burned powder.

I saw no newspapers, had no radio, read nothing, heard nothing. I knew nothing about the conduct of the war, about where it was being fought or who was winning or losing it. Nor did I waste my time thinking about it. It had simply fallen on me from out of the blue, and I accepted it for what it was.

Forgotten fragments, like scenes from a dream, came back to me now.

When the fighting began, before I was sent to Mount Zion, I spent a few days in an Arab neighborhood of Jerusalem called Musrara, in a rear position near the broadcasting station. There had been a piano in one of the studios there, and I used to shut myself up in the dark, soundproofed room and hammer away on it, though I knew nothing about music at all.

All the houses of Musrara had been abandoned, as though in a dream. In some of them, food was still left on the tables, yet you couldn't find a living soul in them. From time to time Jews would come, soldiers or civilians, to loot what rugs, furniture, or radios were left. What they wanted any of it for was beyond me. The world was totally spiritual then, totally religious: all its conventions and givens had melted away, shells whistled through the air like flying angels of death, and one could have really died at any minute. Yet even I made off with something, a small reproduction of Van Gogh's *Sunflowers* that I found on somebody's wall. It cheered me to have it, because Van Gogh and Gauguin were my two favorite painters in those days. I can still remember that yellow.

Afterward, in Abu Tor, a neighborhood separated from Mount Zion by hell on earth, I found an abandoned house with a room that was empty except for an armchair and a large mirror. I used to sit for hours in the depths of the chair, opposite the mirror, writing poems on a pad of stationery that bore the letterhead of an Arab commercial firm.

I liked best climbing onto the roof of that house in Abu Tor, a neighborhood named after a comrade-in-arms of Saladin, and throwing hand grenades from it at the Arab position down the street. It didn't accomplish much, but I had a weakness for the sudden flash, and for the thud of the explosion that followed.

Later, on Mount Zion in the Church of the Dormition, from which the Virgin Mary supposedly ascended in her sleep to heaven, I used to sit for long periods in the forsaken cells of the monks. Thus

I managed to live in a variety of times at once, among them my own and the Middle Ages.

Now and then I would descend into town. The connecting passageway was a low, narrow tunnel that had been dug to the Jewish neighborhood of Yemin Moshe. You had to traverse it doubled over, like a worm burrowing through the earth. Once in the city, I went to see two girls I knew, Hava and Ada. Sometimes, walking along a deserted street, it would occur to me that I was living to see the fulfillment of Nietzsche's words that man's destiny in life was to be a warrior and woman's to be his paramour. The thought amused me, since—with a helmet shaped like a chopping bowl on my head and army pants a size too big for me that kept threatening to fall off—I looked like anything but a prophetic vision of the Übermensch. In general, though, those walks were a strange hallucination of empty city blocks, bloodstained sidewalks, suddenly shrieking shells, thirst, and a smell of sperm and sweat.

Those days were distant. Now I stood on the mount by the Old City wall, opposite Zion Gate, but neither mount, wall, nor gate was what it had been. Those days belonged to such another world and such another time that I could almost have believed that the war I took part in had been fought in crusader times, or back in the age of Joshua.

ME'A SH'ARIM

The streets are narrow here. They wind among the columns of the houses like the spaces between the lines on a page of the Talmud.

Small, crooked alleyways, like letters of Rashi script.

Me'a She'arim, Bet Yisra'el, Batei Ungarn, Sha'arei Hesed.

How many nocturnal hours I spent wandering through these alleys during the years I lived in the area. Deathly silent hours of the night, when you could hear a pin drop. When the only sound was the echo of my footsteps on the cobblestones.

In the houses, behind latticed windows, Jews were covered by slumber as the fallen Israelites in the desert were covered by sand.

Sometimes I would pass a house of study. Through the window, by the light of a feeble, yellowish electric bulb, I would see two or three young students bent over their books, rocking softly back and forth while they chanted the ancient Aramaic words of the Gemara in a melancholy murmur: *Thus say the rabbis . . . wherefore Rabbi Levi bar Hama differs with Rabbi Hanina . . . on the one hand, this one says . . . and on the other hand, this one . . .* the torts and case laws of the Talmud . . . the world of Rava and Abayei, of Rav Ashi and Rabbi Abahu. . . .

Sometimes I would stop to read one of the placards affixed to the walls. Proclamations, prohibitions, excommunications. "In the name of our rabbis and officers of the Law, may they live in peace, amen . . . Be it hereby made known . . . For as when the time of the Messiah grows nigh, heresy and apostasy stalk the streets . . . And whereas on account of our innumerable sins the wicked thrive and prosper . . . Wherefore the Holy One Blessed Be He bestows on them success that we may be brought into temptation and withstand it . . . May the Compassionate One have mercy on us and save us . . . For Thou alone, O Lord our God, shall rule over us . . . And may it be granted us to see the coming of the Redeemer. . . ."

Today I have come here on a workaday afternoon. Women are shopping in the market. Men are about their business. My eye is caught by a large notice on the wall. "Help!!!" it says. Its contents are trivial, but I know that all such cries here are essentially addressed to God.

Nearby stands a pretty boy with a proud, wise look on his face. A little scholar of the Law.

To tell the truth, I could never identify with these people (for if I could, I would have come to live with them as an observant Jew) who live by the rule of the Torah and its codes. To be religious, in my terms, means to understand that life is a parable of which God is the meaning—that is, to live life as a struggle to make contact with the divine. Somewhere else I have written about the instructive historical fact that the official codification of the Bible in the days of Ezra the Scribe was accompanied by the cessation of prophecy—in other words, by the drying up of the previously renewable source of human contact with God.

And yet still I feel close to them, these people who live as though in a fortress under siege, surrounded by a secular world they disdain and by a "culture" that revolts them. Their life is without compromise, without concessions. It is a waiting for the Messiah.

When I was called to the army in the War of Independence, it grieved me to think that I might have to die defending the Hebrew University, or the bourgeoisie of Rehavia, or the offices of the press. These and many other things meant nothing to me then and mean nothing to me now, nor do I hesitate to say so. But the Torah is something else. I have no difficulty understanding that whoever believes in it must be ready to die for it. One must never refuse to be a martyr for God. There can be no other significance to life beside worshipping Him. The rest is simply a question of how one understands this worship—that is, of how one understands God.

Worshipping God, as the phrase suggests, has nothing to do with pleasure or cultural frills. It is work, hard work, like paving a road, or farming land, or building a house. In general, I don't believe that the purpose of life in this world is to snatch a little pleasure here or there. If it were, we might as well have been born bedbugs. In whatever we live and do—in our happiness, our suffering, our love, our hate, our passions, our thoughts—we must live and do it not just for itself, but as a parable, as a question, as a war. As work. As worship.

What is man? Man is a question. God is the answer. If the answer were available here, in this life, the question would be unnecessary. The painful tension between the two gives life its energy.

(TRANSLATED BY HILLEL HALKIN)

THE NINTH GATE

Jerusalem in Modern Poetry

The synagogue of Judah Chassid in the Old City, August 1937
(Central Zionist Archives; with permission)

The subject of Jerusalem is important in modern Jewish poetry writen in Hebrew and other languages even if it is no longer as dominant as it was in medieval times. The aspect of holiness remains, but one also hears about Jerusalem as a city of history, of beauty, of memory, of love, of everyday life, and even as a subject of humor. The poetry here has been arranged neither by chronological order nor by author, but in a way as to lead from one theme to another by connection or by contrast.

From Jerusalem: A First Poem
Gabriel Preil

Under these historic skies
I am older than Abraham and his stars,
and I am the young father of the children
playing among pink trees.

On Alharizi Street, on a violet afternoon,
such an hour of grace
gazes out of an arched frame
as sometimes whispered to the prophet
weary of fires,
who dreamed of a village
cool among the stars.

(*Translated by Robert Friend*)

The First Day
Marcia Falk

High wind and a blackbird
push the sky across
the pale Judean hills.
The windows shake. She pulls
herself out of the blankets,
a flash strikes the eastern walls
of houses. It is morning,
the city a cup full
of light, a bright

The Judean hills near Jerusalem, ca. 1935 (Central Zionist Archives; with permission)

flask of wind

to rise to.

IN THE JERUSALEM HILLS
Leah Goldberg

I lay like a stone between these ridges,

In grass orange and blighted and summer-burnt,

Inert and silent.

Pale skies touch rock.

From where came the yellow-winged butterfly here?

Stone among stones—I know not

How ancient my life

Or who will yet come

With foot shoving me

And I will roll downhill.

Perhaps this is beauty frozen forever.

Perhaps this is

Eternity moving slow.

Perhaps this is

The Dream of death

And the one love.

I lay like a stone between these ridges,

in thorn and thistle,

Across from the road flowing townward.

Come wind blessing all

To caress pine-tops

And mute stones.

(TRANSLATED BY AURA HAMMER)

JERUSALEM

David Rokeah

Your stones I shall polish into a mirror

For in them is my yearning,

Pines' loftiness and their hearts' resin.

In dawns' topazes
I shall store
The reflection of your day
Rising early on the city wall
Like a stream of light
On a slope of flint
In a bronze mortar sheath.

Your stones I shall polish until my dreams course in you
Like a flow smashing your rocks—
Your yearning, wanderer.

(Translated by Ruth Finer Mintz)

On Nevi'im Street (The Street of the Prophets)
Yehoash Biber

Shadows of large trees
lash the surface of Nevi'im Street.
As on a shaky ladder I will go down to Damascus Gate.
To the voice of the wind's howl, the street will move beneath me,
and many a time drop from under my feet,
shake me about,
hang me
above a vast abyss.

I will cover my face and listen
to God's voice
roaring in Zion.

(Translated by Aura Hammer)

Street of the Prophets, date unknown (Central Zionist Archives; with permission)

LONGING (I)
Ruth Finer Mintz

In the translucent light of Jerusalem
I go at four o'clock to greet,
The Prophet Isaiah.
And he greets me as I greet him
with silence.

I stand looking toward his sanctuary
shaped like a clay jar, keeping his scroll
guarding his peace, thousands of years:
from the desecrations of man
and from the desiccation of time.

Now it rests here, in time out of time,
in Jerusalem, a fragment of eternity.

Its letters are black on white, clear
as at their recording. Parchment
preserved in dried earth. Earth
from which Adam was first created.
Earth to which Adam returns, crumbling.
Thus a scroll is like a man, fragile crumbling
yet preserving for thousands of years
words, ideas, beliefs.

One, Three. Seven.
Love, The Presence. Peace.

Here their shadow falls upon me in the shade of a tree.
Now their light overwhelms me, transfiguring
limestone to pointing fingers of ivory upon parchment.
And the light rests where all revelation must rest,
in words, till the heart of stone turns flesh.

This Valley, these hills are unbelievable
Therefore, they exist in the age of unbelief.
To deny the law of gravity which is downfall.
To contradict the law of optics.

Even as I know that all that was lost
has been returned to us, from the cave of our disaster:
The longing possess me utterly, yet escapes

my suppliant fingers, my outstretched hands.
For it rests, half underground, in the sanctuary
of wrought stone, above the olive valley.

And in the translucent light of Jerusalem
The Olive Valley burns with green Grace.
The expanse of God flickers before my eyes.

RELIGIOUS QUARTER
A. C. Jacobs

Grandfather, to-day I walked in Mea Shearim
And it was a little like it must have been
In Vilna seventy years ago.
                                    Small boys
Walked between their dangling curls
With already the strange sensuality of talmud
Scholars. Merchants, in fur coats, relaxed
In the slow pace of their closed, coinless
Sabbath; matrons went with their love blown
Away into a nagging over-all welfare
And young girls were concealing their sex
In a terrible kind of shapelessness.
                                    And all this

Under the hot sky of Jerusalem.

It was a little, grandfather, of the sea
Of the past, out of which you sailed

Inhabitants of Meah Shearim, date unknown (Central Zionist Archives; with permission)

To leave me in the north,

                        whose speech
I take to tame, oh, centuries of such
Isolated quarters striving in my blood.

BUILDING PARTNER
Elisha Porat

I also want to be a partner
in the building of Jerusalem. With you
sing hymns to her with a great voice
in the assemblage of her mutes;

with you encompass her wall
in a glory-march among her lame celebrants.
I have the right to be a partner, after all
I spilled the fury of my youth on her:
fights with zealots and night patrols
in the shadow of fences, sniping from her lattices.
Wait, don't finish without me, I've
bought rough sandals and white linen
to flourish with you on her towers,
before I smash myself on the squares
and am pounded by her stones like you
powdered fine
coveting the dust of her saints.

(*TRANSLATED BY RIVA RUBIN*)

TO MY CITY JERUSALEM, 1967
Amir Gilboa

I knew in the dream the dream wouldn't fly like a dream.
I knew in the dream that in me myriads are dreaming the dream.
I woke. Midnight. Who turns the dark of night into the light of
day?
The sun stands still in the window in the dream as on that day in
Gibeon I recall.
Look, here comes the night that is day and not night
and the endless day comes in the midst of the night. And it will
never darken.

And morning light glows. I wake. Look, here before me, Jerusalem.
And I see it. I see it with myriads of eyes.
Was there ever anything like this—
a dream dreamed at the same time
by myriads where they dream.
(*Translated by Shirley Kaufman and Shlomit Rimmon*)

Homage to Jerusalem; Jerusalem 1967
Yehuda Amichai

This year I travelled far
to view the quiet of my city.
Rocking soothes a baby, a distance soothes a city.
I lived in my longing. I played a game
of four severe squares of Yehuda Halevi:
my heart, my self, the East, the West.

I heard bells ringing in time's religions,
but the howl I heard within
is still from my Judean Desert.

Now that I'm back, I cry again.
At night the stars come up like bubbles from the drowned.
Each morning I cry the scream of a newborn baby
From the blind chaos of homes and all this great light.

Light against the Tower of David, light
on the Church of Maria, light on the Fathers
asleep in their double-graves, light on your face
from within, light on the transparent honey
cakes, light on the clock face, and time
is lighted passing between your thighs
when you take off your dress.

Lighted the round cheeks of my childhood,
lighted the stones that wished to be
lighted, with those that wished to
sleep in the darkness of squares.
Lighted the spiders of railings, and
cobwebs of churches and acrobats of
spiral stairs. But of all these, most
is lighted, the true and terrible X-ray
in letters of white bones and lightning:
Mene   Mene   Tekel   Upharsin.

ॐ

In vain you'll look for barbed wire fences,
You know such things
don't disappear. Another city, perhaps,
is now cut in two: two lovers
separated; other flesh tormented
by these thorns, refusing to be stone.

In vain you'll look. You lift your eyes unto the hills.
Perhaps there? Not these hills, accidents of geology,
but The Hills. You ask
without raising the voice, without question mark,
to do your part in asking questions
gone now. But a great tiredness wants you with all your heart and
gets you. Like death.

Jerusalem, the only place in the world
where even the dead have a right to vote.

☙

It's not time that takes me from my childhood,
but this city and everything in it. Now
to have to learn Arabic, to reach Jericho
from both sides of time; and length of walls
added to heights of towers and domes
vast without limit. All these
widen my life and force me
to migrate anew from the smell
of rivers and forest.

My life's stretched out; thinning like cloth,
transparent. You can see through me.

☙

The city plays hide-and-seek between names
Jerusalem, El-Kuds, Shalem, Jer, Yeru,

whispering: Y'vus, Y'vus, Y'vus, in darkness.
Weeping with longing: Aelia Capitolina, Aelia, Aelia.
She comes to all who call her
at night, alone. But we know
who comes to whom.

❧

Jerusalem stone is the only stone
that hurts. It has a network of nerves.
From time to time Jerusalem gathers
to mass protest like the tower of Babel.
But with big clubs God—The Police beats
her back: houses razed, walls torn down,
and then once more the city disperses, midst jabbering
prayers complaint and random cries from churches
and synagogues and minaret shout from mosques.
each one to his place.

❧

I and Jerusalem like blindman and cripple.
She sees for me
until the Dead Sea, until the end of days.
And I hoist her on my shoulders
and walk blind in my darkness beneath.

❧

On this clear autumn day
I build Jerusalem anew.
Foundation scrolls
fly in the air, birds, thoughts.

God is angry with me
because I force him, always,
to create the world from Beginning:
Chaos, Light, Second Day, to
Man and back again.

☙

In the morning the shadow of the Old City falls
on the New. In the afternoon, the reverse.
Nobody profits. The muezzin's prayer
is wasted on the new houses. The ringing
of bells rolls like a ball, and rebounds. Seraphic
praise from synagogues will fade like grey smoke.

At the end of summer I breath this air,
the parched and aching. A silence
like many shut books is thought:
many closed books, most of whose pages are
stuck like eyelids in the morning.

☙

I go up David's Tower
a little above the most exalted prayer,

halfway to heaven. Some
of the ancients succeeded: Muhammad, Jesus
and others. But didn't find rest in heaven,
they entered a higher excitement. But
the applause for them hasn't let up
below.

❧

Jerusalem is built on vaulted foundations
of a held-back shout. Without a reason
for the shout, the foundations would give, the city would totter;
if the shout is shouted, Jerusalem would explode skyward.

❧

Poets come with evening into the Old City
and leave it loaded with images
and metaphors and little maxims
and twilight similes between vaults and rims.
Darkening fruits and
wrought-iron filigree of the heart.
I lifted my hand to my forehead
to wipe the sweat
and brought up Else Lasker-Schüler
by chance. Light and small as she was in her life,
how much more so in her death. But her poems!

❧

Jerusalem, port city on the shores of eternity.
The Holy Mount is a hugh ship, a luxurious pleasure
liner. From the portholes of her Western Wall happy
saints look out, travellers. Chasidim on the dock wave
goodbye, shout hurrah till we meet again. She's
always arriving, always sailing. And the gates and the docks
and the policemen and the flags and the high masts of churches
and mosques and the smokestacks of synagogues and the boats
of praise and waves of mountains. The sound of the ram's horn is
heard: still
another sailed. Day of Atonement sailors in white uniforms
climb among ladders and ropes of seasoned prayers.

And the trade and the gates and the gold domes:
Jerusalem is the Venice of God.

(TRANSLATED BY HAROLD SCHIMMEL)

LESSON IN GEOLOGY
Elisha Porat

"The anomaly of Jerusalem is not simple to perceive.
At a glance, transparent: mountain platform and chalkstone,
an elevated Holy Site."
He tapped with his stonemason's hammer,
chipping crimson flakes off a stone taken from a wall.
"The flawless Red stone of Jerusalem testifies
that there in the subterranean depth of the city,

all is broken burst and smashed.
Like a gigantic inverted funnel—
a cistern for Jewish blood pumping,
draining into it from all worlds."
I remember his lesson as if it was yesterday:
the city afloat, the street suddenly swaying,
the veins of rust and dim and deep beneath me,
the rustle and seethe of a primeval river.

(*TRANSLATED BY RIVA RUBIN*)

JERUSALEM, 1968
David Rokeah

I

You want to know the number of gates
in Jerusalem. I count seven gates open
to you, four barred to me,
a golden gate for the lingering Messiah.

II

In deciphering letters
that burn on a cold stone
you will explore the language of darkness
and the language of shadows. Motionless
in prayer, like a hunchbacked olivetree,
you will search for keys
lost by God in the wadi of Kidron.

Jewish Quarter and New Synagogue; from Palestine in 1860 (Glasgow: 1860) (Photograph by John Cramb. Collection of Mr. William P. Wolfe, Montreal; with permission)

III

Formed out of stony earth

of solitude fencing this town

where the sorrow of the defeated

is a yashmak veiling the faces of women

where candles of life never set

I am digging in time built

into walls beneath walls.

    (TRANSLATED BY ALAN BROWNJOHN)

JERUSALEM
Else Lasker-Schüler

God formed out of his spine: Palestine
Out of one single bone: Jerusalem.

I wander as through mausoleums—
Our holy city turned to stone.
Stones lie along the bed of her dead waters
Instead of the water-silk at play: flowing and ebbing.

Transfixed by earth's cold stare,
The wanderer founders in the starry chill of her nights.
There is a fear I cannot overcome.

Were you to come . . .
Wrapped in a snow-bright Alpen-coat
And take the twilight of my day—
My arm would encircle you, framing a holy image.

As once, when I suffered in the dark of my heart—
There were both your eyes: blue clouds.
They took me from my melancholy.

Were you to come—
To this ancestral land—
You would reproach me like a little child:
Jerusalem, arise and live again!

We are greeted by

Living banners of the One God,

Greening hands, sowing the breath of life.

(TRANSLATED BY AUDRU DURCHSLAG AND JEANETTE LITMAN-
DEMEESTERE)

AUTUMN IN JERUSALEM

Oded Peled

And I heard thee wandering the Hebrew Land / southward and
eastward your gaze turns:

A n d   t h e   r a i s i n   o f   t h e   w o r l d
i s   s t i l l   i n t a c t

lo, a thin white in the tropic of the eye will accompany thee in
the streets of Yerushalem*/

come I will show thee summer blaze like a handful of
consciousness blinded by tweaks of light / come out to the balcony
facing eastward and southward:

Ramat Rachel and a nearby Arab village (Zur Baher?) a sketch

on the forehead of light forehead of light, border of the Judaean
desert Dead Sea

stain like distant azure—here, at dawn, ye shall wake to the
winged flutter of

sparrow scurrying in the high boughs of the window,

his Strength and Song is the Lord:

*Yerushalem: the ancient Cannanite name of Jerusalem.

lift up your heads oh ye heavens and your eye a frontlet of
wisdom, above your chiefest joy she will rise, her days are yet to
come—

for he whose lips are seraph will shed genuine light and an exile
in his heart will return to God's Land:

(*Translated by Aura Hammer*)

A View of Jerusalem

To Tamara

T. Carmi

1

Soft light, green
of treetops—one green,
the fir; another,
the pine. A blue nest in the middle
for the morning bells—one bell
for the fir; another
for the pine.

That is what the eyes see,
that is what the ears hear
in the northern window. There is nothing,
nothing like Jerusalem,
in which this distance says
something obscure, muted
and explicit.

The birds see the sound,

my wife sees the birds,
and I cannot lie to her.
There is nothing.

2

Child, child, little flower,
can I already play with you at words?
If I say to you that mine is ours,
that the button opens and none can close,
that the flower closes and none can open—
come here beside me.
Even when the sun is shining,
walk in the middle of the street.
When the street-lamp is before us,
put your shadow in mine.
When the street-lamp is behind us,
your hand in mine.
Always be visible,
within range of eye and voice,
and I will teach you games of hide-and-seek.

3

Naked. Bone, stone, sky.
Sirens drain our blood,
air foams in the wake of their sound.
Open wide. Dust—blind—and ashes.
Windowpanes make room for eyes,

eyes for the sound of sirens.
That is all a man is, now.

       Take off your clothes.

I have to touch you.
Now.

  4

Everyone speaks in song:
thinks one thing,
and says another;
says one thing, and thinks.

A winter landscape filled with clocks.
A man puts on his smile like a coat.
Don't look at the lining.

The mine is a name.
The raid is a door.
The trap is a part.
There is no thing
that does not compel its opposite.

A grammar of fears.
The rules—extremely sudden,
and it's hard to talk.

One thing is clear:
everyone plays.
And another thing:
you are no exception.

5

Now. Tomorrow will surely come,
in my window.
And the walls without a window?
The windows covered with stone?

My wife sees the birds
hidden,
her eyes wide open.
I see my wife:
in the noon of night,
a silver dome at her right hand;
in the dark of day,
at her left a dome of gold.

Sirens in the eyes
and stones from a wall.
(Flash of entangled horns.
A nail glittering in the Roman sun.)
A stone rises
like a small cloud—

child, child,

little hand,
can I already say to you Jerusalem,
soft light, tomorrow, another green.
(AFTER THE MAHANEH YEHUDAH EXPLOSION, 1969)

(TRANSLATED BY STEPHEN MITCHELL)

Crowds looking at a building on Ben Yehuda Street
demolished by a car bomb February 22, 1948 (Central Zionist
Archives; with permission)

CITY OF WOUND

Haim Guri

I have another city of my own blood containing too much wine
and too much tar.
City of large stones and torn iron.
Half of her in rock;
Half of her flying, gliding, to Kings' Heaven above her,
Pleasant light till the night.
City of hills, I'm a stranger to her, falling toward ravine,
She faints there
Shattering.

She leaps up
Higher and higher in the loneliness of her towers,
In love with the sky.
City of yearning, another city
built of strangled cries.

I have a city of wound.

(TRANSLATED BY AURA HAMMER)

HOUSE DOG
Uri Zvi Greenberg

Never have I raised a veil across my face before the abyss.
Nor covered my eyes from encountered fear:
Only once here I tried covering my eyes with my own hands:
Not to see the abyss of Jerusalem opening—
And I saw through the hand, shut-eyed, much fearing:
The third fire in hiding—
Now my eyes are open, lashes singed from the fire.

(TRANSLATED BY AURA HAMMER)

JERUSALEM
Moshe HaNa-ami

On the road to Bethlehem I live.
And in Emek-Refaim my friend
Bakes small cakes, scatters sugar
In the German colony. Amazing

How the old to the new is joined
Like sewage pipes on an old wall
In this Jerusalem, as if on canvas
A painter added, here flower, here tree—

And here me with detective novel,
And there old woman, and here railroad tracks,
And church, and Ethiopian priest.

And one man who for his messiah waits.
And a hand which on wall writes:
Holy place, pissing not allowed.

(*TRANSLATED BY AURA HAMMER*)

THE WARM STONE ON THE HILL OF JERUSALEM
Ayin Tur-Malka

To attach our cheeks to the warm stone on the hill of Jerusalem:
this stone softer than softness.
That within her rigidity waves of voices
which rise in the ear's imagination.
That within her hardness abysses pull.
To rest the head on her like resting it
on water.
Within her sun-heat and rain combine.
A settling of dense delight.

And when our father Jacob the loving
crowned by the retribution of love

(which warmly reaches to the root of pain)
rested his head on the stone
and the stone mellowed the headrest of his spirit
carried on to heights—

(*TRANSLATED BY AURA HAMMER*)

JERUSALEM'S WALLS
Israel Efrat

From late afternoon on,
are lit the stones of Jerusalem's walls.

From the King's street, through Mount Zion,
and in the semi-circle to Katamon westward—
like tall torches Jerusalem's walls.

Like priests' foreheads as they push back their tallit
after lifting their palms,
like a tune silent-silent burning.

From gaping light like a great recollection,
to saffron and gold, to crimson-torment-deep-
each hour and the color of its flame—
until buds of fire float in a lake of air.

Look, look
all the roads reach for Jerusalem,
and she herself?
For what does she burn so forcefully?
Toward what is she road?

Until night comes from behind, from Temple Mount,
lingers a while,
and in a dark veil hushes the city walls.

(Translated by Aura Hammer)

ABU-TOR
David Rokeah

Since evening
the hill hasn't moved. The stones that absorbed
tales of a thousand and one nights
continue to dream. My memories
are outdated. The shadow of my love
between the stones like a wire.

(Translated by Aura Hammer)

EVENING IN JERUSALEM
Yehuda Karni

The evening here does not approach in stealth,
   With feline bounds;
Night is no velvet of luxurious wealth
   To wrap you around.

The evening never oozes from the soul
   Until the last small drop is gone,

Nor does Night's curtain slowly fall
  Between the bright and dun.

The evening seizes, fetters,
  Hands on to the night;
The latter clutches, batters,
  Kills and buries tight.

(TRANSLATED BY ABRAHAM BIRMAN)

JERUSALEM MOON
Gabriel Preil

The moon has risen above the festive city.
It is not now a silver vessel on an azure sea,
nor any other metaphor that drops
from rhetoric's tired trees.

  In the great city
  of sleeping kings,
  I rise with the moon,
  the single slice of bread
  to feed my hunger—
  an explication, perhaps,
  of the festivity.

No longer am I caught on the horn of renunciation.
A violet morning prophesies: It is never too late.

(TRANSLATED BY ROBERT FRIEND)

I DON'T KNOW IF MOUNT ZION
Abba Kovner

1

I don't know if Mount Zion would recognize itself
in the fluorescent light at midnight
when all that remains of Jerusalem
is her beauty wakeful
in the milky light spreading over her limbs
still wings raising it above the desert which sank away
so slowly above the stars
this eerie seashell floating from the midst of night
a transparent giant
so much sky sweeping over it
I don't know if Mount Zion looks
into my heart which holds its breath now behind a latticed
window
out of torment and delight and for whom it's meant
in the heart of night.

2

These olive trees
which never bowed with the hidden knowledge
and the grooved wrinkles that this whole blue fan
over the Gehenna road
I don't know if Mount Zion sees the things

Mount Zion, the Dormition Abbey, and the walls of the Old City, ca. 1912 (Central Zionist Archives; with permission)

that changed our image

beyond recognition. The hands that touched it daily

like a mother touching her son's forehead fell

elusively into the slumber

of the Dead Sea

Does it hear the cry

from the Marketplace of Gates or the thrust of my prayer from the shade—

What good are friends who watch from the balcony

while our heart wrestles on the stage

and what use are we poets if we

don't know how to speak
—Does Mount Zion really exist or
is its light like our love beaming from a source
rising every
night
(TRANSLATED BY WARREN BARGAD AND STANLEY F. CHYET)

MORIAH

Levi Ben Amitai

My days have marched unto
The fragrant mount.
My feet have stood upon
The mount eternal joy.

I close my eyes and see
The whiteness of the stone
The skies of Moriah.

What can man add to
The glory of these things!
All I have are words
So poor and few.

I say unto my soul:
It is enough, enough.
(TRANSLATED REUVEN HAMMER)

CITY OF DAVID
Zerubavel Gilad

By daylight she is a village
Wrapped in the smell of smoke
And dung.
But in the dark, as her lights blossom
With a young girl's laughter,
I am reborn at her feet
And like my father's father's father
When young,
I hear on her streets at midnight
The melody of
David's harp.

(*TRANSLATED BY AURA HAMMER*)

JERUSALEM
Yaakov Fichman

Jerusalem! Cry of the hungry heart, oblivion's
garden beyond the hills when refugees fled the storm—
Silence you are, submission and rebellion.
Because of you, heart shudders, the griefs swarm.

By green of your earth I swear and by your sunlight.
I inherit the desolation that remains.

I stand like a tree in stone, by you held spellbound—
soul woven with soul, my root in your dry veins.

I love what survives in you as in cold lava,
the rejoicing sound of ancient days,
echoing still from your white rocks of silence.

But with your holiness is now my strife,
and I have come to small rocks into clods.
Dead spendour rests on furrows of new life.

(TRANSLATED BY ROBERT FRIEND)

PENALTY KICK
Ronny Someck

You'll never walk alone Beitar Yerushalaim.
In the Mahane Yehuda market they sew your Shabbat dress,
and a ragball heart rolls
between a pound of tomatoes
and an olive tin.
In these streets they brewed history over a paraffin stove.
Jesus was a bench player and Josephus Flavius
an acquisition for Italy's national team.
Close your eyes Beitar Yerushalaim
time is a penalty kick of both kicker and kicked.

(TRANSLATED BY AURA HAMMER)

LEAVING JERUSALEM
Marcia Falk

I've worn through the soles of my shoes—
my feet so tough they no longer feel the ground
where cyclamen split rocks, recklessly.

I've put on a lizard's skin,
the Salt Sea slides down my neck
like oil in the sun.

Now I'm heading west,
my suitcase stuffed with chunks of halvah,
sacks of chickpeas and almonds.

Tomorrow I'll beat my clothes
like the Bedouin women at the streams,
but the viscous scents will cling

like musk to the skin
where the body claims its home.

JERUSALEM: LADDERS OF LOVE
Gabriel Preil

I've returned to New York. For months
I am struck by the Jerusalem moon.
The stones of Jerusalem tell me wine,
testing the hues of my love.

So will it be if I too
reach the very white years.

Montefiore Quarter, date unknown (Central Zionist Archives; with permission)

The dreams that will walk in me then
will thunder like lions in their thirst.

Meanwhile mother Jerusalem
sends me regards
more peaceful than flocks
to a tower-burdened son.

(TRANSLATED BY GABRIEL LEVIN)

FROM THE STREETS OF JERUSALEM
Abba Kovner

When did the flocks pass from the streets of Jerusalem?
We went out into her street and there were
no flocks in Zion Square Jerusalem.

When was the wolves' howl silenced in the nights of Jerusalem?
In that winter we awoke
for the desert had retreated from the bounds of Jerusalem.

When did the camel caravans cease in the avenues of Jerusalem?
Yesterday an old man died
he had yet seen camels make their way through the dust of
Jerusalem.

And do mad dogs yet wander through the alleys of Jerusalem?
I saw a blocked up well in Yemin Moshe and
there is a new moon, why should
wild dogs be missing within Jerusalem.

And how does a man die in Jerusalem. In turn
each man is bequeathed one day
his own death. Even if flock by flock
they still fall on the altars of Jerusalem.

And when is there none so beautiful as Jerusalem—always
when I hear two Jerusalemites
saying to each other: Let us go home
and make ourselves a light.

(TRANSLATED BY AURA HAMMER)

TOURISTS
Yehuda Amichai

Visits of condolence is all we get from them.
They squat at the Holocaust Memorial,

They put on grave faces at the Wailing Wall
And they laugh behind heavy curtains
In their hotels.
They have their pictures taken
Together with our famous dead
At Rachel's Tomb and Herzl's Tomb
and on the top of Ammunition Hill.
They weep over our sweet boys
And lust over our tough girls
And hang up their underwear
To dry quickly
In cool, blue bathrooms.

Once I sat on the steps by a gate at David's Tower, I placed my
two heavy baskets at my side. A group of tourists was standing
around their guide and I became their target marker.

"You see that man with the baskets? Just right of his head there's
an arch from the Roman period. Just right of his head." "But he's
moving, he's moving!"

I said to myself: redemption will come only if their guide tells
them, "You see that arch from the Roman period? It's not
important: but next to it, left and down a bit, there sits a man
who's bought fruit and vegetables for his family."

(*Translated by Glenda Abramson and Todor Parfitt*)

THE TENTH GATE

Jerusalem in Jewish Folklore

Zion Gate, May 1968 (Israel Government Press Office; with permission)

King David's Tomb in Jerusalem

Folk Tale

Eighty years ago, in a Polish yeshiva, there were two pupils who were aroused with a longing for redemption. Both of them eagerly desired to ascend to Eretz Yisrael, the Land of the Fathers. They especially wished to see King David's tomb. Day and night they dreamed about it, and at last they began to think how to turn their dream into reality. They did not have money, so they decided to ascend on foot. As they decided, so they did. They set off taking only sticks and knapsacks. On the way they met with many obstacles, but with the help of God they overcame them all and arrived at last at the holy city of Jerusalem. They trembled and were happy in their hearts to be at the holy place and to arrive safe and sound at their destination. Still overcome with joy, they found themselves suddenly just opposite the walls of Mount Zion. They did not know, however, exactly where King David's tomb was or which road led there. While they were wondering, Elijah the Prophet, of blessed memory, appeared before them and showed them the way.

"Now my sons, when you reach the tomb and when you enter and go down the steps, keep to the bottom of the tomb. Your eyes will be blinded by all the visions of desire that you see there, silver, gold, and diamonds. Woe if you should lose your senses! You must look for the jug of water at King David's head. Pour water from the jug onto King David's hands as he stretches them toward you. Pour water three times over each hand, and then the King will rise up and we shall be redeemed. For King David is not dead; he lives and exists. He is dreaming, and he will arise when we are worthy of it. By your virtue and the merit of your longing and love, he will arise and redeem. Amen, that this may come to pass."

As Elijah the Prophet finished these words, he disappeared. The young men then ascended Mount Zion, guarded by Elijah, the Prophet. They went down into the depth of King David's tomb. Just as Elijah the Prophet had said, so it was. King David stretched out his hands to them, and there was a jug of water at his head. But because of our many sins, the riches around blinded the young men's eyes, and they forgot to pour water onto the hands outstretched toward them. In anguish the hands fell back and immediately the King's image disappeared.

The young men were startled when they realized that through them the redemption had been delayed again and the *galuth* would go on longer. They both wept from bitter anguish because the mitz-vah of redemption had been in their hands and they had let it slip through their fingers.

May it come to pass that silver and gold will no longer dazzle our eyes. And when the right hour comes again, let it not be delayed. Amen and Amen.

(RECORDED BY NEHAMA ZION FROM
MIRIAM TSCHERNOBILSKI BORN IN POLAND.)
(TRANSLATED BY GENE BAHARAV)

LEGENDS OF JERUSALEM

Zev Vilnay

> *The late Zev Vilnay was the most famous of Israel's guides. He collected stories about Israel and especially Jerusalem from numerous sources to enrich his legendary walking tours. The following is a brief sample.*

HOW DID DAVID CONQUER

When King David went out to fight against the Jebusites in Jerusalem, he said to his followers: "Whosoever smiteth the Jebusite first, shall be chief and captain."

What did David's commander, Joab, do? He brought a green cypress tree and fixed it by the side of the wall of Jerusalem. Then he climbed on David's shoulders, bent down the flexible head of the cypress, and hung onto it. The tree straightened itself, lifting him up to the top of the wall, which he then scaled.

What did the Almighty do? He shortened the wall, and David climbed after Joab, for David said in his book of Psalms: "In the day that the Lord delivered him from the hand of all his enemies . . . For by Thee I run upon a troop; And by my God do I scale a wall."

THE SYNAGOGUE OF ELIJAH THE PROPHET

Many centuries ago there was a very small Jewish community in Jerusalem, consisting of only nine men all told. Once when they assembled together on the eve of the Day of Atonement, there was no minyan (required quorum of ten for prayer). The day was already late when suddenly an old man entered, weary and covered with dust, looking as if he came from a great distance.

The men rejoiced upon seeing him, gave him the seat of honor, and began the service. The next day when they completed the service, each turned to the old man to invite him home for supper, but he was no where to be found. Then they understood that it was Elijah the prophet who had come to complete their minyan. They called the synagogue by his name and preserved the chair he sat in for many generations.

THE MIRACLE IN ELIJAH'S SYNAGOGUE

In the synagogue of Elijah the prophet, in old Jerusalem, in the southern wall there is a closet where Holy Bibles and prayer books for the use of the worshippers are kept. Here a great miracle was wrought by the saintly Rabbi Kelonimus, who saved the Jewish community of his city from a terrible danger.

The synagogue of Elijah the Prophet restored following the Six Day War, (Photograph by David Harris; with permission)

One Sabbath eve, a short while before Passover, a Christian priest stole into the synagogue of Elijah and placed within the book closet the body of a slain boy. Next day, on the morning of the holy Sabbath, angry crowds led by their priests broke into the Jewish quarter and streamed to the synagogue, shouting menacingly, "You have murdered our child! Your hands have shed this innocent blood! We shall avenge ourselves sevenfold! Now your bitter end has come!"

At this moment Rabbi Kelonimus entered the synagogue and saw the unruly mob pointing to the body of the dead child in the closet. Before the threatening multitude, although it was the holy day of the Sabbath, he wrote on a piece of paper the ineffable Name in full and placed it on the dead child's forehead. Immediately, to the astonishment of the people, the boy stood up, and in answer to the questions of the rabbi he designated a man in the crowd and said, "This is the priest who tormented me, then killed me and brought me here under the dark cloak of night."

People looked at each other in amazement. The chief of the priests rose and ascended the platform, where he confessed his grievous error and craved the pardon of the rabbi and all his congregation.

Thus through the merit of Rabbi Kelonimus, The Jews of Jerusalem were delivered from dire distress, and they finished the Sabbath day in rejoicing, singing psalms to the glory of the Guardian of Israel. Since then, they called their rabbi "Kelonimus baal ha-ness-the miracle-maker."

MOUNT OF ABRAHAM

In the midst of a beautiful grove, high upon a mountain peak south of Jerusalem, stands a splendid edifice—formerly the residence of the British high commissioner for Palestine. Today the building is occupied by officials of the United Nations.

The peak of the mountain, called in Arabic *Ras al-Mukkaber*—the Mighty (Mount)—rises 820 meters above sea level. From it one may view a magnificent panorama of ancient Jerusalem and its surroundings. In the distance can be seen Mount Moriah, the Mount of God, to which the patriarch Abraham journied to sacrifice Issac, his son. The Torah narrates:"Abraham lifted up his eyes, and saw the place afar off . . ."

In the Middle Ages people said that from the Mighty Mount, Abraham stood and gazed upon Mount Moriah.

On the outskirts of Jerusalem and on the sides of roads leading to her, many stones are scattered and strewn. Where did all these stones come from? Who put them along the roadsides?

It is told that when any Jew in exile remembers Jerusalem in her destruction, he feels as if a heavy stone presses his saddened heart. If the blessed day should come when he is granted the privilege of ascending to Jerusalem, the first glance at his desired site relieves him of his burden. It is as if the very stone that pressed him is lifted. He takes the stone and places it on the roadside as a faithful testimony that here he was comforted by the sight of the Holy City.

One wish is in his heart, and one prayer on his lips to see his city, Jerusalem, rebuilt and flourishing.

Did King David Erect the Tower of David?

Abraham E. Millgram

The Tower of David has stirred the imagination of all lovers of Jerusalem. The eastern walls of many Jewish homes were once adorned by stylized pictures of either the Western (Wailing) Wall or the Tower of David—signs of attachment to the Holy City and hope for its restoration. These two ancient relics were regarded as the most genuine symbols of Jerusalem. Christians, too, gazed at the Tower of David with intense interest, because King David was, according to Christian tradition, the ancestor of Jesus. Prior to modern times, neither Jews nor Christians questioned the authenticity of the tradition that the tower was erected by King David. But modern research uncovered a different origin.

The Tower of David, adjacent to the Jaffa Gate, is part of Jerusalem's Citadel. This "massive fortress of five mighty towers" occupies the area where once stood the palace of King Herod. In its present configuration the Citadel dates back to the early fourteenth century with some sixteenth century additions. In recent years the Citadel has been extensively excavated and restored and made into a museum on the history of Jerusalem.

The Tower of David is the northeastern tower of the Citadel. It is a relic of three towers which King Herod erected and named in honor of his three favorites": his brother Phasael, his friend Hippicus, and his wife Marriamne. These towers were spared demolition when Jerusalem was destroyed by the Romans in the year 70. These three towers were finally demolished by the Moslems in 1219. Only part of the Tower of Phasael was spared.

When this relic first came to be called the Tower of David is not known. Historians of the Crusading period already called it the

The Tomb of David on Mount Zion in 1900 (Central Zionist Archives; with permission)

Tower of the Citadel of David. The association of the Tower with the ancient Jewish monarch was generally accepted and was adorned with imaginative details. The most intriguing of these is one that tourist guides used to tell pilgrims and other "innocents"—that it was from this tower that King David gazed at beautiful Bathsheba as she was taking her bath, whereupon he fell deeply in love with her. Pilgrims were shown the exact spot where the King stood, the "window" through which he gazed, and the spot where Bathsheba was taking her bath. The fact that the most ancient section of the tower was erected a thousand years after King David's reign made no dent in this romantic story. Pilgrims loved to hear of the royal romance and guides enjoyed telling it.

The lower section of the so-called Tower of David is easily identified as one of the famous constructions of King Herod. The massive stones resemble those of the Western Wall. They are inferior in size, but they bear the same distinctive marks of that architectural era. Each stone is of prodigious magnitude, and is exactly fitted, the joints being perfectly true. Their definitive earmark is the beveling around the edges of each stone. The Herodian section of the tower rises about thirty or forty feet. The rest of the tower is a Turkish addition. The contrast between the massive grandeur of the Herodian workmanship and the relative frailty of the more recent section is striking.

700 YEARS OF SANCTITY

Meir Ben Dov

> *Meir Ben Dov is one of Israel's leading archaeologists. Among other things, he has served as Deputy-Director of the excavations at the Western Wall.*

During the Six Day War the forces of the Israeli Army stormed into the Old City through the Lions' Gate, going from there to the court of the Temple Mount and one of the most beautiful buildings of the ancient world, the Dome of the Rock. The radio announced,"The Temple Mount is in our hands." The magnificent Muslim structure from the seventh century was erected near the site of the Second Temple, the most holy and honored of all Jewish structures.

When the first storm of emotions had passed, the group of paratroopers—the first conquerors—make their way to the Western Wall where they unfurled the flag of Israel. From their point of view, their task was accomplished. They had reached the spot which was most holy and most symbolic of all sites in the eyes of the Jewish people. Throughout the generations both Jewish leaders and the masses had become accustomed to separating themselves from the Temple Mount and clinging to that bit of an outer support wall—the Western Wall.

The motivation of masters of Jewish law in past generations was the assumption that if something cannot be attained, but will only arouse riots and a storm of useless emotions, it is better to turn it into a heavenly possession, something abstract, that one can aspire to, while leaving the actual right to possess it to the Messiah.

This assumption was well fortified by laws which subsequent generations erected. Obviously the masters of Jewish law did not accept the Messianic-nationalistic ideas which guide such groups as the Temple Mount Faithful.

Although it would appear that sanctity was first ascribed to the Western Wall on the day of the destruction of the Temple, the 9th of Av in the year 70 C.E., in actuality the status of sanctity was granted the Wall only 500 years ago or possibly in the 13th century, some 700 years ago, but certainly not prior to that.

From the point of view of architecture, the Temple stood on the top of a mountain with slopes on all sides. In order to create a large plaza which would permit the populace to enter and observe both the structure and the rituals performed outside of it, the planners were forced to build walls on the slopes which would support the plaza. This was done when King Solomon built the first Temple and the builders of the second Temple did the same thing. At the time of Herod, the numbers who came on pilgrimage reached new highs. Therefore it was necessary to double the size of the plaza of the Temple Mount from 70 dunam (70,000 square meters) to 145 duman (145,000 square meters)—a gigantic plaza unknown in any other sanctuary in the ancient world. Four retaining walls were built around it. They are the walls of the Temple Mount—the eastern, the southern, the western and the northern.

The longest wall outside the plaza of the sanctuary—certainly not part of the walls of the sanctuary itself—is the Western Wall which is 485 meters long. In its southern half there are extant the remnants of four gates. Two gates are in the lower part of the wall and two in the upper part. The remnants of arches and platforms which led to them are known as "Robinson's Arch" and "Wilson's Arch" after the men who first revealed them. The gates are also known by names of those who discovered them, "Barkley's Gate" and "Warren's Gate." The southern most gate is the Mograbi Gate. Part of its lintel can be seen at the right side of the womens prayer space and consists of a stone which weighs more than 100 ton.

In the midst of the great space thus created the Temple itself was erected. The Ark of the Covenant stood near its western wall. In the Second Temple the Holy of Holies was completely empty, except for the "rock of the foundation," which was thought to be the rock on which the world was founded.

Obviously at the time of the Second Temple no sanctity was ascribed to the supporting walls of the Temple Mount, including the

Western Wall. Along that wall ran a street lined by shops on both sides. The shops on the eastern side were part of the wall and reached a height of 3.5 meters.

On the 9th of Av in the year 70 the Temple Mount was conquered and the Temple destroyed. On the 8th of Elul, a month later, the Upper City—in our days the Jewish quarter, the Armenian Quarter and Mount Zion—was conquered. The area of homes was plundered, destroyed and burned, and all the inhabitants were exiled from the city. The Roman imperium decreed that Jews were not permitted to live in Jerusalem or to visit there. The destroyed city served only as a camp for the Roman legion which remained there as a stationary force. After the Bar Kokhba revolt (135 C.E.) the Emperor Hadrian decreed that the city was to be rebuilt and renamed Aelia Capitolina in honor of the Emperor Aelius Hadrianus and the Capitoline Hill in Rome upon which stood the Temple of Jupiter.

The decree forbidding the entrance of Jews to Jerusalem remained in force during the hundreds of years of the Byzantine Empire which followed Rome, until the Persian conquest in 614 and, later, the Arab conquest in 638. On rare occasions Jews managed to enter the city or to visit the area of the Temple Mount, but always at the risk of their lives.

During those more than 500 years, if a Jew wanted to contemplate the holy places, he would climb up to the Mount of Olives and gaze upon the ruins of the Temple Mount and the Sanctuary. The wall which could be seen was the eastern wall, which became the most honored and sacred part of the Temple Mount.

When Jews were permitted to settle in the city, they held their prayers at the southern wall which, in the days of the Second Temple, had been the entrance with two gates leading into and out of the Temple area. Nor was the eastern wall neglected. Now they could cling to its actual stones.

Until the crusaders came and destroyed the Jewish community of Jerusalem (1099 c.e.) we have reports of Jews worshipping at the bottom of the Temple Mount, but only at the eastern or southern walls. The western wall is never mentioned.

It would seem that the tradition of praying at the foot of the western wall began with the renewal of the Jewish settlement in Marmeluke Jerusalem. This took place in 1267 when Nachmanidies came to the city. Nachmanidies began to repair the Jewish quarter including the synagogue, the area which is still known as the Jewish Quarter of the Old City. Unfortunately we do not have exact information. In the middle of the 11th century, the size of the area of Jerusalem was reduced and the southern wall of the city was built following the line of the later wall of Suleiman's, that is from El Aqsa mosque to the heights of Mont Zion. This excluded most of the southern wall, especially Hulda Gate, from being within the city.

Going to pray at those sacred sites became very dangerous for Jews. In their search for an alternate place of worship, it appears that they found a part of the remaining western wall with gigantic stones from Herod's construction. They began to pour out their prayer at that section of wall.

We know that organized prayer at the Western Wall began in the days of the Ottoman Sultan Suleiman the Magnificent, who built the walls of Jerusalem in the first half of the 16th century, i.e. 450 years ago. Suleiman wanted to draw Jews exiled from Spain and Portugal who were scattered throughout Europe and North Africa to his kingdom. Amongst the enticements this sultan offered was an orderly palace for prayer at the Western Wall.

When Jews began to pray at the Western Wall, whether at the time of Nachmanides at the end of the 13th century or in the days of Sultan Suleiman in the first half of the 16th century, it was necessary to make the place precious to Jews. This was accomplished mainly by connecting it to the tradition of holiness which in our sources was attached to "the Wall." Never mind that the tradition was not really attached to the support wall of the Temple Mount; they managed to transfer it to that wall.

In the first years of the common era, it seems that the western wall of the Temple building itself still existed. Thus it is reported in one source: "It was decreed from heaven than it should never be destroyed. Why? Because the Divine Presence is in the west." To this was joined the legend which says that when the Romans conquered the Temple Mount, Titus gave the work of destruction to four commanders of the legion, one wall to each of them. They all began destroying the walls except for the commander Pengar, an Arabian count, in whose section was the western wall. When Titus asked him why he had not carried out his orders, he contended in his defense that he wished to leave a vestige standing so that people would see and marvel at Titus' destructive force and at the size of the Temple he had destroyed (Lamentations Rabbah 1:30). Our sources tend to ascribe the fact that this wall was not destroyed to the personal intervention of Heaven since the Divine Presence was found in the western wall of the Temple.

In those days, when those tales were told, the western wall of the Sanctuary still stood in place. When they began to pray at the western retaining wall of the Temple Mount, the prayer-site of our time, they transferred the legend to the western retaining wall of the Temple Mount. In the course of time, that stretch of wall where prayers were held became the holiest place for the Jewish people, even though the tradition of its holiness was born only 700 years ago.

A 700 year old tradition is not to be sneezed at. The prayers, the emotions and the memories of those years contributed to the holiness of the Western Wall—a holiness which drew hardened fighters from the site of the Sanctuary itself to the Wall.

THE ELEVENTH GATE

Archaeology of the Old City

Jerusalem from the air, photographed by a German pilot in 1917 or 1918 (Central Zionist Archives; with permission)

WALKING THE OLD CITY: A JERUSALEM TOUR

Herbert Alexander

> *Herbert Alexander, formerly professor of psychology, is now a guide and lecturer in Jerusalem.*

There is a saying: "When the world was created, ten measures of sorrow came down to earth. Nine fell on Jerusalem and one on the rest of the earth." No city has known more conflict and suffering. Though conquered by foreign invaders some thirty-seven times in her more than four-thousand-year history, she remains the symbol of man's noblest visions of peace. The proverb continues that nine-tenths of the world's beauty and holiness also rained upon the city, bringing into existence a place full of vibrant tensions: between darkness and light, spirit and substance, war and peace. Those tensions, for all their modern guises—souvenirs for sale amid the shrines, soldiers patrolling the holy streets—still confound and fascinate.

This walk is tailored to fit into two days, but you could rush through it in one—or, better, savor it in seven.

Montefiore's Windmill, across from Liberty Bell Park, and the Mishkenot Sha'ananim building below it were the first built outside the Old City walls, in 1860. The Yemin Moshe neighborhood was the beginning of modern Jerusalem. From its observation platform, the Old City spreads out before you. To the left is Jaffa Gate, with banners flying from the Tower of David. The Old City walls, built by the Turks only 450 years ago, are in fact the newest city walls. They sit on the remains of Crusader walls from 1100, which sit on Byzantine remains from 550 and follow almost exactly the Roman walls from 135, which replaced the walls the Romans destroyed in 70.

The valley before you, Gai Ben Hinnom—*gehenom*, Hebrew for hell—has been by turns the site of pagan idol worship, Canaanite child sacrifice, a leper colony, and tombs. "Yes, though I walk through the valley of the shadow of death"—this is it. As the border between Jordanian-occupied Jerusalem and Israel from 1948 to 1967, this valley also bears some of the deepest scars of the long Arab–Israeli conflict. Arab Legion troups occupied the Old City walls, firing sporadically into the Yemin Moshe neighborhood, which became a boarded-up slum. The destruction in Jerusalem during these years saw 90 percent of the Jewish Quarter reduced to rubble. Beyond is the Judaean Desert.

Nineteenth-century *Yemin Moshe* is the "new" Jerusalem. Restored after the Six Day War, it is now a charming neighborhood of high-priced homes where noted artists have studios.

Descending Yemin Moshe Street, at the bottom of Yemin Moshe, bear right and cross the bridge to the foot of Mount Zion. A path to the left takes you up the hill to the southwest corner of the wall, with spectacular views of the New City along the way.

The tour of the Old City could begin at Zion Gate, but we recommend the more spectacular Ramparts Walk from (1) *Jaffa Gate*. Follow the path to the Citadel, turn right before entering Jaffa Gate, then walk over the wall and around the Armenian Quarter to (2) Zion Gate. From the top of Zion Gate, the Jewish Quarter, the Temple Mount with the gold Dome of the Rock, and the lead-domed Al Aksa Mosque come into view. Beyond the Old City you can see the Hebrew University on Mount Scopus, the *Mount of Olives* with the churches at *Gethsemane*, and the ancient *Jewish Cemeteries*; and, to the southeast, the Judaean Desert stretching to Jordan.

Descend at Zion Gate and step outside. The pockmarks are damage from the fighting in 1948. This became the border after the evacuation of the Jewish Quarter. On re-entering, turn right, follow the street to and across the parking lot, and turn left to the (3) *Four Sephardic Synagogues*, all largely destroyed between 1948 and 1967 and reconstructed after the Six Day War. Built in the early 1600s, the Yohanan Ben-Zakkai is the largest and one of the most beautiful in Jerusalem. Two-thirds of this three-story synagogue was built below street level, so as not to challenge Muslim architectural domination of the landscape. Continue along the street to the reconstructed arch of the (4) *Hurva Synagogue*. Built in the late 1850s, this was the largest in Jerusalem in 1948 and was intact at the time the Jewish Quarter surrendered to Jordan. It stands today as a memorial to the destruction of 1948.

(5) *The Cardo* (below street level), the main business avenue of Roman, Byzantine, and Crusader Jerusalem, was discovered in excavations in the Jewish Quarter in the 1970s. The northern part of the street, built by the Romans in about 135, starts at *Damascus Gate* and runs between the Muslim and Christian quarters to David Street. A small portion at Damascus Gate has been excavated. The Byzantines extended the street through the Jewish Quarter in 550, and the Crusaders rebuilt part as a closed shopping mall in the 1100s. In the days of the Byzantine Cardo, columns supported a covered sidewalk on both sides, and arched shops lined the street—some can still be seen. Note that only half the width of the street is exposed.

Continue north. The pointed Gothic arches indicate the covered Crusader Cardo, occupied by modern shops. Prices on the Cardo tend to be fixed, but it never hurts to say, "It's nice, but I didn't want to spend that much," and see what happens.

Midway along the Cardo is the (6) *Cardo Culinaria Restaurant*, a first-century kosher Roman restaurant. The furnishings and decor are based on excavations in the Jewish Quarter, the menu on a Latin cookbook of the period.

The following labels appear on the map:

- Golden Gate
- TEMPLE MOUNT
- **20** Dome of the Rock
- **19** Al Aska Mosque
- Excavations
- **18** Islamic Museum
- VIA DOLOROSA
- WESTERN WALL TUNNEL
- Iron Gate
- **14** Western (Wailing) Wall
- Mograbi Gate
- MUSLIM QUARTER
- **15**
- Excavations
- **16**
- **17** Dung Gate
- **13** Western Wall Plaza
- Mount of Olives
- Gethsemane
- Jewish Cemeteries
- To Jordan
- OLD CITY
- ¼ mile
- Damascus Gate
- START
- YEMIN MOSHE
- Mount Zion
- Mishkenot Sha'ananim
- Montefiore's Windmill
- JEWISH QUARTER
- **12**
- Hurva Synagogue
- Church of the Redeemer **23**
- **21** Souk (Market)
- **9**
- **11**
- **6**
- **10**
- **4**
- **3**
- Church of the Holy Sepulchre **24**
- **22** Archway
- **7**
- **8**
- **5**
- The Cardo
- HABAD ST.
- Parking lot
- CHRISTIAN QUARTER ST.
- DAVID ST.
- ARMENIAN QUARTER
- 100 yards
- N
- CHRISTIAN QUARTER
- **25** Citadel (David's Tower)
- St. James Cathedral
- Zion Gate **2**
- Jaffa Gate **1**
- ••• Below street level
- START
- HATIVAT YERUSHALAYIM
- HATIVAT ETZIONI

Walking tour map, courtesy of Condé Nast Traveler. Copyright © 1993 by The Condé Nast Publications, Inc.

Just above the Cardo, at 34 Habad Street, (7) *Archeological Seminars* offers in-depth walking tours in the Old City. To the south on Habad Street, search in (8) *Sachs Gallery* and the *Cardo Center* for ancient coins and antiquities.

Go back down again to the Cardo and turn right past the Culinaria. Go up four or five steps to street level. To the left, just before the Muslim Quarter, is (9) *Tamar*, a shop barely big enough for two. The owner works mostly in silver. Back down the street near the Hurva, (10) *Baruch Hadaya* has very elegant modern pieces.

Halfway between Hadaya and Tamar, a side street takes you to the (11) *Broad Wall*. Built by King Hezekiah before the Assyrian siege of Jerusalem in 701 B.C.E., this was the northern border of the city twenty-seven hundred years ago. Under a nearby school stands the gate through which the Babylonians captured the city in 586 B.C.E., ending the First Temple period.

Return to the Hurva area and cross to the (12) *Wohl Archaeological Museum (Herodian Quarter)*. Beneath Yeshivat HaKotel are the remains of six mansions that belonged to wealthy priests in Herodian times. The structures were burned by the Romans in 70 C.E., but mosaics, frescoes, furniture, and ritual baths survived.

You come out down the hill on your way to the (13) *Western Wall Plaza*. The Temple Mount ahead of you is crowned by the gold Dome of the Rock, built in 691 after the first Arab Conquest. Muslim tradition says that Mohammed ascended from this spot to heaven on his Night Journey. The Dome sits on or near the site of the Sanctuary of the great Second Temple, destroyed by the Romans in 70. It had, in turn, replaced the First Temple of Solomon, which had stood for about 350 years before its ruin by the Babylonians in 586 B.C.E. For Jews this is the holiest place on earth; for Muslims, the site of the third holiest mosque, Al Aksa; for Christians, the site of major events in the life of Jesus. So if you come here on a Friday afternoon, you will hear the call of the muezzin from the mirarets, the peal of bells from the Church of the Holy Sepulchre, and the singing of Jews greeting the Sabbath Bride.

For the last thousand years, the Jews' most sacred place of prayer has been the Kotel of (14) *Western Wall*, of the Temple Mount. It was long believed to be the only remains of the Temple and closest to the site of the Holy of Holies, though both of these claims have been disputed by recent scholarship. Still, this is the place where a Jew has the greatest sense of standing with the generations whose most fervent prayer has been "Next Year in Jerusalem." On Friday evening, song and dance greet the Sabbath. For festivals, tens of thousands of people fill the plaza in front for prayers. At noon on Friday, the Holy Day for Muslims, thousands flock to the Al Aksa Mosque. At three, the Franciscans walk in procession along the Via Dolorosa to the Holy Sepulchre.

Two recent excavations reveal the extent and magnificence of the Temple Mount. North of the plaza the (15) *Western Wall Tunnel* was dug under the Muslim Quarter to the northwest corner of the Temple Mount. Inside is a replica of the Second Temple, Herodian masonry, and much more. Walk to the huge (16) *South Wall Excavation*, where you can see Crusader, Umayyad, Byzantine, and Second Temple Jewish remains, and to the southeast the original steps and pilgrim gates to the Temple Mount.

Had enough for the day? The No. 38 bus just outside (17) *Dung Gate* will take you close to our starting point in about three stops. But if you want to continue, a ramp to the right of the Western Wall leads to *Mograbi Gate*, which is the visitors' entrance for the (18) *Islamic Museum*, (19) *Al Aksa Mosque*, and the (20) *Dome of the Rock*, all of which are open to non-Muslims some hours of every day, except Friday and Holy Days. Strolling around the Temple Mount is free, but buy tickets for the Muslim buildings at one of the kiosks.

And dress modestly—in other words, don't wear shorts—to visit this place of great sanctity.*

Follow the path around the Temple Mount and back to the Western Wall Plaza and take the stairs to the Street of the Chain. Turn left and continue up the hill toward Jaffa Gate. When you crossing the Cardo, the street becomes David Street. You are now in a medieval (21) *Arab souk* with shops selling spices, clothing, brass and copper, jewelry, and souvenirs. Bargaining is absolutely expected. Your opening offers should be about half the asking price; where you end up depends upon how much you want the thing. There are tremendous bargains on things you don't want.

At Muristan Street, turn right through the arch into the (22) *Christian Quarter*. The Lutheran (23) *Church of the Redeemer* at the end of the street, the Protestant church nearest the Holy Sepulchre, was built in the 1890s on Crusader ruins. Turn left to the (24) *Church of the Holy Sepulchre*. For sixteen hundred years this has been the focus of Christian pilgrimage to Jerusalem. Constantine built the original Byzantine church in about 333 at the site of the Crucifixion and Tomb of Jesus. The church was damaged many times; its destruction by the

---

*There are different opinions concerning the halakhic permissability of entering the Temple Mount area. The Chief Rabbinate of Israel has posted signs warning that it is forbidden to do so. Some Orthodox authorities, such as Rabbi Shlomo Goren, were of the opinion that at least part of the area was not included in the prohibition. The Law Committee of the Rabbinical Assembly of Israel (Masorti-Conservative) has issued an opinion stating that it is permissible to enter the Temple Mount, but not the Dome of the Rock or the raised platform surrounding it. A minority opinion stated that the entire area is permissible except the place where the Holy of Holies was situated (i.e., the central area within the Dome of the Rock) and that in all cases proper dress and an attitude of reverence are required. It was suggested that Psalm 15 be recited before ascending to the Mount.—ed.

Muslim caliph Al-Hakim in the eleventh century inspired the Crusades.

Today's Crusader structure was built in the twelfth century on the site of the much larger Byzantine original. Property rights today are divided among Roman Catholics, Greek Orthodox, Armenians, Syrians, Copts, and Ethiopians, but the keys have been kept by a Muslim family since the days of Saladin.

Inside the church are what are traditionally regarded as the last stations of the Via Dolorosa. A balcony to the right of the entrance encloses what some believe to be the hill of Golgotha, where Jesus was crucified. Directly ahead is the Stone of Unction, where his body was prepared for burial. To the left we come to the reconstructed Byzantine Rotunda and the Anastasis, or Chapel of the Resurrection, with the Tomb under the great dome. The rotunda and dome inspired the Dome of the Rock in 691, which reflects the same interior architectural plan.

In the crypt below the church is an ancient stone quarry, now the Chapel of Saint Helena, named for Constantine's mother, who in 326 claimed she found the True Cross there. The quarry dates from the time of Herod. It is thought that some of the stones of the Western Wall match those in this quarry.

It's a typical Jerusalem story. Muslims have the keys to the church where Helena found the Cross in an abandoned quarry that Jews are said to have used to cut stones for the Second Temple.

On leaving the Church of the Holy Sepulchre, turn right; walk to Christian Quarter Street and make a left, then walk to David Street, turn right, and walk to the (25) *Citadel* at Jaffa Gate. This ancient structure, which has archeological remains going back two thousand years in some places, houses the Tower of David Museum of the History of Jerusalem. A walk though a series of chambers takes you through the entire history of Jerusalem, with models, audiovisual displays, and film clips. Don't miss the twenty-minute animated film.

The 360-degree view from the top of the Tower is spectacular. In the late afternoon light, the city takes on a pink and then a golden glow as flecks of mica in stone reflect the setting sun.

Many believe there is a heavenly Jerusalem just above the earthly one of tension and conflict. It is a city of perfection, with streets of gold and buildings of sapphire and pearl, where everyone lives in perfect harmony with his neighbor and his God. A thin gold chain hangs down from this Celestial City, just over the gold dome on the Temple Mount, waiting for the Messiah to pull it down and make the two one. From the top of the Tower, as the sun sets and turns the stones of the city to gold, you may catch a glimpse of it.

TWENTY-FIVE YEARS OF EXCAVATIONS IN JERUSALEM, 1967–1992

ACHIEVEMENTS AND EVALUATION

Hillel Geva

> *Hillel Geva, an archeologist working with the Israel
> Exploration Society, assisted the late Prof. Nahman Avigod in
> his work in Jerusalem.*

The reunification of Jerusalem in 1967 sparked a dramatic surge of archaeological activity in the ancient city. Widespread investigation of the ancient remains was initiated on a scale which overshadowed all such previous work. Excavations were conducted throughout the entire extent of ancient Jerusalem, including places within the Old City walls where the spade of the archaeologist had never broken ground. Building and structural remains, and the artifacts that have come to light in the course of the last twenty-five years of intensive archaeological research in Jerusalem, now make it possible to re-evaluate and summarize some of the key questions concerning the topography and architectural features of the city during various periods of its history. As a result, much of our understanding of the city's past has been revolutionized.

One cannot summarize the decades of archaeological research in Jerusalem without mentioning the enormous and often insoluble difficulties—some of them specific to Jerusalem—that have always been inherent in archaeological excavations there. Most of the urban area of ancient Jerusalem today lies within the walls of the densely built Old City and the adjacent neighborhoods. This severely limits the possibilities for excavating large areas, which is the only way to obtain a comprehensive overview of the city's topography. Religious sensitivity and political factors also hinder archaeological research in key parts of the city. Jerusalem has been inhabited continuously and intensively for thousands of years. On the slopes upon which the city was built, and in the surrounding valleys, archaeological deposits consisting of layers of occupation and accumulated debris were later covered by large, deep dumps. Buildings constructed upon steep hillsides collapsed and suffered erosion, leaving only foundations in some places. With each subsequent rebuilding, foundations had to be sunk more deeply through the previous occupational levels to achieve the necessary stability. Earlier structures were dismantled and their building stone reutilized. Sometimes, as a result of official building activities in the city, such as the construction of the Temple Mount in the days of Herod, all previously existing structures along its outer sides were razed to make room for the new foundations. In view of the difficulties and limitations on the investigation of Jerusalem's past, the overwhelming achievements of archaeological activity, and particularly the excavations of the last twenty-five years, are the more remarkable.

THE BRONZE AGE

The excavations by Y. Shiloh in Area E on the eastern slope of the City of David in 1978–1985 revealed significant remains of the earlier settlement of the city, indicating a limited occupational presence in the Chalcolithic period—as early as the fourth millennium B.C.E. During the third millennium B.C.E., in the Early Bronze Age, the first structures were erected on the bedrock of the steep eastern slope of the hill above the Gihon Spring. In the course of these excavations, a long segment of the city wall of the beginning of the second millennium B.C.E. was uncovered. This was part of a southern extension of fortifications first found by Kenyon in the 1960s. A succession of remains of Middle and Late Bronze Age settlements discovered in Kenyon's, and mainly in Shiloh's, excavations presents firm evidence for occupational continuity in the City of David in its early days.

THE FIRST TEMPLE PERIOD

So far no evidence has been encountered at the City of David for its conquest by members of the tribe of Judah or, at a later date, by King David, as described in the biblical narrative. These recorded events of the earliest history of Jerusalem still remain without satisfactory explanation from an archaeological point of view and perhaps manifest the need for re-evaluating the correlation of the historical and archaeological data.

Shiloh's work in Area G provided new evidence that the stepped stone structure at the top of the northeastern slope of the City of David, previously excavated by Macalister and Duncan, and later by Kenyon, dates to the tenth century B.C.E. Shiloh assigned these remains to King David's Fortress of Zion mentioned in the Bible. Recent analysis of finds from this area for final publication has led J. M. Cahill and D. Tarler, members of the Shiloh expedition, to propose the possibility that the stepped stone structure was constructed in the days of the Canaanites-Jebusites (thirteenth–eleventh centuries B.C.E.) before David's conquest of the city.

Warren's Shaft, the ancient water supply system of the City of David, was uncovered and cleared in the framework of Shiloh's excavations. However, there still is no conclusive dating for its construction.

In the eastern part of the Ophel, south of the Temple Mount, B. Mazar and E. Mazar uncovered a complex of monumental buildings attesting to royal construction activities during the ninth–eighth centuries B.C.E. This complex consists of several contiguous construction units which together formed a massive fortification system—the eastern defense wall of the city—during the First Temple period. Among these buildings are a tower and remains of an adjacent structure which the excavators identified as a four-chambered gatehouse—the biblical Water Gate.

Discoveries by N. Avigad in the Jewish Quarter have finally resolved the long-standing debate concerning the date of Jerusalem's westward expansion over the Western Hill of the ancient city. The many structures and artifacts he found on bedrock throughout the Western Hill, particularly the remains of the Broad Wall, indicate that settlement on the hill began as early as the eighth century B.C.E. At the end of that century, King Hezekiah fortified the Western Hill by encompassing it with a strong wall. Additional sections of fortifications excavated by Avigad north of the Broad Wall probably indicate a second phase of fortification-building activity toward the end of the First Temple period—to strengthen the northern side of the city, which lacks deep natural barriers. These remains of fortifica-

tions exposed on the Western Hill confirm Josephus's account that
the First Wall of Jerusalem dates originally to the time of David and
Solomon (the First Temple period). It is also clear now that portions
of the early city wall of the end of the First Temple period were later
incorporated into the reconstruction of the First Wall erected around
the Western Hill by the Hasmoneans in the late second century
B.C.E. As a a result of numerous excavations and studies conducted
along the western sections of the First Wall above the Hinnom
Valley, there is growing evidence pointing to the existence of fortified segments dating to the end of the First Temple period on this
side of the city. To my mind, it conclusively confirms the view held
by most scholars that the late First Temple period city wall encompassed the entire Western Hill up to the present Jaffa Gate, and continued southward above the Hinnom Valley around Mount Zion,
and down toward the southern tip of the City of David. A minority
opinion visualizes a smaller city on the Western Hill.

Shiloh's excavations brought up evidence for the existence of a
sparse extramural residential neighborhood in the eighth century
B.C.E., located outside the eastern wall of the City of David and contemporary with the early stage of the settlement of the Western Hill.
An unfortified squatters' neighborhood north of the Western Hill (in
the present-day Christian and Muslim Quarters) began to develop
during this period. A contemporary workshop building, discovered
by M. Broshi outside the western wall of the city, should also be seen
in the context of such extramural construction. It would seem that
the impetus for construction of residential areas outside the walls of
Jerusalem at the late First Temple period ceased with the Syrian siege
by Sennacherib in 701 B.C.E. and the resulting deterioration of security. Unfortified quarters were probably abandoned at that time, their
residents preferring to live within the walled city.

The First Temple period cemeteries around Jerusalem have also

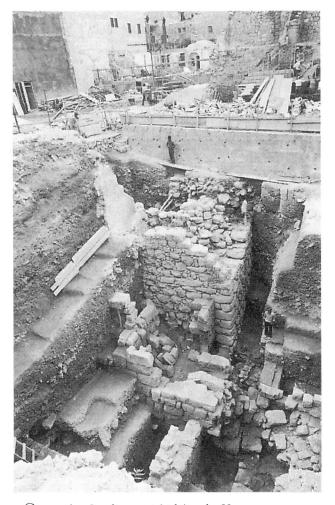

Corner of an Israelite tower (right) and a Hasmonean tower abbutting it (left) as uncovered in the Jewish Quarter (Ancient Jerusalem Revealed. Israel Exploration Society; with permission)

been thoroughly investigated in the past twenty-five years. Over a hundred First Temple period tombs are known to us from surveys and excavations around the city, although, regrettably, only a few were found with their contents intact.

In 1968–1970 D. Ussishkin surveyed and documented tens of burial caves in Silwan Village on the eastern slope of the Kidron Valley opposite the City of David. We now have a comprehensive picture of this sumptuous cemetery, which served Jerusalem's upper classes during the First Temple period (ninth–seventh centuries B.C.E.).

Several groups of burial caves dating to the end of the First Temple period (eighth–sixth centuries B.C.E.) were excavated on the slopes of the Hinnom Valley by M. Broshi, A. Kloner and D. Davis, by G. Barkay, and by R. Reich. Their location provides further evidence for the city's westward expansion at the end of the First Temple period. Among the many artifacts discovered by Barkay in the Ketef Hinnom cemetery are two small, rolled silver plaques bearing the biblical priestly benediction from Numbers 6:24–26.

A few rock-cut tombs of the end of the First Temple period were reinvestigated and published by G. Barkay, A. Kloner and A. Mazar. Two such tombs in the grounds of the Saint Etienne Monastery are the largest and most luxurious of that period known to date in Jerusalem—or elsewhere in the Land of Israel. Their unexpected location is indicitive of the northward expansion of Jerusalem's unfortified residential areas at the end of the First Temple period. Although it is difficult to establish whether they can be identified as the royal tombs mentioned by Josephus to have been situated in this vicinity, they probably give an idea of the monumental sepulchers in which the kings of Judah and high-ranking officials were buried.

Avigad's excavations on the Western Hill, B. Mazar and E. Mazar's excavations at the Ophel, and Shiloh's work in the City of

David provide archaeological evidence that sheds light on the biblical account of the destruction and burning of the city by the Babylonians in 587/6 B.C.E. The most important testimony for this event comes from Area G in the City of David, where fragmentary remains of several burnt buildings containing assemblages of vessels characteristic of the period were discovered. In one of the rooms, which once contained an archive of documents, were more that fifty clay bullae that had been fired in the conflagration. This important epigraphic find provided a long list of Hebrew names, two of which have been identified with biblical personages active in Jerusalem on the eve of its destruction by the Babylonians: Gemariah son of Shaphan and Azariah son of Hilqiah.

Unique artifacts relating to the Temple and to the political administration in Jerusalem at the time of the First Temple have been published recently. The most important is a small ivory pomegranate bearing the Hebrew inscription: "sacred donation for the priests [in] the house of Yahweh." It apparently belonged to a group of objects utilized in the Jewish Temple in Jerusalem, of which no architectural remains are yet known. Also of great interest are two identical bullae depicting two figures, a king and a high personage facing each other. Beneath them is the Hebrew inscription: "governor of the city." These impressions were most probably made by the seal of an official under one of the last kings of the Judean monarchy.

THE SECOND TEMPLE PERIOD

Finds from recent excavations of the City of David have provided new information on the extent and urban features of Jerusalem during the Persian and early Hellenistic periods, before the renewed expansion of the city toward the Western Hill. For the first time, an occupational level of the Persian period was uncovered—by Shiloh at the City of David—in a clear stratigraphic context. Kenyon's and

Shiloh's excavations also provide important evidence that the remains of fortifications on the crest of the eastern slope of the City of David were originally constructed during the Second Temple period, and possibly even as early as the time of Nehemiah (mid-fifth century B.C.E.)—but not in the Bronze Age (the Canaanite period) or the Iron Age as had been thought previously. This shows that at the beginning of the Second Temple period the earlier line of fortification of the City of David, at the lower part of the eastern slope above the Gihon Spring, was abandoned in favor of one better placed, along the crest of the hill.

In all, the information gleaned from the new excavations clearly indicates that settlement in Jerusalem after the destruction of the First Temple and until the Hasmonean period (sixth–second centuries B.C.E.) was once again confined only to the traditional boundaries of the City of David, the Ophel, and the Temple Mount.

The exact location of the Seleucid Akra fortress, known from historical sources to have been erected in Jerusalem during the second century B.C.E., is still enigmatic after a hundred and fifty years of archaeological research in the city. The absence of any supportive finds on the Western Hill no longer justifies looking for it at the western side of the city, as had been suggested by some scholars. Several locations proposed more recently for the Akra focus upon controversial archaeological remains in the southeastern part of the Herodian Temple Mount precinct or on the Ophel. So far, such proposals remain inconclusive. The information we do have may lead us to reconsider one of the other hypotheses: that the Seleucid Akra was one in a series of citadels erected from the time of the Ptolemies (and perhaps even earlier, during the First Temple period or the return from Babylonian exile) until the construction of the Antonia fortress by Herod on the dominating hill next to the northwestern corner of the Temple Mount.

*Remains of Hasmonean construction uncovered in the
Jewish Quarter (Ancient Jerusalem Revealed. Israel
Exploration Society; with permission)*

All the excavations on the Western Hill attest to a resumption of
permanent settlement there during the second century B.C.E. This
process apparently reflected a change in the status of Jerusalem during the middle of that century, when it became the capital of the

merging Hasmonean kingdom. Toward the end of the Hasmonean period, in the mid-first century B.C.E. and particularly from the time of Herod, large, elaborate, lavish dwellings were built in the wealthy suburb on the Western Hill known as the Upper City. At the beginning of Hasmonean rule (the second half of the second century B.C.E.) the First Wall was rebuilt around the Western Hill along the line of the circumvallation at the end of the First Temple period. The excavations along the line of the First Wall in the north, west and south exposed long sections of the wall and several of its towers. Evidence was found for the incorporation into the Hasmonean First Wall of older sections of fortifications of the late First Temple period.

In the Tower of David Citadel, R. Sivan and G. Solar brought to light impressive testimony of the siege of Jerusalem by the Seleucid King Antiochus VII Sidetes in 134–132 B.C.E., which left hundreds of ballista stones and arrowheads at the foot of the wall.

Only traces of the foundations attributed to Herod the Great's palace that stood at the northwestern corner of the Upper City were uncovered in excavations by K.M. Kenyon and A.D. Tushingham, by R. Amiram and A. Eitan, and by M. Broshi and D. Bahat in the area of the present-day Tower of David Citadel and the Armenian Garden south of it. This extensive palace is believed to have occupied most of the area of the present Armenian Quarter up to the Old City wall in the south.

Avigad's excavations in the Jewish Quarter revealed remains of large, sumptuous private dwellings in Jerusalem's Upper City from the days of Herod the Great (the second half of the first century B.C.E.) until the destruction of the city in 70 C.E. Of these, the most impressive is a palatial Herodian mansion that included several dozen rooms arranged around a central courtyard. The dwellings built in the Upper City at that time had some particularly splendidly decorated rooms with colored mosaic pavements, and fine-quality plastered, frescoed and stuccoed walls. In the houses, Jewish ritual baths (*miqva'ot*) were found cut into the bedrock.

One of the most outstanding finds in the Jewish Quarter excavations is a graffito of the Menorah on two plaster fragments. This has come to be considered the most detailed, authentic early depiction of the Menorah that stood in the Temple in Jerusalem during the Second Temple period.

B. Mazar's excavations at the Ophel exposed the massive foundations of the southern wall and the southern corners of the Herodian Temple Mount platform. These discoveries followed up and complemented the thorough investigation along the outer walls of the Temple Mount started by Warren a century earlier. Abutting the walls of the Temple Mount, remains of impressive Herodian public works now uncovered to their full extent include wide, paved streets, flights of stairs, and plazas used by those who came to the Temple.

Robinson's Arch was found to be part of a series of vaults that supported a staircase giving access from the level of the main street in the Tyropoeon Valley to a gate once located high at the southwestern corner of the Temple Mount.

The Western Wall of the Temple Mount was exposed along its entire length, north of the present prayer plaza, by means of a tunnel excavated with considerable difficulty beneath the buildings of the Old City under the supervision of M. Ben-Dov and later by D. Bahat. The dating of Wilson's Arch remains uncertain. Some scholars consider it to be the original arch—part of the bridge built during the Second Temple period over the Tyropoeon Valley; others prefer an Early Arab period dating and consider that it was built over the remains of the original arch. In the Wall north of Wilson's Arch, a gigantic stone weighing over 300 tons (!) was discovered. Further north, the façade of Warren's Gate, as it was rebuilt in the Early Arab period, was entirely exposed. At the northern end of the Western

Wall, the builders of the Herodian Temple Mount had to cut into the living rock of the hill in order to continue building the Wall in a straight line. The pavement of the street hugging the Wall here remained unfinished for some reason. Still further north, a rock-cut aqueduct, apparently of the Hasmonean period, that had been reported by Warren, was rediscovered and investigated anew. It seems to support the increasingly prevalent view that Herod's Antonia fortress was confined only to the rock outcrop between the Temple Mount and the Convent of the Sisters of Zion to the north.

The location and date of the Second Wall still remain unresolved problems in the topography of Second Temple period Jerusalem. Avigad's discovery at the northwestern side of the present Jewish Quarter of the remains of a fortification system in the line of the First Wall, which he identified as the Ginat Gate complex, is perhaps indirect evidence that the Second Wall indeed passed north of there, along a course largely corresponding to that proposed by Kenyon.

The long-standing controversy among scholars concerning the precise line of the Third Wall of Jerusalem, constructed at the northern side of the city during the reign of Agrippa I in the first century C.E., now seems to be near resolution. The accumulating evidence conclusively confirms Sukenik and Meyer's identification of the fortifications remains north of the Damascus Gate as the Third Wall, and clearly shows that the Third Wall did not follow the course of the present north wall of the Old City.

Surprisingly, a number of excavations along the conjectured eastern and western line of the Third Wall have not yielded any results. A possible explanation of this may be inferred from the excavations along the northern line of the Third Wall, which seems to have been extensively robbed of its stones, mainly for the building of Aelia Capitolina, leaving only fragments of its foundations. It may be, therefore, that those eastern and western sections of the Third Wall that were closest to Aelia Capitolina were dismantled to the last stone without leaving a trace. A hypothetical reconstruction of the line of the eastern and western portions of the Third Wall would perhaps have it running slightly inside the present wall of the Old City.

A. Mazar's new archaeological survey and study, in the late 1960s, of the remains of ancient aqueducts that supplied water to Jerusalem brought to light new information on their exact course and the engineering details of their construction. Segments of the Lower Aqueduct were recently uncovered south and west of the city limits. Particularly impressive is the long tunnel piercing the Armon Hanaziv ridge (the Hill of Evil Counsel).

The extensive cemeteries which surrounded Jerusalem during the Second Temple period have been the subject of intensive excavations and research in the years after 1967. Tens of new tombs excavated primarily north of the city, in the area of Mount Scopus and the new Giv'at Hamivtar and French Hill neighborhoods, have raised the known number of Second Temple period burial caves in Jerusalem cemeteries to over 830. Notable among recently discovered tombs is the burial cave of the Nazirite family excavated by N. Avigad, and a burial cave uncovered by V. Tzaferis in which an inscription was found mentioning one "Mattathiah son of Juda[h]," identified by some scholars with Mattathias Antigonus, the last king of the Hasmonean dynasty. Another tomb, excavated by Tzaferis, contained an ossuary bearing the inscription: "Simon the Temple builder" and the bones of a man executed by crucifixion. South of the city, Z. Greenhut recently excavated a tomb containing an ossuary inscribed "Joseph son of Caiapha"—perhaps related to the family of the Jerusalem high priest Caiaphas mentioned in the New Testament in connection with the crucifixion of Jesus.

For the first time we have vivid, concrete evidence for the violent conquest of Jerusalem by Roman Legions in 70 C.E. and the intensive destruction of its buildings. Deep accumulations of stones from walls and buildings of the Temple Mount were encountered in B. Mazar's excavations next to the southern and western walls. These substantial remains, which included ornamented architectural fragments, covered destroyed buildings and streets alongside the Temple Mount. Next to the southwestern corner of the Temple Mount, a fragmentary Hebrew inscription incised in stone was found, reading: "to the house of the trumpeting to pr(oclaim)." This stone was originally embedded in the masonry high at the top of the corner here. Avigad's excavations in the Jewish Quarter uncovered evidence of the total destruction of the luxurious structures of the Upper City. The destruction wrought by the Roman conquest is particularly evident in the Burnt House found buried under a thin layer of charred remains and collapse. A stone weight inscribed "[belonging] to bar [son of] Kathros"—the name of a well-known priestly family of Jerusalem during the Second Temple period—was found in this building.

THE ROMAN PERIOD

(SECOND–THIRD CENTURIES C.E.)

Recent excavations have shed new light on the construction activities of the Roman Tenth Legion, which, after 70 C.E., built its camp on the Western Hill of Jerusalem over the ruins of the Upper City of the Second Temple period. A small unit of the Tenth Legion occupied several scattered buildings on the Western Hill, of which many fragmentary remains came to light mainly in the vicinity of the Tower of David Citadel.

The northern gate of Aelia Capitolina with its tripartite arched entrance flanked by two towers, located under the present Damascus Gate, was entirely exposed by M. Magen. The gateway is built mainly

of large ashlars taken from destroyed Second Temple period buildings. Magen's work confirmed that this monumental gateway, mod-
elled on Roman triumphal arches and preserved to an impressive
height, was originally constructed at the time of the foundation of
the Roman colony Aelia Capitolina by Hadrian at the beginning of
the second century C.E. The excavation results seem to indicate that
Aelia Capitolina was an unfortified city, with the possible exception
of the three massive Herodian towers and the western section of the
First Wall, which, as Josephus tells us, were left in place to protect
the camp of the Tenth Legion stationed in the city after 70 C.E.

Information concerning various public and religious buildings in
the northern, civilian, portion of Roman Aelia Capitolina is still
very fragmentary. We are mainly familiar with Roman street pavements and plazas. Inside the Damascus Gate, M. Magen uncovered
part of a massive Roman pavement which is firmly identified with
the open plaza depicted on the Madaba mosaic map. The pavement
in the basement of the Convent of the Sisters of Zion, northwest of
the Temple Mount, venerated as the Lithostrotos in Christian tradition (the courtyard of the Antonia fortress) can now be dated more
confidently to the Roman period. Apparently, it was part of the eastern forum of Roman Aelia Capitolina, where a tripartite triumphal
arch stood—of which the central, highest archway is the Ecce Homo
arch in the Via Dolorosa.

Structural remains attributed to the Roman period were discovered from the 1960s on in a survey and in excavations of limited
extent conducted by V. Corbo and others during the restoration of
the Church of the Holy Sepulcher. The most impressive of these
Roman remains are the walls attributed to the raised platform
(*temenos*) constructed here by Hadrian in the second century C.E.
next to the forum. Other walls may have been part of the foundation
of the Roman temple, and possibly also of a basilica that stood here.

The remains of several buildings of the Roman period uncovered by B. Mazar's excavations south of the Temple Mount and next to its southwestern corner are of great interest because of their locations and functions in connection with the activities of the Roman Tenth Legion.

THE BYZANTINE PERIOD

Several architecturally uniform sections of the Byzantine city wall and its towers are known today from both past and recent excavations. These seem to indicate that the Byzantine city wall stretched along the line of the Damascus Gate in the north, the Jaffa Gate in the west, around Mount Zion in the south, and along the eastern side of the City of David and the Ophel in the east. It was probably erected originally as one concentrated construction project at the beginning of the fourth century C.E., and several of its sections were reconstructed during the late Byzantine and the Early Arab periods.

Important, unique discoveries by Avigad in the Jewish Quarter gave a new perspective on the development and urban character of the Byzantine Zion Quarter. Remains of the southern portion of the main north–south street of Jerusalem—the Cardo with its two colonnades as depicted in the Madaba mosaic map—were discovered, thus extending the northern part of the Cardo, which dates to the period of the foundation of Roman Aelia Capitolina in the second century C.E. The archaeological evidence shows this southern portion of the Cardo to have been constructed in the mid-sixth century C.E., during the reign of Justinian, to connect in a straight line the Church of the Holy Sepulchre with the new Nea Church.

At the southern end of the Cardo, in the southern part of today's Jewish Quarter, several sections of foundation walls of the Nea Church complex, also built by Justinian in the mid-sixth century C.E., were uncovered and identified by Avigad, thus enabling us to appreciate its huge dimensions and massive construction. The estimated length of the church proper is 115 meters (!) The southern part of the church complex was supported by the vaults of an immense underground cistern. An inscription in plaster on one of its walls commemorates the emperor Justinian and this monumental project.

The Kenyon-Tushingham excavations in the Armenian Garden, Broshi's excavations on Mount Zion, and Y. Margovsky and Ben-Dov's excavations on the eastern slope of Mount Zion all revealed many additional remains of streets and private, public and religious buildings that densely covered the Zion Quarter during the Byzantine period.

B. Mazar's excavations at the Ophel uncovered remains of a residential quarter established there already at the beginning of the Byzantine period. The structures are more-or-less uniform in plan. They include many rooms arranged around central courtyards, many of them paved with mosaics. Their well-preserved remains give us a clear picture of the domestic architecture in Jerusalem at that time. Later in the Byzantine period, this neighborhood became more crowded with additional construction. In one of the structures near the southwest corner of the Temple Mount unexpected evidence attests a brief period of Jewish settlement there at the end of the Byzantine period, perhaps following the Persian conquest of the city in 614 C.E. The finds demonstrate that some of the Byzantine buildings continued to be used alongside the palaces constructed south and west of the Temple Mount at the beginning of the Early Arab period.

The picture which has emerged from excavations north and west of the Old City, regarding the extensive Byzantine construction beyond the city walls, is both important and innovative. North of the Old City several Byzantine-period structures serving religious functions were previously known. The most famous of these are the

Armenian and the Orpheus floor mosaics. Near these Ben-Arieh and Nezer uncovered the remains of a large building which they identified as a Byzantine monastery. Additional monastic buildings were discovered nearby by Tzaferis and others. These include a large number of rooms, burial chapels with a mosaic pavement, and many tombs. Remains of another monastery which belonged to the Armenian community in Byzantine Jerusalem were uncovered by D. Amit and S. Wolff. The excavated finds illustrate the development, during the latter part of the Byzantine period (fifth, and mainly sixth, centuries C.E.), of an unwalled urban quarter of Christian religious character, north of the city wall. At the same time, remains of commercial complexes with workshops were excavated by A. M. Maeir and R. Reich just beyond the present-day Jaffa Gate—outside the western Byzantine city gate.

THE EARLY ARAB PERIOD

Finds of the period following the Muslim conquest attest to the efforts of the new rulers in changing the city's Byzantine-Christian character. The most important discoveries dating to the Early Arab period are the remains of two large palaces and several other royal buildings uncovered in the course of B. Mazar's excavations at the Ophel and near the southwestern corner of the Temple Mount. These impressive palaces—part of a royal administrative center— were constructed next to the walls of the Temple Mount during the rule of the Umayyad caliphs toward the end of the seventh and beginning of the eighth century C.E. They are contemporaneous with the foundations of the earliest mosques on the Temple Mount and incorporate also restorations of parts of the destroyed walls and gates of the Temple Mount. The palaces follow a nearly identical plan with a central courtyard surrounded by porticos and rooms. Building materials taken from collapsed and destroyed walls of the Second Temple

Remains of a columned room of the Crusader period uncovered in the southern part of the Jewish Quarter (Ancient Jerusalem Revealed. Israel Exploration Society; with permission)

period Temple Mount, as well as columns and various architectural components from destroyed Byzantine churches, were utilized in their construction. The palaces were in use for only a short time. They were severely damaged by the earthquake that shook Jerusalem in 747 (or 749) C.E. and were subsequently abandoned. Various structures were erected upon their ruins during the Fatimid period.

In the context of royal building activity in Jerusalem at the beginning of the Early Arab period, a new fortress was erected in the area of the present Tower of David Citadel south of the Jaffa Gate. Apparently at the same time, several sections along the line of the

Byzantine city wall, which continued to protect the city during the Early Arab period, were restored.

The decline of Jerusalem as a Christian city began with the inception of Abbasid rule in the mid-eighth century C.E. and continued through the ninth century. During this period the city gradually became Muslim, both architecturally and demographically.

Avigad's excavations along the southern wall of the Old City uncovered a section of fortifications—the earliest city wall found along this line —with a gateway protected by a pair of inner towers dated to the end of the Early Arab period (tenth–eleventh century C.E.). This indicates that the southern city wall was not shortened before this period to the line of the present-day southern wall of the Old City, leaving Mount Zion, the City of David and the southern issue of the Tyropoen Valley outside of the walled area of the city.

THE MEDIEVAL PERIOD

New information is now available about the fortifications of Jerusalem in the Medieval period. Digs conducted by Ben-Dov, Avigad and Broshi along the southern and western lines of the present Old City wall and at its foundations, from the Tower of David Citadel in the west and as far as the Dung Gate in the south, uncovered long sections of an earlier city wall with towers and gates. The foundations of the new wall were laid during the Ayyubid period (or perhaps previously, under the Crusaders) over the line of the even earlier wall of the tenth–eleventh centuries C.E. Inscriptions uncovered on Mount Zion by Broshi also clearly indicate fortification-building activity there at the beginning of the thirteenth century C.E. But as we know from literary sources, this construction was purposely dismantled shortly afterwards by the Muslim rulers. At the northwestern corner of the Old City wall, D. Bahat and M. Ben-Ari uncovered remains of the façade of the Medieval Qal'at Julad (Goliath's Tower) and the moat which protected it from the outside. During the Crusader period the Damascus Gate was refurbished by the addition of an outer fortified gateway, the remains of which were excavated by Kenyon and Hennessy.

The digs conducted in the Tower of David Citadel have exposed only fragmentary remains of the foundations of the Medieval fortress. It seems that the present Ottoman Citadel, which dates originally to the Mamluk period, had the same proportions and plan as the one constructed there by the Crusaders.

Within the Old City, several underground Mamluk building complexes, west of Wilson's Arch were cleared and re-examined. These consist of a series of vaulted subterranean rooms along a central vaulted passageway which served also as substructures of the houses above. In the Jewish Quarter, A. Ovadiah cleared the ruins of a Crusader monastery comprising a church and other buildings on two levels. Along the course of the Byzantine Cardo Avigad uncovered a two-stories vaulted Crusader bazaar with buildings added at some indeterminate time. A public building, probably of monastic character, its central room having a roof supported by four heavy, round stone pillars was also found by Avigad in the southern part of the Jewish Quarter. In the Armenian Garden, Bahat and Broshi uncovered a few remains of the royal Crusader palace.

For the first time, the archaeological investigation of Jerusalem is accompanied by wide-ranging restoration and preservation projects comprising excavated remains of all periods. It is now possible to visit many sites that illustrate and bring to life much of ancient Jerusalem, and to follow and understand the urban and architectural history of the city—from its beginnings, thousands of years ago, through the Ottoman period.

THE TWELVETH GATE

Jerusalem: Toward the Future

An aerial view looking toward the Rockefeller Museum with the Italian Hospital, now the Ministry of Education (front), 1937 (Central Zionist Archives; with permission)

JERUSALEM

Avraham B. Yehoshua

> *Avraham B. Yehoshua, usually called in Hebrew simply "Aleph Bet Yehoshua," is one of Israel's formost novelists and commentators on the social scene. This article was first published in 1981 and reflects his thinking on issues of the future of Jerusalem which have become even more critical than they were then.*

Every month for some years now it has happened in the same way. It is Saturday evening, the close of the Sabbath, at the first shades of twilight (the twilight in the Middle East is very short). We are driving towards the west, on the main road which runs between the thinly wooded mountains. Jerusalem has already disappeared behind us, all at once, between the mountains. The children are silent in the back seat and try to find a place amidst the bags of sweets, cakes and pots of jam which my mother lavished on us at the end of the family visit. In the boot, wrapped in an Arabic newspaper, is some "find"—a little rug, a veil, a blouse bought in the *suq* (bazaar) of the Old City. A weariness and a sense of relief overtake us at the prospect of returning to our home in Haifa. The burnt-out skeletons of military vehicles from the War of Independence on the sides of the road show that we are approaching the end of the mountain area. Here bloody battles were fought then to keep the way open to a besieged Jerusalem. We are at Sha'ar ha-Gai ("The Gates of the Valley"). All at once, the mountains end, and the plain, lit by the last rays of the sun, come into view and spreads out before us, and, immediately, a dampness and a heaviness penetrate the clear air. Something darkens over. This is where Jerusalem ends and where it begins. The rocks become flat and low, the dust loses its coppery tinge and grows grey-ish brown; the earth becomes richer and heavier.

Where does a city begin and where does it end? Is this merely an administrative question with an administrative answer? In which abandoned street of Levalois or Ivry does one feel that Paris comes to an end? Once the way in and out of a city was through a large gate in the walls. Nowadays, this gate has become a small faded sign between two tired traffic lights, hidden behind a parked car. So how, in our days, does one demarcate a city's boundaries? What starts up the symbolic radar in one's mind which suddenly arouses on approaching a city which one loves, the feeling of "Here I am!"? What causes it? The way people are dressed?

Jerusalem for its part, has no suburbs in the ordinary sense of the word. Around a relatively small centre with octopus-like tentacles, various neighbourhoods spread out, scattered over the hills of the city. From the centre you can, if you wish, take a short trip of ten minutes in any direction you like, and find yourself in a cultivated field, on the wooded slope of a mountain, among the thickets of a deep valley, or in complete desert—yellow, barren and desolate. Drive on for five more minutes and you will find residential areas—houses, pavements, shops. On its western side, however, the radia-tions of the city extend to this point where the mountains end, and anyone coming up to Jerusalem from the coastal plain will feel, here, the nearness of the city from the sudden change in the air. And here, at this point when Jerusalem is behind us and our car picks up speed on a road straight as a ruler, my wife always addresses me as follows:

"Don't you want to go back and live there?" She asks me. "No," I answer quickly, "not yet. . . . Perhaps in a few years . . . We'll see . . . Not yet . . . To die there, certainly . . . I mean, our last years . . . Even before . . . But, for the time being, no . . . I feel really relieved every time I leave the place." And yet, every time we come to Jerusalem, during the twenty-four hours we spend there, we swoop down upon the city like tourists who are only passing through it; we are astonished more at its beauty, its charm, its singularity, and between one family meal and another, between two loaded visits to friends, we never stop touring the city. On Friday at the approach of the Sabbath, as soon as we arrive, we unpack our case, leave the children and set out for a drive through the quiet streets of the religious quarters in the north of the city and see how the Sabbath comes in there. Then we head East, toward the Arab part of the city, and drive along the southern wall and come to a halt in a narrow road, in a denuded landscape without a blade of grass; we look at the Arab children scrutinizing us darkly, raise our eyes to the two lofty towers marking the eastern boundary of the city (facing the desert) and register the lightning-flash of the golden roof of the Dome of the Rock, and the sense of the hard stoniness of the city, which is built only of stone by municipal decree. Now we focus our attention on the Jewish cemetery, which pours its white marble over the side of the Mount of Olives, the place where, as tradition has it, the resurrection of the dead will begin. We again look upwards and see the luxurious Intercontinental Hotel built by King Hussein, with its arches of reddish stone, and lower our gaze once more onto the broad valley and the dusty, fenced-in areas of archaeological excavations whose successive layers reveal civilization upon civilization. And suddenly we see above us, on the broken line of the wall, an Israeli soldier in his greenish uniform holding a sub-machine gun, looking as if he were floating in the sky.

Back in our car, we enter the main street of east Jerusalem, where a noisy weekday's activity is drawing to a close. We go into a toyshop or a chemist's to buy something from the mustachioed and polite Arab salesman who speaks to us in English and gives us the feeling that we are shopping in a foreign city. We go back, walking among the black-gowned Arab peasant women, barefoot and erect, carrying high straw baskets unswervingly on their heads, and carve a way through a group of tall Scandinavians with huge knapsacks. Again we get into our car, and within five minutes we are back in the Jewish part of the city, skirt some streets closed to vehicles during the Sabbath, and reach the centre of town, driving carefully on account of some skull-capped American Jewish tourists making their way, with proprietary ease, along the middle of the road to the main synagogue.

And then, when evening comes, we have still not had enough. Late at night, after a visit to friends, we return, making a detour through the official area of Jerusalem, with the stolid government buildings situated on a hill of rocks and the Knesset building lit up with a murky, yellowish light, go quickly back towards the Old City and arrive at the forecourt of the Western Wall. We do not go up to the great stones, but look from a distance at the black-garbed Jews, members of extreme religious sects, who at night take possession of the Kotel (the Wall), pray, weep and sway backwards and forwards with a powerful rhythmic motion. I try to follow their glance, to make some sort of connection with them, but their look passes me by as if I were air, as if I were nothing. They do not recognize me, they do not recognize this state; they are directly linked to eternity—metaphysical beings who fascinate me, whom I hate and who hold an attraction for me. Somebody touches me on the shoulder and I start back with surprise: without speaking, an old toothless Arab holds out to me a paper skull-cap to cover my head. A Holy Place . . .

Next morning, we again feel a physical need to wander around the city. Between two telephone calls, between literary or political discussions, in the relentless Jerusalem sun, with the children or without them, we do not cease for a moment travelling around Jerusalem, and, driven by some indefinite urge, we are again in the narrow and crowded street of the *suq* and hunt around it amidst the colours and aromas, and then go off to Mount Scopus and look at the desert, near and far, the Mountains of Moab and the other side of the Jordan, glimpse the end of the Dead Sea like a streak of blue lightning, and come back and climb an impossibly steep hill to the Russian Church, that looks like a little Kremlin, and return discovering new corners, strange people, other possibilities. In Jerusalem we are eternal tourists.

And yet I was born in this City; I lived here for twenty-seven years. My father, my grandmother and her forebears for five generations were born there and lived there. It is the everlasting and inexhaustible subject of my father's documentary books describing the life of its inhabitants—Jewish and Arab—at the beginning of our century, and giving an account of each house, each quarter, each political and social event which had taken place there in the past. All my best friends and most intimate acquaintances still live there. In a certain sense it will always be my home, but for my children home is the city of Haifa. Jerusalem, for them, is an alien city.

CONFLAGRATION

Thousands of books have been written about Jerusalem, and thousands more are still to be written. It is one of those cities whose physical being is detached from and oppressed by their spiritual and national significance. Jerusalem is one of the most complex cultural, religious, national and human admixtures, and in a period of violent religious renaissance it is a dangerous political explosive which could give rise to an uncontrollable conflagration. It is an inexhaustible source of nostalgia, for pilgrimages steeped in fantasy and romance. It is fixed in the consciousness of millions who have never set foot there and who never will.

Yet, nevertheless, taken all in all, it is only a rather small city, situated at an altitude of nine hundred metres, with quiet residential quarters, whose population consists of officials, university teachers, some tradesmen, and simple people, without any significant middle class. It has a small, dismal commercial centre which has recently been brightened up. But at its heart, inside the not very lofty Turkish stone walls, lies the hard nucleus of *Yerushalayim shel Ma'ala*—the Heavenly Jerusalem.

Within a radius of half a kilometre, there are famous sites. There is the small damp Church of the Holy Sepulchre, which throughout history has seen numerous Christian denominations quarrel for possession of every inch, of every key. From there, via the Via Dolorosa, you reach the gigantic wall of stones which has survived from the Jewish Temple enclosure: a high, isolated wall linked to nothing, a kind of perpetual reminder of a destruction which will never be forgotten and the obstinate promise of something which will never be built—an intermediate situation which is so well suited to Jewish life. Above it, bestriding an immense stone esplanade, are two mosques, the Dome of the Rock and the Mosque of al-Aqsa, Muslim holy places built over the ruins of the Jewish Temple. And again, a short distance away, there is an Orthodox church, next to it an Armenian church, and, between the two, a yeshiva; nearby is a Protestant mission school, next door a Muslim school, and so on. Religion beside religion, religion beneath religion, religion wedged into religion, religion threatening religion. Religion upon the ruins of another religion. Every place has a history of destruction, of attempted change of identity (the Holy Sepulchre was destroyed by the Muslims, the mosques of the Temple Mount were transformed into churches by the Crusaders). Mingled stones, mixed beliefs. In academic gatherings in Europe, in congress halls, amiable professors, cultured theologians, enlightened men of religion can meet quietly and speak of cooperation, brotherhood and common roots. But here, a stone is moved and it's a note from the Security Council, some pipes are repaired and it's an ecumenical question; a wall is knocked down, and it's a national provocation.

In history, there have been cities in which various changes of civilization have taken place; churches have been transplanted by mosques, and vice versa. These, however, were painful historical processes which have come to an end. Here, on the other hand, the struggle is alive and unceasing, and any accommodation that is made is only temporary. A hurried tourist can go quickly from one famous site to another, happy that he is able to "do" so many famous places in a short time, but a thoughtful visitor will feel the weight of an enormous tension. A hard city. . . .

PROPHECIES

"When your ancestors were playing with monkeys in the forests of London and Oxford, our ancestors were listening to the noble moral preachings of the prophets in the streets of Jerusalem!" In these words, the Zionist leaders answered the cold, thin British High Commissioners who governed the country until the middle of the century, in an attempt to convince them of the Jewish people's deep connection with this city.

Indeed, it was here that Jeremiah, Isaiah and Micah walked the streets—extraordinary, wonderful men who came up from Galilee, Samaria or the desert and prophesied, and it was to this city that John the Baptist and Jesus finally made their way. Men burnt by the sun came up to Jerusalem to speak to it. In alleyways similar to those of today but lower (two or three meters lower according to the archaeologists) they moved around and made their prophesies of anger and admonishment, consolation and love.

But do these help us today, or do they merely make things more difficult? Will the wonderful spiritual power poured out over this city help us to find a path towards life, and some human status quo for this mixture of people flowing through the city so that blood will no longer flow there? For blood has always flowed in Jerusalem, and it is still flowing there today. Every house, every corner can tell a story of war and destruction, recent or long distant. Every archaeological stratum which is uncovered reveals the root of a great fire, signs of shattered stones. One part of the city always attacks the other part, besieges, bombards it. A city of struggle . . .

Jerusalem exemplifies in concentrated and almost absurd fashion one of the most burning problems of our time—the achievement of

Ben Yehuda Street, May 12, 1937, decorated in honor of the coronation of King George VI and Queen Elizabeth (Central Zionist Archives; with permission)

unity within disparity, cooperation with the preservation of one's identity, international brotherhood, but within carefully defined limits—and as long as Jerusalem cannot solve this problem, we will feel the weight of the anguish. My own short biography alone covers three phases in the life of Jerusalem, three dimensions: I am still expecting the fourth one.

There was the Jerusalem of my early childhood, a city united under British rule: foreign domination for all its inhabitants. A city of hypocrisy in which there were polite but wary contacts between Arabs and Jews, who lived as minorities with equal rights but with no sovereignty. A relationship in which intercourse was mingled with enmity, and below the surface, a constant preparation for the approaching hour of combat.

And then, there was the war of 1948, a cruel struggle between the two parts of the city. An attempt of the Arab, eastern part to dominate the Jewish western part—an attempt which failed—followed by an opposite attempt which also failed. There was an armistice. The front line, frozen, became a fixed frontier raised up in the middle of the city, high, concrete walls and barbed-wire fences were erected, windows were sealed and look-out posts went up. Each part of the city became a complete entity in itself, lived its own existence and decided its own character.

Then, after nineteen years, came the third period. A lightning war, a sudden, unexpected unification, this time under Israeli rule. The frontier was demolished and a stream of Jews flocked in to settle in the "conquered" or "liberated" eastern part. Electric cables were connected up, piping systems laid down, and the frontier which had been like a deep scar in the heart of the city was erased, and when I look for traces of it to show my children the places where it zigzagged across the city, such as the remains of a bullet-ridden wall, a destroyed house in the centre of the city or a concrete anti-tank

The protective walls near the Jordanian section in divided Jerusalem prior to the 1967 War (Israel Government Press Office; with permission)

barrier still standing in the city park, they think that I am showing them archaeological discoveries.

The frontier-line, however, whose physical remains I am searching for, is like a sort of hallucination crying out for a new political identity, failing which Jerusalem, like a deadly mine, will explode any agreement that is made.

It is now summer, the holiday season. People would prefer to read human-interest stories and avoid political problems, but there are some cities in the world such as Belfast, Berlin and, of course, Jerusalem, in which the political clouds which brush lightly against other places are settled like a thick fog, penetrating every nook and cranny. I cannot think of my city, my home, without associating it with political concepts. Politics weigh down upon them, and they also weigh down upon me. Here in these streets, within this difficult admixture, a cool head, imagination and courage will be needed in order to find a lasting solution in the near future. The city must remain united from the human point of view, but diversified from the point of view of sovereignty; it must be a single city for all its inhabitants, yet at the same time two capitals for two peoples; it must function as a single whole, yet divided up between its various religions and national entities. Several flags ought to fly here in mutual toleration. The city is too important to its inhabitants, is too much part of them, to be controlled by sterile UN forces consisting of Swedes and Nigerians under an Austrian officer. The solution must be an organic one, coming from within through a process of patience and goodwill.

Its history is against it: a gloomy, pessimistic history. Will the city have the power to oppose that history, and at the same time to preserve it? Jerusalem is held as a kind of threat against itself.

JERUSALEM—TODAY AND TOMORROW
Teddy Kollek

> *Teddy (Theodore) Kollek was born in Vienna and settled in then Palestine in 1934. His career as a public servant began in 1940 with the Jewish Agency and culminated in his serving as Mayor of Jerusalem from 1965 to 1994. He was therefore the first Mayor of united Jerusalem. Of this article he says, "Although this was written in 1980 and, were I to write it today I might change some details, in general it still reflects my views."*

The place of Jerusalem in the process of seeking peace in the Middle East is unique. Its historical, emotional, and international complexities set it apart from other issues that may be solved on the basis of mutually agreed-upon boundaries. The Jerusalem question cannot be decided by drawing a line. The future of Jerusalem cannot be resolved by division.

This does not mean that Jerusalem is an insoluble problem. It means that Jerusalem's people of differing faiths, cultures, and aspirations must find peaceful ways to live together other than by drawing a line in the sand with a stick. It is no solution to rebuild concrete walls and barbed wire through the middle of the city.

The problem of Jerusalem is difficult because age-old and deeply felt emotions are encrusted over the rationality necessary to find solutions. But I am convinced that these solutions can be found by people of goodwill.

To be perfectly candid, what I dread most is that this city—so beautiful, so meaningful, so holy to millions of people—should ever be divided again; that barbed wire fences, mine fields, and concrete barriers should again sever its streets; that armed men should again patrol a frontier through its heart. I fear the redivision of Jerusalem not only as the mayor of the city, as a Jew, and as an Israeli but also as a human being who is deeply sensitive to its history and who cares profoundly about the well-being of its inhabitants.

Jerusalem is, of course, one of the oldest cities. Signs of human habitation have been found dating back at least four thousand years. In the course of these millennia it has been coveted and conquered by a host of people: Canaanites, Jebusites, Israelites, Babylonians, Assyrians, Persians, Romans, Byzantines, Arabs, Seljuks, Crusaders, Mamluks, Ottomans, British, Jordanians, and Israeli. But throughout those thousands of years, Jerusalem has been divided for less than two decades, from 1948 to 1967. It must never again be divided. Once more to cut this living city in two would be as cruel as it is irrational.

Why have all these various peoples sought this city? It has no natural resources; it has no port; it has no material wealth. It has been coveted primarily for spiritual reasons; it was the site of the Temple of the Jews, the site of the Crucifixion of Jesus; and the place from which, according to tradition, Muhammad rose to heaven.

The fact that all three great monotheistic religions find meaning in Jerusalem cannot be a random accident. I think the reason is clear. First of all, Jerusalem is a beautiful place set in the mystical Judean Hills, conducive to meditation and thought and wonder at the meaning of life. And second, for all their tensions and exclusiveness, the three great religions are historically deeply interrelated. Jesus came to Jerusalem because he was a Jew who made the pilgrimage to the City of David and the Temple. Muhammad, whose roots were in Mecca and Medina, still the main Holy Cities of Islam, is said to have visited Jerusalem during his night ride because his ideas and his vision were interrelated with Judaism and Christianity. We must live with the reality of these connections. For centuries men have fought and died because of them. But I am not alone in feeling intensely that men can also live in brotherhood because of them.

These very connections make any division of Jerusalem a senseless exercise. The remaining Western Wall of the Temple enclosure, the Church of the Holy Sepulchre, and the Dome of the Rock are all in the Old City within yards of each other. The Dome of the Rock is actually atop the Temple Mount, the very site of the Temple of the Jews. . . . The centrality of Jerusalem in Jewish faith and tradition and the intensity of Jewish feeling about Jerusalem are reflected in the two-thousand-year-old prayer repeated throughout the centuries, "Next year in Jerusalem." This symbolizes not only a religious hope but memories of ancient glories under Jewish rule and an unyielding struggle for their revival. All this is expressed for Jews in the word "Jerusalem." The Jewish people cannot give up Jerusalem, nor can they, nor will they ever again, remove their capital from Jerusalem.

But independent of these intense feelings, internationalization will not work for pragmatic reasons. Past experience, whether in Trieste, Danzig, or Shanghai, has shown its unworkability. In the case of Danzig, indeed, it contributed to bringing on a world war.

A city cannot be run by a committee, particularly a city of such complexity and diversity as Jerusalem. Before building a road or a sewage system, the committee members would have to refer back to their foreign offices or to a UN bureaucracy. And who would pay the bills? . . .

When I look at the future of Jerusalem there are two premises with which virtually everyone in Israel agrees: that Jerusalem shall remain undivided and that it shall remain the capital of Israel. Most Jerusalemites of every persuasion would agree that, under whatever political solution, the city should remain accessible to all and the rights of every religion to its Holy Places should be preserved.

These two conditions have now existed for thirteen years, since the city was so unexpectedly unified after the Jordanians attacked Israel in the June 1967 War. And I think that the history of relations in Jerusalem among Jews, Muslims, and Christians during this decade points to the kind of solution we should eventually evolve for Jerusalem.

Tensions do exist in the city and nobody can deny them. But it was a much less happy city when walls and barbed wire divided it; and it was certainly a more violent city than it is today. We have made progress toward a city of tolerant coexistence in which common interests are emerging, and we have established crucial principles that made continuing progress possible. Four of these principles are

- There shall be free access to all the Holy Places regardless of creed or nationality, and they shall be administered by their adherents.

- Everything possible shall be done to ensure unhindered development of the Arab way of life in the Arab sections of the city and to ensure the Muslims and Christians a practical religious, cultural, and commercial governance over their own daily lives.

- Everything possible shall be done to ensure equal governmental, municipal, and social services in all parts of the city.

- Continuing efforts shall be made to increase cultural, social, and economic contacts among the various elements of Jerusalem's population. And, in fact, civic affairs, law enforcement, infrastructure services, urban planning, marketing and supply, and to a great extent, specialized medical services are centrally provided to all Jerusalemites. . . .

For some time now, I have envisioned a future structure in Jerusalem under which the city would be governed through a network of boroughs. Each borough would have a great deal of autonomy over its own municipal services and its lifestyle. It would decide its own needs and priorities. It would be modeled not on the boroughs of New York but on those of London, which have their own budgets and a great deal of independence.

Of course, the borough idea is not a panacea. The Arabs will want the Temple Mount to be in their borough, and no Jew would agree to that. But the proposal does suggest an approach under which many of the aspects of everyday life can be delegated to local authorities and the people of the various neighborhoods can feel some increasing control over their own lives and the decision-making process. . . .

We do not want to make Jerusalem a parochial city but to restore its ancient glory. We have built a handsome Israel Museum, perhaps the major museum of international art and archaeology between the eastern Mediterranean and Tokyo. The Jerusalem Museum of Islamic Art and Culture, opened a few years ago, is one of outstanding excellence. The Jerusalem Theater has given us a home for the performing arts. . . . We have built an embryonic center for writers, artists, and musicians at Mishkenot Sha'ananim.

☙

Jews care intensely about Jerusalem. The Christians have Rome and Canterbury and even Salt Lake City; Muslims have Mecca and Medina. Jerusalem has great meaning for them also. But the Jews have only Jerusalem, and only the Jews have made it their capital. That is why it has so much deeper a meaning for them than for anybody else.

When the city was reunited, all Jews, not only the religious but also the secular, felt the ancient prophecy fulfilled. Jerusalem was our capital even when few were here—for two thousand years. Since the Muslim conquest only the Crusaders and the British ever made it the administrative capital of the country. On the two occasions when the Arabs could have made Jerusalem their capital, they did not. In the Middle Ages they chose Ramleh, near Lydda on the way to Jerusalem, and in 1948 they chose Amman, which they preferred to Jerusalem.

We do not aspire to find solutions to all the problems of the Middle East in Jerusalem. This is a complicated city with conflicting interests, and it is impossible to satisfy the wishes of everybody.

Sometimes people outside the Middle East ask: What is the relevance of what we are doing in Jerusalem in making the city viable, beautiful, and peaceful to the ultimate question of the sovereignty of the city? We can only look at the situation realistically. If, at worst, Muslim and Jewish differences prove irreconcilable, we will have to live in tension for a long time. All the more reason to care for the city as much as we can to ensure its welfare and well-being in spite of the strains and stresses. If, at best, Jews and Arabs find accommodations that are acceptable to the aspirations of all three faiths, no one would argue that what we are doing for Jerusalem today has been irrelevant. . . .

Within an undivided city, everything is possible, all kinds of adjustments can be made, all kinds of accommodations can be considered, all kinds of autonomy can be enjoyed, all kinds of positive relationships can be developed.

These have been my ideas for many years, and now even more so with the new reality created by the peace agreement signed between Israel and Egypt. The new reality exists, but it should be stressed that we are at variance with ideas expressed by Egyptian spokesmen, which also reach us from time to time from Jordan, namely, that Jerusalem come under dual sovereignty. It is emotionally inconceivable to divide any city, certainly not Jerusalem, which was a united city from its inception four thousand years ago until 1948. Nor can this work from a practical point of view. How could one city have two sets of laws, two different courts, different police forces? Within no time there would be frontier barriers, and the walls and the barbed wire would return to where they had been for nineteen years. Anyone who really cares for Jerusalem cannot even fathom this situation, Moreover, more than one hundred thousand Jews now live in areas beyond the former border. On the other hand, Jerusalem has shown in practice that coexistence is possible. In Jerusalem, there already exist many of the aspects of autonomy that the Israeli government has proposed as part of an over-all peace settlement. Thus I believe that the ideas expressed here answer this new reality.

In 1967, when attacked by the Jordanians, the Jews were willing to sacrifice their lives for Jerusalem. They would again. Israel gave up Sinai; some Israelis would give up the Golan and some the West

Bank and Gaza. But I do not think you can find any Israelis who are willing to give up Jerusalem. They cannot and will not. This beautiful golden city is the heart and soul of the Jewish people. You cannot live without a heart and soul. If you want one simple word to symbolize all of Jewish history, that word would be "Jerusalem."

EPILOGUE

David's Tomb on Mount Zion, date unknown
(Central Zionist Archives; with permission)

Jerusalem, Holy City

R. J. Zvi Werblowsky

> *Prof. Werblowsky is Professor of Comparative Religion at the Hebrew University, Jerusalem, and author of numerous scholarly articles and books.*

One way in which people have experienced and, as it were, crystallized their sense of holiness, was in relation to space. There are holy lands—that is lands which are considered holy by virtue of the bond that binds human groups to the earth on which they live. It is a bond of gratitude and love that often, and at times imperceptibly, turns into veneration. In one of the temples in Benares the object of worship is a map of Mother India. *Bande mataram*! There are holy places as distinct from holy lands, places where the divine became manifest, in one way or another, to the eyes of believing men and women, and which were cherished or revered as concrete, tangible, spatially defined testimonies to the reality of the divine as it had become visible in experiences or traditions of theophanies, revelations, miracles, or the lives of saintly men. There are holy cities as distinct from holy places: cities that acquired their holiness as a result of historical circumstances or events, or cities that are holy because either in theory or in actual fact they were constructed so as to reflect cosmic reality—a kind of micro-cosmic spatial reflection of the cosmos and its underlying divine ground as conceived and spelled out in mythological tradition. There are cities which are holy because they harbor and possess a holy object, or shrine or relic. We can think of Mecca, Benares, Lhasa, Angkor, Roma (Roma Quadrata!) and many others. As a modern example we may instance Tenri (near Nara) in Japan, which is a holy city not only because it is built around the "navel of the earth," the sacred *Skanrodai*, but also because it is constructed according to a divine plan. Hence also the importance which students of religion attach to that branch of their science which is called *geographia sacra*.

The case of Jerusalem is in many ways unique, since this city is a focus of devotion, piety and religious symbolism for three related religions, two of which are universal religions counting hundreds of millions of followers. Nevertheless, it is the third which, for our purpose, is the first—and not merely for chronological reasons. Judaism is a non-universalistic religion which specifically conceives of itself as the religion of a particular (and incidentally rather small) people. But it is this religion which became the "mother" of the attachment of Christianity and Islam to this Holy City. It is this triple attachment which is the cause of the complicated, and often tragic, history of the city. Mecca is of no interest to Hindus, and Buddhists care little for Benares. Jerusalem is charged with profound emotions of piety, devotion, ardent longing, theological symbolism and—alas—fanaticism and desire of domination for three hostile brothers.

The pre-history of the city, fascinating as it is for archaeologists, is not our concern here. A careful reading of the Hebrew Bible record shows that the City played no role during the early period of the settlement of the Israelite tribes in Canaan. The main cultic centers were Beth El, Gilgal, Shiloh and others. The episode of the meeting of Abraham with Melchisedek, the priest-king of Shalem (Gen. 14) probably reflects later, post-Davidic ideology, bent on cementing the association of the Holy City with the ancestor of the nation. Jerusalem entered Jewish history and historico-religious consciousness with its conquest by David, who realised that in order to unite the tribes into a nation he had to establish his capital in "neutral" territory, not associated with any tribe (thus avoiding the suspicion of aspirations of hegemony by the tribe of Judah), but solely with his personal prestige as king and the Lord's Elect. National/political and cultic center, royal residence, and temple of God—in antiquity the two often went together. (Cf. e.g., Amos 7:13 à propos Beth El: "Royal sanctuary.") Jerusalem–Sion–City of David: City of God. Surprising and, indeed, unique is the rapidity with which the ideas of God's Covenant with his Chosen People, with the Promised Land, with the Chosen City and the Temple, and with the Chosen House of David merged into one integrated symbol (see the Book of Isaiah, the Psalms, or Jeremiah 31:34–39; 33:14–26). The name of the city soon acquired a historical, indeed existential significance superimposed on its original geographical meaning. When the prophets bewail the agony, suffering and exile visited upon the people, they never speak of the people of Israel. They say: Jerusalem sheddeth tears, the daughter of Zion crieth. And when they speak of the final redemption and the ingathering of the exiles, they say: rejoice O Jerusalem, exult O daughter of Zion. In the tradition the destroyed and ruined city, now in the hands of "enemies," also served as a symbol of hope and trust in God's eternal promise for a suffering and persecuted and massacred people. It is not surprising that the modern movement of national renaissance did not call itself "Jewish risorgimento" but "Zionism."

Jesus was the teacher and master of a group of Jewish disciples. His career, as the Gospels testify, took place in the Jerusalem-centric framework of contemporary Judaism. Even his attacks on the Temple and its unworthy priests and worshippers, even his prophecies of destruction, were not much different from those of other and earlier prophets (see especially Jeremiah). The consummation of his terrestrial ministry, his passion, burial, resurrection and ascension took place in specific sites in Jerusalem (and it does not matter, for our purposes, whether the places indicated by pious tradition or eager tourist guides are historically "authentic" or not). From the fourth century on, largely through the activities of the Emperor Constantine's mother, Helena, Jerusalem rapidly became a center of pilgrimage not only in the Byzantine empire but for Christendom as a whole. Christ (the word is the Greek translation of the Hebrew term for the Lord's "Anointed") being, by definition, the Messiah Son of David (see Mat. 1), the link between Christianity and the "City of David" was obvious. Center of devotion, piety, pilgrimages—the very name of Jerusalem was capable of provoking (in combination with other factors) powerful movements, and even leading western Christianity to one of its saddest and most unchristian adventures: the Crusades. But the role of Jerusalem in Christian spirituality is far more complicated than that. The universalist element in the message of Jesus necessarily led to a universalisation of the traditional Israelite notions of a "chosen people" and a "chosen land." The holy people was henceforth the Church, that mystical body of which Christ was the head, and the holy land was the whole world to the extent that the life of Christian holiness was lived there. But this omnipresent terrestrial Jerusalem was a mere reflection of the true celestial Jerusalem, "the mother of us all." The latter concept also stems from Judaism, but there it plays only a secondary role whereas in Christianity it became primary. In the world of the medieval poet:

Urbs Sion unica, mansio mystica, condita caelo.

And every terrestial church, reflecting the heavenly Jerusalem, is dedicated (in the Latin rite) with the beautiful hymn:

Urbs Jerusalem beata
Dicta pacis visio
Quae construitur in caelis
Vivis ex lapidibus.

The case of Islam is, from the historian's point of view, the most remarkable. How did Jerusalem gain such importance in a religion that originated, and developed, far away from the city, in the part of the Arabian peninsula known as the Hedjaz? And yet, during the first years of Islam the prescribed direction of prayer (*gibla*) was toward Jerusalem. Even after the Prophet changed the *gibla* in the direction of Mecca, one of the names of the City remained *'ula al-giblatheyn* ("the first of the two giblas"). At the time the Arab peninsula was heavily populated by Jewish and Christian tribes, and the traders reaching Mecca with their caravans must also have contained many Jews and Christians. It is not, therefore, surprising that many biblical influences were absorbed by the Prophet during the crucial period when his message as it were "incubated" and matured. Jerusalem was integrated into the Muslim heritage of belief by being linked to the ministry of the Prophet himself: The references in the Koran (Sura 81:9, 53:1ff. and 17:1) to the Prophet's miraculous nocturnal journey and to his ascension—the *'isra* and the *mi'radj*—were combined into one event and linked to Jerusalem. Another Judeo-Christian heritage was the role ascribed to Jerusalem in Muslim eschatology. In due course Jerusalem became the third holiest city after Mecca and Medinah. But it always remained a purely religious center, and never was a capital—political, administrative or merely provincial. Islam, however, has a political dimension also as a religion (cf. the division of the world into *dar al-Islam* and *dar-al-harb*). It is therefore inconceivable to a Muslim mind that a territory or a city, let alone a holy city, which had for over a thousand years been under Muslim domination, should now be under the rule of infidels. The rise of a new and specifically Palestinian nationalism renders the problem even more acute.

All these elements together make up the unique character of the city which a popular (but incorrect) etymology has traditionally interpreted as "the city of peace" but which, in reality, has more often than not been a city of conflict and violent clashes. Few cities in the world, not to speak of "holy" cities, have seen so many wars, conquests, and blood flowing in its streets than this "city of peace." Perhaps the popular etymology reflects not so much a reality as a hope or even challenge to the three religions concerned: will they ever succeed in transforming this place of hated, violence, competition and political intrigue (often masked as "religious") into a center radiating peace? The true mystery of the city may well be in its future rather than its past, a future prepared for it by those who (in the words of the psalmist) "love Jerusalem" and who seek in and through it that Peace of God that passeth all understanding.

The animal market at the Sultan's Pool in 1900 (Central Zionist Archives; with permission)

JERUSALEM THE IRREPLACEABLE

André Neher

> *The late Professor André Neher, born in Alsace, became one of the leading figures of French Jewry after the Second World War. He held the chair of Jewish Studies at Strasbourg and later divided his time between Jerusalem and France.*

The intertwining of Jerusalem and of the irreplaceable has never been felt by human consciousness with as much obstinate strength and poignant evidence as by the very consciousness that discovered it on the banks of the rivers of Babylon and which, ever since, without respite, pause or parenthesis, has sensed it, sung it, cried out for it throughout the course of history—Jewish consciousness,

Indeed, Christian consciousness very rapidly found another Jerusalem in Rome and in the heavens; Moslem consciousness too, from the time it came into being, built one in Mecca and Medina; finally, agnostic consciousness erected still others in Paris, New York and Peking.

Only the Jews, long before there were any Christians, Moslems or believers in a third testament, *would have no other* and have, ever since, with fierce steadfastness, persisted in their refusal to replace Jerusalem, though it be only ruins and dust, by another Jerusalem, though it be heavenly or like Paradise.

We will have no other, cried the Jews, during the nights of bitter weeping and in the first light of dawn; we will have no other, said the Jews, gritting their teeth or with the ghost of a bitter smile, every time that, on the road of their long Exile, they were offered in exchange a final and peaceful stopping place within a Jerusalem other than that which, lying there, on its rock, seemed quite dead and could only present them with the stones of an aging Wall, the access to which, moreover, would soon be denied them.

I will have no other because, indeed, the Exile has never been to me a fortuitous march without a compass. Never, in the worst of my flights, have I been a wanderer without landmarks. Every step had a meaning; never have I been the Wandering Jew. I have always been the Pilgrim of Jerusalem. Every wandering was oriented towards it. Never have I felt settled anywhere: my prayers, my offerings, my yearnings, and often my steps made me the everlasting Lover of Zion. Every martyrdom was a sacrifice, because the endless dreams of my people brought the humblest, but also the most sorrowful of my ashes to the Mount of Olives.

Thus, Exile itself was a road, the road returning to Jerusalem. And now that this road has brought me back to Jerusalem; now that its name is Israel and that there it exists, built up, lined with tears, laughter, trees and human-beings as manifold as the millions of irreplaceables—who, while they lived and when they died, had no other name upon their lips but Jerusalem; now that Jerusalem is not anymore the *symbol* of the irreplaceable but stands for its *reality*; now, do you believe that I, a Jew, would love another, have another, accept another one?

Pray for the Well-Being of Jerusalem

S. Y. Agnon

> *The Nobel Prize–winning author, S. Y. Agnon, expressed the meaning of Jerusalem to him in this rather sarcastic reply to a letter asking him to answer certain questions about his attitude toward the city.*

It would have been better, Madam, had you not sent me your queries, and now that you have, it would have been better had I not been

View of the Temple Mount and the horizon of new Jerusalem from Mount Zion, July 1981 (Israel Government Press Office; with permission)

pressured to answer them. I am a man preoccupied with my own queries, to which I have as yet found no answer. However—for the honor of Jerusalem I will do what I can to attempt to answer your queries. That which God puts in my mouth, I shall speak.

You ask: what does Jerusalem symbolize for me? You ask me? Ask rather the sages of all generations throughout the ages from the time of the first prophets until our own day what Jerusalem is and what they have said. What does a man like myself have to add and of what importance is it if I reinforce their words? For it is from their words that I live and I guide my thoughts by theirs. If only I were worthy to behold Jerusalem in my peak hours as they beheld her in their most trivial ones. Jerusalem never departed from their hearts during their entire life times. They needed no "symbols." If you have read my book *A Guest for the Night* you know my opinion of symbols.

That is my answer to your first query: what does Jerusalem symbolize for me.

Now that we have disposed of one query, perhaps we can dispose of the second one.

You ask: why did I choose Jerusalem as my dwelling place?

I must candidly admit that such a query never occurred to me in all my days. I live in Jerusalem because I was privileged to be among those that God chose to permit to live in His city which is called by His name. Perhaps it would be better to say: God was merciful to me when He perceived that I had made up my mind to go up to Jerusalem, and from the time that I was so privileged to go up, I paid no attention to all the troubles that have come upon me in Jerusalem, be it the earthquake of 5687 or the riots of 5689 or the noise of vehicles which gives me no peace day or night—not even on the Sabbath or Festivals. It seems as if He agreed to permit me to be gathered into His city.

Now, Madam, I shall attempt to answer your third query which is the most difficult of all. You ask: in what lies the superiority of Jerusalem? Has it not already been stated that "The Lord loves the gates of Zion more than all the dwellings of Jacob. Glorious things are spoken of you, O city of God" (Pss. 87:2–3)? If God—who possesses the entire world—who loves all of the Land of Israel—loves the gates of Zion more than all the dwellings of Jacob—shall not a mortal man—dust and ashes who has nothing but what he can attain all his days and after length of days and years, would that he would be worthy of possessing even one grain of the dust of Jerusalem—shall not such a one love Jerusalem more than all the dwellings of Jacob? To say nothing of all the other places in the world.

And now, Madam, I shall attempt to answer your fourth query: how do I perceive Jerusalem?

All moments and days are not equal. We have the Sabbath and Festivals, and then there is Tisha B'Av. Nor am I the same all moments and days or hours, but would that I could truly perceive Jerusalem for one day, one hour or even one brief moment!

I see that your fourth query really contains another question as well which is itself two-fold: what places in Jerusalem are particularly precious to me and why?

I have nothing to say regarding the first part since all of Jerusalem is precious to me. From the moment that that part of the city which is within the walls was taken from me for the time being, I perceived all of Jerusalem which remains in our hands until the Redeemer shall come as one precious entity. If I may use the language which is unique to Jerusalem, I would say that all of Jerusalem is holy unto me.

As for the second part of the query, i.e. "why?" I know not what to reply. All the answers in the world would not be sufficient.

I assume, Madam, that you are not satisfied with my answers. But I must tell you that I too am not satisfied with my answers, although not for the same reason. You expected to receive answers from me that would be acceptable to the general populace, that is matters which any normal person who speaks the language of normal people would reply, while my answers were quite far from that.

This, Madam, this is the punishment of one who makes inquiry of a man such as myself, who sees nothing problematic in any of these queries. This is the punishment of the man who must answer queries such as these which are not queries to him nor in themselves.

I have finished my words. From now on, I want to return to my own queries to which I seek answers. But I tell you, I am willing to give up all the answers for one day of repentance, so that I shall be worthy to dwell in Jerusalem.

∾ Afterword

In 1996, Jerusalem will reverberate with the sounds of celebration marking three thousand years since David, the King, made this hilltop town the capital of his Jewish kingdom.

Since its founding, Jerusalem has been the heart of the Jewish people, the focus of its faith and central thread of its historical memory. There is an eternal tie between Jerusalem and the Jewish people, a tie which has no parallel in the history of nations. The Temple was erected in Jerusalem and pilgrimages were made to it; chapters of the Bible were written within its wall and there the prophets prophesied. The eternal symbol of the hopes, dreams and aspirations of the Jewish people, Jerusalem is the source of inspiration to Jewish artists and visionaries the world over.

Today, Jerusalem is also a vibrant, modern and progressive capital with well-preserved historical sites and a rich cultural life. It is a cosmopolitan city, the home of a varied mosaic of different races, peoples, religions and sects, which have lives together for generations. And Jerusalem is an international destination, welcoming millions of visitors from a hundred nations.

Jerusalem is unique in history and unique in the world and the tri-millennium celebrations will be a unique year for Jerusalem. Hundreds of thousands of visitors will relive the splendor of the historic ancient city as it has blended into the landscape of a thriving capital. They will attend a myriad of cultural events, from a monumental sight and sound spectacular, to opera, poetry, concerts, gospel choirs, pageants, banquets, theater, dance, exhibitions and much more. The tri-millennium activities reflect

474

Jerusalem's enormous artistic and spiritual heritage and above all Jerusalem's unique power to inspire artistic, spiritual and intellectual expression.

The essence of Jerusalem's uniqueness flows through the pages of this special anthology which has gathered so many wonderful examples of how this city has inspired Jewish poets, writers, philosophers and scholars—through the ages and throughout the globe. And with this volume, once again, Jerusalem has been the source of creative endeavor and its pages promise that Jerusalem will continue to be an inspiration for the Jewish people for many millennium to come.

Reading through these pages, I am reminded once again what an immense and humbling responsibility it is to hold the office of Mayor of Jerusalem. Jerusalem is so much more than a city—it is the symbol of a nation, the focus of attention both in Israel and the world; a universal spiritual center with room for all religions, peoples and traditions.

Ehud Olmert
Mayor of Jerusalem

ॐ A Selected Jerusalem Bibliography

The following list of books in English includes both books excerpted in this volume and others that may prove of interest to the reader.

ॐ

Adler, Elkan Nathan. *Jewish Travelers*. London, 1930.

Adler, Marcus Nathan. *The Itinerary of Benjamin of Tudela*. London, 1907.

Agnon, S.Y., *In The Heart Of The Seas*, New York, 1947

al-Harizi, Judah. *The Book of Tahkemoni*. Translated by David Simha Segal. Oxford, forth-coming.

Alon, Amos. *City of Mirrors*. New York, 1989.

Amichai, Yehuda. *Great Tranquility*. New York, 1983.

———. *The World is a Room*. Trans. by Elinor Grumet. Philadelphia, 1984.

———. *Poems of Jerusalem*. Jerusalem, 1980.

———. *Songs of Jerusalem and Myself*. Translated by H. Schimmel, New York, 1973.

Ancient Jerusalem Revealed. Ed. by Hillel Geva. Jerusalem, 1994.

An Anthology of Modern Hebrew Poetry. Selected by S. Y. Penueli and A. Ukhmani. Jerusalem, 1966.

An Anthology of Modern Hebrew Poetry. Ed. and trans. by Abraham Birman. New York, 1968.

The Apocrypha and Pseudepigrapha of the Old Testament in English. Vol. 1. Ed. by R. H. Charles. Oxford, 1913.

Aristeas to Philocrates. Ed. and trans. by Moses Hadas. New York, 1951.

Avigad, Nahman. *Discovering Jerusalem*. Jerusalem, 1980.

Bellow, Saul. *To Jerusalem and Back*. New York, 1976.

Ben-Arieh, Yehoshua. *Jerusalem in the 19th Century: The Old City*.Jerusalem, 1984.

———. *Jerusalem in the 19th Century: The Emergence of the New City*. Jerusalem, 1986.

Ben-Dov, Meir. *In the Shadow of the Temple.* Jerusalem, 1982.

————. *Jerusalem, Man and Stone.* Tel Aviv, 1990.

Bentwich, Norman, and Bentwich, Helen. *Mandate Memories, 1918–1948.* New York, 1965.

Benvenisti, Meron. *The Torn City.* Jerusalem, 1976.

The Book of Tobit. Trans. by Frank Zimmerman. New York, 1958.

Brandwein, Chaim. *In the Courtyards of Jerusalem.* Trans. by Hillel Halkin. Philadelphia, 1967.

Burstein, Chaya M. *A Kid's Catalogue of Israel.* Philadelphia, 1988.

Carmi, T., and Pagis, Dan. *Selected Poems.* Middlesex, 1976.

Collins, Larry, and Lapierre, Dominique. *O Jerusalem!* London, 1972.

Deem, Ariella. *Jerusalem Plays Hide and Seek.* Trans. by Nelly Segal. Philadelphia, 1987.

The Diaries of Sir Moses and Lady Montefiore. Ed. by Dr. Louis Loewe. Chicago, 1890.

The Diaries of Theodore Herzl. Ed. by Marvin Lowenthal. New York, 1956.

The First Book of Maccabees. Ed. and trans. by Sidney Tedesche. New York, 1950.

Falk, Marcia. *This Year In Jerusalem.* Brockport, NY, 1986.

Folktales of Israel. Ed. by Dov Noy with the assistance of Dan Ben Amos. Chicago, 1963.

Frankel, Ellen. *The Classic Tales: 4,000 Years of Jewish Lore.* Northvale, NJ, 1989.

Gilbert, Martin. *Jerusalem: Rebirth of a City.* Jerusalem, 1985.

Goldberg, Leah. *Selected Poems.* Transl. by Robert Friend. San Francisco, 1976.

Gruber, Ruth. *Israel on the Seventh Day.* New York, 1968.

Har-El, Menashe. *This Is Jerusalem.* Jerusalem, 1977.

Hareven, Shulamith. *City Of Many Days.* Trans. by Hillel Halkin and the author. San Francisco, 1993.

Hazzaz, Haim. *More Sa'id.* New York, 1956.

Hazelton, Leslie. *Jerusalem, Jerusalem.* New York, 1986.

Heilman, Samuel. *A Walker in Jerusalem.* New York, 1986.

Heschel, Abraham Joshua. *Israel: An Echo of Eternity.* New York, 1967.

Holtz, Avraham, ed. *The Holy City: Jews on Jerusalem.* New York, 1971.

The Image of Jerusalem. ADAM International Review. 1968. Ed. by Miron Grindea. Rochester, NY, 1968.

Israel Argosy 8. Ed. by Isaac Halevy-Levin. New York, 1962.

Israeli Poetry. Ed. by Warren Bargad and Stanley F. Chyet. Bloomington, IN, 1986.

The Jerusalem Cathedra 2. Ed. by Lee I. Levine. Jerusalem, 1982.

Jerusalem—City Holy and Eternal. Ed. by B. Dworkin. New York, 1954.

Jerusalem Eternal. Ed. by Azriel Eisenberg. New York, 1971.

Jerusalem: 5,000 Years of History. Les Dossiers D'Archeologie. Paris, 1992.

Jerusalem: Its Redemption and Future. New York, 1918.

Jerusalem: Most Fair of Cities. Ed. by Henia Stein and Franklin Jagodnik. Jerusalem, 1977.

Jerusalem: Problems and Prospects. Ed. by Joel Kramer. New York, 1980.

Jerusalem Revealed: Archaeology in the Holy City, 1968–1974. Jerusalem, 1975.

Jerusalem through the Ages. Jerusalem, 1967.

Joseph, Dov. *The Faithful City.* New York, 1960.

Koestler, Arthur. *Promise and Fulfilment.* London, 1949.

Kolleck, Teddy. *For Jerusalem—A Life.* Jerusalem, 1978.

Kolleck, Teddy, and Pearlman, Moshe. *Jerusalem: A History of Forty Centuries.* New York, 1968.

Kroyanker, David. *Jerusalem Architecture.* Jerusalem, 1994.

Kurzman, Dan. *Genesis 1948.* London, 1970.

Else Lasker-Schüler. *Hebrew Ballads and Other Poems.* Philadelphia, 1980.

Letters of Jews through the Ages. Ed. by F. Kobler Frazn. London, 1952.

Lever, Walter. *Jerusalem Is Called Liberty.* Jerusalem, 1951.

Levin, Harry. *Jerusalem Embattled.* London, 1958.

The Life and Works of Flavius Josephus. Trans. by William Whiston. Philadelphia, no year.

Meir, Golda. *My Life.* London, 1975.

Millgram, Abraham E. *Jerusalem Curiosities.* Philadelphia, 1990.

Mintz, Ruth Finer. *Jerusalem Poems, Love Songs.* Tel Aviv, 1976.

Modern Hebrew Poetry. Ed. and trans. by Ruth Finer Mintz. Berkeley and Los Angeles, 1966.

A *Narrative of a 40 Day's Sojourn in the Holy Land*. Montefiore, Sir Moses. London, 1875.

Navon, Yitzhak. *The Six Days and the Seven Gates*. Jerusalem, 1978.

Narkiss, Uzi. *The Liberation of Jerusalem*. London, 1983.

New Writing in Israel. Ed. by Ezra Spicehandler. Tel Aviv, 1976.

The Old Testament Pseudepigrapha. Ed. by James H. Charlesworth. New York, 1983, 1985.

Phillips, John. *A Will to Survive*. New York, 1976.

Philo. Vol. V, VII and X. Trans. by F. H. Colson. Cambridge, MA, 1962.

Prawer, Joshua. *The Latin Kingdom of Jerusalem: European Colonialism in the Middle Ages*. London, 1972.

Preil, Gabriel. *Sunset Possibilities and Other Poems*. Trans. by Robert Friend. Philadelphia, 1985.

Rabinovich, Abraham. *The Battle for Jerusalem*. Philadelphia, 1972.

———. *Jerusalem on Earth*. New York, 1988.

Raphael, Chaim. *The Walls of Jerusalem: An Excursion into Jewish History*. New York, 1967.

Retrievements: A Jerusalem Anthology. Ed. by Dennis Silk. Jerusalem, 1977.

Rose, Pauline. *The Seige of Jerusalem*. London, no year.

———. *Window on Mount Zion*. London, 1973.

Saadia Gaon, The Book of Beliefs and Opinions. Trans. by Samuel Rosenblatt. New Haven, CT, 1948.

Samuel, Edwin. *A Lifetime in Jerusalem*. Jerusalem, 1970.

Selected Religious Poems. Trans. by Israel Zangwill.

The Seventh Day. English version by Henry Near. London, 1970.

Shalom, Shin. *On Ben Peleh*. Trans. by Victor E. Reichert and Moses Zalesky. Jerusalem, 1963.

The Story of Jerusalem. Ed. by Dr. Beno Rothenberg. Trans. by M. Kohansky and Ben-Ami Sharfstein. Tel Aviv, 1967.

Tracks to the Promised Land. Ed. by Nahman Ran. Tel Aviv, 1987.

Steckoll, Solomon H. *The Gates of Jerusalem*. Tel Aviv, 1968.

———. *The Temple Mount*. London, 1972.

Uris, Leon and Uris, Jill. *Jerusalem—Song of Songs*. New York, 1981.

Vilnay, Zev. *Legends of Jerusalem*. Philadelphia, 1973.

Weilerstein, Sadie Rose. *The Best of K'tonton*. Philadelphia, 1980.

Weizmann, Chaim. *Trial and Error*. Philadelphia, 1949.

The Western Wall. Ed. by Meir Ben-Dov. Ministry of Defence. Tel Aviv, 1983.

The Western Wall. Ed. by Menahem M. Kasher. New York, 1972.

Wiesel, Elie. *A Beggar in Jerusalem*. Trans. by Lily Edelman and the author. New York, 1970.

Wilhelm, Kurt. *Roads to Zion*. Trans. by I. M. Lask. New York, 1948.

Wilson, Sir Charles W. *Jerusalem—The Holy City*. Jerusalem, no year.

The Wisdom of the Zohar. Fischel Lachover and Isaiah Tishby. Trans. by David Goldstein. Oxford, 1989.

Yaari, Avraham. *The Goodly Heritage*. Jerusalem, 1958.

Zion in Jewish Literature. Ed. by Abraham Halkin. New York, 1961.

The Zohar. Trans. by Harry Sperling and Maurice Simon. London, 1933.

☙ Index

Places in Jerusalem appear in boldface, a page number followed by f. indicates an illustration.

Abraham, 88, 399, 464
  gate of, 155
  Jerusalem as called by, 113
Absalom, Monument (Hand) of, 153, 156, 167
Abu Dis, 329
Abu Tor, 311, 329, 346, 380
Adam, 88, 358
Aelia Capitolina, 365, 405, 431, 432, 433, 434, 435
Agnon, S. Y., 242–55, 333–38, 470–73
Akiba, Rabbi, 132
Al Aksa Mosque, 147, 406, 412, 415, 416, 448
Alharizi Street, 353
Allenby, Edmund, 226–27, 230–31, 232f., 235, 236
Allenby Square, 264
Alliance School, dormitory of, 324f.
Ammunition Hill, 391
Anastasis, 418
Antiochus, 77
Antonia, tower of, 332
Antonia fortress, Herod's, 427, 431, 434
Apocalypse of Baruch, 88–89
Apocalyptic writing, 72
Aqueducts, 432
Arab Legion, 266, 269, 270, 310, 341, 412

Arab quarters, 260
Arabs, 166, 222, 236
  attacks by, 237, 242–43, 246, 247, 265–66
  boroughs for, 457
  neighborhoods of, 329–30
  in Old City, 335
Arab souk, 417
Archaeology. *See* Excavations
Archeological Seminars, 415
Arches, triumphal, 212
Aristeas, description of Second Temple by, 73–76
Ark of the Covenant, 3, 5–6, 26, 113, 122, 166, 176, 404
Armenian Garden, 436, 440
Armenian Quarter, 266, 429
  conquered, 405
Ashkenazim, 164, 207, 209, 224, 309
Athens, 4
Ayyubid tower (or gate), 154f.

Babylon, 4
Bait Vegan, 260, 263
Barkley's Gate, 404
Baruch
  Fourth, 90–91
  Second, 88–89
Baruch Hadaya, 415
Batei Mahse, 279, 281, 283
Batei Ungarn, 347

Bath-houses, 207–9
Batrik Street, 207
Bayit ve-Gan, 329
Bazaars, 165, **440**
Beersheba, 3, 227
Ben Gurion, David, declares State
    of Israel, 264
Benjamin of Tudela, 154–57, 344
Benjamin's Gate, 153
Ben Yehuda(h) Street, 260,
    377f., 450f.
Bet Hakerem, 328
Beth El, 3
Beth Hakerem, 260
Bet Yisra'el, 347
"Bevingrad," British compound,
    261f., 264, 275
Binyanei Ha'ooma, 293
Bridegrooms, customs concerning,
    178, 179
Brides, customs concerning, 179
British Army, liberates Jerusalem in
    1917, 230–31
British zones, 260
Broad Wall, 37f., 415, 422
Bronze Age, 427
    excavations of, 421
Burial caves, 425, 432
Byzantine period, excavations of,
    435–37
Byzantine Rotunda, 418
Byzantines, 411, 413, 417, 418

Caesar, and destruction of Temple,
    104, 106, 107, 109
Cafés, 260
Cardo, 413, 435, 440
Cardo Center, 415
Cardo Culinaria Restaurant, 413
Caves, burial, 425, 432

Cemeteries, 156, 412, 445. *See also*
    Grave-yards; Sepulchre(s);
    Tomb(s)
    excavations of, 432
    First Temple period, 423, 425
    Ketef Hinnom cemetery, 425
    on Mount Herzl, 269–70
Chapel of Saint Helena, 418
Chapel of the Resurrection, 418
Chelo, Isaac, 159–61, 163
Christianity, 464, 465, 466
Christian Quarter, 417
Christians, 467, 469
Church of Maria, 363
Church of the Dormition, 344,
    346
Church of the Holy Sepulchre,
    214, 416, 417–18, 448, 455
Church of the Redeemer, 214, 417
Citadel, Tower of David, 71f.,
    75–76, 203, 211, 400–2,
    418, 419, 429, 439, 440
City of David, 24, 25f., 344,
    386, 435
    excavations of, 421, 425–26
    fortifications in, 427
Convent of the Sisters of Zion,
    pavement in basement of, 434
Crucifixion, site of, 417, 418
Crusader period, 401, 440, 466
    remains of columned room from,
    438f.
Crusaders, 406, 411, 413, 418, 448
Customs, concerning Jerusalem,
    178–79
Cyrus of Persia, 36–38

Damascus, 228
Damascus Gate, 111f., 413, 434,
    435, 440

David
  brings Ark to Jerusalem, 26
  gate of, 155
  in Hebron, 24
  legend about, 396–97
  makes Jerusalem capital, 24, 464, 474
  Tomb of, 2f., 157, 343, 344, 401f., 461f.
  folklore concerning, 395–96
Dead Sea, 311, 365, 372, 384, 447
Dead Sea Scrolls, 72
  psalms in, 85
Degania, 16
Dome of the Rock, 147, 177, 291, 330, 403, 412, 415, 416, 417, 418, 445, 448, 455
Dormition Abbey, 384f.
Dung Gate, 293, 416, 439

Early Arab period, excavations of, 437–40
Ecce Homo arch, 434
Ein Karem, 269
El Aksa Mosque. *See* **Al Aksa Mosque**
Elijah the Prophet synagogue, 397–99, 398f.
Emek-Refaim, 378
Etzion bloc, 310, 314
Even Sh'tiyyah. *See* **Foundation Stone**
Even Yisrael, 206–7
Excavations
  Bronze Age, 421
  Byzantine period, 435–37
  of City of David, 421, 425–26
  difficulties of, 420–21

Early Arab period, 437–40
First Temple period, 421–26
Medieval period, 439–40
Roman period, 433–35
Second Temple period, 426–33
of Temple Mount, 416
Ezekiel
  predicts restoration of Jerusalem, 54
  prophesies destruction of Jerusalem, 48–49
Ezrat Yisra'el, 329

First Wall
  excavations of, 429
  western section of, 423, 434
Folklore, Jewish, 393–407
Fortifications
  Early Arab period, 438–39
  First Temple period, 422–23
  Medieval period, 439–40
  Second Temple period, 427, 431
Fortress of Zion, 422
Foundation Stone, 14–15, 147, 175–76, 177f.

Gai Ben Hinnom, 412
Gaius, 92–96
Gate of the Tribes, 290
Gates. *See also specific gate names*
  of Jerusalem, 155, 369
  to Temple Mount, 121–22
Gate(s) of Mercy, 153, 155, 160, 161, 166
"Gates of the Valley," 443
Gaza, 226, 227, 460
Geonic period, writings of, 142–50
Geonim, 142
Gethsemane, 289, 412
Ge'ula, 329

Gikhon, Upper pool of, **198**
Golan, 459
Golgotha, 418
Gomorrah, 7, 43, 48, 167
Goren, Shlomo, 294–96, 295f., 417
Gottfried de Bouillon, 330
Grave yards, 167. *See also*
    Cemeteries
Greenberg, Simon, 239–40
Gushpat, gate of, 155

HaCohen, Jacob, 153
Hadassah City Clinic, 262
Hadassah Hospital, 269
Haganah, 264, 266, 267, 345f.
Haifa, 443, 447
Hasidim, 207–8, 209, 224, 306,
    368
Hasmonean period, construction
    during, 427, 428f., 429, 431
"Ha-Tik'vah," 16
Hebrew (language), 207, 234–35
**Hebrew University, 8, 269,
    332f., 349**
    dedication ceremony, 239f.
    foundation stone laid for,
      233–35, 234f.
    **on Mount Scopus, 226, 233,
      239f., 269, 332f., 412**
Hebron, 3, 24
Help of the Needy (settlement),
    204–205f.
Herod, 73, 94, 331, 400, 402, 404,
    418, 420, 427, 429, 431
    expands Second Temple, 97–102
    palace of, 400, 429
Herod's Gate, 288
Herzl, Theodore, 15, 211–21, 221f.
    Tomb of, 391
Heschel, Abraham Joshua, 314–16

Hezekiah, 29–30, 31, 32, 415, 422
Hirschberg, A. S., 222–24
Holocaust Memorial, 390
Holy of Holies, 130–31, 132, 139,
    155, 166, 176, 177, 291, 404
Hot Bath of Al-harem, 207
Hula Valley, 16
Hulda Gate, 121, 406
Huldah, tomb of, 161, 167
Hurva Synagogue, 413

Intercontinental Hotel, 445
Isaiah, 357
    denounces Jerusalem, 43–46
    predicts good future for
      Jerusalem, 51–53
    as prophet of Jerusalem, 30–31
Islam, 464, 466–67
Islamic Museum, 416
Israel, State of, declared, 264, 275,
    276
Israel Museum, 457–58
Italian Hospital, 441f.

Jaffa, 221, 225, 227
**Jaffa Gate, 19f., 141f., 198, 202,
    203, 268, 270, 333, 411,
    412, 435, 437**
Jaffa Road, 218f., 260, 321, 322
Jehoiachin, 34
    Jehoshaphat
    gate of, 155, 156
    valley of, 153, 156
Jeremiah
    denounces Jerusalem, 47–48
    hides Temple vessels, 90–91
    predicts restoration of Jerusalem,
      53–54
Jericho, 228

Jerusalem
aerial view of, 409f.
destruction of, 109
in First Temple period, 34–36
in rabbinic literature, 123–28
in future, 132–36, 443–60
"heavenly," 130–31, 145–46, 419
map of, 62f., 414f.
naming of, 21–23, 113
**Jerusalem Museum of Islamic Art
and Culture, 458**
Jerusalem Theater, 458
Jesus, 415, 455, 465
sepulchre of, 207, 417, 418
**Jewish Agency building, 221f.,
260**
**Jewish Quarter, 154, 370f., 412,
413**
Arab attacks on, 265, 266
Broad Wall in, 37f.
conquered, 405
excavations in, 429–30, 433,
435–36, 440
repaired by Nachmanidies, 406
view of, 319f.
wall designs in, 81
Jews, return to Jerusalem, 131f.,
147–48
Jordanian section, protective walls
near, 452f.
Joseph, Dov, 265–271
Josephus Flavius, 72, 387
writings of, 97–104, 106–107,
109
Josiah, 33–34
Judaean Desert, **412**
Judah, 80
Judah Chassid synagogue, 351f.
Judah Halevi, 182–88
Judean hills, **353, 354f., 455**

Kaddish prayer, for Jerusalem, 150
Karo, Joseph, 178
Katamon, 312, 314, 330, 380
Kerem Avraham, 329
**Kerem Moshe Ve-Yehoodit, 198,
201**
Ketef Hinnom cemetery, 425
Kidron, Valley of, 34, 369
King David Street, 345f.
King Feisal Street, 291
King George Avenue, 260, 264
King Solomon's quarries, 153
Kiponus, gate of, 121
Kiryath Shmuel, 272
Knesset building, 446
Kollek, Teddy, 453–60

Ladino, 207
Lamentations, 65–69
Laws, concerning Jerusalem,
137–39
Lions' Gate, 257, 289, 290, 403
Loeb synagogue, 171
Lower Aqueduct, 432

Maccabees, First Book of, 77–80,
82
Magreb Gate, 301
Magreb Quarter, 222
Maimonides, 178–79
Malha, 269
Mamillah Road, 264
Mamluk building complexes, 440
Manasseh, 32–33
Mandelbaum Gate, 287, 288f.
Mattathias, 79–80
Mazkeret Moshe, 206, 207
**Me'ah She'arim, 198, 329,
347–50, 359, 360f.**

Medieval period, excavations of, 439–40
Mehane Yehuda market, 387
Mekor Hayyim, 329
Messiah, 145–46, 349, 369, 403, 419
    arrival in Jerusalem, 131f.
Micah
    denounces Jerusalem, 42–43
    predicts good future for Jerusalem, 50–51
Mighty Mount, 399
Ministry of Education, 441f.
Misgav Ladach Hospital, 208f.
Mishkanot Yisrael, 206, 207
Mishkenot Sha'ananim, 411, 458
Mishneh Torah, 178–79
Mograbi Gate, 404, 416
Mohammed, 415, 455
Monasteries
    Byzantine, 437
    Crusader, 440
    Saint Etienne Monastery, 425
    Saint-Simon Monastery, 330
Montefiore, Moses, 197–201, 208, 214, 329
Montefiore Quarter, 389
Montefiore's Windmill, 198, 411
Monument of Absalom, 153, 156, 167
Mosaics, 437
Moses, 88, 145–46, 329
Moses Praeger, 168–73
Moshav Zekenim (Home for the Elderly), 204f.
Moshe ben Maimon. See Maimonides
Moshe ben Nahman. See Nahmanides
Moslems. See Muslims

Mosque of al-Aksa. See Al Aksa Mosque
Mosque of Omar, 214, 237, 290, 291, 301
Motza, 220, 220f., 221
Mount Herzl, 269–70
Mount Moriah, 188, 385, 399
    God's presence on, 114
    holiness of, 6
    Isaac sacrificed on, 14
    as site of Temple, 15, 21–22
Mount of Olives, 122, 153, 161, 163, 405, 412, 445
    graves on, 167, 251, 344
    view from, 215
Mount of Qarantal, 331
Mount Scopus, 288, 333, 447
    Hadassah Hospital on, 269
    Hebrew University on, 8, 226, 233, 239f., 269, 332f., 412
    tearing of garments on, 132, 138
    terrorist attack on, 260–62
Mount Sinai, 5, 6, 88, 114
Mount Zion, 153, 176, 276, 277f., 343–47, 383–85, 384f., 435. See also Temple Mount
    Arab Legion on, 266
    in Book of Maccabees, 80, 82
    Byzantine remains on, 436
    conquered, 405
    holiness of, 5, 6
    in Lamentations, 69
    in Psalm 48, 60, 61
    sepulchres on, 156, 161
    Tomb of David on, 2f., 343, 344, 401f., 461f.
    view of Temple Mount from, 471f.

views of New City from, 412
war on, 46
Mugrabis' Gate, 291
Muhammad. *See* Mohammed
Muslims, 147, 437, 439, 469
Musrara, 311, 330, 346
Mystical literature, Jerusalem in,
174–77

Nablus Gate, 287. *See also*
Damascus Gate
Nablus Road, 288
Nachalat Shivah, 329, 336
Nahalat Ahim, 329
Nahmanides, 157–59, 173, 406
Nea Church complex, 435–36
Nebuchadnezzar, 34–35
Neighborhoods. *See specific*
neighborhood names
Nevi'im Street, 356, 357f.
New City, 366
Mount Zion views of, 412
New Gate, 271
New Synagogue, 370f.
Notre Dame, 311

Obadiah Da Bertinoro, 163–67
Ohel Moshe, 207
Old City, 8, 259, 264, 366, 367
Arabs settled in, 335
burning in War of
Independence, 272, 274
defenders taken captive in War
of Independence, 278–86
Jaffa Gate to, 141f.
liberated in Six Day War, 286–93
tourists in, 337
walls of, 384f., 411
in War of Independence,
265–69, 270, 271

Zion Gate to, 193f.
Omar, Mosque of. *See* **Mosque of**
Omar
Omar ben al-Khatab ('Umar I),
147–48, 155, 160
Omariyyah, 329
Ophel, 105f., 422, 425, 427,
430, 435, 436, 437
Ottoman Citadel, 440
Oz, Amos, 307–13

Palace of Queen Helena, 161
Palace(s)
Crusader, 440
Early Arab period, 437–38
Herod's, 400, 429
of Queen Helena, 161
Pavements, Roman, 434
Phasael, tower of, 332
Philo Judaeus, 72, 92–96
Poetry
liturgical, 149
medieval, 180–91
modern, 351–91
Pogrom, in Jerusalem, 235–38
Princess Mary Street, 261f., 264
Psalms, 60–65
noncanonical, 85–87
of Solomon, 83–84

Qal'at Julad (Goliath's Tower), 440
Quarries, of King Solomon, 153

Rabbinic literature, nature of, 112
Rachel, Tomb of, 391
Ramat Rachel, 372
Ramban. *See* Nahmanides
Ramparts Walk, 412
Rehaviah, 259, 260, 264, 349
Rehoboam, 28, 29

Riots of 1929, in Talpiot, 242–55
Rivoli Hotel, 287
Robinson's Arch, 404, 430
Rockefeller Museum, 287, 289, 297, 441f.
Roman legions, 432, 433, 434, 435
Roman period, excavations of, 433–35
Romans
  pavements built by, 434
  walls built by, 434
Rome, 4
Romema, 329
Ruhama, 329
Russian Church, 447
Russian Tower, 215

Sachs Gallery, 415
Saint Etienne Monastery, 425
Saint-Simon Monastery, 330
Salah e-Din Street, 287
Samuel, Tomb of, 228
Schneller Woods, 311
School for Sewing at the Schneller Woods, 201f.
Second Isaiah, predicts restoration of Jerusalem, 54–58
Second Wall of Jerusalem, 431
Seleucid Akra fortress, 427
Sephardim, 207, 209, 222, 224, 309
  synagogues of, 413
Sepulchre(s), 156–57, 161, 167.
  See also Tomb(s)
  of Jesus, 207, 417, 418
  of Solomon, 157
  of Uzziah, 156
Sha'arei Hesed, 329, 347
Sha'ar ha-Gai ("Gates of the Valley"), 443

Shcharansky, Anatoly, 316–17
Sheikh Jarrah, 261, 269, 312, 329
Shiloah, water of, 148
Shulhan Aruch, 178
Siloam, waters of, 153, 156
Silwan, Pool of, 162f., 293
Silwan tunnel, 32f.
Six Day War, 456, 459
  crowds at Wall after, 304f.
  monument to fallen soldiers, 342f.
  Old City liberated in, 286–93
  soldiers' recollections of, 296–301
  Temple Mount captured in, 403
  Yemin Moshe restored after, 412
Sodom, 7, 43, 48, 167
Solomon
  builds Temple, 26–27, 28f.
  Psalms of, 83–84
  sepulchre of, 157
  song of songs, 176
  tefillin of, 298
  Temple of, 151f., 155, 404
Solomon's Palace, as one of seven wonders, 161
Song of songs, 176
Souk, Arab, 417
South Wall Excavation, 416
Stambuli Synagogue, 273f.
Stone of Unction, 418
Street of the Prophets, 356, 357f.
Streets. See also specific street names
  Herodian, 108f.
Sukkat Shalom, 206–7
Sultan's Pool, 468f.
Sweat-baths, 207–9
Synagogue Court, Ashkanazi, 164, 171, 172

Synagogues, 117–18, 206–7
  Elijah the Prophet, 397–99,
    398f.
  Hurva Synagogue, 413
  Judah Chassid, 351f.
  Loeb synagogue, 171
  New Synagogue, 370f.
  Sephardic, 413
  Stambuli Synagogue, 273f.
  Yohanan Ben-Zakkai
    synagogue, 413

Taddai, gate of, 121
Talbiyyah (Talbieh), 264, 329
Talpiot, 311, 329
  1929 riots in, 242–47, 248f.,
    249–55, 251f., 255f.
Talpiyot. *See* **Talpiot**
Tamar, 415
Temple
  architecture of, 403–4
  called Lebanon, 120–21
  as center of Jerusalem, 113
  cleaning of, 147
  destruction of, 35–36, 118, 123,
    124, 126, 128, 405
  direction of prayer in, 139
  in future, 134
  gives holy status to Jerusalem,
    6
  God's presence in, 129, 143–44
  in heaven, 145
  Jerusalem's worthiness of, 114
  mourning customs for, 178–79
  in Psalm 122, 61, 63
  rebuilding of, 38–39
  restoration of, 33
  Solomon as builder of, 26–27,
    28f., 151f., 155
  song of songs about, 176

  tearing of garments upon seeing,
    138
Temple, First
  Dome of the Rock and, 415
  excavations of, 421–26
Temple, Second
  Aristeas' description of, 73–76
  destruction of, 102–4, 106–7,
    109, 124, 126
  Dome of the Rock and, 415
  excavations of, 426–33
  Herod's work on, 97–102, 117
  model of, 128f.
  statues to emperor in, 92–96
Temple Area, 214
Temple Mount, 43, 105f., 132,
    147, 412, 415. *See also*
    Mount Zion
  aerial view of, 11f.
  altar stones stored in, 80
  ashlars at, 75f.
  captured in Six Day War, 290,
    403, 405
  conquered, 405
  construction of Wall at, 431
  customs concerning, 122
  excavations of, 416, 433, 436,
    437
  gates to, 121–22
  Hebrew inscription on, 127f.
  Herodian public works at, 430
  Herodian street at, 108f.
  permissibility of entering, 417
  psalm for ascending, 61, 63
  Romans conquer, 407
  search for fortress on, 427
  soldiers at, 298
  view of, 471f.
Terrorist attacks, 260–62, 377f.
Third Wall of Jerusalem, 431–32

Titus, and destruction of Temple, 102, 103, 104, 106, 407
Tomb(s). *See also* Sepulchre(s)
  excavations of, 432
  First Temple period, 425
  of Herzl, 391
  of Huldah, 161, 167
  of Rachel, 391
  of Samuel, 228
  Tomb of David, 2f., 157, 343, 344, 401f., 461f.
  Tombs of the Kings, 161, 215, 216f.
Torah, 114, 120, 349
Tour, walking, 411–19
  map, 414f.
Tower of David, 153, 155, 160, 363, 366–67, 411, 418, 419. *See also* Citadel, Tower of David
  legends of, 400–2
  views from, 213–14
Tower of David Museum of the History of Jerusalem, 418–19
Towers
  Hasmonean, 424f.
  Hippicus, 109
  Israelite, 424f.
  Mariamne, 109
  Phasaelus, 109
Travelers' accounts, of Jerusalem, 153–61, 163–73
Turks, in World War I, 226, 227–28, 229, 230

Upper City, 405, 429
Uzziah, sepulchre of, 156

Valley of Ben-hinnom, 23, 34, 412

Valley of Jehoshaphat, 153, 156
Valley of Kidron, 34, 369
Valley of Rephaim, 23
Valley of the Cross, 322
Vespasian, 118, 124, 125, 126
Via Dolorosa, 214, 290, 416, 418, 434, 448

Walking tour, 411–19
  map, 414f.
Walls
  city, 109, 411
  Roman, 434
War of Independence, 8, 260–62, 265–86, 349
Warren's Gate, 404, 430
Warren's Shaft, 422
Water Gate, 422
Wedding customs, 178, 179
Weizmann, Chaim, 8, 224–26, 233–38, 234f.
West Bank, 293, 459–60
Western Hill, 422–23, 427, 428
Western Wall, 153, 155, 455
  Austrian soldiers and Jews at, 225f.
  beggars at, 213, 222
  construction of, 166–67
  excavations of, 430–31
  God's presence at, 129, 407
  Herodian street at, 108f.
  Hirschberg's visit to, 222–24
  Kotel of, 416, 446
  liberated in Six Day War, 291–93, 301–3
  as one of seven wonders, 160, 161
  paratroopers at, after Six Day War, 302f., 403

prayer at, 200, 204, 206, 209,
  222, 223–24, 333–34, 406, 407
Rabbi Goren's speech at, 294–96
sanctity of, 403–7
soldiers at, 298
as symbol of unity, 300–301
tourists at, 391
Wiesel's visit to, after Six Day
  War, 303–7
on Yom Kippur, 209, 240–42
Western Wall Plaza, 415–16
Western Wall Tunnel, 416
Wiesel, Elie, 303–7
Wilson's Arch, 404, 430, 440
**Windmill, Montefiore's, 198,
  411**
**Wohl Archaeological Museum
  (Herodian Quarter), 415**
Women Workers' Farm, 243
Workers' Brigade, 243, 245

Yegia Kappayim, 329

**Yemin Moshe, 329, 347, 390,
  411, 412**
Yiddish, 207
YMCA, 324–25
  East Jerusalem, 287
**Yohanan Ben-Zakkai synagogue,
  413**
Yom Kippur, Western Wall and,
  209, 240–42

Zechariah
  Monument of, 167
  predicts restoration of Jerusalem,
  58–59
Zedekiah, 35, 278
**Zion Gate, 155, 193f., 266, 268,
  270, 289, 347, 393f., 412**
Zionism, 194, 211, 224, 465
Zion Quarter, Byzantine remains
  on, 436
Zion Square, 259, 389
Zohar, 174–77

✍ About Reuven Hammer

Reuven Hammer received his ordination and doctorate in theology from the Jewish Theological Seminary. He holds a Ph.D. in Communicative Disorders from Northwestern University. After serving as a chaplain in the U.S. Air Force and a congregational rabbi for 15 years, he and his family made *aliya* to Israel in 1973 and have lived in Jerusalem ever since. He has taught Jewish studies and special education at various institutions, including the Hebrew University, David Yellin College, and Oranim.

Rabbi Hammer served as dean of the Jewish Theological Seminary of America's Jerusalem Campus and was founding director of the Seminary of Judaic Studies. He has taught and lectured throughout the world and is the author of five books. He is currently at work on a JPS High Holy Day companion, which explains both the holidays and the accompanying Mahzor.